AFTER A STROKE STRIKES

AFTER A STROKE STRIKES

A LONG NIGHT'S SPIRITUAL
JOURNEY INTO DAY

Charles W. Kegley & Debra J. Kegley

Advance Praise for *After a Stroke Strikes*

"Life brings many unexpected twists and turns that shape our identity, our beliefs, our faith and our future. This touching story about one couple's journey from stroke to recovery, and how it brought them closer to each other and to God, will tug on your heartstrings and offer inspiration and hope for dealing with adversity in the face of seemingly insurmountable circumstances."

—Dr. Shannon Lindsey Blanton, Dean of the Honors College and Professor of Government, University of Alabama at Birmingham

"The internationally influential scholar and author Charles W. Kegley and his wife Debbie have chronicled their journey following her strokes and their experiences at the edge of life. Regardless of your personal spiritual beliefs, *After a Stroke Strikes* will force readers to evaluate what is truly important in their life."

—Dr. Greg Carlson, Ph.D., CEO of the Center for Neurosciences, Orthopedics and Spine (CNOS)

"Among many demands of stroke recovery, the love and faith of this couple shine through every step of their journey."

—Pierre Gehlen, former President of the District Court of Luxembourg and former President of the Public Cultural Radio of Luxembourg

"I have observed Debbie's remarkable recovery firsthand, and attest that her inspiring rehabilitation illuminates what can be achieved through perseverance, faith, and skilled treatment."

—Dr. James R. Herman, M.D., Diplomate American Board of Internal Medicine

"This testimonial exploration of near-death casts light on the dark corners of human existence, and the engaging witness to faith provides a road to discovery that will provoke deeper thinking about fundamental metaphysical and spiritual questions for all of us to ponder."

—Dr. Charles F. Hermann, Brent Scowcroft Chair in International Policy Studies, Bush School of Government & Public Service at Texas A&M University

"This is a gravitating and gripping story about love, faith, and human physical endurance. A stroke took Debra Kegley to the edge of life, and her beliefs and her relationship with her husband, Chuck, brought her back. The Kegleys have portrayed the stages and extraordinary persistence and exertion of slowly pulling back from the end of life. This story captures the emotional effort by both wife and husband to create normalcy and restore both mind and soul."

—Llewellyn D. Howell, Ph. D., LMT, Emeritus Professor of International Management, Thunderbird School of Global Management at Arizona State University

"Unexpected dramatic things can happen to all of us. Many people call these events 'fate.' They are independent of our will or any action. A sudden stroke is one of these terrible turning points in life which lead to the question: 'Why me?' If we are lucky to survive without major repercussions, the question can also be: 'Why me?' Then comes the second part that now depends on our will and action, our faith and courage, our determination to make the best out of the situation, which also depends on the support from our partners, from those who love us, from those who can give us professional support. This book provides an absorbing presentation of the different aspects that follow a stroke and thereby change life. For me personally the person afflicted is a very dear friend, and the story of this couple's courage, determination, love and faith will encourage all who suffer."

—Dr. Jean H. Klinger, M.D., Retired Swiss Pediatrician, President of the Association Verein Partnerschaft Kinderspitalar Biel-Haiti and former President of the Association of Pediatricians of the Swiss Canton of Bern

"The power of Christ's healing and redeeming presence courses through this remarkable story of determination, dedication, love and friendship. This book educates and inspires."

—Dr. Jan Love, Dean and Professor of Christianity and World Politics, Candler School of Theology, Emory University

"The Lord often brings us to a place where we have nowhere to turn but to Him, only to find that He is always all that we need. How He worked in Debbie Kegley's life is a manifestation of His miraculous power on her behalf. This testimony is a prophetic word that what He did in Debbie's life He can do in yours. The Lord is no respecter of persons, and He is the same yesterday, today and forever. This should be an encouragement to us all."

—Dr. Gregg W. McKenzie, D.D.S.

"*Ecclesiastes (7:8)* states 'Better is the end of a thing than the beginning...' In this book, Dr. Kegley provides the informed and informative spiritual toolbox every individual needs to assure that their life will end better than when it began. *After a Stoke Strikes* reminds us how important it is to learn from and value each moment during our life's journey in order to finish and complete our God-given purpose and destiny with honor and integrity."

—Evangelist Adrian Moldovan, Founder and President of *Tell Hell No Ministries*

"*After a Stroke Strikes* lies at the confluence of science and spirituality. At one level it is a wondrous, inspiring saga of a woman's strength and courage, her husband's faith and devotion, and the skill of a compassionate medical team during a life-threatening crisis. However, at another level, it is a powerful, uplifting story about the meaning of human existence, the eternal, and the blessing of transcendent love."

—Dr. Gregory A. Raymond, Frank Church Distinguished Professor of Public Affairs Emeritus, Boise State University

"This loving couple's fight for survival and recovery after life-threatening crises will touch you and invigorate your faith."

—Dr. Alpo Rusi, Ambassador and former Chief Advisor of the President of Finland

Selected Books by Charles W. Kegley

A General Empirical Typology of Foreign Policy Behavior
After Vietnam: The Future of American Foreign Policy
The Domestic Sources of American Foreign Policy
Controversies in International Relations Theory: Realism and the Neoliberal Challenge
After the Cold War: Questioning the Morality of Nuclear Deterrence
International Terrorism: Characteristics, Causes, Controls
The Long Postwar Peace: Contending Explanations and Projections
The New Global Terrorism
New Directions in the Study of Foreign Policy (with Charles F. Hermann and James N. Rosenau)

With William D. Coplin:
A Multi-Method Introduction to International Politics
Analyzing International Relations

With Patrick J. McGowan:
Challenges to America
Threats, Weapons, and Foreign Policy
The Political Economy of Foreign Policy
Foreign Policy and the Modern World System
Foreign Policy: USA/USSR

With Gregory A. Raymond:
International Events and the Comparative Analysis of Foreign Policy
When Trust Breaks Down: Alliance Norms and World Politics
How Nations Make Peace
A Multipolar Peace? Great-Power Politics in the 21st Century
Exorcising the Ghost of Westphalia: Building World Order in the New Millennium
After Iraq: The Imperiled American Imperium
From War to Peace: Fateful Decisions in International Politics
The Global Future, five editions

With Eugene R. Wittkopf:

American Foreign Policy: Pattern and Process, seven editions

World Politics: Trend and Transformation, sixteen editions (five with Shannon Lindsey Blanton)

Perspectives on American Foreign Policy, two editions

The Global Agenda, six editions

The Nuclear Reader: Strategy, Weapons, War, two editions

AFTER A STROKE STRIKES

A LONG NIGHT'S SPIRITUAL JOURNEY INTO DAY

§

Charles W. Kegley & Debra J. Kegley

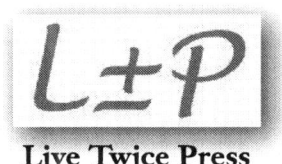

Live Twice Press

Published by Live Twice Press ™
Distributed and available for purchase from
CreateSpace.com/6299641 and/or
Amazon.com

Kegley, Charles W. & Debra J. Kegley
After a Stroke Strikes: A Long Night's Spiritual Journey Into Day,
by Charles W. Kegley and Debra J. Kegley

ISBN-13: 9780997652802
ISBN-10: 0997652802
ISBN: 9780997652819 (eBook)
Library of Congress Control Number: 2016909530
Live Twice Press, Blythewood, SC

To our Lord and Savior

CONTENTS

MEET YOUR AUTHORS

§

Charles W. Kegley was born in Chicago and raised in Columbus, Ohio. A past President of the International Studies Association, he holds the title of Pearce Distinguished Professor of International Relations Emeritus at the University of South Carolina. He has served for two decades on the of Board of Trustees of the Carnegie Council for Ethics in International Affairs. A graduate of the American University (B. A.) and Syracuse University (Ph. D.) and a Pew Faculty Fellow at Harvard University, Kegley previously served on the faculty at Georgetown University and has held visiting professorships at the University of Texas, Rutgers University, the People's University of China, and the Institute Universitaire de Hautes Études Internationales in Geneva, Switzerland. He has published more than sixty books and scores of peer-reviewed journal articles on international affairs.

Debra J. Kegley was born and raised in Fairmount, Indiana. She obtained a B. A. degree in business administration from Grand Valley State

University and has received several awards for speaking achievements. She is the CEO of Kegley International, Inc. (a publishing, research, and consulting foundation). In her professional career, she served as Manager of Human Resources for various businesses and organizations, among other positions. She has also been an entrepreneur in the health sciences field and is the former owner of 3-Way Fitness.

Chuck and Debbie Kegley live in Blythewood, South Carolina, and Wytheville, Virginia.

PREFACE

Astroke can strike anyone, anytime, anywhere. One out of every five people will suffer a stroke by the age of fifty. Strokes are the third-leading cause of death. Our tale is a true story about what happened in the wake of a life-threatening stroke to a particular victim at a particular time in a particular setting.

This book describes how near-death experiences provided an eye-opening education. After looking at death in the face, we are almost grateful for the adversities and anxieties we withstood. Catastrophic crises brought us closer to God. We found renewed faith and also began to find our "true selves"—who we were always meant to be. Moreover, when all seemed lost, we found just how much we loved one another.

It may take a life-threatening experience to confer meaning on an otherwise meaningless existence. That's what happened for us as we walked through the valley of the shadow of death. In the wake of a series of near-death crises, many thoughts within thoughts surfaced, and we discovered that what happens is less important than how we think about and respond to them.

After a Stroke Strikes has been written not solely for stroke victims and their loved ones but for everyone—because sooner or later all will experience a life-threatening crisis, contemplate ultimate destiny, and seek understanding and comfort. Anyone, therefore, might benefit from learning what we learned during our long journey from night into day. The larger picture beyond what happened to us is applicable to what can happen to anyone. You too can emerge from crushing medical crises forcing you to face death, more confident of God's miraculous power and more resilient than ever imaginable. Follow the path we took, and you might restore hope and expand your spiritual imagination.

Part I: Trials On An Uncharted Trail

I held my breath as the surgeon's scalpel split open my wife's skull. Was this the last time I would see her alive? If she survived, would she retain any of her former capabilities? Would she be a different person? I needed God like I needed air. These were the dark thoughts that raced through my mind at the stroke of midnight. My young wife had had a stroke, and it struck fear into the depths of my soul. That was then, and this was now. Want to hear what happened?

CHAPTER 1

LOST IN THE DARK?

§

*None of us can help the things life has done to us.
They're done. And once they're done, they make you do
other things, until you've lost your true self forever.*

—EUGENE O'NEILL

These words penned by Eugene O'Neill were carefully typed and
posted on the wall by Chuck Robinson. He was my college roommate and remains my best friend.

O'Neill's iconic autobiographical play, *A Long Day's Journey into
Night*, provokes despair and hopelessness. It describes how, abruptly or
gradually, anyone can slip into someone they previously weren't. Life
usually begins full of promise, but as it evolves, events happen which
change both our behavioral habits and our conception of who we are.
As our lives unfold, it commonly becomes increasingly clear that who
we once imagined ourselves to be may never be truly recovered. Haven't
you at times felt like a cork in a gushing stream, pulled on a course over
which you had little control?

O'Neill captured a sad truth: unexpected events alter perceptions of
who we are. Things happen, and in the aftermath, they unleash chain
reactions that change who we think we are and what we will become.
Our "true" selves can easily be lost.

Anyone can lose his or her self and identity in huge leaps or in small steps. Never in our wildest imaginations did my wife Debbie or I expect O'Neill's message to be so profoundly relevant. O'Neill's insight seemed to capture what would assuredly happen whenever an unanticipated medical emergency takes the victim to the edge of death. In their wake, all sense of our true selves can, as O'Neill predicted, be lost. Insidiously, a larger sense of well-being fades, as anxieties and gloom pull the victim down into night's darkness.

However, that is *not* what happened to us. This book documents the possibility of a very different outcome. It records how a totally unexpected life-threatening event produced surprising rewards, revealing how light can break darkness when pain turns our heads around.

A disaster can come in many forms. What struck Debbie, my beautiful young wife of only fifty-four years of age, was one of the worst—a massive hemorrhagic aneurism that assaulted her brain and led to paralysis of her body. There were no prior symptoms and therefore nothing that could have been done to prevent this tragedy from occurring. We will never know why this happened.

This destructive brain attack abruptly terminated the course on which our lives had been traveling. What life can suddenly do to life on earth cannot be helped. O'Neill had been right—terrible events sometimes happen. They change instantly who we are and clear a path influencing what we will become.

In the aftermath of Debbie's strokes, a long journey began along a long, dark twisting path. Did we lose, or find, our "true selves?" Adversity can become a powerful teacher. Contrary to O'Neill's prophecy, our traumatic experience ushered into being a time when life started to mean something. Through suffering and grief, we reevaluated our values, ourselves, and our relationships with our Lord. At death's door we also earnestly began to seriously reassess our philosophy of life, moral code, and religious faith. We desperately called on our Creator for help, and discovered the remarkable extent to which our loving God answers prayers. His healing power enabled us to see His hand more clearly.

Conscious like never before of God's loving presence within our souls, we began to find our true selves, and learned some valuable lessons about how to face death and find faith.

But we are getting way ahead of our story. Let's start at the beginning and recount what happened at the advent of our learning experience, tracing the trials, tribulations, and trepidations after our grim travels commenced.

CHAPTER 2

DARK BLACKENS A BRIGHT DAY

§

January 8, 2014, was a day that abruptly changed our lives. It began on a very cheerful note. We awoke to a clear and crisp morning in our Wytheville, Virginia, home resting atop the Blue Ridge Mountains. The spectacular view of the prominent landmark Queen's Knob and the Seven Sisters peaks on the edge of the Jefferson National Forest met our eyes. Our hearts were warmed the sight of the cattle grazing on the 350-acre Kegley Farms, where our cousin Andy and his family practice the art of organic farming.

"IT WAS THE BEST OF TIMES"

That morning our elevated mood was further heightened by the glow of a warm fireplace. Debbie and I sipped coffee and counted our many blessings. These were halcyon days. We had just concluded a wonderful two weeks over the Christmas holidays hosting the family of my thirty-year-younger brother Stephen Lincoln Luther Kegley, and our spirits were appreciatively lifted by the opportunities their travels from California afforded to play and pray.

We reflected on our good fortunes. We enjoyed great health and great churches led by outstanding pastors. We also benefitted from our two homes. The first was located on the University Club golf course in Blythewood, South Carolina; we had married there twelve years earlier. The second was our Wytheville home we had named Twin Oaks. We had experienced the best years of our lives. Life was good. We were comfortably complacent. To twist an adage, we found ourselves between a pillow and a soft place. We felt truly blessed.

"It Was the Worst of Times"

A hiatus from carefree days was about to unexpectedly end. We were driving on cruise control, unaware that as we talked clouds were gathering, darkening our horizon. We had no warning that within hours a catastrophic event was about to happen. We were unprepared for a life-threatening blow that would strike like a bolt of lightning.

The plan that fateful day, January 8, 2014, was to return to South Carolina to take down the two Christmas trees Debbie had magically decorated for our visiting California family, open the mail, and attend to business before returning to our Virginia home and skiing at the Winter Place Resort conveniently located an hour's drive away.

"Do you want to close the house and drive straight to our South Carolina house?" Debbie asked. "Or should we first get in a quick workout at the Wytheville Community Center athletic facility, shower, and then head back?" We chose the latter. For breakfast, we each ingested only a single hard-boiled egg, planning to eat the turkey sandwiches Debbie had packed after our exercise. "Meet me at the community center's front door at exactly noon; I'll drive first," Debbie said.

Well, engrossed in a locker-room conversation, I was late, as was my bad habit. It wasn't until 12:20 p.m. that I arrived to join her. Debbie was behind the wheel, and I rode shotgun.

"Sorry I'm late," I apologized.

"No problem," she said. So Toby (my nickname for Debbie) peeled away in our Honda CR-V minivan and headed south on Interstate 77. As Debbie drove, I tried to strike up a conversation. "What's on your mind? Anything you care to share? You're so quiet. You okay?" "I'm just a bit tired," Debbie explained. "Let's talk later. Put on your seatbelt.

Let's listen to the fifties music CD Pat Larson gave us at church." And off we went.

At 2:00 p.m., I suggested that we switch drivers at the next rest stop. "Sounds good. Do you want to use the restroom so we can continue the two-hour trip home without stopping?" We agreed that was the best choice.

A TERRIBLE TURNAROUND

Upon Debbie's exit from the rest-stop door to the women's room, life veered in an unexpected direction. In our wildest dreams, we could never have imagined that what happened would happen. We were propelled into a different world.

The first sign that life had dealt a cruel blow came out of the blue. I waited patiently outside the women's restroom. Debbie stepped forward, expressionless. She began to wave both her arms, up and down, as would a butterfly in flight. She was shaking like a leaf. "Now, Flapper, you're flapping," I said. "Flapper" is another of Debbie's many pet names. "Very funny, sweetie," I said. But she continued wavering. "Okay, that's a good one. Enough is enough, though." At that point, Debbie sat on the stone floor and then rested her head on the floor. Was this some kind of seizure?

"Should we call for help?" inquired a nice couple from Ohio.

"No, I'm okay." Debbie dismissively announced as she rose to her feet on her own power. "Just got dizzy. So let's go," she insisted. She marched to the car under my watchful eye.

The Ohio couple mumbled, "We're not so sure she's all right. Maybe you should call 911 for medical assistance."

Always stoic, Debbie shrugged off her momentary vertigo. "I probably got lightheaded because I had worked out for an hour without hardly anything to eat. Here are the keys, Chuck. Why not get the sandwiches I made so we can hightail it to Blythewood without stopping?"

So off I drove onto Interstate 77. About three minutes later, Debbie bent over in the passenger's seat and gagged, trying to vomit.

"I'm sorry," she apologized. A dreadful plea followed: "I think I need help. My head hurts. This is the worst headache I've ever had. What can you do?" she urged as alarm bells rang in my ears and dark clouds suddenly blocked the daylight.

Thus began a long day's journey into night. A stroke hit Debbie fast and hard. In an instant, daylight disappeared. It was as if someone had turned off the lights, letting darkness overcome the glow of light that had been shining moments earlier.

"There is only one option: trust in the Lord, and look for rescue," I anxiously tried to reassure her. I was out of my mind. I sped on the interstate at eighty-five miles per hour, the only option I could think of was to find a hospital and get her there immediately. There was no place to turn around, and 911 could not quickly get Debbie the emergency assistance she desperately needed.

AN EXIT?

That's when the first of a series of God's subsequent miracles occurred. In less than two miles, the next exit came into view, with a huge blue "H" sign indicating a hospital was near! It was not just near; it could be seen from the exit ramp off the superhighway. Lake Norman Hospital was within sight, less than one hundred yards from the exit ramp.

Pulling up to the hospital's emergency entrance, I gasped, "Hold on, Debbie; I'll get help." I rushed into the reception room. The receptionist behind the counter pointed to a waiting area. "No," I screamed, "my wife is having a stroke. We need immediate help. Now! She's outside in our car."

An army of attendants appeared from nowhere, swept Debbie onto a stretcher, and hastily carted her off to the emergency operating room. I was forced to pause long enough to sign some necessary paperwork. Within two minutes, I was by her side. She was surrounded by two doctors, who began temporary treatment in preparation for an MRI brain scan. All this, from her first headache to initial treatment, had consumed less than seven minutes.

Had we not stopped at that particular rest stop when we did, called 911, or had she been struck a minute earlier or a minute after passing the exit ramp to the hospital, there would have been no chance of her survival. She would have died. Why did this crisis happen exactly where and when it did? The crisis's location and timing could hardly be called sheer luck; the odds that the circumstance was mere happenstance were as remote as winning a mega lottery. The fortunate time and location of this catastrophe, we later concluded, was a miracle— a blessing from our Savior. Survival was a possibility. Potential was not certainty, however. As I barged into the emergency room, the smell of death saturated the air.

"I'm Dying"

The scene in the emergency room was dazing and dizzying. "I'm dying," Debbie whispered.

"No, you're *not* dying," I nervously rebutted.

But she was sure that she was about to die. She prayed, saying the same prayer three times in succession: "Father, please forgive me for my many past sins, and accept me into your heaven. Chuck, I love you with all my heart and will be waiting for you when your time comes." She trailed off as the painkillers and other meds took away her consciousness.

Stunned and shocked and drained of all sensation, the psychological defense mechanism of denial failed to provide relief from the hell I was experiencing. How could this be happening? Is this just a terrible nightmare? Or had day, in the blink of an eye, really turned into the pitch blackness of night? I was lost.

Darkness Drowns Light

As I waited impatiently, minutes seemed like hours. This was pure agony. "A stroke? This really can't be happening," I repeated to myself over and over again. I could not escape the punishing pain. I was adrift in suffocating, purgatorial air. The same dreadful thought kept passing through my spinning head—that her words "I'm dying" and her prayer might be the last words I might ever hear her say. Was this the last time I would see my Debbie alive? My dread was uncontrollable. I was like a child repetitiously tapping a loose sore tooth, even though each touch caused pain. I kept reliving my indescribably hurtful and fearful thought that I might lose my beloved wife. The fear could not be blocked.

Next came a dark, startling pronouncement: "We are sending Debbie by emergency helicopter to Carolinas Medical Center in Charlotte. A team of surgeons will be waiting for her. Some blood vessels in your wife's brain have burst, and blood is flowing out of a ruptured aneurism and flooding her brain. These hemorrhages damage brain tissue and are almost always fatal. She has a chance, however. She has been sedated, and her CT scan and MRI data have already been forwarded to the neurosurgeons in Charlotte. You cannot ride with her in the chopper because of weight issues and regulations. So drive there, now. The distance is twenty-seven point eight miles—about thirty-two minutes. Here are the directions. The emergency room there will tell you her condition and what to do. Good luck."

As I approached our car, I witnessed the helicopter rise from the platform, and my tears fell. The sight and sound of that helicopter lifting my Debbie and the fear that this might be her last trip were overwhelming. Trembling, I lost my balance and stumbled. This was the most frightful scene I had ever seen in a lifetime that included many past hair-raising scares. We desperately needed a lifeline. "Please, God, save her," I prayed. "Let her live."

What would I find in Charlotte at Carolinas Medical Center (CMC)? Would my Debbie still be alive? My panic clouded my thinking about the myriad possibilities. The worst-case scenario was too painful to envision. But I could not erase it from my petrified imagination. This moment was an experience nobody should have to endure. Anyone who has been informed of the death of a loved one knows the unbearable grief that that kind of news always provokes.

Fear leads to deadly despair. However, extreme danger and approaching mortality can have the opposite effect—they can instead breed hope derived from faith and from the search for meaning. The sermon Debbie and I had recently heard took on real meaning, although at this time of crisis there was no space left in my befuddled mind for abstract reasoning. Pastor Stephen Ridenhour had explained that God had created both day and night and had separated them; we are called to accept His created darkness and to live through the shadows of night as we await the light that assuredly will follow. At this terrifying moment, all was pitch black. In the night no light could be seen. That could change later, I prayed. But at this horrific moment darkness smothered all light.

COULD LIGHT BREAK THE DARK OF NIGHT?

On the interstate driving from Lake Norman Hospital while Debbie was being flown to Charlotte, I darted past and around vehicles in heavy traffic. Mercifully, the congestion did not cause any of Charlotte's notorious bumper-to-bumper backups. The agonizing drive was awful. But it was fast. I rushed with distress lights blinking while maneuvering at ninety miles per hour. A blur of images masked my incoherent and unconnected memories. I recall little except speeding in heavy interstate traffic while crying my eyes out. People I passed in other vehicles looked at me in horror. I made the trip in twenty minutes.

Was Debbie's arrival by helicopter at CMC another mysterious miracle? Why did she look at death in the face here of all places, where, I was to learn, her chances of survival through the CMC team were without parallel? Carolinas Neurosurgery & Spine Associates has one of the best teams of brain surgeons in the world. Why was Debbie so blessed? Was her arrival here at this time just a lucky coincidence? That was doubtful. Debbie's circumstances enhancing her prospects for potential survival were too improbable. They happened for a reason. There could only be one answer.

Recklessly pulling our Honda CR-V into the cavernous CMC four-story hospital parking garage, I rushed to search for Debbie while praying that she was still alive. The emergency room attendants flinched as they received me and directed me to the operating rooms on the hospital's fourth floor. A team of eight brain surgeons and their assistants sighed in relief when I arrived. They were anxious to issue a report. What did they want to tell me face to face?

CHAPTER 4

Traversing the Valley of the Shadow of Death

§

The news from the CMC surgeons nervously awaiting my arrival was alarming. "Your wife is very fortunate to still be alive. Few victims of a brain aneurism survive, and she certainly would be dead had she not received stabilizing treatment at Lake Norman Hospital so promptly." I felt like a walking dead man, unable to hear my own footsteps. This news was only a shade less dark than the worst outcome. Was there a basis for hope?

Sounding the Alarm

The surgeons' initial disclosure of Debbie's condition was dismal. "The CT scan shows that Debbie has suffered a major severe hemorrhagic aneurism in the posterior of her brain, the part that controls many mental and physical functions, and there could be other smaller vessel ruptures hidden by the flood of blood. The visible perforated aneurism is small," Dr. Hunter Dyer reported.

"Small is good," I prematurely concluded.

"No," Dyer cautioned, "that makes closing the broken vessel harder. Worse still, the hemorrhage is shaped like a 'hot dog' balloon, not like the usual 'pimple,' which is easier to treat with a tubular 'pipeline' or 'stent' duct inside broken blood vessels to stop the blood leaking into the brain and to restore the vital oxygen-supplying blood flow. In addition, the aneurism is located where two vessels intersect, increasing the dangers. My colleague Dr. Joe Bernard refuses to attempt to reach the perforated vessels by threading a stent from the groin through the less-invasive arteries leading to the brain vessels. He said the location of the hemorrhages make this procedure much too risky, probably lethal. Given this dangerous circumstance, we simply must split open Debbie's skull to try to stop the deadly cerebral bleeding and stabilize the blood flow in her brain's vessels. This is absolutely necessary if we are to save her life. We aim to put a metal clip on her broken aneurism. Despite the risks, it's the only remaining surgical option. We are going to try hard. Very hard."

The choice seemed like a choice between facing a firing squad or being hanged. I hanged my hopes on God's intervention.

"There's a slim chance that Debbie will survive without some perhaps serious and permanent loss of function," Dr. Dyer grimly warned. "If you want to proceed, here are some forms to read before giving consent."

"Are you kidding?" I cried. "You just said there's no alternative but to operate, or she will die! I don't want to waste a single second reading these legal forms. So let me sign, and please get started immediately."

Appreciatively, Debbie's surgeons did not take umbrage at the desperation in my adamant voice and jumped into action, giving the "go ahead" to start preparations. As the surgeons and assistants gathered over and around Debbie lying on the anesthesiologist's table, I asked if I could offer a prayer. We all held hands. I cried out to the Lord: "Dear heavenly Father, I ask for Your help. You see our need. Debbie has skilled surgeons poised to save her life. Please empower them to use all their talents in their efforts to save Debbie, and guide them as they exercise those skills to serve Your purposes, if that, beloved Savior, is Your will." Misty-eyed and energized, this team thanked me for my words of support, insisted I leave the surgery room, and prepared to begin the surgery.

I was forced to exit. But first I said to my sedated Debbie, "I love you more than I ever have before. You are safe. God is with you." I suspected that my words penetrated her subconscious mind. I couldn't bear the thought that I might be speaking to her for the final time on earth; my hopes faded like mist in the sun but rose immediately when I called on God to intercede to save Debbie from destruction and return her to me.

As instructed, I was required to leave the operating room and wait in the waiting room for the surgery to be attempted. As I shuffled zig-zag down the hallway, I held my breath as I pictured the surgeon's scalpel splitting open Debbie's skull. The next image appearing in my dark imagination was the surgeon's tools attempting to breach the lesion where her aneurism had broken—just below the dangerous point where a metaphorical fuse meets a powder keg. The results could be gruesome, maybe fatal. I trembled. Had I seen her for the last time? I prayed that she would survive but knew that if she did, she probably would lose some of her former capabilities. She might be a very different person, but I didn't care as long as she survived, and I could be with her to love and care for her. I didn't want to live if she didn't survive. This surgery struck fear into the depths of my soul.

Debbie's team of surgeons had warned me that the difficult surgery would be very long. That wait became more unbearable because the surgeons had advised me to use my time securing a copy of our last will and testament and obtaining a permission form to pull Debbie off life support if her survival looked hopeless—a grim reminder that the operation might not succeed. (Our will included a clause that in the event of her death, Debbie had elected to be an organ donor so her transplanted vital body parts could enable other dying patients to live.) The only thing that carried me was my belief that anything is possible through a loving and healing God. The words Eugene O'Neill wrote in his 1928 play, *Strange Interlude*, rose from my deep memory: "Our lives are merely strange dark interludes in the electrical display of God the Father." I counted on God's electrical intercession as I prayed that this nightmarish, strange interlude would be only that—a temporary interval that someday could be buried in the past.

HIGH RISKS FOR HUGE STAKES

Harsh realities sucked the air out of the waiting room as I tried to face Debbie's uncertain fate. I could hardly breathe. I quickly became aware of the risks confronting all who experience a hemorrhagic stroke. The handout from the CMC defined a brain aneurism as "a balloon-like bulge in the wall of a brain vessel. If this bulge tears and bleeds, a stroke occurs." The handout went on to summarize what happens when a blood vessel in someone's brain bursts. A stroke "may happen if the blood vessel wall is weak, or if a blood clot gets stuck in a blood vessel. Blood then either flows out of the vessel or the blood vessel is blocked. In either case, brain tissue is damaged or destroyed."

Strokes are horrific beyond words. A stroke can damage a brain in countless ways, including literally killing brain functionality as the victim becomes "brain dead." Because strokes can result from multiple threats, many neurosurgeons think the term "brain attack" better captures what is commonly called "a stroke." The brochure I was given did not mince words in identifying the risks confronting stroke victims who survive surgery:

> You may bleed more than expected during surgery. You may need a machine to help you breathe. You may have another stroke or go into a coma. You may be paralyzed on one or both sides of your body. You may not be able to care for yourself or live alone. You are at greater risk of falling. You may develop muscle shortening or bedsores. Even with treatment, you may have lasting problems talking, thinking, or moving your body. Without treatment, your risk for another stroke increases. You may die from a stroke.

I was later to learn more about the terrifying dangers. Joshua Rothman, a seasoned neurosurgeon, writes candidly:

> The anxiety begins long before surgery, with the decision to operate in the first place, which could easily be wrong. A brain scan

is mute on many all-important questions, and a catastrophe is very possible. Brain surgery is slow and dangerous—like defusing a bomb. A quarter of the body's blood courses through the veins and arteries of the brain; the basilar artery carries blood to the brain stem, which regulates the rest of the brain. When any vein or artery tears or breaks, brain tissue is destroyed. Unlike the rest of the body, the brain and the spinal cord rarely heal. If a neurosurgeon makes a mistake, the damage is often permanent.

Another information booklet did not improve the picture. To address a brain aneurysm, it explained, the surgeon has

to make his way deep into the brain, exposing the small, deadly balloon of arterial blood so that, without rupturing it, it can be sealed off using a miniature clip. At risk is the mysterious substrate of all thought and feeling. Often, there's a question of how far to go; if an aneurysm is not quite perfectly positioned, the surgeon must face the risk of repositioning it, which can cause a catastrophic hemorrhage. Neurosurgical disasters can be cruel. A patient can wake up and appear healthy only to die, a few days later, of another stroke or hemorrhage that's related, in "some unknowable way," to the first surgery. And patients can live on—sometimes for months and years on end—in a state of vegetative numbness without feeling.

Could Debbie's precarious situation get any worse? Had I actually read these warnings when the surgery-permission forms were shoved into my hands, I might have rethought this procedure. But what alternative was there? The surgeons knew that without prompt surgery, there was no chance that Debbie would survive. The best course of action was the one taken, upon reflection it seemed certain. Debbie's brave surgeons had to be admired for their courageous efforts to fight grim odds. They were asked to go into battle weakly armed, like taking a toy water gun into a gunfight. They forged ahead, knowing they, like me, would have to anxiously wait after the surgical efforts to observe their results. I had to wonder how, while performing such an unpredictable operation, her brain surgeons could strike a balance between optimistic hope and dreadful realism.

In *My Stroke of Insight*, Dr. Jill Bolte Taylor, a brain scientist who in her mid-thirties underwent a severe stroke, pinpointed the dangers of a cranial invasion. She feared that if surgeons penetrated her skull, "I would never be able to recover my body or any of my cognition. I made it perfectly clear to everyone that under no circumstances would I ever agree...to open my head." Dr. Taylor subsequently changed her mind and authorized this highly calculated risk, which enabled her survival. Surgery, too, was Debbie's only option. God granted us confidence to proceed. Debbie was poised for a set of miracles.

This instantaneous decision to take this passage into the unknown took me into dark and turbulent uncharted mental waters. This gush of distressing information flooded my mind; I was psychologically drowning, feeling like I had been drinking from a fire hose. To the extent that I could think rationally, there percolated in my hazy mind the vague realization that something profoundly transformational was unfolding—not simply big but life-changing, possibly life-ending. Debbie's life was exceedingly perilous. The worst possibility—fatal mortality—was a grave potential outcome.

Nothing makes life more precious than the prospect of imminent death. The thought of Debbie's end made me appreciate, like nothing else, life's value. But more than that, at the abyss I stood somewhere between being and not being, existence and nonexistence, and at that threshold I began to reevaluate my values and life's meaning. I didn't clearly see it then as Debbie stood at the edge of existence, but her brush with death launched into consciousness a whole gamut of metaphysical and theological thoughts. It took a dark tragedy for life to start to mean something. Facing death was broadening and deepening understanding of what life and death might mean. What a strange time and way to begin a journey to grasp the meaning of life and strengthen faith! Terrifying circumstances were generating unintended consequences in the midst of utter agony. Benjamin Franklin wrote, "The things that hurt, instruct." My education began as hurt escalated.

CHAPTER 5

A DEAD END?

§

I was forced to sit out the outcome in the waiting room while Debbie's preparations for surgery were underway. This is what people do in waiting rooms. They wait. That was my plight. It was a nerve-racking predicament. I was grieving and frustrated. Wait? Wait? This is one of the many things in which I am highly deficient. I am not a patient person but had no choice but to practice patience waiting for the verdict. I was ill equipped to sit this crisis out.

THE DAY TIME STOPPED

I would like to be able to say that I remember well what was happening at this terrible time. That was not the case. I was in a state of psychological shock. I tried to collect my thoughts. I failed. In my nervous angst, all I could think about was the horrible realization that my vulnerable Debbie was lying on an operating table and that surgeons were busy opening her brain cavity to stop the bleeding from her broken vessels. I tried mentally to block this image but couldn't. All I could do was picture her fighting for her life. I was not just beside myself; I was out of my mind. In the shade and shadows, I do not recall many details.

Some degree of solace and serenity came from the firm belief that God was in control and that prayers are heard. I knew Debbie and I could potentially get by with the help and prayers of our families and friends.

So how to occupy time productively while hysterical? Better inform loved ones. Andy answered first and asked what they could do.

"Please tell our family and friends what has happened," I answered, "and ask for their prayers, but do *not* come to Charlotte. Under the best of circumstances, Debbie will survive surgery necessitating cutting open her skull. Pray. If she makes it over this hurdle, she will be alive but heavily sedated. There's really nothing you can do for me now. Company will not help." Uncharacteristically candidly blunt, my hasty message made its point clear. Imagining how my grim words sounded hit a raw nerve. But they expressed the dark truth about the gravity of the situation.

Pastor George Crow responded immediately to my second call. He offered an inspiring prayer, asking God to uplift and protect His cherished child and keep her safe. George boosted my hope and my faith.

I didn't know it at the time, but God answered my prayers and those of a rapidly growing number of friends and family in this, the most precarious period of Debbie's life. I knew that there was only one path for deliverance, and that was by God's grace. I firmly believed that I was not worthy but could pray for loving and healing help from God. This was not because of illusions about our own worth warranting God's intervention on our behalf. Instead, faith rested on the Lord's promise to look with compassion on those who throw themselves at His feet, crying out of the depths of darkness and despair. Psalm 139:12 voices the comforting message that in dark times God can pierce anyone's gloomy mind and instill assurance of His tender care, and that the darkness can't hide us from Him.

- **Finding Our Fate**—The waiting room staff witnessed my anxiety and offered special attention and consolation. A message board informed all of each patient's status: pre-operation, operation, and, where possible, post-operative recovery. The receptionists could see my grief from the tears in my terrified eyes and were taken by my disclosure that I believed that only God could provide the protection for which I prayed. They whispered to me that they would disregard protocol and page me ahead of any postings when they received news, as the board was rarely current. They even volunteered to make a call to the surgeons' assistants if there were serious delays between updates.

Three agonizing hours passed without any news beyond the message that the team of surgeons had promptly begun the operation. Then, contrary to my previous request, Andy and Nan Kegley muscled their way into the waiting room. They were not to be denied. Following my call, they jumped into their car and headed for Charlotte. I was immediately gratified that they had ignored my request. They were right. I really needed them and their advice and encouragement.

They greeted me warmly, but try as they might, they could not hide their fears. However, they floated an idea: while waiting for the operation to proceed, Andy suggested that we should use the time productively. I suspect their real motive was to get me moving to shake the endless stupefying worrying from my mind. The tension was so thick I felt it could be cut with a knife.

Andy led me, staggering, to the nearby Hospitality House, where the doctors had reserved room 308. In the interim, this excursion was prudent. It was necessary to pay for my assigned room in order to hold it. I prepaid for five days but had no intention of leaving Debbie's bedside in the intensive care unit if she survived. I am devoid of a sense of direction, so Andy's guidance through the tangle of parking lots to the Hospitality House about five hundred yards from the hospital enabled me to gather some clothes from our vehicle and take a hurried shower. While this was taking place, Nan tended the waiting room armed with a cell phone to announce any developments.

Ever efficient, Andy called family and friends in Wytheville while I finished dropping a few items in my room. Andy had notified others of Debbie's situation, and passengers in three cars were traveling to Charlotte when Andy reached them. His e-mail prior to their departure had summarized the bleak situation: "Debbie had a seizure and ruptured aneurism while they were driving to South Carolina. Chuck is extremely distraught and is waiting on the doctors to decide how to best close the hemorrhaged brain vessel. He discouraged the idea of us trying to come down, saying he doesn't need company, but I think friends would really be helpful for them. We are leaving now to be with him."

Others acknowledged that a crowd would not be helpful and reluctantly accepted my frantic request not to visit, and Andy's report of my request convinced the travelers he had contacted to turn back and postpone their visits.

We returned to the waiting room, and the clock ticked at a snail's pace. The sound system blurted "Would Mr. Kegley come to the desk?" My heart sank and soared at the same time. I learned that the surgeons called to report to the waiting-room staff that the anesthesia and many other medications including vaccines, morphine, antibiotics, and hemoglobin transfusions had taken effect. After reviewing additional MRI and CT scans, they said that Debbie was now prepared for the operation to open an incision into her skull in order to try to close the bleeding aneurism. The operation would soon begin. Movement forward to the operating stage meant she remained alive and that progress might be possible, while the nightmare of disaster persisted.

- **Suspense Mounts**—Was it possible to fear no evil, even while comforted by knowledge that God was with me? Can we really control our minds? It is doubtful that people are masters of their thoughts. Leo Tolstoy understood. In his youth, he recalls, his boyhood friends had formed a club. To join, as an initiation test, potential members had to lean against an oak tree and, for a full minute, *not* think of a white bear. Everyone seeking membership who claimed they successfully managed that challenge was denied inclusion—they were liars. We simply cannot impose by will control over what we think. So it is especially with angst and fear; we are incapable of directing our thoughts away from ideas suggested to us, and this holds especially for our deepest dreads. Debbie's potential death was deeply dreaded, and no amount of denial could dispel the despair that the thought of her loss provoked. I could not control my thoughts.

Watching the clock made matters worse. Time seemed to move at a glacial pace. With each minute, dread increased, for the longer the operation lasted, the more likely it was that the challenges for the surgeons also were increasing. But wait. No word meant that Debbie was still alive and the surgery might be safely proceeding. Fear and hope seemed to alternate in ever-changing ratios. (An anecdote captures the lack of control in this kind of situation, with a small dose of humor. Once when I was looking downcast, a friend counseled, "Cheer up. Things could be worse." So I cheered up, and, sure enough, things got worse.)

I never felt, during those frightening hours, so afraid. But every time I hit rock bottom psychologically, I was lifted up by constantly renewed awareness that God was with Debbie and me, and therefore we should not be afraid. Assuredly He was there for us. I knew He cared. Nonetheless, I was haunted by the realization that our heavenly Father might call Debbie home. I could not imagine living without her. Indeed, I quickly concluded, in that case I did not want to live; I would gladly welcome the opportunity to join her in an afterlife, in a better place. I mumbled that I wished it had been me, not her, who stood at death's door.

The spell was broken by an abrupt announcement booming through the waiting room's speakers. "Will the family and friends of Debra Kegley please come to the reception desk?" Heart pounding, I leaped into action. There Angela and Greg greeted me with cautious smiles, with Andy and Nan trailing. "Chuck, one of the surgeons' assistants just called from the operating room. She said to tell you the surgery was progressing and that 'so far, so good.'"

Two more hours passed, and the sun was beginning to set and the sky was darkening. At 5:30 p.m., the voice once again boomed loudly, summing me, Andy, and Nan. "The operation is nearing completion," Angela happily announced. "The chief surgeon, Emmet 'Hunter' Dyer, will brief you on Debbie's condition in the oak-lined private consulting room through that doorway where I am pointing." We headed there and nervously waited. The consulting chamber was built like a church or funeral-home parlor. The three of us huddled and quietly braced ourselves for the crucial verdict destined to point to some kind of road to the future.

- **In the Dark: Life or Death?**—Time continued to look like it stood still. It was now 6:50 p.m., and my heart was racing. "What is taking so long?" I fretted. Debbie had been in the surgery recovery room now for over two and a half hours. Was she really recovering? Or was something wrong—maybe terribly wrong?

   Our wait ended shortly thereafter. Dr. Dyer arrived from the surgeons' quarters, looking exhausted with wrinkles from worry lining his face as he prepared to issue a report. I was glad Andy and Nan were by my side. They helped to dispel some of my confusion, and they chimed in to ask some questions which I, unnerved, didn't have the wit to ask. And they were alert and better able to comprehend and remember Dr. Dyer's appraisal. I was afraid to ask for Dr. Dyer's report. Andy broke the ice for me: "What's the prognosis in your opinion?"

   Dr. Dyer began his briefing by disclosing a stubborn fact. "While there are commonalities among stroke victims, no two are alike. Every case is unique. Each individual is truly an individual. So we have no basis for predicting what Debbie's future holds." Dr. Dyer continued, "The surgery did go reasonably well," he understated. "Better still, Debbie's vital signs appear moderately encouraging—for now. We will watch her closely in the recovery room. The operation on her brain vessel to install a metal clip to seal the aneurism seems to have worked. If by tomorrow morning we see that her bleeding has stopped, the stitches closing her head wounds will enable the incisions to begin to heal. But, as I said, only if all goes well tonight."

"However," Dr. Dyer continued, "there are serious threats ahead. If Debbie stabilizes sufficiently within two to three hours, she will be carried on a roll-cart transport platform accompanied by a full array of life-support aides such as a respiratory feeder to supply oxygen. She will be assigned to a private room in the Intensive Care Unit [ICU] where you can join her. But if that happens, don't expect her to show awareness. She will be heavily sedated, in a coma-like state. Be prepared, Chuck, for the ICU staff to ask you to look at legal papers permitting the suspension of life support if her cognitive skills are damaged beyond recovery; the request is standard operating procedure. Oh, by the way, count on this additional bit of information: after Debbie is ready, as I hope she will be, to be transported from post-op to her assigned ICU room, I will stop in and give you three the latest report on her condition."

Within minutes Dr. Dyer's prophecy was fulfilled. Angela and Greg gave me a reassuring look and gave me the information I sought: "The surgeons called. Your wife will be transported to room 9-A of the stroke unit in intensive care on the ninth floor within an hour. Go ahead to her room so you can be there when she arrives."

THE DAWN'S EARLY LIGHT?

Debbie was still alive. Her condition was uncertain. But there remained a decent chance that she would survive. Thank you, God! She lives because You love. This bridge over troubled waters had not been crossed, but there was hope that the bridge might carry her to safety. A little bit of light filtered through the dense darkness.

There was nothing more that could be done at that time. We could only brace ourselves for whatever might happen next. Anything was possible. What would we find, tonight or tomorrow? No one could foretell the future.

Dr. Dyer concluded his post-surgery evaluation in the consultant's chamber. He urged, "I suggest you get something to eat while you try to digest the information I am able to supply at this point in time."

I thanked him and offered prayers of appreciation for his amazing contribution to Debbie's opportunity to live. So Andy, Nan, and I shuffled our way to the third-floor cafeteria. The music piped to the diners was from the '50s. The lyrics hit hard:

Oh where, oh where, can my baby be?
The Lord has taken her away, from me!
She's gone to heaven, so I've got to be good,
So I can see my baby when I leave this world.

CHAPTER 6

INTENSIVE CARE

§

With Andy and Nan's assistance, I found my way through the maze of corridors to the hospital elevators and ninth floor to Debbie's assigned room in the stroke victims' section of the Intensive Care Unit (ICU). My nervous excitement and alarm had erased all memory of our navigational route. This trip was a complete blur—even my entry through the security doors that barred intruding visitors.

Debbie's designated room was rather roomy. Three windows opened to the skyline, now darkened by the onset of nighttime. The darkness covered all thoughts.

The night nurse, Katie, was caring and compassionate. She would be attending Debbie and one other stroke patient in the adjoining room (occupied by a thirty-one-year-old woman with a remarkable resemblance to my Debbie, who also had been victimized by an asymptomatic burst aneurism; tragically, she met her Maker two days later). "There is a stuffed recliner chair available," Katie pointed out, "if you want to spend the night in Debbie's room." "Of course I will. I refuse to leave her."

In the meantime, other assisting staff attendants arrived. As Dr. Dyer warned, they asked me to send for a copy of Debbie's living will, which requested that her vital body parts be donated to critically ill victims who were praying for a donor to supply organs. The ICU staff also pressed me to make available consent forms if her brain function stopped and the life-support systems could be turned off. (I never complied with the latter request; her life was in God's hands and no one else's.)

The wall clock showed 8:17 p.m. when at last the sound of movement could be heard outside the entrance to Debbie's ICU room. I tried to rearrange my face to greet the attendants escorting Debbie on a roll cart into her ICU room. Andy and Nan's eyebrows rose in anticipation. Debbie was carefully transferred to her bed. She lay there so motionless that I wondered if she was in a coma. She was surrounded by what appeared to be an endless tangle of tubes and wires that fed her limp body with painkillers, sedatives, spinal fluids, heart monitors...you name it. A ventilator supplied oxygen, an IV drained excess spinal fluid from her brain, and nameless other devices protruded from her body.

DR. DYER'S DIRE REPORT

Dr. Dyer walked into the ICU room with two assistants, all looking like exhausted prize fighters at the sound of the bell signaling the end of a hard-fought round. Dyer, businesslike, was, well, dire. "Here's the news. As you know, the flood of blood that had burst into Debbie's brain was immediately drained when Debbie first arrived by helicopter at the hospital. As you will recall, in the operation, we shaved half of Debbie's head and opened a thirteen-inch incision into the rear portion of her skull to clamp and close the aneurism. The gap was sealed with a clip to stop additional bleeding and prevent further damage. Unfortunately, as the scans had shown, the aneurism was in a difficult place to reach. We found another balloon-like bulge on the opposite side of the aneurism where the vessel broke. This is worrisome. We will have to carefully watch for another rupture. An additional operation may be necessary."

"Now all we can do is wait and see. Debbie will be monitored by the panel of devices that measure her heart rate, respiratory pulmonary intake, blood pressure, cerebrospinal fluid, temperature, et cetera. Throughout the night, the attending nurse in the ICU, Katie, will observe these indicators. If and when any functions vary outside the acceptable range, sounds will peep to signal a warning. Chuck, you can watch from the chair by her bedside. Don't expect Debbie to awaken—the morphine and other pain-killer medications will keep her asleep. If all goes well, she may regain consciousness sometime tomorrow—but if she does, she will not remember anything; no stroke-attack patients ever do for the first two weeks. My surgery associates and I will examine Debbie's condition early next morning, providing she successfully clings to life."

Andy, Nan, and I tried to consume this troublesome surge of distressing information. We conferred and compared our interpretations. However, the only conclusion was that we were dealing with a bundle of known unknowns. Only time would tell. Andy and Nan then exited to travel back home to Wytheville, begging me for constant updates. We hugged and said our good-byes, trying to put a cheerful face on a dreadful situation. We could not know if Debbie would recover.

"The Lord is my shepherd; I shall not want," I told myself. "I am not alone. God must be with me and Debbie as she travels through the valley of the shadow of death." Nan had left Debbie a loving note, in her famously neat block letters, to be read if and when Debbie awoke. "Debbie," it read, "you are great. We love you. PS: I could do without your mohawk haircut—ha-ha." She added this touch of humor about Debbie's half-shaved head to lighten the depressing situation.

Always wondering and worrying, I had no idea if Debbie would begin her journey from darkness to light. Had she lost her true self…perhaps forever? Or, with God's healing and expert medical care, would Debbie regain a large percentage of what had been lost? Was it possible that she might come out of her travels renewed, perhaps even reborn? Another outcome floated through the tension—if resuscitation led to recovery, might Debbie emerge a new person? This was another possibility; Dr. Dyer had disclosed that people after brain surgery frequently develop new personalities. Life can be transformed in countless ways. Change is the only thing that is constant. We accordingly have no alternative but to accept the things we cannot change.

CHAPTER 7

DAYLIGHT OR DARKNESS?

§

This first evening at Debbie's bedside was an incredibly dark period—a virtual black night of danger and dread. "Darkness" is an appropriate adjective. It describes what is associated with what is bad, in stark contrast to the adjective "light," which is universally associated with what is good.

That first night was the paragon of dark circumstances. It was filled with doom and gloom. "Darkness" covers a lot of ground within the human experience (whereas in heaven there will be only shining light; "there will be no more night," Dr. Randy Alcorn posits). To call this first black night in ICU "dark" is a gross understatement, but it defines just how black the dark can get. "Dark" is appropriately descriptive of the utterly black negative sensations I experienced during that bleak cold January night.

My dark hours at Debbie's bedside that first night set into motion what was to become a deeply entrenched pattern. It became as ritualized as an eighteenth-century dance. Sitting and praying at Debbie's bedside as she lay motionless, as if on autopilot, I first stared obsessively at her beautiful face, waiting for her eyes to open or body to move. Then I shifted my focus, fixating on the panel of lights and signals that recorded eight different indicators of her constantly changing condition. Every time a beep sounded, I jumped in fright. This happened often, signaling that some change in Debbie's vitals (heart rate, blood pressure, oxygen intake, et cetera.) had vacillated outside the normal range, either high or low.

My mental alarms sounded, and I would instantly spring into action to seek the always-attentive nurse Katie (and the subsequent sequence of capable nurses who took her place). They seemed to tolerate—no, openly applauded in appreciation my untiring vigilant attention to Debbie—and promptly reacted, usually by trying to calm my needless anxieties. In this thunderstorm of tumult, I lost all sense of time. Every minute seemed like an hour, and every hour seemed like a minute.

This ritualized routine continued without interruption. This interlude was interrupted only by rare calls to family and friends and trips to the restroom. I did not spare time from my vigil to fetch food at the hospital cafeteria. I had no appetite. I remained steadfast at Debbie's bedside.

ENLIGHTENMENT?

We survived that first night. The early morning of January 9—the day after Debbie's travels started—began the next stretch of her long journey. Would daylight bring a basis for hope? I waited in anticipation, constantly watching Debbie and her monitors. A new day at dawn offered the possibility that some positive answers to many questions might be found.

Andy encapsulated well the situation that had unfolded during that long night. His e-mail put the news this way: "Debbie's nurse Katie told me that Debbie is 'stable.' I know Chuck is on pins and needles. Dr. Dyer reports that he feels good about the surgical procedure to put a clip on the aneurism, but they have collected a fair amount of bleeding from the procedures they did last evening when we were there with Chuck at the hospital. The surgeons decided not to do the vascular procedure from the groin as the aneurism's location—behind the ear—because it was difficult to get to, so instead it became necessary to perform the surgery by cutting through the skull. Keep them in your prayers. Many miracles happened yesterday to get them here."

So here we were, thanks to miraculous treatment under God's magnanimous management. That morning was *not* a time of mourning.

Debbie had survived the night. She was still not conscious. Some light began to become visible. I was with her, poised to discover where we were heading.

As promised, Dr. Dyer and his colleague Dr. Bernard arrived very early the next morning. I sat, shaking, as I awaited the latest analysis. Dr. Dyer started his briefing slowly and deliberatively. He broke the silence by stating the obvious in his introduction to his summary evaluation: "Debbie made it through the night. This is a good start," which meant she had not slipped away. "The aftermath of her surgery could have gone in a different direction. It didn't. So we have something to build on. Better still, her vital signs appear to be stabilizing. We are heartened by what we now observe and by what our team has found reading Debbie's computer records since her surgery."

I interrupted Dr. Dyer's briefing to give him and his associates the heartfelt thanks they deserved. They earned it tenfold. They had masterfully and miraculously performed an exceedingly challenging operation, deploying great skill and experience to keep Debbie alive.

Resuming his report, Dr. Dyer again warned, "We have no way of confidently predicting if and when consciousness, muscle mobility, and respiration will resume. Anything can happen," he pessimistically cautioned. "We shall just have to wait and see." (Thankfully, Dr. Dyer did not use that overused expression "It is what it is." That says nothing. It skirts the issue of defining what "it" is. To me, that trite tautology is like saying "it isn't what it isn't.")

So the good news was that Debbie's departure on her journey's flight had lifted and her condition had stabilized. The situation could have been far worse. She might be poised for a new start. I took this as a sign of progress, however modest. But the worrisome news was that survival did not mean that she would necessarily improve. Her destination remained unknown. True, she was living and receiving oxygen through a respiratory ventilator, and the possibility existed that some level of functional recovery could eventually commence. She conceivably could regain consciousness and possibly be able to speak and comprehend others' words. So a basis for hope had been created. She was not necessarily permanently grounded.

About 10:00 a.m. on that bright January 9, Pastor George Crow arrived from Columbia. He somehow secured permission to enter our ICU room; it was hard for the security guard to reject a request by a man of the cloth! George shot like a speeding bullet into our ICU room.

George was all excitement and encouragement. He came to offer blessed assurance. George cupped his hands on Debbie's brow—a "laying of hands" gesture to comfort the ill dating back to the time of Jesus Christ. George offered an inspiring prayer. Never at a loss for words, George provided the spiritual comfort and relief that were craved. If only my Debbie could hear and understand. Or could she? Maybe she could! George's words to our Savior conceivably could seep into her subconscious mind. Was Debbie a silent participant in this moving conversation? Was Debbie able to intuitively grasp George's words, even if she could not hear them? Humankind has not scratched the surface of knowledge about how the subconscious mind works and how it can sense intuitively unseen and unheard hidden realities. This possibility could not be ruled out, just like people often intuitively sense their deep inner communication and relationship with their God-in-us, as Saint Augustine did in picturing God "closer to me than I am to myself, more intimate than my very innermost point."

As if on a strict schedule, Dr. Dyer, Dr. Bernard, and two other neurosurgery assistants reappeared from nowhere later that morning to conduct a second assessment of Debbie's post-surgery condition. Their evaluation was to the point. The words flowed off Dr. Dyer's lips, confirming the prior diagnoses while repeating the grim warnings. The surgery team then exited and said they would return that afternoon for still another inspection. I suspected that they had hope that by then the sedatives and pain medications would have worn off and Debbie's eyes would open, but knew that the bases for their hopes could be groundless. So there was nothing to do but continue waiting.

THE SETTING FOR SUBSEQUENT ACTIVITY

As time slowly passed, two developments transpired during this second day that gave shape to the ICU environment in which Debbie and I found ourselves thereafter. The first enabled a window to open to allow others to keep informed about what was happening. The second was a rule imposed by the ICU that posed a barrier to others' ability to see Debbie in the hospital and observe her changing condition for themselves.

* **Communications Central**—In the first scenario, a communication service was created. Andy Kegley, fully aware of my ineptitude with anything technological, especially computers, kindly offered to assist with communications through the Internet. He launched e-mail communications carrying news I reported about Debbie's evolving circumstances to family and friends.

  His offer established an extremely helpful network service without which I could not have managed. I was swamped with calls and could not give the many concerned people the time or detail they sought. Personal updates simply were impossible, even though everyone deserved to hear individually an account from me about what had happened and Debbie's prospects for survival. I apologized, through Andy's e-mail, for my inattention and begged all to understand why I could not allocate time to share the dramatic news with each loved one individually. Free time to keep people informed simply did not exist. And to be frank, I wished to avoid the psychological stress that I knew I would encounter telling and retelling the traumatic events that were occurring moment by moment. Each personal effort generated a flood of tears. When I tried to talk, I was so choked with emotion that I was inarticulate and hard to hear. So I gave up. Updates would have to be spread by Andy's invitation to include whomever asked to be added to his e-mail list. That list grew like a wildfire.

  Andy's e-mail for Debbie set an important precedent. For example, Andy summarized the situation for George Crow, who immediately forwarded the message to the many members of Northeast Presbyterian Church as well as to members of Holy Trinity Lutheran Church in Wytheville. What is more, into the situation stepped our energetic friend Hilel Salomon and my twin brother, John Kegley, and his Internet-savvy wife, Mary. They also promptly set up their own Debbie Kegley report lists. As my telephoned news to them went viral, the three networks quickly expanded to other sets of concerned people (such as my Alpha Tau Omega fraternity brothers, who had met Debbie at three reunions). It was very gratifying to learn that almost from the beginning, our three primary Internet volunteers shared their updates with each other and, when pressed for time, forwarded the others' updates to those on their own server lists. What a gift in what was the most stressful period, without parallel, in my lifetime!

- **Visitors Prohibited**—In the second scenario, the ICU created a barrier to friends and family who wished to contribute by coming to Debbie's hospital room to provide comfort and aid. They were barred from visiting us.

  The ICU enforced a strict rule. Their established regulations prohibited any visitors and immediate caregivers other than me into Debbie's room or, for that matter, into the entire stroke victims' unit. This rule was not only to avoid infections, it also was to prevent any overstimulation and energy-draining excitement at the sight of visiting loved ones, should Debbie regain consciousness. Survivors of a stroke, I later learned, needed inordinate amounts of sleep and quiet while the brain struggled to connect neurons that allow cognition, speech, and body mobility.

  As noted, on that first dark night, Andy and Nan had been able to overcome this hospital rule, and I was thankful because their presence and participation were extremely helpful. Yet after they departed, it became evident to me that the last thing I then needed was a rush of other visitors. I needed only to be with Debbie, instead of consuming time in the visitors' waiting room. What could they do? I questioned. "But we want to be there for you, Chuck," some insisted. My reply: "I am not the person who needs help. Debbie is the person in need, and I must devote all my energies to her. At this time, she will not be aware of your presence and will not be able to see flowers or understand 'get well' cards and letters."

If truth be told, I wished to avoid being seen as the emotional wreck that I was. Frankly, telling people what had happened drained my endurance and sapped my energy, because it required me to relive the painful experience and put my emotional fractures on display. It was depressing for both listener and talker.

John and Mary forwarded my sentiments:

> Chuck has felt all of your care, concern, compassion and prayers. We told him we were packed and ready to be there with him and support him in any and all ways possible. However, he said that this would be appreciated, but would constitute almost interference at this time. He has asked us to request no visitors or phone calls until further notice, because this would be exhaustive and unproductive. We talked with Pastor Crow who is with him today. He reinforced the rationality of this approach. Chuck did say that meaningful information about Debbie's status will be forthcoming as it unfolds. We will pass this information on to you.

Quite candidly, I really was in no mental condition to judge how my interests would best be served. Whatever the wisdom or folly of my request, my plea was reluctantly honored, and its communication cut the travel plans to Charlotte of not only John and Mary but also the others who had planned to visit. This seemed to be the most prudent policy at this time. It generated some sound decisions. For example, my request to stay away for now was the message Debbie's sister, Karen, and her husband, Mark, needed; they were understandably inhibited by the thought that if they traveled to Charlotte, if then conscious, Debbie might think that the reason for their presence was to say good-bye for the last time because she was about to die.

Countless others may have felt abandoned, left outside the loop, by my request. (An exception did occur later: Hilel and our friend, Herman Rich, could not be deterred and drove from Columbia and somehow managed to sneak through the security doors. I must confess that their words of encouragement and cheerfulness provided a dosage of comfort, even though a long visit in the ICU waiting room was repeatedly interrupted by my frequent runs to see if Debbie was regaining consciousness and if she was receiving the constant attention from the attending nurse that was promised. Hilel's never-ending wit and humor in efforts to lighten my mood managed, momentarily, to do just that. His cheerful chuckle and jokes lifted me up. Where he comes up with his endless supply of funny material is anybody's guess. One example of his quick wit: adjacent to the CMC hospital is the Levine Children's Hospital. Hilel mused, "Boy, that guy Levine must have had a lot of children."

The sleepless hours following Debbie's brain surgery were interrupted only by assessments from our nurse, calls to our e-mail team, and quick trips to the restroom. And in the midst of these terrible trials in the fog of the unknown, a remarkable event occurred.

CHAPTER 8

EYEWITNESS TO A NEAR-DEATH EXPERIENCE

§

I sat by Debbie's bedside, hanging onto hope. I felt like a rock climber clinging by fingertips to prevent a long fall into a deep canyon. Contrary emotional states fell and rose like an elevator. I heard voices in my head. My thoughts oscillated between fatalistic pessimism and expectant optimism as I tried to imagine what Debbie was thinking, if she was capable of rational thought. Her eyes remained closed, so there were no visible light flickering from her blue eyes to suggest what, if any, sensations might be racing like deep dreaming within her subconscious mind.

Moonlight streamed through the windows to brighten the thick darkness during my second all-night session, and I was exhausted. In the throes of shifts between panic and confidence, at the stroke of midnight, I gave myself permission to rest my eyes for a ten-minute break in my bedside chair. Many hours without sleep was taking a toll. This is when, in the dark, I found God at work. It was a sensational sensation that I will never forget. Here's what happened in the blink of an eye.

No sooner had I closed my eyes for a few seconds when, instinctively, I reopened them to look at Debbie. Then it happened: a distinct brilliant light about the size of a blazing blueberry shone directly on Debbie's motionless body and began slowly to rise above it. Steadily the shining dot ascended about four feet. Then astonishingly the transcendent ray of light blossomed into a picture-perfect image of her smiling face, as unmistakable as she would appear in a mirror. She directed her gaze straight at me. Her face radiated supreme serenity—she hovered at some level of anesthetic calm, without a trace of agitation but with the appearance of animated comprehension. Her facial expression communicated a singular reassuring message: "Everything is good." Then, puff! Her head expanded and dispersed in thin air, like an exploding firework in the night sky. Her image imploded, disappearing from sight. More accurately, her soul—for I am convinced that is what I saw—vanished from sight.

I gasped in wonder. This was far outside any measure of normal experience. I am sure my sigh could be heard in heaven. I surmised that I had witnessed Debbie's spiritual soul levitate outside her body while she remained fully alive in her hospital bed. No monitors beeped indicating that her heart and respiratory rates had flat lined or her stationary corporeal body had died. She had been neither fully alive nor dead—an ephemeral force that had been lifted between the place where mortality and identity converge as the soul heads toward heaven. But God had sent her back. Her soul reunited with body; she had returned to earthly existence. I was certain this was a sign for me.

SEEING IS BELIEVING

I can only infer what Debbie experienced. She was heavily medicated and ostensibly comatose, so she retained no memory of the sensations which flowed, I suspect, through her spiritual subconscious mind into what William James termed the mind's "unconscious memories" which are automatically stored deeply in the cortical substrate brain. It is possible that, although unconscious, segments of her experience had lodged into her brain and been implanted in the deep recesses of her memory for potential retrieval when awake. Science has affirmed that an unconscious person retains a dim awareness of their experiences, such as blurred thoughts in deep dreams.

I have no idea what imagery of Debbie's spiritual sojourn might have been retained in her subconscious mental landscape. However, my imagery was vivid. I can only ask you to rely on my lucid eyewitness testimonial recollection of what I so clearly saw—the shining light floating upward, her blissful face, her reassuring gaze at me, and her amazing vanishing act. Because she lived and breathed normally afterward, I presume that her spiritual soul then rejoined her physical body.

I really don't know how this transfiguration happened. I wish I could find someone else who has watched another person undergo a "near-death experience" (NDE), so comparisons can inform my judgment about how NDEs look to external observers. Then again, such comparisons could be misleading, like comparing apples and oranges. Just like no two strokes and no two people are exactly alike, so no two NDEs are exactly the same. What I saw may have been unique.

My sight of Debbie's experience was personal. No one else was in the room able to verify my eyewitness account, but I am sure that had anybody else been present they would have seen what I saw. Admittedly, what occurred happened so fast that I momentarily had difficulty overcoming my natural initial cognitive dissonance about this phenomenal ocular event, but my confusion ended at the speed of thought. I shook my head and quickly organized my perceptions into a coherent conceptualization of what I had just witnessed. The picture was perfect, and amenable to no rival interpretation. Undoubtedly, Debbie's soul had risen outside her body. The kinetic image rippled from my retina to my brain's neural circuitry, hardwiring neural connections so that this spectacular optic sensation was imprinted permanently in my memory. I can vividly reconstruct the image of Debbie's out-of-body journey in full detail. Any time I need inspiration, I revisit in my mind's eye what I observed. I do so frequently. These visual paroxysms provoke no apprehension or agitation, only joyful equanimity. I am dead certain Debbie's soul had been briefly escorted beyond her body by the Holy Spirit, which is present, as the Bible maintains, inside the soul. God's awesome light showed His almighty power. I had seen a miracle—a fleeting peek at life beyond the body—what the book of Revelation describes as a light as brilliant as "a stone most precious." Debbie's soul had traveled to death's door, seen heaven's candle, and returned to her bodily essence where it had always been—an emanation of the Father.

As a brief aside, I should share that I do not think I could have seen this spectacular event in the absence of deep faith. I first had to place faith in God in order to overcome my myopia. Without faith, I was blind. I could not see the light. But with belief, when trust was placed in God's love, I could then see what God can do. The adage "seeing is believing" sees it backward; believing enables seeing, not the other way around. I believed. I am convinced that I was able to see the Holy Spirit at work during Debbie's sojourn between life and death precisely because of my prior belief. We can't see a spiritual world unless we think an invisible other world exists. My belief made my vision of Debbie's near-death journey possible.

The biblical story of Saul's epiphany and acceptance of Jesus as his Savior illustrates how belief allows us to see truths that were formerly hidden. On the road to Damascus, suddenly a blinding light flashed from heaven, and Saul fell to the ground and heard Jesus ask, "Saul, Saul, why do you persecute me?" For three days Saul was without sight, until God sent Ananias to fill Saul with the Holy Spirit, and immediately "something like scales" fell from Saul's eyes, and his sight was restored. Saul believed, and belief enabled him to see. Adopting the name Paul, he began to proclaim Jesus in the synagogues, saying "He is the Son of God" (Acts 9:1–20). The lesson: Believing empowers sight. Faith is the author of what can be perceived.

What did Debbie really experience during her near-death journey? I can only speculate what kinds of thoughts and sensations were implanted in the inner depths of her subconscious mind. But surely her sojourn had spiked a higher consciousness of self-awareness, similar to the intense sense of reality that emerges after a deep sleep when our minds create what psychologist Carl Jung called "big dreams." Her subconscious mind must have intuitively grasped God's spiritual presence alive within her. "What keeps faith alive," David Steindl-Rast notes, "is always experiential knowledge of God's spirit within us." Christianity maintains that

God acts within our deepest soul. Debbie must have understood that she had not been alone, that she belonged and had been accepted, and that therefore fatality was not final—death did not presage solitary confinement or nonexistence. There was something beyond this life, something much better (Phil. 1:21). As her soul traveled back to resume her "near-life" experience, some kind of subjective reminiscence of her sojourn likely was preserved and if so was certain to have lifted and sustained her future spirits. While nearly dying, the line between life and death is obscured, and at the cusp of experience I surmise that Debbie's pre-stroke intuitive convictions about God and eternity were reaffirmed, similar to how an electrical charge ignites a dead car battery. It is reasonable to infer Debbie had rediscovered old truths as the neurological ties that bind experience to faith became more binding. The neural bridge is sturdy because the borderline between earthly existence and the heavenly kingdom requires no passport beyond belief to cross. In this mystical spiritual realm, where the essential is invisible to the eye, Debbie must have subconsciously sensed her freedom from fear as well as the inextricable interconnection with God's entire infinite and everlasting cosmic universe.

As I reconstructed what I had observed, the attending nurse, Katie, bounded into our ICU room. She froze in her tracks as she looked at me. "What happened? Did something just happen? You should see your face! Is Debbie okay?"

I stammered, "Everything is under control." I couldn't put into words what exactly had just happened. I wasn't sure how to describe my ineffable and incredible mystical sensation. To be honest, still stunned, I didn't really then know how to connect the dots to frame an explanation. All I knew for certain was that my mind-boggling vision was real and good. Very good.

When Katie departed, satisfied that Debbie was safe and that I was not having some kind of psychological fit, I gave thanks to God. I knew the loving source for the miracle I had witnessed. My mood lifted in the darkness because I had seen the light—God's light, which moves faster than the speed of light in a vacuum. This light was deliverance. The amazing phenomenon I had observed suddenly made sense—it was the devine presence within Debbie's soul, the spiritual force driving her true self. "There is a light within a person of light, and it shines on the whole world," the Gospel of Thomas (24) proclaims. I had seen that light shine for me.

Why God chose to orchestrate the miracle I saw will never be known. We cannot know His plan, although there was no questioning the spiritual consequence of this witnessed miracle—the blessed assurance of His presence. I am confident that Debbie's reunion of body and soul was His doing. In the dark, the light of God at work became visible. I found God at the darkest hour. My faith knew no limits.

WHAT'S REALLY FOR REAL?

Emotions usually cloud visions, but intense emotions can also clarify vision. What I had seen was seen with 20-20 eyesight. What I witnessed was the kind of normally invisible ultraviolet "black light" made visible—what is known to theologians and to scientists as a veridical vision. I am utterly certain that what I saw was real. Okay, I admit that my jaw dropped in amazement when I first saw the bright pinhole of light begin to rise from Debbie's prone body; "What is that?" instinctively was my first thought. But what I witnessed was so evident that any subconscious doubts instantaneously vanished. This was not an apparition. Debbie's soul, her spirit, was active, mobile, and transformed before my very eyes.

"Perception is reality" is a well-known cliché. To an extent, we are all captives of the things we perceive, whether those things are figments of our imagination or visions rooted in reality. In perceiving Debbie's soul rise above her body, was I simply hallucinating? Was what I saw really real? Was I crazy—out of my mind? Admittedly, what I saw sounds suspiciously outside the conventional wisdom regarding what takes place at death's approach. As you read my account, your eyebrows may rise in disbelief. I can't provide proof.

Nonetheless, the epistemological principle that "seeing was believing" is popular for good reasons. Induction is a potent path to knowledge. I believe what I saw really happened. I am absolutely certain that the Holy Spirit carried Debbie's soul and escorted its return from near-death to life on earth. This was no hallucination. Her soul's journey was not a mirage manufactured in my imagination.

You may question my perceptions of Debbie's sojourn outside her body. I am making bold claims. It is natural to wonder about proclaimed wonders. For all kinds of reasons, you might rightly ask, "Was my wonderful vision merely a metaphysical delusion?" You could readily dismiss the validity of my vision, suspecting, for example, that my visionary experience was a fantasy induced during intense emotions by chemical reactions which disrupted my cerebral cortex's management of my perceptions. Or you could classify my ocular event as the kind of paranormal anomaly and extrasensory perception that clairvoyants and psychics assert they can lucidly see. However, these hypotheses are neither verifiable nor plausible.

Perceptual psychology firmly supports the proposition that expectations shape perceptions. A skeptic could also conclude that my vision was based on my expectations, or that I saw what I wanted to see. This can't be true. What I saw was the last thing I ever expected or wanted. I had never dreamed I would see Debbie's soul rise from her body. I never expected it, and certainly did not want to see her soul rise, shine, and depart from life to die. Why would I? To be sure, the mind can play tricks on our vision, making us see what we hope for. Still, even though desires can induce misperceptions, the horrific idea of Debbie departing from me forever would have been my worst nightmare. Wishes could not have been the parent of my vision.

In the midst of this short experience I began to sense that the mystical blazing pinhole of rising light was Debbie's levitating soul. As I saw her head materialize and then dematerialize in thin air, I suspected that her soul had returned to and reunited with her body. This mysterious feat was a cause for celebration—a spiritual defeat of death. I would have liked to have been able to foresee this victory before it happened, to banish the dreadful inference that Debbie's soul was heading to the afterlife. But the process unfolded too quickly to deduce the likelihood that in actuality her soul was in the process of rejoining her body to resume earthly living. When I grasped this, my fright turned to bliss as I saw the blessed drama play itself out, with a great ending.

I am sure that my vision of Debbie's levitating soul was not an instance of what psychologists call *photisms* to define the kind of hallucinatory or spurious misperceptions of luminous phenomena which people sometimes claim they see. The ascending light I saw firsthand could not have been an illusion because the blazing light exploded into a full picture of Debbie's head and smiling face; her radiating soul was unique, unlike the flooding luminous mystical light common to others' mystical photisms. The mobile phenomena I witnessed was individualized, so it is inconceivable that it was hallucinatory. As Josiah Royce noted, "the training of the imagination cannot occur apart from a fitting training of the senses" through previous conduct, and I had neither that training or prior experience to train my imagination with a predilection to observe such an astounding phenomenon. There was no stream of consciousness to predispose my mind to see what I saw, which laid beyond my most fantastic imagination. The image and its meaning was spontaneous, vivid and self-evidently interpretable, in much the same way as was Saint Paul's vision on the road to Damascus and was Emperor Constantine's perception of a shining cross in the sky.

I was an eyewitness to what occurs at the intersection between death and rebirth. Her sojourn had to be blissful. A soul taken away from the body is more alive than ever before; the souls of the departed are headed to God's kingdom (1 Cor. 15:19–20). Our merciful heavenly Father picked another path, reuniting Debbie's soul with her corporeal body. She was reborn in a safe, earthly place with me by her side.

Many months later, reflecting on my veridical vision, it struck me how, after His resurrection and return to earth to give instructions to his disciples, Jesus' reappearance at first provoked disbelief among some of His most devoted followers. The disciples were shaken by their sight of what they never expected—their Lord returning to earth in flesh and blood. Jesus had to show his disciple Thomas His wounds from the cross for Thomas to believe. "Doubting Thomas" was emblematic. Once the apostles overcame their natural instinct to mistrust their perception of what they understood could not be true, their faith became firmer and firmer. They then knew, consistent with mystical Jewish traditions, that their visions were veridical and not illusionary.

The miracle I saw in Debbie's mobile spiritual soul was as veridical a vision as is possible. I have no doubts. I derived this lesson: there are spiritual sensations that lie beyond sight and explanation. Her soul's sojourn was one of them.

In order to believe that which appears unbelievable, we must open our minds to the existence of supernatural spiritual phenomena. Where does reality end and inner spirituality begin? If there is a line, it must be extremely thin—smaller than the width of a row of aligned atoms. To draw a border between objective reality and supernatural or mystical phenomena is to make a distinction without a difference. The two cosmic dimensions are inseparably intertwined. I witnessed their fusion and the benefits of their synergistic interactive interdependence. I saw the coexistence of the spiritual and the material realms.

The sight of Debbie outside her body had to be a sign sent from God of His presence and participation that I needed most at my tormented moment of hopeless despair, when it seemed all hope for my Debbie was lost. God had answered my prayers! I knew that His intervention was not just for me but for Debbie. In the aftermath, the view of my Debbie contentedly lying peacefully in her bed suggested that she had been remade whole but better and nearer to her true self. I was relieved, like a skydiver must feel when the parachute opens.

GETTING NEAR TO NEAR-DEATH EXPERIENCES

The grounds for my conclusions about the Holy Spirit's role along life's journey are supported by what has been learned from others who have analyzed reports of people who have personally undergone a near-death experience and revealed their recollections.

With hindsight and study, I deduced that the astonishing episode I had lucidly seen was an instance of a near-death experience. I am sure this is what happened to Debbie. I witnessed the loss of life reversed. It is striking that what I observed is highly congruent with the customary characteristics described by those who have reported their own moving near-death experiences. Moreover, my vision conformed to the numerous resurrections from near death recorded in the Bible.

Fortunately, we have empirical evidence about NDEs to inform our interpretation. As the *Journal of Near-Death Studies*, *The Handbook of Near-Death Experiences*, and the publications of the International Association for Near-Death Studies document, thousands of people have reported that they remember temporarily departing this world and then returning. NDEs are estimated to be a part of the life story of one out of every twenty-five people. Their testimonies provide a large sample to extract the attributes of near-death experiences.

- **Evidence of Near-Death and Renewed-Life Experiences—** Firsthand accounts of NDEs consistently report very common sensations. They usually include a separation of consciousness from the person's physical body, passage through a tunnel toward a brilliant shining light, vivid alertness, intense emotions of being embraced by love and acceptance inducing feelings of peace and tranquility, visualization of an otherworldly heavenly realm (sometimes populated with other people or escorting spirits), loss of a sense of time and space, and a return to the body. When Debbie approached the edge of eternity, it is probable that her brief journey subconsciously included most of these positive experiences. In contrast, some people without faith dominated by repressed guilt for past sins report that their encounter with near death was fraught with painful visions of torment, suffering, and acute awareness of approaching nonexistence or estrangement from awareness of the self (similar to the classical image of hell's eternal void during which the tormented suffer alone in the absence of a transcendent relationship with God.)

NDEs have been reported throughout the globe and date deep in antiquity. A composite picture emerges that is remarkably similar. Unbearable pain and stress are followed by confusion, which suddenly ends, and the person perceives themselves departing from his or her body and floating somewhere, when a very peaceful state of consciousness usually takes command. Even when the heart stops; the brain doesn't. Some level of awareness continues when the person nears death; electrical surges in the brain preserve consciousness or what interchangeably is called the psyche, the mind, the self, or the soul. This survival of consciousness beyond death suggests that the soul never really dies.

In this state, many travelers report receiving a panoramic view of the life they have lived. Every thought, every word, every deed, every good thing, every bad thing, every cruel thing, and every kind thing ever done are all rendered available for evaluation. For most who recall standing at this gateway, the nearing afterlife appears bright and extremely auspicious. These people report feeling they had turned a corner, that they were full of creative energy and enthusiastic about the next surprise awaiting the next stop on a euphoric ride to the final destination. No regrets. No sense of loss. No pain. Sheer gratitude for the opportunity to proceed to the other side.

Those having positive near-death experiences usually remember receiving the same message from a shining spirit, communicating to them in so many words that "your life is not finished. There are things for you to do, and you need to go back." Participants taking an NDE journey all report finding themselves suddenly back in their earthly body and often that they regret their return from their blissful trip.

The affirming feelings of rapture and visions of mystical unity and eternity reported by the majority of those who have had near-death experiences could not be by chance. Recollections of near-death experiences have been recorded across age, location, gender, race, religion, nationality, and all other categories by which demographers classify populations. NDEs cannot be just a fantasy, because the odds of this uniformity are a statistical impossibility.

If you remain doubtful, consider the recollections of the eminent psychologist Carl Jung who had a "life after life" encounter. Jung wrote that he floated in space, washed by a gleaming light, and that his experiences "were utterly real; there was nothing subjective about them; they all had a quality of absolute objectivity." This from a famous world-class scientist. Then also consider brain scientist Jill Taylor's conclusion following her stroke, when her kinesthetic right brain dominated her intuitive senses of well-being and cosmic harmony. She wrote that she was given a "feeling of deep inner peace… completely committed to the expression of peace, love, joy, and compassion in the world." How better to describe the blissful look of fearless connection with me and the entire universe that captured euphoric Debbie's facial expression when her soul materialized from a risen ray of light for me to see?

• **Near the Edge of Eternity: Attributed Attributes**—Dr. Judson Booker from Wytheville Virginia conducted interviews with people who had had near death experiences and drew on published research to broaden understanding of the key elements of the phenomenon. Booker presented his findings in a public lecture. Danny Kegley's transcript of Booker's lecture expands our overview of this phenomenon's salient properties. Consider a selective paraphrased sample of some of Booker's salient ascriptions, with key passages of his lecture directly quoted.

   • In this place, space doesn't have meaning. "People can instantaneously move from one place to another just by thinking, 'I want to be there.' They don't pass through space, they're instantly there."
   • Time is not a straight-line sequence. It does not have the same meaning as measured on earth. Time repeats itself endlessly,

moving in an enduring cycle at different rates. Time is timeless. This bodes well for eternal life in heaven.

- "One's body is spiritual. The body is sometimes described as an energy field, like a collection of electrons or electricity that's all put together. Some people describe it as a rainbow of light. The spiritual body has arms, legs, a head area, it can reach, it can walk if it wants to, but the body is like a spiritual body.... All other people in this other world also have these spiritual bodies."

- "Mental telepathy is the language of communication in this other world, which is instantaneous. Nothing can be hidden. Whatever you think is instantaneously accessible to others. You cannot hide anything, and you communicate directly not just words, but whole thoughts, whole concepts which spread instantaneously."

- Booker asks the single question most pertinent to Debbie's momentary spiritual departure from her body: "When they come back to this life, what is the thing that is uppermost in their minds? What is it that we are here to do? That is to love each other. That's what the being of light tries to communicate: that it is our relationship to each other that is so important.... When this love is described by those experiencing near death, they are describing love in the Christian sense, not love in the romantic sense. Love in the Christian sense means that we are caring for what happens to our fellow persons." Believers are not likely to be surprised by this disclosure; just reread holy scripture.

- "Near-death experienced people come away with the impression that learning is constant, and continues even after death." This speaks directly to what Debbie probably learned during her soul's journey outside her body. "When they want to know something, all they have to do is think, 'I'd like to know how the universe began.' Suddenly, they know. Just like that. They can take any mystery, and all of a sudden they know it. One of the greatest disappointments when people come back is that when they felt in tune with the universe, they knew everything, but when they came back they lost that knowledge."

- No one who has enjoyed a positive near-death experience has regretted it. All see it as invaluable, transforming completely their prior dark view of death. "They are never the same again. They become more reverent of life, and no longer fear death."

If Debbie regained consciousness, I planned to ask her if she had experienced near death and if these attributes and attitudes of NDEs would describe her disposition. I hoped so. Nothing could provide her better spiritual armor to contend with the challenges she would face; the Holy Spirit's enlightenment was the best medicine to deal with recovery from disability and to conquer any fears she might harbor about her ultimate destiny.

For my part, my astonishing vision invigorated my spiritual confidence, and the meaning of life and death began to become clearer. Death is our enemy (1 Cor. 15:25–28), which is why its finality is dreaded by those nonbelievers who fail to see to it as enabling something far better beyond the suffering intrinsic to material life—entry into a heavenly home. "To die is gain" (Phil. 1:21). Death is not to be feared because there *is* an afterlife. Life beyond human existence is a path to that paradise, a universe in which our souls, our true selves, will be thoroughly immersed in God's unending loving presence, living in God as God lives in us. Mortality is a means to a welcome end.

If on her soul's sojourn Debbie had passed death's door, both of us were better for the experience. We were both awakened. Paradoxically, fears heighten faith, and faith subdues fear. A vision had cast light on the dread of night and exterminated the fear of death by providing a glimpse of eternity

- **Existential Implications: Imagining Heaven**—Put these glimpses together, and assemble the ascriptions of NDEs. What you see is what you get—a pretty good idea of the afterlife as many verses in holy scripture picture it. In relying on these NDE accounts, however, keep in mind that not a single person reporting his or her NDE actually traveled through the end of that tunnel to death and exited on the other side. These people only came to the border between living and death, like an airplane making its approach to the tarp but lifting up at the last second to resume flight. They did not land. However, they saw in a state of near death the proverbial "light at the end of the tunnel." The light shone brightly to illuminate some characteristics of the afterlife—a universe where everybody and everything is interconnected and inextricably interwoven in a shared, eternal web of consciousness.

That said, the afterlife is destined to remain beyond humanity's capacity to comprehend. Heaven is literally "over our heads." We cannot understand this imponderable any better than we can define abstractions like "eternity" and "infinity." The lyrics of one of Debbie's favorite songs, *Some Enchanted Evening*, put well our dependence on faith for life's most important existential questions, such as what happens after life: "Who can explain it? Who can tell you why? Fools give you reasons. Wise men never try."

The most important implication of NDEs is the central question that is powerfully raised: Did the loving God who created us give us the capacity to think not only during but also after life? If so, this gift means that our capacity to think persists after death, so that consciousness survives once it is severed from our deceased brains and bodies. If human consciousness never does die but can live for all eternity with God, then death is only an exit from this world and an entrance to a better afterlife. As Dr. Mark Berkson frames the issue, "If it could be established that consciousness can exist separately and independently from the body and brain, it would mean that the disintegration of our bodies and brains does not mean the end of us. So research into near-death experiences could have profound implications for how we understand what kinds of beings we are and what lies beyond death."

Debbie's stroke and witnessed NDE forced a confrontation with, and contemplation of, existential questions like nothing before. Light cleared a path to finding some revealing clues to the mysteries of existence and eternity, clues which reinforced the core of our religious convictions about an afterlife.

You may be one of the many skeptics who reject what cannot be seen or proven—supernatural phenomena such as an external spiritual force. Many people cannot conceive of a supreme power beyond themselves. If you are one of them, you're missing what life is all about. In the dark, you will not understand the meaning of life and the afterlife and will be doomed to wander through life without a lamp to guide your path and give you hope and happiness. A Supreme Being exists beyond our world, powerfully influencing who we are and what we will become. I saw the Holy Spirit carrying my Debbie's soul to safety. I believe.

I didn't know it at the time, but when I saw Debbie's soul rising, God was busy. I knew neither Debbie nor I could be delivered from death without God's grace. I firmly believed that I could pray for loving and healing help from God, because the Lord has promised to look with compassion on those who throw themselves at His feet, crying out in the depths of darkness and despair. We were in those dark depths. Debbie was breathing but comatose. Would He deliver?

CHAPTER 9

REBORN?

§

The dawn broke the silence of a suspenseful, sleepless, and spectacularly eventful night. The sunrise brought a bright new day. I was invigorated by my astonishing vision of Debbie's near-death experience. I had spent the entire night riveted on her soul's out of body levitation. It had to signal that blessings had been provided. The dramatic episode augured well. Expectations were rising. I was dying to discover if and when more encouraging signs would be forthcoming. I didn't have to wait long.

AWAKE!

At dawn's break, the light of day revealed what would happen next. My prayers and the prayers of many were answered. As Debbie's painkillers and sedatives wore off, she began to turn on! First, her eyelashes fluttered. Then her beautiful blue eyes opened. Next, her radiant smile appeared. She was alive, awake, and displaying motion and emotion.

My dreams were coming true. Debbie had escaped mortality, and her true self was emerging; it felt like a resurrection had occurred. This was the advent of a new beginning, opening up the path to auspicious possibilities. There had been a chance that Debbie would pass through the point of no return. Now there was a chance for better things to come. My joy and relief blossomed. Debbie's prospects suddenly looked promising. I gave God a prayer of thanks for His care.

I couldn't wait until Debbie's surgeons could see her responsiveness. I didn't have to wait long. The neurosurgery team was already making their rounds and arrived in her room as the sun began to flood the room with light. They were stunned. Dr. Dyer was the first to speak. "I didn't expect Debbie to be so awake and alert so soon. This is very unusual. Debbie, let's see if you can understand me. Try to squeeze my finger."

She nodded, and he gave her a finger (not his middle one!). She weakly squeezed it. Dr. Dyer's wide smile spoke volumes. Debbie had understood and had responded. She had grasped what was said to her and reacted! Cherished memories of this breakthrough are burned in my memory.

I said nothing to the doctors about the near-death experience I had witnessed, I guess because I did not want the doctors to think I was losing my mind and also because I didn't want to divert their attention from Debbie's evaluation. Hunter was on a hunt. I did not want to risk distracting him. He found that for which he was hunting and did not expect to find—a conscious and responsive Debbie. The expression on his face was like that of a golfer watching his tee shot fall into the cup for a hole in one.

Maybe I should have told the two surgeons about my vision during the night and shared my conviction that Debbie had benefitted from the greatest Helper in the entire universe He had created. I lost a golden opportunity to testify to God's unlimited power, and later regretted it. I guess I didn't want to confirm their worst suspicions about my sanity in the face of stress and sleeplessness.

The dedicated surgeons were cheered, and I wanted their mood to stay upbeat. That was not to be. "These are very encouraging signs for now," Dr. Dyer dryly cautioned, "but as I told you previously, we have no basis for a prognosis. We must continue to watch hour by hour and see how Debbie responds. So far, so good." "That's what the poor fellow who fell off the roof of a skyscraper was overheard saying halfway down," I feebly tried to joke. But Dr. Dyer stood by his script, adding that "many obstacles on the road to recovery remain, and reversals are not unlikely. If Debbie is able to continue periods of alertness and responsiveness, remember that these phases are normally short. There will be periods of lucidity followed by periodic pauses, plateaus and mental sluggishness. Right now Debbie is on a roll. That pace is unlikely to persist. Several steps do not make a trend. I'll check back later today to see how Debbie's responses develop."

It didn't take long for me to throw Dyer's precautious pessimistic verdict to the wind. I took full advantage of Debbie's newfound alertness. Compulsively, incessantly I talked to her to stimulate her thinking. I dwelled on and on about how much I loved her and how together we would overcome any challenges. I dared not go into detail about the drama I had witnessed during the night. This was not the time to quiz her about her near death. She was barely conscious and could not mentally focus to comprehend a complicated account of an astounding experience. To say the least, her mind was very fuzzy. I delayed trying to test her recollections and teasing out any subconscious memories she might have retained during her soul's levitation above her body. What was the point? She could not talk to express her thoughts, and I was uncertain whether she was even able to cognitively comprehend abstract ideas such as an encounter with near death. Exploring the boundaries of her subconscious memories would have to wait.

Dr. Dyer had told me, "Debbie will not be able to remember anything after her surgery for a long time. If she survives, that's when the real fight begins." Well, here we were. The first round of the fight had begun, and she was winning. But she faced many additional long rounds.

A LIGHT IN THE DARK

Only about an hour after the doctors' departure, I lost my balance and almost fell over in excitement. My most frequent petition to God was then answered. Light began to shine much sooner than anyone expected. A very faint whisper emerged from Debbie's lips! Debbie quietly spoke in a complete sentence that made perfect sense! Her mumbled first words:

"I love you." These were the words I most craved. She spoke them! A new beginning to a new life may have begun.

I was thrilled. My emotions shone like the sun. This achievement must be God's doing. I firmly believe He had brought Debbie back from death's doorway, and undoubtedly it was for a purpose. God would not have performed the miracle of a tour to heaven's gate, just to then let her survive comatose. She could comprehend me and whisper her thoughts. It was clear He had other goals.

What did Debbie remember? Did she know that she had had a stroke? Were her last memories her prayers and farewell to me in the Lake Norman emergency room? And now, I earnestly wondered, did she have any sense of her spiritual soul's journey outside her body? I hoped her subconscious mind had stored this blissed sojourn, which would bring her psyche much comfort. I prayed that her near-death tour was imprinted in her brain, from which she might draw inner courage and perhaps someday pull into consciousness. We would see.

What I could then see was Debbie's complete confidence and fearlessness. When she regained momentary alertness, I pressed her hard to use her new consciousness and exercise her mind, and this exchange revealed some aftereffects attributable to her sojourn to the edge of eternity. Our brief, heartwarming conversation went something like this:

"How do you feel?" I nervously asked.

"What? Do you think I look different?"

"No, you look more beautiful than ever. But you seem different. You're remarkably content and happy. Debbie, you've been through a lot. Are you feeling different?"

"Yes, I feel unusually happy. There's nothing to worry about. I know I am in good hands. Why shouldn't I be content?"

"You have every reason to be calm and confident, darling. I know you're in God's care. He is with you, as am I. I know you feel God's presence."

This reconstruction of our conversation provided the clue that Debbie's mind was active and that her mood had been elevated while she was unconscious when her soul had risen above her body. Today she had come back reborn and recharged. The clouds began to vanish, and light began to replace darkness. Her journey, which had begun after her stroke less than three days earlier, looked like it would be lit by lamplight from God.

Andy's upbeat updates summarized Debbie's great leap forward. He wrote, "Friends and family—Chuck has checked in after a good night. He reports that Debbie is alert, responding to questions with nods and even a few tears. She is still on the ventilator. Chuck then announced he had a surprise—he put Debbie on the phone and we had a nice though short conversation! Very coherent, very appreciative of everyone's prayers. She's on some new pain meds. All in all, incredible progress. Blessings."

All in all, indeed. It really was a new day, a new beginning. Debbie had regained consciousness. She was thinking. She had spoken. Her words were coherent. Her cognition was excellent. She was moving forward. She was way ahead of everyone's expectations.

When Dr. Dyer returned that afternoon, Debbie was still awake and able to communicate with him. Hunter could not hide his surprise. His pessimistic cautions about the likely slow rate of Debbie's progress, interrupted with delays and setbacks, had proven to be premature. Within a few hours, Debbie had taken another huge leap forward. Dr. Dyer's most optimistic estimates had already been surpassed. He discovered that Debbie was able to talk, after all, and now—not days, weeks, or even months in the future. He was elated to learn that Debbie could carry on a meaningful conversation. Her sentences were complete and logical. This was huge. It boded well.

Several tangential events occurred after Debbie's breakthroughs that thrilling day:

- **Banned at Night from the ICU**—As many doors opened to encouraging new possibilities, another closed. I had spent more than seventy uninterrupted hours at Debbie's side since our trials had erupted on January 8. The thrill of Debbie's breakout into consciousness was an adrenalin rush that had energized me. However, the effects of sleep deprivation concomitant with emotional swings between anguish and excitement were showing. I was exhausted.

The doctors and nurse assistants insisted that I *not* stay in Debbie's ICU room overnight anymore. They instructed me to start using the Hospitality House at night to regain my own strength and alertness. Dr. Dyer did not mince any words. "Chuck, you need to preserve your strength. If Debbie continues her journey to recovery, she will need you on all cylinders to help her. So prepare yourself. To protect her, protect yourself. Get some sleep. Start eating again. Give Debbie a break from your constant hovering presence. She needs lots of sleep. And expect the unexpected. A burst aneurism in that part of Debbie's brain can produce all kinds of changes, and you must be ready to adapt to them. Remember, I told you that her personality could change. If so, you will have to adjust. Another change could also happen with which you might have to deal: she might lose the ability to distinguish right from wrong." (The odd thought struck me at this news: have nearly all politicians experienced a stroke?) "So prepare yourself, and learn to be more flexible. You must give Debbie more quiet time. Give her a break by taking a break."

Okay, I was being kicked out. I fought this hard, but could not win this battle. But I managed to bargain for a concession: I would spend the evenings at the Hospitality House if, and only if, I had permission to call the night nurse at any time of night to get a report on Debbie's condition. The ICU staff readily agreed and actually expressed appreciation for my compulsive caring even though my calls would interrupt their nightly routines. And I secured a corollary promise: I would be called immediately if any indicators signaled that medical treatment might be necessary or if Debbie requested my presence. Above all, I asked the attending nurses each night to tell Debbie, if she should awaken, that I was nearby and that I loved her. I asked them to call me if she wanted to see me. Some of my anxiety declined when I remembered that the Hospitality House's warm abode for patients' caregivers was only a ten-minute hike away. So I would not be far away.

- **A Surprise Gift**—When I reluctantly dragged myself to my Hospitality House room, I opened the door and nearly tripped over a large box on the floor. A note was taped to the cover, saying, "Maria and I thought you could use some support, brother. Here's an uplifting Bible passage and assorted clothes, meds, and supplies. We are praying for Debbie and you. Your friend in Christ, Don Sanders." Don had driven all the way from Blythewood to deliver this package.

   The Christian caregiving that the staff at Hospitality House provided also was uplifting. On my bed someone had left a message: "So do not fear, for I am with you; do not be dismayed, for I am your God. I will strengthen you and help you; I will uphold you with my righteous right hand—Isaiah 41:10." These words helped dispel despair and desperation; as I cried for God's help, I knew He would answer (Ps. 18:6, 40:1–2).

- **Striking a Balance?**—Andy encapsulated my difficulties trying to balance approach/avoidance on behalf of Debbie's need for both my presence and need to avoid my overattentiveness: "Chuck was excited seeing Debbie reacting to his voice. But the nurses have continued to warn him to not make her excited or over-stimulated. So he's been a little better in stepping away and giving her more space and time. I've noticed an increased reflection of what that time and space is meaning to Chuck, as treatments will take a good long while and many more prayers."

   An underlying principle guided the physicians' request. Andy's e-mail summarized why "the doctors and nurses told Chuck to let Debbie rest, and not to be talking to her so much." Patients needed time to escape from brain stimulation, and the best way to avoid stimulation overload was to minimize conversation with others. Too much attention and talking drained the patient's energy. Our friend, Steve Hibbard flew all the way from San Francisco to wave to Debbie from her ICU doorway, and his short visit was sufficient to lift her spirits—she chuckled "Hi Hibbard."

To be honest, I was so eager to take advantage of every moment of Debbie's awareness that I did not religiously follow this advice. In some ways, I doubled down by doubling up the things I tried to do for her in her precarious position. I had problems controlling giving as much care as possible. For example, I tirelessly performed various passive exercises, such as stretching Debbie's fingers and arms, and each night prior to prayers, I gave Debbie foot massages and applied skin creams—a practice that, to Debbie's delight, never ceased once I started it. In hindsight I deeply regret any delay and disruptions my zealous but inadvertent efforts to mentally connect with and rehabilitate Debbie may have caused. In short, I was impatient when it came to attending to my beloved patient. I carry a measure of guilt with me. Good intentions do not always lead to good consequences.

- **Bemusing Declarations**—Andy spread the latest news: "Friends—Chuck has left a couple of messages, and we finally talked this afternoon while I was unrolling a bale of hay near his house here on the farm. Much good news to pass along from him. Debbie is alert, talking up a storm, and telling jokes. The docs talk of her imagining things as part of her reconnecting the dots from before the aneurysm—called stenosis I think he said. For instance, when she heard Chuck was washing her laundry, a surprised Debbie replied 'reeeally?,' and after another nap she asked if he remembered to put her clothes in the dryer. Taking bets. She told Chuck she was ready to 'come home to Wytheville,' which brightened his day, and at a later point asked about a dinner date with friends tomorrow. A swallowing evaluation has been scheduled to determine whether the feeding tube can be removed."

- **Moving Forward**—I was beside myself with joy at the great advances Debbie had so quickly begun to make. To encapsulate the promising direction of developments during these first four days in ICU, again listen to Andy's update through communications central: "Debbie is growing in strength so rapidly that her nurses have insisted putting mittens on Debbie's hands at night to impede her ability to pull tubes out. Chuck has begun keeping written notes about Debbie's remarkable achievements and improving condition, and says he has over twenty pages of memos he's compiled—publishers, you've been warned. He found a walking nature trail outside the hospital by a creek, and it sounds like his short walk while Debbie was sleeping was very therapeutic, as is Debbie's ability to reset her sleep cycle. He and Debbie are deeply appreciative of your thoughts, prayers, messages and cards. A few more names have joined my email list of over fifty, and John and Hilel have many more on their email lists as well. Keep the prayers coming."

Those many prayers were needed, and their cry was assuredly heard in heaven. Lord Jesus had answered. He promised He would always be there for us, and His power was displayed continuously. Debbie's awakening had awakened many others to the Lord's loving care. They should have known all along from the Bible that Jesus would be present in times of trouble; after all, Jesus had allocated huge portions of his missionary activities on earth healing the diseased and the dying and even raising the dead. Why would that loving commitment end after His resurrection? Not a chance.

In summation of the highlights of those first four days in Charlotte, where there had been nothing but the black of night, there had instantly appeared the light of day. A basis for optimism had been delivered. A true set of miracles had taken place. Light had broken the blackness. With her talented surgical team's skill and God's guidance, Debbie had survived an extremely challenging surgical operation, had regained consciousness, and had begun to vocalize her thoughts.

What ideas were circulating in Debbie's mind was unclear. Her thinking was affected heavily by her intrusive brain surgery and by the interference to cognition caused by her massive doses of sedatives and sleep aides. When Debbie next spoke, her mumbled words sent chills down my spine.

- **"I'm Not Supposed to Be Here"**—I spent a good portion of my nighttime in the Hospitality House between calls to Debbie's nurse every two hours wondering not whether Debbie was thinking, for obviously she was, but what she was thinking *about* in her sleepy drift in and out of alertness. Was she dreaming? What thoughts received her attention?

  Insight into Debbie's state of mind was provided the next morning after my first night in the Hospitality House. I bounded into her room at daybreak. She was still asleep. My eyes drifted to the eraser board, and my jaw dropped. During the night Debbie had awoken and urged nurse Katie to write three things on the eraser board so they would be remembered. Katie obeyed. There in large letters was written: "(1) Speakers: Cathy and Teresa; (2) my IRA distributions; (3) Permission for Chuck." What in the world?

  The mystery was not hard to solve. Katie explained Debbie's instructions, and when Debbie herself awoke, she was able to fill in the blanks. Salient in Debbie's mind was her death. The speakers referred to Cathy Crow (Pastor George's wife) and Teresa Amick, her best friend since childhood in Indiana. Debbie wanted to make sure they were designated speakers at her funeral! She apparently thought she would soon die. Her IRA referred to her desire to escalate the pace at which she wanted me, the executor of our last will and testament, to distribute her specified allotments. Here Debbie was preoccupied with having her wishes met after she died, which presumably she believed was soon. Was this because her soul had approached heaven's gate?

  Her third request was directed to me and pierced me like a bullet. "Chuck," Debbie clarified, "I want you to feel free to remarry after I'm gone." The words stung.

  I protested, "I do not want to live in a world without you. The last thing I want is to imagine what life would be like without you; I don't want to live if you are not here. Don't you know that you are the woman of my dreams and that there could never be a replacement?

Debbie, you are the center of my universe, my reason for living. When I vowed in our marriage ceremony that I would 'love you, in sickness and in health,' I meant every word. It was a pledge to God. There is no acceptable license to the other words I reluctantly recited in our wedding vows—'till death do us part.' My love is for only you, and it will never die. Death will never part us. My love will never leave you. I do not want to live without you."

Her message spoke volumes about Debbie's thinking. She was preparing to die! Had she had a nightmare? That horrific hypothesis was reinforced that afternoon when Debbie awakened from her needed sleep. I called Debbie's sister, Karen, and told her Debbie was with me as I handed our cell phone to Debbie. The first words out of Debbie's mouth were mystifying: "I'm not supposed to be here." What provoked this exclamation? What did it mean? Was her belief based on her hazy memory of her prayers in the emergency room at Lake Norman hospital, when she told me she was "going to die" and that she loved me? Or was her assertion that she wasn't "supposed to be here" based on a deep-seated inner recollection of her soul's near-death sojourn? God has "set eternity in the human heart" (Eccl. 3:11); had she been looking forward to joining God in heaven and understandably disappointed to discover she was here and not there? Was her statement that she was not meant to be here a reflection of her amazement that she was still here on earth? The aftereffects of her unconscious experiences defied interpretation.

Whatever the root causes of the underlying ideas behind Debbie's statement following her revival, it is clear that she had not expected to return from the gateway to heaven. Surprise! A merciful and loving God had reached the fathomless depth of her soul and provided a passage to continuing life on earth. God's reach had reached and restored her soul, giving her the will to cheerfully overcome the terrible limitations imposed by her stroke. Would she continue on that path? Could we both "run with endurance the race that was set before us" (Heb. 12:1)?

CHAPTER 10

A ROAD TEST

§

Prospects were looking up, but the dark downside could not be denied. I continued to remain in bondage to fear and anguish, continuously worrying. Recall the obstacles standing in the way to a restored way of life. After a stroke strikes, most people die. The majority who survive a first stroke experience in its wake a number of additional strokes. Add to this grim picture the evidence showing that strokes are the leading cause of disabilities, and that one of every four stroke victims remain disabled for the rest of his or her life.

Given these grim realities, I had no real basis for confidently assuming that Debbie would continue her journey from darkness to light. The barriers to progress were many. Like the stroke itself that struck without warning, a wide range of additional threats to her rehabilitation and potentially her life was extant. Anything could happen—even the worst.

Dark apprehension could not be exorcised. A bright horizon was in sight but seemed to recede as I approached its promise. Hope could be extinguished in the blink of an eye. It was even conceivable that Debbie could lose her true self, perhaps forever. Or, on the bright side, with God's healing and expert medical care, there was a chance Debbie could regain a high percentage of what she had lost and in time eventually come out of her journey renewed and reborn. In the wake of brain surgery, stroke survivors take divergent directions; different individuals emerge with different experiences, adopting different personalities and different new convictions. The range of potential transformations is wide.

The darker face of the probabilities cast a long shadow over the sun that had begun to shine. There were many reminders of Debbie's continuing vulnerability. Her nasogastric (NG) tube from her nose to her stomach to receive liquid food still disfigured her pretty face, and her pneumatic boots pulsating air pressure to help prevent deadly clots were another constant reminder of persisting dangers. Include the multitude of IV lines, cerebrospinal fluid pumping, respiratory support, and monitoring devices into the portrait, and you can imagine why worries diminished the hopes her recent mental and vocal alertness had inspired. Still, her travels that morning had taken an easy path, unlike the rugged route up the steep mountain that Debbie had climbed fighting to survive since her stroke. This day Debbie took a huge first step on her journey.

EPISODIC EVENTS IN THE ICU

A series of events occurred in this interim post-surgery period in ICU that opened my eyes and opened my mind to reexamination of ingrained habits of thought. The things that happened in this interval formed a collage of memories.

In this period, I was flying solo. I retained and could recall most events, but Debbie could not yet contribute to the telling of our story because for a prolonged period after brain surgery no stroke survivor ever remembers anything. In contrast, my memories of those first two weeks are packed with vivid recollections—big and small, heartwarming and painful. I highlight the most prominent developments.

In general, the next twelve days were fraught with a constantly shifting admixture of progress and setbacks. The overall trend line moved in the right direction but with perturbations—highs and lows—around Debbie's trajectory. The trend line fluctuated crab-like, with periodic pauses in changes, zigs and zags, and improvements and reversals. The vacillations jumped up and down like the stock market. We had been forewarned about this probability. Every journey has its ups and downs, and Debbie's performance conformed to the law of gravity—"what goes up must come down." The ICU chorus repeated a familiar refrain "Two steps forward and one step backward" to project the expected hills and valleys on Debbie's daily progression, overshadowed by the threat that after a stroke, anything that can happen might happen.

A number of events on this segment of our long journey identify what can happen after a stroke strikes. Place them into the portrait you may be painting in your mind if you are attending a loved one enduring life-threatening circumstances.

- **A Shrink Calls**—During this interregnum, Debbie never displayed frustration or remorse. Her spirits were downright up—a happiness I ascribe to the unconscious memories and sensations she experienced on her near-death tour of post-mortal existence. Her positive attitude undoubtedly contributed to her progress. She seemed able to somehow calmly ride the roller coaster on which she was traveling, drawing on invisible inner strength. I, on the other hand, lived with constant fear. I was painfully aware that there was no guarantee that she would recover. She was still walking a tightrope from which she could easily fall. The dire danger had to be faced—Debbie sat on the threshold between life and death. Any second, another breakdown could destroy everything that had so quickly been regained.

  The days and nights following the strokes did not pass quickly. Debbie looked like an octopus with so many wires and tubes protruding from her little body. I sat by her bedside doing best what I had always done since childhood: I worried. The gloom in the room was as thick as black bean soup. There was no relief. As the hours ticked away, the number of real or imagined problems confronting Debbie multiplied. So much could go wrong. The threats seemed like a spreading cancer.

  Prayer brought momentary peace from such pregnant worries. "Thank you, God, for Your protection," I whispered as I recounted the marvelous turnabout. But quite frankly, given Debbie's precarious condition, the alarming magnitude of life-threatening dangers appeared beyond human control. My intractable anxiety went way beyond paranoia—itself sometimes a heightened state of awareness.

I was a nervous wreck. When attendants asked how I was doing, I tried to make light of the situation. "Have you ever leaned on the back legs of a chair, lost balance, and wavered back and forth, nearly falling backward? Well, that's how I feel all the time."

That remark caused the staff to send for the hospital psychiatrist. The shrink was concerned about my mental and psychological state. I can see why. Moments of tearful hysteria were experienced, and so were manic moments of tearful joy when Debbie's condition improved. Like a bipolar manic-depressive, I rotated between the depths of despair at every sign of Debbie's vulnerabilities and the heights of hope every time she showed the least sign of progress. Outpourings of tears were frequent. This became so common that I accumulated some strange but appreciative nicknames from the affectionate staff; I learned that "the town crier" and "the weeping willow" were among them. At this precarious point, for me to claim that I was in control would be extreme hyperbole. I was an apprehensive mess, and everyone could see it.

The CMC psychiatrist tried to steady my nerves. She did not succeed any better than had the noble efforts of my twin brother, Dr. John Kegley—a seasoned psychologist in full stride in his professional skills. My free-floating anxiety and hushed mention of suicide if Debbie did not survive alarmed the psychiatrist, who accepted the fact that I simply did not wish to live without Debbie. I learned how much I needed and loved Debbie when I came close to losing her.

In desperation, to get my mind off these kinds of thoughts, the psychiatrist inquired, "Did you ever think about keeping a diary?"

"Well," I replied, "if Debbie recovers partially or even fully, I doubt that she would like to learn about these dark days."

"No, Chuck, silly. Think outside the box," she ordered.

Phooey, I thought to myself, I'll think outside the circle...the sphere...anyplace if that would help me cope.

She continued, "The diary is not for her. It's for you. It may help you in unforeseen ways to have a record. Keeping track of changes and the thoughts they provoke could be somewhat medicinal, if for no other reason than clearing your cluttered mind of painful, repressed memories that will continue to haunt you."

I was immediately persuaded by her logic and advice and began that day to more accurately expand my shorthand, one keyword notation of each event in the stream of unfolding changes. This memory aid also reduced some tension because I could refer to my primitive diary when recalling for Hilel, Andy, and John and Mary what happened each day that had defined Debbie's current status.

- **Evaluating Our Hospitable Hospital**—Each day was spent observing Debbie closely and taking time to inform loved ones of what was happening and not happening. Try as I might, I could not help but wonder about the quality of the hospital in whose hands Debbie's life depended. Was it sufficient? Capable? Professional? Dedicated?

Those doubts disappeared when I was informed about the high stature and reputation of Carolinas Medical Center in general, and Carolinas Neurosurgery & Spine Associates in particular. Both were highly rated. Hilel passed on needed encouraging information that dispersed some of the shadows and clouds. His sons, Josh and Alex, are both physicians, and Josh had just received tenure in Harvard's medical school. "Dad," Josh told Hilel, "tell Chuck that Debbie is at the best hospital for brain surgery east of the Mississippi River. There is none better anywhere. It doesn't get any better than this."

Several days later, an anecdote confirmed this superlative evaluation of the special stroke unit at CMC. A television celebrity, who shall remain anonymous, was escorted by an army of personal managers. The celebrity's administrative head had been vacationing in the Carolinas when she had a stroke and was rushed to CMC. The celeb's staff insisted on twenty-four-hour personal care from private physicians and then hesitated and screamed, "This hick southern hospital isn't good enough. We will take her to New York, where real experts can provide the care she needs." The call did not go as expected. That famous hospital informed the caller to have the patient to stay put at CMC: "Carolinas Neurosurgery & Spine is the best brain facility in the entire United States, and we would have sent her back to CMC." This place works!

- **Debbie Pens Her Nighttime Thoughts**—Could it be that a welcome signpost was coming into sight? Another memorable event suggested as much. Debbie's sleeping aides and painkillers were reduced, and this turned her restoring sleep cycle upside down. She was wide awake during the night and drowsy during the day. She used her alertness to her advantage. Asking her nurse, Katie, for a pencil and paper, Debbie scribbled her thoughts in tiny cursive letters. In the far-left top corner, she wrote, "Tom and Candi—I love you—DK"; below that, she penned, "Teresa & Larry—I love you—D." Her penmanship grew smaller and less legible, but her letters suggested the words "Brooklyn Rudi & Lucy, I love you." Then she targeted others: "Karen & Mark—I Love you," ending with "Cruck [sic], I LOVE You—D. K." My heart melted, and my spirits soared at this achievement and the sentiments her words expressed. Now this was encouraging!

- **The Rascal Behaves Rascally**—Soon thereafter another setback occurred. This time Debbie, also known wide and far by the affectionate nickname "the Rascal," acted in a way that accidently created a large bump in the road. While I was making notes for my diary, I happened to look up to see if Debbie had awoken. To my horror, she was wide awake and in the process of pulling her nasogastric (NG) feeding tube from her nose. That Rascal! I screamed. But it was too late.

The tube had to be completely removed and a replacement inserted from her nose to stomach. This procedure was difficult and required x-rays to ascertain that the tube was properly positioned in her stomach. Sadly, the first effort failed, so another procedure and x-rays had to be performed. The second try was a charm—the tubing was successfully positioned.

This was high drama. The episode had elements of both comedy and tragedy—somewhat amusing albeit scary. Debbie had had a smirk on her beautiful face as she had proudly pulled at the nuisance intruding into her nostrils. She was showing off her skill and independence, and, I'm sure, never dreamed that her maneuver would be dangerous. The Rascal desired to participate in her personal treatment and could not resist the temptation to take matters into her own hands. To be fair, no one can blame Debbie. The tubing had to be terribly uncomfortable and irritating. Her reflex sought to remedy the situation.

To prevent a reoccurrence, during both night and waking periods during the day two very large padded mittens looking like boxing gloves were tied around Debbie's little hands. There was no indication that she disapproved. Maybe she understood that the mittens were for her protection. And I drew confidence that Debbie was being watched from above. If her tube-tugging stunt had happened at another time when I was not there to intervene, she could have brought disastrous harm to herself.

- **Spasm-Speak**—The first Sunday following surgery was sunny. Despite a restless sleep, Debbie was in full command—way ahead of expectations. All signs on the monitor were great, and Debbie was talking clearly, and what she had to say made perfect sense. Debbie called me "Charlie"—a nickname I had only permitted her to use.

  Dr. Dyer tried to prepare me for likely developments. It was a good thing, because sure enough some other surprises materialized. "Expect this certainty," he informed me. "Debbie will experience 'vasospasms' in her brain's vessels, at irregular intervals. These spasms result when the fluids in her brain cavity compress her vessels, preventing the blood from flowing freely and potentially igniting more strokes. They also occur when the fluid pressure weakens, and the vessels open like a drainpipe, causing the reverse danger. Vasospasms exert a very predictable cognitive dysfunction—they generate hallucinations and strange thoughts. Debbie may then say almost anything. Some of her visions and things she says may sound funny—others possibly scary. Do not take anything she might say seriously; weird thoughts and fantasies are induced by random spasmodic vessel-bloating or vessel-restricting fluctuations." He added that the expected "vascular spasms normally begin six to ten days after brain surgery." They had already begun, as suggested by Debbie's exclamatory "reeeaaaly?" when she was informed that I was doing laundry. Now they were increasing in frequency and introduced some amusement into the story of our journey. Her outbursts were entertaining.

Dr. Dyer's prediction and warning were fulfilled a number of times that day and during the week that followed. "What's Steve Spurrier doing on the ceiling?" was one of Debbie's first hilarious statements that day. Next came her claim that "John and Mary were here. I saw them."

"No," I reassured her, "they unpacked and cancelled their trip when I told them that no visitors were permitted."

"But I saw them—right where you are standing," Debbie insisted.

"No, they weren't. Ask nurse Elizabeth," I suggested.

"Elizabeth, were Chuck's brother, John, and his wife, Mary, here last night?" Debbie asked. "No. You had no visitors," Elizabeth confirmed.

"Elizabeth, you are a terrible liar!" Debbie challenged. We had many a laugh about that one later.

Add another memory to the record. Debbie also chimed, "I don't think we will be able to go to church today." She had hopes for the impossible. Another spasm may have been the catalyst when she informed me that we will still be able to "go on our scheduled trip in two weeks to Tuscany and on to Switzerland." To dampen her disappointment, I suggested we postpone that trip but was delighted to learn that Debbie entertained hope that our normal life might someday resume.

- **Manufactured Hopes**—To try to overcome the suffocating gloom that fear of the unknown breeds, Debbie and I avoided all discussion of the dreadfully unpredictable future. An unmentionable possibility cast dark shadows—that cures and health would not be part of our lives, at least for a long time, and that confinement to a wheelchair or worse, bed, would be Debbie's ultimate destiny.

  To avoid facing this kind of depressing thought, we talked about promising possibilities. One salient example stands out among our many efforts to construct a scenario that might provide a happy image of some semblance of a restored normal life. "Tell the nurse, Debbie, what we plan to get when we can go home," I urged. "A dog! A dog!" Debbie announced. "She will be a Dalmatian like my favorite dog growing up, and we will name her after that dog, Dale. She will give us company and love."

  This probably was not the best idea, given the constant care a dog would require. But the idea served its purpose: providing a symbol of a hopeful future. I could easily picture a devoted puppy curled up by Debbie to keep her company.

- **"You Can Have This World…"**—My occasional hushed disclosures to the nurses about my wish to take Debbie's place were sincere. In my mind, we should have switched places, with my sixty-nine-year-old body in the ICU after my stroke and my vibrant fifty-four-year-old Debbie attending to my needs. I made the mistake of repeating my wish not to go on living should I lose Debbie. Enough people heard my self-destructive thoughts to provoke their concerns that the psychiatrist had not alleviated my depression. So, for better or worse, in this period, the ICU staff instructed a resident hospital chaplain to pay me a visit.

  Collected and compassionate, he asked if we could talk.

  "Sure. I could use any available counsel, especially from a minister," I said.

"Tell me what you're feeling, Chuck," the Reverend asked.

"I feel desperate, without any control over ever-present dangers, scared, and consoled only by trust that God is with us."

He responded, "Are you angry? Are you angry at God for letting this happen?"

"No, I don't see our fate this way at all. I do not hold God responsible. I am grateful for the many blessings He has bestowed. I feel no anger toward God. I remain convinced that illness and disease are not punishments for sins administrated by an angry God, any more than are natural disasters like destructive hurricanes. God is not the source of the world's problems, and He never deserves blame for things that happen that cause humans to suffer. Why hold God accountable? I can never look to God in anger; He is not culpable and worthy of gratitude for preventing Debbie's death. However, I feel an urge to end my life if Debbie's life ends. Thoughts of suicide—a cardinal sin—have crossed my mind."

In St. John's Lutheran Church cemetery, a distant ancestor, Emmett Harlow Kegley (1874–1929), had inscribed his tombstone with this message: "You can have all this life. Give me Jesus." That view captured my sentiments when I faced the possibility that Debbie might not survive; in that case, I felt I had embraced the view that I, too, had had enough of this sinful world, and without her I was ready to see Jesus.

"Do not feel ashamed at the depth of your despair," this kindly preacher answered. "Permit me to tell you what happened to me. Six years ago I lost my wife and three children. I hit rock bottom. I admit I became very angry at God. I tried to kill myself, but obviously, my attempt at suicide failed. So I turned to God. He must have saved me for a purpose. I received His call and went to the seminary to train for a life professing God's gospel—His good news—to others. I now sit before you an ordained minister, performing His larger purpose. God surely has a plan for you too. Your challenge is to find it, to listen to your heart for guidance. God's plan may include Debbie also living to serve Him."

What a relief! Things happen that cannot be helped. Those things can help us find a new path, a new mission, in life's journey. When Debbie survived her brain surgery, we were given potent incentives to help ourselves by serving our Lord and helping others also.

- **A Candle Emits Light**—Debbie's blood tests and pathology reports gave no clues as to the cause of her aneurism but had not produced evidence that something systemic was deteriorating the blood vessels throughout her entire body.

  She had had no follow-on seizures, and with the passage of time without another vessel breach, the odds that Debbie could avoid another hemorrhage were improving. In fact, my optimism began to build. "The types and degree of disability that follow a stroke," a National Institutes of Health brochure summarizes, "depend upon which area of the brain is damaged and how much it is damaged. It is difficult to compare one individual's disability to another, since every stroke can damage slightly different parts and amounts of the brain. Generally, stroke can cause five types of disabilities: paralysis or problems controlling movement; sensory disturbances including pain; problems using or understanding language; problems with thinking and memory; and emotional disturbances." In Debbie's case, so far, none of these disabilities were conspicuously present, and only some scary but modest debilities resulting from her burst cranial blood vessel were exhibited. Her condition until now was more positive than anyone had expected.

  This was the good news. The bad news was that there was no assurance that further damage would be avoided. A look at Debbie's many tubes and life-support devices served as a constant reminder that she was still very vulnerable. For example, the NG tube running from her nose to her stomach to provide food and water was like a giant facial billboard warning of danger and dependence. Nonetheless, I began to envision the proverbial light at the end of the tunnel.

The days in ICU started to unfold thereafter at a faster clip. A technician showed me how to connect to the ICU Wi-Fi, and with great difficulty, with his guidance, I managed to track some e-mails. I was thrilled and told Debbie that she had received more than four hundred e-mail messages of love from far and wide. Debbie was charged up!

- **Driving Downhill to Find Helping Friends**—Debbie was beginning to respond, even though her energy was very low and her speech was weak. But she could give clear voice to her thoughts. She exclaimed, "Charlie, you're beginning to get on my nerves. Why don't you drive home and pick up the mail?" Our holiday mail was being held at the Blythewood post office, 120 miles away. Her proposal showed me that she was increasingly aware that she was making progress.

Hesitantly, despite my exaggerated sense of usefulness at Debbie's bedside, I took her advice and rushed toward home. I made a hasty premature turn at Providence Drive (was its name a coincidence?) and headed for what I hoped was south. Fortunately, my wrong turn onto Providence providentially enabled me to find along its path an entrance ramp to Interstate 485, which, within twenty-five miles linked to Interstate 77 at the North-South Carolina border. So from there I quickly made it home without getting a speeding ticket. I picked up the mail and dashed the half mile to our Cobblestone Park home to pick up some clothes and prescriptions.

While I was packing, the front door swung open, and in came our neighbor Forrest ("Fo"). "Doc, give me a hug and put me to work. I'm here to help." And help she did. Within minutes, she assisted with the packing, obtained a key to the house, and, with Maria Sanders, agreed to take down our two Christmas trees and house decorations and wash and remake all the beds from our California family guests. After I departed, Fo took on all kinds of chores, including driving our 2006 Mercedes to keep the batteries charged, recruiting a housekeeper, and taking measurements of doorways and ramps in anticipation of the time, we prayed, I could bring Debbie home in a wheelchair.

While this was happening, in bounded another neighbor, Dr. John Moore, who also volunteered to help in any way I requested. This offer culminated in his agreement to use a spare key to pick up our subsequent mail at our community mailbox station. This help proved invaluable. Friends performed courier service carrying bundles of mail from John and Susan's home to us at Carolinas Medical Center. Needless to say, Fo and John spread the news of Debbie's stroke throughout our neighborhood; nearly everyone followed the daily bulletins closely and said prayers, often joined by their entire churches.

Other kinds of acts of loving kindness and expressions materialized, too numerous to count. Several stand out and illustrate the surprising amount of unsolicited support we later received, sometimes from unfamiliar people and churches. For example, Nancy Kegley mailed a prayer shawl that our church had made for Debbie. Likewise, dear Cathy Crow made Debbie a gorgeous quilt. Another example was the artwork gift designed by mixed-media artist Christine Raymond, who made Debbie a beautifully encased golden heart to brighten her spirits.

As you might expect, many friends from near and far crowded our ICU room with flowers. That stopped abruptly when the hospital staff informed me that flowers were not permitted in an ICU room because they consume too much oxygen, and our faithful network aides sent a message about the policy, causing many others to cancel their orders; still, it was the thought that counted.

I sped back to Debbie, arriving within four hours of my departure despite another mindless detour from the route I had planned to follow. Recall that one of my many limitations is a missing sense of direction; I get lost easily and often. This time I made my way.

When I returned to Debbie's ICU room, I encountered a pleasant surprise: Emily Crow had talked her way into Debbie's room for a visit. "I can't believe Debbie's progress," Emily told me, and Debbie shone when she overheard Emily's amazement. Emily's words gave Debbie needed reassurance beyond my constant cheering.

- **The New Routine Resumes**—Progress continued. Debbie had somehow managed to catch some sleep even though her caregivers woke her every other hour to conduct tests, monitor things like blood sugar, turn her on her sides to prevent bedsores, supply food and medicines, and the like (this was routine every night). Hilel traveled to Charlotte, as promised, showered Debbie with love, and brought a bundle of mail, including Christmas gifts.

Andy described my mood: "Chuck's call a little while ago continues to be upbeat and positive. Debbie is talking a lot, especially in the mornings, but isn't able to swallow yet so is still being fed through the nose. Numbers are improving, and no spasms today. Chuck said to thank all for prayers and love, and to pass along that they can't accept flowers though several have sent them."

In my shorthand note I scribbled, "A good night for 'Toby'—my favorite affectionate pet name for Debbie. Toby told the night nurse that she had a headache and was given a painkiller. She was still sleeping like a babe at 9:30 a.m. When Debbie awoke, she told me, 'I kind of like having you around but please stop talking all the time.' I got it. The docs removed the IV cerebrospinal line from Debbie's head and replaced it in her back at her lumbar to reduce the risk of infection. I love my Toby."

- **What's New?**—When Dr. Dyer made one of his frequent second daily rounds, he was overjoyed with what he found. Debbie spoke with him, and he made another discovery. "Anything unusual to tell me?" he asked.

"Yes," Debbie's weak voice announced. "For some reason my vision has improved. I can even read without my glasses the message 'CHUCK LOVES DEBBIE' on the eraser board." My notepad recorded still another promising sign: "Dr. Dyer again asked Debbie to squeeze his finger; she did, and he urged her on by yelling 'Ouch!'

Debbie managed a laugh. She was back! He was amazed and said, 'This is very encouraging.' I stayed in the room all day but held my constant conversation in check."

E-mails again flooded hundreds of loving messages. Debbie saw on TV that President Obama was in Charlotte today and urged me to attend his speech, but I refused to leave her alone. I walked the ICU's hallways while Debbie tried to sleep and peeked in the room every five minutes. At 1:58 p.m. I found Debbie awake. She asked, "Do you want to have some porridge?" I looked puzzled. "You know, oatmeal. I think there's some in the car." This knee-slapper vasospasm was another sign that seemed to justify growing faith in future progress. And these achievements came just a week since the first surgery; she was doing great. But not that great. There were many periods of inaction, some without awareness evident and many when Debbie lay silent and still with a vacant, lost look on her face.

- **"Say Good-bye"**—the monitors tracing Debbie's vital signs suggested trouble might be brewing if preventive actions were not taken. John and Mary reported, "Debbie's eyes briefly opened, so Chuck rushed to her side. Her blood pressure dropped, so the doctors are dealing with that. Debbie is worn out from all the procedures, operations, and medications. In the past few days there have been periods when she has been very drowsy and nonresponsive. To trace potential problems, she will have another CAT scan early tomorrow, and everyone is awaiting the biopsy reports to understand how to attack the vasculitis that appears to be responsible for some of her health issues."

The external drain used to monitor intracranial pressure (ICP) and control the level of cerebrospinal fluid (CSF) in Debbie's cranium appeared to be functioning well. Her doctors and nurses made many adjustments to the pressure released from the encased bedside fluid bag hanging from a pole, raising or lowering the pouch as needed to increase or decrease the pressure. Too much or too little pressure would present a dangerous problem. Gradually, the amount of fluid was reduced in incremental small adjustments, and then stopped altogether for a whole day. "I think Debbie's safe on her own," her skilled primary surgeon in charge of this facet of brain functioning, Dr. Scott McLanahan, concluded. "Let's get rid of the lumbar drain—a first step toward the ambitious goal of no more tubes penetrating a patient's body." Great! "Say good-bye to that instrument, Debbie," I cheered. "We won't have to deal with or see that ever again," I boldly prognosticated.

This last step that week looked like a big step forward. What a relief! It momentarily seemed worth celebrating. My notes wrote, in false hopes, what proved to be mistaken—"sometimes people have to permanently use an implanted internal drain, but not my Toby!" With a blink of an eye, I would soon learn that celebration was premature. New threats were surfacing.

CHAPTER 11

A DANGER ZONE

§

Debbie's staggering post-surgery abrupt starts and stops had not led her to a straight pathway. She was moving forward, backward, and sideways. Her mind and body behaved in a manner that no GPS could sort into a clear set of directions; the messages made about as much sense as saying, "Two wrongs don't make a right, but three rights make a left." Alternate steps pointed to divergent destinies. In the darkness of night, the headlights on the road made clear that another crossroad was approaching.

On Friday, January 17, something startling happened that demonstrated the dangers of making assumptions about the future based on recent precedents. New concerns arose about the shifting levels of cerebrospinal fluids in Debbie's brain cavity, which no longer could be adjusted since the external pouch had been removed. Dr. Bernard ordered another CT scan, which revealed that the levels had not stabilized as had been expected. So Dr. McLanahan insisted on still more CT and MRI scans. It looked like new brain perils were emerging.

This news was frustrating. I thought this "problem" had been solved when the cerebrospinal fluid pouch had been removed. Initially, I was skeptically dismissive of the necessity of another precautionary set of tests. In my mind, these new scans represented a step backward. I quickly pivoted. I had to appreciate every precaution. I consoled myself, thinking, "Better safe than sorry."

Sure enough, the scans and tests confirmed that some brain-drain apparatus was necessary, proving how unqualified I was as a prophet and how unpredictable were changes in Debbie's condition. Reasons had surfaced for creating more effective controls to manage the circulation of Debbie's cerebrospinal fluid, which had been impacted by her subarachnoid hemorrhage. The brain imaging revealed an expansion of the ventricular system. "We must accept the reality," Dr. McLanahan explained, "that a reliable means is required to regulate the level of cerebrospinal fluids. There is no immediate urgency to take action. Debbie needs time to heal and get stronger."

That very day, I found out that the plumbing problems emerging from fluctuating cerebrospinal fluid levels in Debbie's brain were not the worst threat. Another was far more troubling.

CONTAGIOUS CIRCUITRY CRISES?

Andy encapsulated the reigning confusion and complexity. He sent the encouraging news that Debbie's "test numbers this morning were good, including the Doppler test and EEG and CAT scan from yesterday." However, he put his finger on the danger that could culminate in another severe crisis—the possibility that Debbie's vascular system might break down, provoking lethal strokes. "The final pathology report still isn't complete," he warned, "suggesting I think the complexity of what they are looking for which would explain the multiple and varied aneurysms—the connecting thread to all of this."

Finding answers was imperative. The dangers of a systemic or congenital blood-vessel malfunction had to be diagnosed if the dangers were to be arrested. This was made evident early Saturday morning. The night nurse called at 3:30 a.m. to inform me that Debbie had asked for me. So of course I hustled right over. I didn't know what to expect. Debbie had talked coherently, so I thought she would be responsive. However, the morphine had taken effect, and when I reached her bedside, she was then fast asleep. She had oscillated "between short periods of sleep and alertness," like a light switch being turned off and on, the nurse explained. "This was not unusual," he added.

Dr. Dyer stopped by later, bearing terrible news: "We found more than two corroded or blocked vessels—many, actually. Given this finding from the preceding scans, we must operate to clear as many as we can find. Dr. Bernard will lead the surgery team tomorrow. Do not worry. This is a far less-invasive operation than through the skull. Her brain vessels can be reached through an incision in her groin to the cerebral veins, and an inflatable "balloon" intravenous device will allow the large constricted vessels to be cleared to widen the narrowing and restore the blood flow."

Andy broadcasted: "A setback this morning. Chuck just called to say that a Doppler test showed more spasms were occurring, so the doctors have decided to do a precautionary surgery through the groin to check/fix some tightened veins. Not sure of all the details about this, but through the groin is far less invasive than through the skull. This will be sometime later, maybe tomorrow."

What I failed to include in my call to Andy were the dire details of Dr. Bernard's evaluation. Dr. Bernard painted some frightening scenarios based on what the angiogram, MRI, and CT scans had revealed:

There is a lot going on in Debbie's brain vessels that could spell big problems. We have no way of knowing. However, the indicators point to some serious possible threats. The worst is the likelihood that any number of vessels could rupture, either from too much pressure where the 'bumps' and 'blisters' are located, and they are numerous, or from not enough blood pressure so that any number of vessels could collapse and interrupt the blood flow, in which case ischemic strokes will probably occur. To be candid, the neurosurgery team is very worried. The risks at this vulnerable time are high. And there is really not much we can do beyond the operation planned through the groin to enlarge as many of the narrowed vessels as possible with the so-called balloon procedure. Then we can only wait and watch and hope that these pervasive and myriad threats diminish.

This scenario was extremely scary. I did not think it appropriate to mention this frightening assessment in my call to Andy or the others, inasmuch as this terrifying news would only cause them additional worries.

I knew God already possessed this information and saw the complete circumstances. Prayers appealing for Debbie's protection focused on these invisible threats to her life, and I was sure that all prayers were heard.

- **Back to the Operating Table**—"Here we go again," I fretted on Sunday morning. Another surgery operation was about to be performed. Dr. Bernard and assistant Larry Braccia reiterated what Dr. Dyer had disclosed—that this procedure was wise ("necessary" was the implied adjective) to help open the blood vessels in Debbie's brain. This was defined as a "preventive" operation, aimed at lowering the risk of further bleeding and to prevent a spasm from causing the other kind of stroke—an ischemic stroke blocking blood flow in vessels, depriving the brain cells of the oxygen-rich blood necessary for survival. The adjectives "exploratory," "preemptive" and "precautionary" were tossed around. I saw them for what they were—euphemisms.

  A supplementary goal for the operation was to keep Debbie's blood pressure elevated to assure that the blood would flow smoothly, rather than "wait to see if another stroke will happen." The fact that this operation was conducted on a weekend did not escape my notice. It could mean only one thing—that an operation was urgent and needed to be performed immediately. There was nothing mundane or ordinary about this kind of operation; Debbie required it as soon as possible to avert a likely catastrophe.

  So to the operating table went Debbie, accompanied by the entire neurosurgeon A-team. This was a planned surgery, so the chaos of January 8 looked like it could be avoided. That said, Debbie was painfully aware of the dark place this operation would, and did, take her. "I am in pain," she confided, and described the level as a "four on a scale of one to ten. Sometimes I wish I had died. Please help me, Lord." I hoped Debbie's terrible statement was induced by her vascular spasms. That could have been its stimulus—she followed her confessional thoughts about fatality with a puzzling non sequitur: "We won't be able to see Tom and Candi. I need a nap. Did my doctor come?"

At 1:20 p.m. we departed for the pre-op and another CT angiogram. Debbie was awake and aware, but racing through her head were additional disconnected vascular-induced thoughts. "You don't have to buy me anything," Debbie exclaimed, so I responded, "I am—something very special such as a new watch. You look so very beautiful."

Her reaction: "Oh, you rascal! Are you taking me home now?" Her strange thoughts did not end until the sedatives took effect. To the specialist administrating the painkilling medications, Debbie inquired, "How did Chuck find out?" after he had kidded us that he was her secret boyfriend. That Toby! We all had a good laugh. But what was happening was no laughing matter.

At 3:30 p.m. Dr. Dyer gave me a brief in the pre-operation station just before the surgery began. He was encouraging but in a hurry to get started. So off he headed to the operating station, while I limped to the familiar waiting room and was welcomed back by the familiar receptionists.

The wait was mercifully short this time. At 4:45 p.m. Dr. Dyer suddenly appeared. Through the glass doors from the waiting room, I spied him heading to the consulting chamber. I rushed through the doors to greet him. Vexed, I held my breath, anxious for him to tell me what had transpired during the surgery. He got right to the point. "The operation went well," Dyer said. "We found that both vessels were, as we feared, narrow, severe, and tight, and the blood flow was weak. We have addressed that and managed to insert a pipeline stent to get the blood fully flowing despite the narrowed vessel, but we still have a way to go. We will monitor the blood vessels closely for the next two to three weeks." A master of understatement, Dr. Dyer's analysis could be readily translated—this procedure undoubtedly had saved Debbie from one or many likely hemorrhagic or ischemic strokes. Her life had been saved, once again! Put this into the growing list of miracles.

That evening Andy reported,

> Chuck has called in after what he described as the longest hour of his life, saying, "God was looking out for her." The docs said afterward that the vessels they examined were more narrow and severe than they suspected, and that if they had not done this procedure now, the risk was far greater for a subsequent hemorrhage. As it is, the docs told him that evening the risk of a stroke was reduced from 60 percent to 10 percent. They will continue the monitoring closely in ICU another couple weeks and do more Doppler tests and another catheter surgery. She's not out of the woods yet and is still sedated, but her eyes are open, and he says she can hear voices. He said disaster was averted but to keep prayers coming.

That operation truly was short and successful. It had concluded soon after it started, and it did accomplish the main goals. In hindsight, I interpreted this achievement as a great triumph. Dr. Bernard's report was also short: "This procedure turned out to be very important. We stopped what could have caused a series of additional ischemic strokes that occur when the blood flow in the brain is slowed or stopped. This operation lowers the odds of that happening. This does not eliminate reasons for concern. We will continue to monitor the vessel conditions carefully. Yet we should feel good that Debbie's signs now are positive."

- **New Declarations in Shadowland**—That evening, the meds wore off and Debbie's words flowed like a waterfall. Debbie surged into a memorable sequence of loud verbal pronouncements with news blasts about her thoughts (fortunately I preserved these in my makeshift "diary" notepad that night).

  Debbie was obviously using her "spasm speak" language to communicate her bizarre thoughts. She for the second time confused me by again announcing, "I don't think we can go to church today." I had heard that one before. So I was not surprised when the Rascal snorted, "I want to go back to my old room."

  "That's where you are now," I responded, and Debbie met this with, "Oh. What day is it?" Next I said, "I'm not supposed to talk with you too much," to which Debbie retorted, "I don't want to talk with you at all. Let's watch a movie, like last night. Did you remember to turn off the phone? Give it to me," she said. Her fingers randomly smashed a bunch of buttons. "Charlie, you don't know how to use this phone! By the way, I'm hungry." This was followed by three bowel movements in succession (at last, the laxatives were working).

  The trickle of tricks did not end there. Debbie tried to pull her tubing from her nose again, but this time I was able to stop her. She had that same smart smirk on her face, as if to let me know that she was about to get away with something despite it not being in her best interest. I stopped her in her tracks. I scolded her with the warning that "any more stunts like that, and we'll have to put the mittens back on during the day as well as at night."

  "You can't," Debbie replied. "We're going to Charles and Ashley Butt's house today. I think I'll have some applesauce. I would like some frozen strawberries. I want to go back to Wytheville. We get two sides at this restaurant. Guess who's going to speak at my funeral? Cathy Crow."

  I couldn't let this one pass. "There will be no funeral. Cathy said she wants you to speak at *her* funeral."

Then Debbie got serious for a moment: "What happened to me?" she confusedly asked.

I tried to tell her, diplomatically, about the perforated aneurism, but she gratefully lost interest and insisted, "I want some cheesecake for desert. By the way, do you want to use this?" she politely inquired while pointing to her bedpan. To her nurse, after her sponge bath, Debbie thankfully declared, "I can dig it."

These vocal outbursts gave me confidence that her strength and cognition were marching forward, even if the spasms spawned some very curious, entertaining thoughts and many laughs. Full coherence, I felt, was around the corner, providing no vessels burst or blocked.

The rest of that nail-biting Sunday was devoted to prayers and my administration of passive stretching exercises. We were gratified by the success that had occurred, or, to deploy an overly used metaphor, by the premise that we had dodged some bullets. One danger had been averted. The secondary operation to treat collapsed or swollen brain vessels was safe and successful. It provided a heavenly safe haven that we prayed would not be temporary. Time kept moving, and so did continuing adjustments in the ICU to the ceaseless changes and reappearing threats.

- **Intensive Care's Intensity**—I settled into a quasi-routine, calling the nurse attendant every night every two hours, rising at 4:30 a.m. for a quick shower and coffee at the Hospitality House, and then bursting into Debbie's ICU room usually at 6:00 a.m. in time for me to catch her doctors making their morning rounds and hearing firsthand their evaluation of Debbie's status. I stayed at her bedside all day and learned a trick at 7:00 p.m. when the nurses' twelve-hour shift rotated—I asked permission and usually was allowed to overhear the briefing of Debbie's status. This provided valuable information that was unavailable on an hour-to-hour basis. On the rare occasions when permission was denied, I shamelessly eavesdropped to catch the inside information. About 9:00 p.m. I routinely sought to "break in" any new nighttime nurse with my unsolicited advice and instructions regarding my regular calls during the nighttime.

Every hour was spent attending Debbie. I hovered over her almost constantly when Debbie's eyes opened, in the hope of using every moment to engage in what I hoped would be therapeutic activities. These included prayers for her and conducting relentless passive exercises. When she slept, I placed calls to Andy, Hilel and John for their daily updates to their e-mail lists and to her sister, Karen, in Indiana. Breaks consisted of pacing the halls and retrieving takeaway food from the cafeteria to consume some nourishment while Debbie slept. That was my typical fifteen-hour day.

This routine began to take its toll. My left ankle swelled dangerously, and my legs stiffened and atrophied. The doctors and nurses noticed my deteriorating condition. "Chuck," Dr. Dyer warned, "I've seen many spouses doing what you're doing without sufficient breaks, and they literally break down, and then we've had to treat two patients in the hospital. Don't let this happen to you. Give yourself a break now and then. I insist that you take an occasional walk and begin to eat." (I lost 20 pounds the first two weeks—too much for a six-foot-three frame normally weighing 190 pounds.) I reluctantly and partially accepted this command.

To be truthful, I pledged to remain steadfast and hyper-attentive to Debbie's care and advocacy. A wave of acute awareness swept through my fatigued mind: she needed me. Previously self-reliant and fiercely independent, Debbie was now totally dependent on me. Because she needed me, I felt needed as never before. Her need was highly motivating. This crisis provided an opportunity to exercise unrelenting efforts to attend to Debbie. I needed to meet her needs; it felt rewarding. I had a clear primary purpose. I could satisfy my need to meet her needs. This was my magnificent obsession of choice. My personal needs were secondary. Debbie's care came first.

- **A Good Samaritan Insures Insurance**—Another event occurred in this post-stroke period that was unanticipated. I discovered on our cell phone to my chagrin and, frankly, alarm, a dreaded message:

"You can expect a call from a representative of your Blue Cross/Blue Shield SC State Employee health insurance program." This, I presumed, could only mean trouble about coverage for Debbie's treatment, I instinctively feared. My paranoia spun out of control the previous evening when a front-page column in the *Charlotte Observer* reported "Man Charged $89,000 for Snake-Bite Treatment" by a local hospital. Was Debbie not covered or her coverage compromised because the hospitals were out of the state of South Carolina?

I soon learned how wrong I was. Our cell phone rang. "My name is Kathy Morris. I have been assigned by Blue Cross to serve as your caseworker for Debra Kegley," the stranger informed me. My heart skipped a beat or three. "I'm here to assist you," she added. (This reminded me of the old joke that one of the least believable messages to Americans was "I'm from the government and here to assist you.") Was I ever mistaken! Kathy was not only real; she was also really there to assist us. "I will be your advocate with any and all issues and questions that may arise," Kathy explained. "May I come to CMC to see you and Debbie?" she pleaded. And come she promptly did. Kathy spent two hours briefing me on procedures, answering questions, and resolving on the spot at that first meeting several concerns about billing due to inadvertent hospital mistakes about our policy identification. But what most made a difference that day was Kathy's request to see Debbie in her ICU room and offer a prayer! It was beautiful. Kathy and I became instant friends, and her "caring and compassionate professional help," as I described it in a letter of appreciation I wrote months later to her supervisors, "made a huge difference for us." This episode was part and parcel of a pattern of myriad friendly help that emerged as time moved forward. Help from friends was a true blessing.

WHAT'S ON THE HORIZON?
None of us truly can help the things life does to us, as Eugene O'Neill warned. They're done, and once they're done, they lead to other things.

Some are good, and some are bad. Our travels were taking us on a path that included both. The vascular operation was an instance of the former. What lay ahead on the road produced experiences that combined the latter with the former.

On most days since her stroke, it appeared that Debbie was traveling on a safe roadway heading toward regained health. True, the doctors were unable, from the many rigorous blood and pathology reports, to determine definitively if Debbie faced some kind of vessel deterioration that would likely cause one or more additional strokes. No promises were made. There was no option but to follow the advice to take one day at a time. (At dismal times, it was more like "dread one day at a time.")

As time passed after Debbie's surgeries without any major incidents, fears of another life-threatening assault gradually began to recede. The days were now getting a little bit longer each day, providing more and more daylight to brighten spirits. It increasingly looked like our race from night to day was underway. However, my budding confidence was based on a weak foundation, perishable as a wet sand castle built at low tide too close to the shore. Just as these recent crises seemed to pass, additional threats generated new fears.

Two major worries darkened the future. The first was the persisting, pervasive threat that Debbie's entire vascular network was deteriorating, which could only mean that another vessel might hemorrhage, causing another ruptured aneurysm and, conceivably, death. It had to be acknowledged that another stroke, possibly fatal, could happen; the grim statistic is that many people who survive a stroke and are assumed to have a healthy functioning vascular system subsequently experience additional strokes. The second worry was the great danger posed by the existence of a blister on both sides of the same vessel where Debbie's first aneurysm had burst. Her surgeons warned that if Debbie got stronger, sooner or later another major surgery into her skull would have to be performed to deal with the danger. Disconcertingly, the surgical team admitted that they were unable to formulate a surgical strategy to address this latent and lethal problem. This deferred issue posed a hidden, lingering threat. It, too, cast a very long and dark shadow on the future.

Experience teaches us to expect the unexpected. And sure enough, just as a modicum of confidence was beginning to build, storm clouds began to gather and darken the sky. What did they presage about the next leg of Debbie's journey? Was this brightening period the proverbial calm before the storm? What would happen next?

PART II: SOME NEW CRISES AND DANGEROUS DETOURS

§

Better to die once for all, than live in constant terror.

—*AESOP'S FABLES*

CHAPTER 12

LOOKING AT DEATH IN THE FACE

§

Ian Fleming wrote *You Only Live Twice*. The movie version of that James Bond novel failed to explain the meaning of the title. The book filled in the blank: "You only live twice—once when you are born, and again when you stare death in the face."

Debbie's stroke ushered into being the second definition of what it means to live: confronting the reality of death in its full meaning. Her subsequent near-death sojourn is as close as it gets to "living twice"— she had faced death a second time.

Never did we imagine what was to next happen—a dramatic scare that forced staring at death in the face once again, indeed, several more times. Debbie was to confront yet another life-defying crisis, meaning she was about to live not twice but thrice.

CRISIS

Social scientists define a "crisis" as a situation comprised of surprise, threat, and a short time to respond. At 4:00 a.m. on January 21, my bio-alarm rang, and I called the night nurse to see how Debbie was doing. "I was just about to call you, Chuck. We have a serious situation here. Get here as fast as you can." My heart dropped to the bottom of my stomach. "Oh, no!" I groaned.

I feared the worst as I sprang into immediate action, like a swim-mer seeing an approaching shark. Alarm bells sounded in my head. My adrenaline surge was strong enough to animate a corpse. All three elements of a crisis were evident. Shock, danger, and the urgent need to react that accompany a crisis pervaded the darkness as I hiked through the dark night to Debbie's ICU room.

Huddled around a sedated Debbie were four surgeons and several assistants. Their report confirmed my worst fears. "Debbie's belly is full of blood. She looks like she is nine months pregnant. Her blood pressure has plummeted to 60/30, and her hemoglobin count has fallen to almost zero. Sign the papers of authorization, Chuck. We must give her massive blood transfusions. There is no time to conduct a CT angiogram to pinpoint where the hemorrhage has erupted—it could be in her stomach, but we hope not because that's hard to plug. It's probably somewhere in her colon. Dr. Lynnette Schiffern from CMC General Surgery will perform the emergency operation to locate and close the vessel break. This must be done as soon as possible. Debbie could easily die, so say some words of comfort to her now."

My heart skipped. I felt like I had been thrown around in a cement mixer. I prayed for another miracle. "Debbie, I am with you. I love you without limit. We will be together forever, here or in the next world, when we will live a second time in eternity. Please, our Lord and Savior, if it be your will, let her live. I need her, Jesus. Please empower her surgeons to serve Your will."

The element of surprise that helps define a crisis can hardly be exaggerated. Given all that had happened the preceding week, no one expected still another emergency. To be sure, there had been many ups and downs, advances and retreats. Nonetheless, huge hurdles had all been transcended, potential catastrophes had been avoided, and in general Debbie's responses had suggested that a positive trend was taking root. So this surprise was a complete shock. Everyone was stunned. There had been few real warning signs prior to Debbie's recent emergencies, and this nail-biting threat was preceded by absolutely no prior symptoms.

The second attribute of a crisis, a threat, was also evident. Debbie's threats, however, were multiple. No one knew what was going on, but the symptoms of potential catastrophic dangers now were everywhere. Debbie looked pale, her sodium level was dropping fast, and her oxygen supply pumped through a respiratory ventilator had to be increased. Her arteries and veins were bulging, her breathing was not controlled, and although she appeared to recognize me, when asked, she couldn't show me or the doctors two fingers or stick out her tongue. Worse still, her transcranial Doppler levels suggested recurring, frequent spasms in her brain vessels. She was hyper-tense, and a new arterial line was inserted to better measure her vacillating blood pressure. The doctors scratched their heads. Was this a seizure? An infection? An infarct? Vascular deterioration throughout her body precipitating heart failure? The multiple threats were menacing. I nearly fainted when I overheard one of the doctors utter, "We have not lost hope yet."

The third element of a crisis, urgency, was as extreme as that need can get. Some kind of action had to be taken, immediately. But what? At least four massive blood transfusions restored a modicum of hemoglobin, but by 8:00 a.m. Debbie's heart rate jumped to 153. It was urgent to locate and stop the source of the bleeding and bloating to determine if a rupture had occurred in the stomach, spleen, liver, colon, or elsewhere. Ten surgeons quickly assembled in the operating room, where a critical decision had to be reached. It was urgent.

A RETURN TO THE OPERATING TABLE

No surgeon dared to guess what had caused the hemorrhage. Someone proposed performing an MRI to try and detect the source of the bleeding, to which another responded "There isn't time; she will be dead if this rupture isn't located and sealed immediately." The surgeons made a wise collective choice, for which there were no viable alternatives. The only way to find answers and potentially control the damage, they concluded, was to open a long vertical incision from Debbie's breastplate to her lower abdomen to search for and find the tissue that had burst. There was no time for delay. I said more prayers for the ears of Debbie's surgery team and hurriedly signed the permission papers. Drs. Lynnette Schiffern and Beverley Paton led the surgery team, aided and guided by the whole neurosurgery team of experts and five assistants.

Bad news travels as fast as a bullet. Before sunrise Andy spread the alarming news of the new crisis: "Friends—major setback. Chuck just called to say Debbie is in critical condition from internal bleeding, somewhere in the stomach region. Her stomach is puffed, her blood pressure fell to 60 over something, and she has been receiving massive blood transfusions. The doctors can't determine where the hemorrhage is and are getting ready to perform surgery to search for the lesion and stop this bleeding."

The operation began promptly. I was pushed to the waiting room, where I waited in the dark, terrified, for word about Debbie's fate. I could smell fear emanating from my body. I felt like I was on death row, waiting for a pardon.

I nervously paced the waiting room in a vain effort to reduce anxiety while her surgeons went about their work at full speed. They cut a sixteen-inch vertical incision from Debbie's upper abdomen to below her belly button and explored the bloody tissue in search of the spot from which the hemorrhage had released a stream of blood. Expertly, they located the site of the vascular tear at the ventricle tip of the colon and plugged the opening shut. In the process, her surgeons found about four inches of "suspicious looking" colon and elected to remove that portion of Debbie's colon then and there to eliminate threats that segment might pose in the future. While they were at it, they also removed her spleen.

If there was a silver lining, it was that a perforated aneurism in the colon was relatively treatable. Had the rupture occurred in the lining of Debbie's stomach, liver, or another vital organ, the odds were very low that the hemorrhage could have been treated. Debbie would have died.

I did not know it at the time, but Debbie faced the additional danger that the infarct could clog her colon, so blood had to be drained fully, and the secondary consequences of greatly reduced blood pressure were unpredictable, endangering other parts of her brain and body.

Without recounting more details, the hoped-for outcome was accomplished quickly and expertly. The skilled surgeons were seasoned in their craft. They stopped the life-threatening bleeding that had bloated Debbie's abdomen. The opening in her colon where the aneurism had burst was stitched shut, and the severed colon was closed at both ends. This allowed the air in the colon to be released, bringing Debbie comforting relief. Moreover, the four inches of suspicious-looking colon were successfully removed and sent to biopsy for testing. The operation went smoothly and achieved its primary purposes.

The only disappointment was the news that another simple follow-on surgery to reconnect her colon would have to be temporarily postponed until the test results were complete and Debbie could gather more strength. (Later pathology tests showed that no portions of the remaining colon were dead.)

Debbie was still at great risk, and the dark warning was issued that if she experienced more strokes, no treatment would be possible. At this critical phase, her surgeons predicted that Debbie's cognition was not likely to have been seriously affected, but that could change. She was to remain on pain killers and heavily sedated on respiratory support. Little did I know that the crisis had not ended. More problems were about to erupt.

AS BAD AS IT GETS: TWO NEW STROKES

Debbie's colon breach was not the extent of the troubles. Conditions did change for the worst during this crisis, and the changes were horrendous. While the surgeons were searching for and finding the site of the hemorrhage, Debbie's condition had sunk to a frightening new level of vulnerability. Her loss of blood and plummeting blood pressure created the kinds of conditions conducive to strokes. That dreaded possibility happened not once but twice. Necessary treatments to perform the colon surgery had created new vulnerabilities precipitating two more stokes!

Andy reported the nightmare this way: "Terrible news from Chuck. Debbie had two cerebral strokes when her colon hemorrhaged from the combination of massive bleeding and accompanying low blood pressure (it was 60/30 yesterday)."

Hilel rushed to the hospital to lend me support. His take from his visit that dark day put a direct spotlight on the disasters that had occurred: "There have been a series of peaks and valleys with optimism and set-backs since the first January 8 stroke, but the most recent is the worst. The latest crises during the night involved a sudden drop in Debbie's blood pressure and other problems with her vitals, followed by a hemor-rhage in her colon, and during surgery a major stroke struck her brain's left cerebral hemisphere and caused a somewhat milder stroke in her right hemisphere. The doctors are extremely concerned but expressed some measure of hope."

Well, that day, and the daylight it provided, did not end the dark-ness. As darkness enveloped Debbie's ICU room, more information pre-sented many more questions than answers and many more reasons for worry. A physician's assistant elevated my alarm. She began by skirting the main concern, stating first that "for the record, the colon rupture was located near the abdominal belly, close to the juncture where the colon and spleen intersect. The rupture might best be labeled a pseudo-aneuris breach." Then she got to the bleak situation, disclosing that the two new strokes had caused an unmeasurable amount of damage. "To be honest," she candidly revealed, "Debbie's response is slow." Another physician's assistant chimed in, trying to calm me by observing, "The post-surgery CT scan did show that the blood was flowing slowly in Debbie's brain, and that the loss of blood, anesthesia, and surgery ordeal could be the cause of delay in her ability to respond. A delay is acceptable if normal blood flows could resume. But the bad news has to be faced: the scan suggested that there probably were spasmal infarct strokes when Debbie's blood pressure was low, the worst in the left front of the brain that controls most motor and cognitive functions and relatively modest bleeding in the right frontal lobe. During the surgery, Debbie had been given super-injections to get her blood pressure up, and that's when the cerebral bleeding was discovered." This grim assessment was about as calming as a hurricane.

- **The High Price of Two Cerebral Infarcts**—The worst damage of this near-death perforated aneurism in Debbie's colon was the collateral damage that this hemorrhage caused. Prior to and during her lifesaving operation to stop the rush of blood in her colon, her traumatized colon rupture set off neurological alarms and the body's defense mechanisms took charge, rushing all internal help to the danger zone by closing down the energy pulled to defend other vital organs. The suspension and closures to keep Debbie alive while the breach was being sealed resulted in a drop of blood pressure to near-fatal levels, and her hemoglobin count vanished to near zero. Four complete blood transfusions corrected the latter problem. But the loss of blood pressure and efforts to boost it was all it took for not one but two cerebral infarcts to result. This is technically defined as what happens when the blood supply is reduced below a critical level to a specific region of the brain, and the brain tissue in that region dies. The dreadful worst had happened, again. Debbie underwent two strokes, and the thought of her becoming braindead or cognitively challenged was deadening.

  As the doctors suspected, the first and most serious stroke occurred in the left hemisphere of Debbie's cerebral cortex. That is, the most damage occurred in the left cerebral hemisphere where, on average in the United States, strokes are four times as likely as in the right hemisphere. This was extremely threatening because this area is the brain's main source of cognition. The left brain engineers most people's ability to understand verbal language, to speak, to write, and to reason and think logically—to exercise God-given rational thought in order to compartmentalize, distinguish, categorize, and arrange sensations into abstract ideas. In addition, the left brain manages movement on the right side of the body.

Debbie's second cerebral stroke that fateful morning had also seeped some blood into her brain's right hemisphere (but comparatively not nearly as much as had flooded her left hemisphere). This area controls functions on the left half of the body and cognitively relies on intuition instead of deductive, linear reasoning, collecting the data from the left hemisphere and integrating trillions of received bits of information into a synthesis. The right hemisphere functions to activate emotions, nonverbal communication such as facial expressions, intuition and imagination, dreaming, and spatial awareness. A cloudy leaked blood mass on the CT scans revealed that some unknown extent of damage had occurred. Mercifully, however, it appeared that this secondary hemorrhage was likely to be relatively less destructive.

Nonetheless, these twin assaults on Debbie's central nervous system were extensive. Both ruptures spilled blood in and around the brain, depriving brain cells of oxygen. Obviously, and dangerously, the alarming damage could kill the cells and neurons, impairing and disabling her, perhaps forever. Only time and subsequent evaluative tests would tell.

- **"Debbie Deserves a Break"**—Those words spilled from Dr. Dyer's lips when, in dismay, he voiced his initial assessment. "This set of cranial disasters is extremely rare and totally unexpected. How could this happen? The odds of a second aneurism so soon after the first were about as high as a hole in one by a two-year-old golfer. It is mind boggling to conceive of the improbabilities of an additional burst aneurism in a different part of the body leading to more strokes so soon after the first on January 8."

In fact, Debbie instantly became an international medical-case celebrity as news of her strokes went viral worldwide. We soon were to learn that in the past quarter century, there had been only four known previous cases of a torn aneurism within some part of the body occurring in less than a month by a hemorrhagic brain aneurism preceding it. The surprising misfortune that happened to

Debbie was extremely rare; she was a statistical outlier, a deviant case, off the charts. No one desires this kind of fame. This is a limelight to be avoided.

The technical term for the assaults that early January 21 morning on Debbie's brain vessels is a "subarachnoid hemorrhage in a case of segmental arterial mediolysis with coexisting intracranial and intraabdominal aneurisms." That mouthful translates to mean Debbie almost concurrently underwent hemorrhagic aneurisms in both her colon and brain.

Why? Super-specialized pathology and blood tests failed to uncover a cause. And this mystery pointed to a dreaded suspicion (voiced by several surgeons) that the two ruptures were likely to be linked. The most probable culprit, it was then often postulated, was a systemic deterioration of Debbie's entire diseased vast vascular network of veins, arteries, capillaries, and blood vessels that made her vulnerable to further ruptures. The image of hemorrhage after hemorrhage popping like a string of ignited firecrackers was too gruesome to picture. But it was a real danger, to be feared especially because in that case there would be no available cures.

- **Some Light in the Danger Zone?**—At 12:15 p.m. Andy reported that a small ray of light had become visible in this grim situation: "Chuck said Debbie was out of the surgery and was now back in her ICU room. They found bleeding in the area between the spleen and the colon, and they have left the wound only superficially closed in anticipation of her blood pressure stabilizing overnight, and then tomorrow they plan to go in to do another surgery to stitch the wound shut and try to treat the severed colon. For now, the good news is that Debbie is stable and opening her eyes, and she is trying to squeeze Chuck's hand and can hear him. He said this is a 'danger zone' but that God is listening to prayers. Chuck says it is another miracle she has come through this. Still more prayers needed. A friend from Columbia [George Crow] had once again arrived to provide support and prayers."

George had indeed arrived in this, the latest time of need. He was there for us, as always. His presence and words provided needed spiritual and psychological medicine. George listened intently. Dr. Dyer attempted to put a hopeful face on Debbie's horrible situation. He extended his colleagues' preceding assessments by informing us,

> The hemorrhage in the left hemisphere was in a small vessel and situated far to the left, which may reduce the risks of disabling cognition and motor functionality and personality changes. Despite remaining in critical condition, there are a few positive developments. Debbie's vital signs have improved since her surgery. Her hemoglobin has gone up from about 3 to about normal (over 10); her blood pressure has risen from 60/30 to 130/70; her heart rate was abnormally very low but has climbed to 123. We are lowering her sedation.

There wasn't much in this evaluation to provide encouragement, but we welcomed any threads on which we could pin our hopes. George cupped his hands on Debbie's forehead and petitioned our Lord to "protect and preserve this child of Christ." The power of touch was visible—I was certain that George's prayer to God had reached Debbie's inner consciousness, even though, sedated, she was asleep. The mystical mind, a source of spiritual consciousness, is a wonder.

John and Mary tried to clarify my rendition of the fast-paced shifts in the crisis circumstances, adding some post-surgery details later that traumatic day:

> Chuck reported that Debbie had a stroke to the left side of her frontal lobe and a smaller vessel leak on the right side. The left part of the brain affects motor skills. She is not able to respond on the right side of her upper body, or with either leg or toes. She is not responding to verbal and physical cues, so the doctors are reducing the sedatives in hopes of responses. She has

opened her eyes but does not focus. The doctors assume these strokes were the result of the bleeding in her colon and the resulting low blood pressure. She will *not* have more surgery on her colon today—possibly tomorrow; at least that is the plan now. We spoke on the phone with Dr. Dyer, the lead doc in her team of doctors. He acknowledges her precarious situation but is still hopeful. He is dismayed by all the seemingly unrelated life-threatening events that have occurred. As long as there are no more surprises, he is holding out hope for improvement.

These synopses purposely underplayed the brutal fact that during her surgery Debbie had been virtually at the doorstep of death. Debbie had stood at the edge of eternity, having to look at death in the face, and once again God had pulled her from death's door. She had survived. However, her survival had come at an awful cost. Her colon operation had saved her life, but the surgery that had to be performed to enable her survival had so greatly weakened her vascular condition that not one but two new strokes had hit both hemispheres of her brain. There was no telling how much damage to the functionality of her brain had resulted, but recovery at some level remained within the realm of possibility.

We had "been there" before on January 8th and "done that." Now Debbie was back at the starting line to a new race. A feeling of déjà vu darkened the running track. We had to start all over again. The route bore a striking resemblance to the same road that had been taken previously. This was to be a new trip on a far-less-traveled but somewhat familiar path. At least the new journey could commence.

- **A Stitch in Time?**—I stayed with Debbie through the night and was rewarded. Debbie awoke at the next morning's dawn and was somewhat responsive. Rested, she slightly responded to my hand squeeze and eye movement. "You have been through a lot, darling," I told her as I tried to summarize what had happened. "An additional colon surgery is planned for today but has not yet been scheduled. I have been with you the last twenty-eight hours and will remain with you in your room all the time. My love for you knows no limit. God is protecting you, so know you are safe."

That January 22 morning, Debbie's condition continued to evolve. The day featured more signals that prayers were once again being heard. Andy reported:

A stable night, and Chuck sees glimmers of hope this morning. Chuck found Debbie wide eyed this morning. She had a good night, and her vitals are stable. A CT scan shows no change from yesterday. The most recent Doppler test, which measures the flow of blood to detect spasms, was a lot better than last week's high numbers. Yet the new strokes might have caused serious damages. Her right side extremities are still not responding, and her motor and cognitive functionalities are worrisome. On the positive side, Debbie heard and responded to Chuck's voice. She was able to respond to simple commands on her left side. She put up her left thumb, and squeezed his hand and wiggled her left toe. The doctors told Chuck there is still the pain killers and sedatives to account for the lack of response on her right side. The follow-up colon-closing surgery will probably happen sometime soon, in the operating room, but no time has been scheduled. Her docs are cautiously optimistic as long as Debbie has no other events or setbacks. No word from pathology as yet. No responses from the right side yet. Chuck asks for more prayers, knowing that God has heard all of you and is so appreciative.

It didn't take long to receive more news. To my surprise, the next day the neurosurgeons gave the colon surgeons permission to perform surgery in Debbie's ICU room, because a move to the fourth-floor surgery room was too risky. This decision allowed me to watch this follow-on operation to close the severed colon by reconnecting the portion where four inches had been removed along with Debbie's spleen during her emergency surgery. Another goal was set. Her surgeons aimed to perforate an opening in Debbie's abdomen to her upper colon, to enable a colostomy bag to be installed; whenever excrement filled the bag, it would be replaced with a new pouch.

At 3:50 p.m. Dr. Schiffern's team promptly set about to close Debbie's colon, look for and remove any dead colon tissue, and install the colostomy. Hilel pictured the plans that were about to unfold: "As we speak, a team of surgeons will be operating on Debbie's colon in her ICU room. The neurosurgeons gave the green light to operate on her colon but without moving her from her room. Everyone is anxious to determine what the relationship is between the hemorrhage in her colon and her brain aneurism and now the new strokes. When I hear from Chuck, I will post anything he reports."

This surgery was performed efficiently and successfully, while I nervously watched from the corner of the ICU room. Not only were all the goals met, without complications, but also another accomplishment was achieved. Remarkably, Debbie's surgeons had been able to close her abdomen with staples rather than having to cut a wide horizontal incision across her stomach. (This was ironic, I thought, because had a horizontal incision across Debbie's stomach been necessary, as had been expected, it would have intersected with the preceding vertical incision to make the sign of a cross. That would have produced a memorable sign, although it was not a cosmetically attractive place to display a cross.) The stapled solution was safer and had enabled the operations to be conducted without any complications. The colostomy transected the places where the opening was made, without interfering with the staple closures. All this was managed with almost no bleeding or infection. Some small blood clots were found around the previous colon surgery; these were not a cause for worry, inasmuch as they sometimes naturally occur and rarely travel to the brain.

THE LIGHT DIMS AND BRIGHTENS

This positive development notwithstanding, no one had ever said that the path to regained functionality would be straight. Sure enough, on the very next day, I had to share my distress and despair. As John and Mary put my mood,

> Chuck is discouraged. Debbie hasn't moved all day. They are wean-ing Debbie off of her many medications in hopes that she will be better able to respond to stimuli. But, so far, there has been insig-nificant movement or cognitive response. The nurses have given Chuck a pep talk. They think yesterday's surgery, weaning her off medication, reducing her oxygen support, and lowering her blood pressure can create extreme exhaustion and may be the reason she is not responding. They are giving her small drops of substances by mouth to encourage her stomach and intestines to begin func-tioning once again. Pressure-support to the lungs may be needed. One of the nurses tried to cheer Chuck by telling him that a body undergoing the stress of surgery can wear down like a battery, but a battery can be recharged.

As if by magic, reasons for cheer appeared, breaking the spell of unmitigated fear. Debbie's condition dramatically improved. My trust in God proved to be well placed. After lying motionless and almost coma-tose the entire day while I helplessly watched for signs of her awakened consciousness, Debbie awoke—just as the 7:00 p.m. nurse shift was tak-ing place. Debbie opened her eyes, moved her left toes, and raised her left thumb for me. Her left arm displayed a tremor, but this shaking was not unexpected given the fluctuating dosage of medications she was receiving. The doctors set as a goal elevating Debbie's blood pressure above 130 to assure a steady flow of blood through her brain's vessels, with some success.

Another step forward had been achieved! In great relief, I rejoiced as I was shooed out of her ICU room for the night to prevent me from interrupting my beautiful wife's sleep. I ventured in an elevated mood to the elevator, where the receptionist who controlled the ICU's security doors said she was worried about me. She had nicknamed me "Deuce" because "you are my second favorite after my nephew." Dr. Schiffern was standing by and said, "Chuck, take care of yourself." "Don't worry about me," I responded. "Just continue to give Debbie such wonderful care." "But I am worried about you," she insisted. "You are wearing yourself out. It shows. The load is too heavy. You're trying to do too much. You need to get sufficient rest to recharge your batteries so you can be strong enough to continue to give care to Debbie." I wondered, how could I? I didn't listen or obey. I am that persistent. I couldn't wait to resume my oversight of Debbie's care when I could rejoin her early the next day.

CHAPTER 13

A CRISIS OF CONFIDENCE

§

The realization sunk into my gray matter that our dark long journey would be much longer. The emergency operation on Debbie's colon rupture had saved her life. But at what a price! The two cerebral strokes did untold damage. Her paralysis was much worse than it had been within two days after her first stroke, and far more threatening. Debbie was fragile, and her flaccid body looked like skin on the bone. This was a very dark period. The road ahead looked much steeper.

To put it mildly, a floating sense of crisis persisted., for good reasons—new threats, surprise, and the urgent need to react to crises had arisen with repetitive regularity. A whole series of emergencies had erupted out of the blue. More crises could come. My anxieties escalated; crisis after crisis had conditioned my mind to anticipate new threats. There was no alternative but to try to summon the courage to change the conditions we could change, and hope that the terrifying things that had happened would be the last and worst of our trials. We were mistaken.

MORE HEMORRHAGIC ANEURISMS AND STROKES?

The greatest threat was that more strokes would strike my Debbie if more cerebral vessels either exploded or imploded. The myriad threats stoked my fears. Was something sinister eroding Debbie's entire vascular system, leaving her prone to further vessel perforation?

The question on the minds of all Debbie's doctors was why her totally unexpected burst aneurism in her colon and the twin strokes in its wake had occurred. The causes of Debbie's latest brush with death remained a mystery.

Rival plausible hypotheses were advanced. Some of the doctors speculated that medications might have exacerbated existing debilitations. Others speculated that the colon rupture was simply a random hemorrhage in a weak aneurism that might have happened by chance independent of the previous stroke and that the loss of blood and plummeting blood pressure had then triggered the two cerebral strokes.

Most often, to my alarm, the doctors suspected that the first stroke and those ruptures that had just occurred were linked by an underlying vascular disease. Andy noted, for example, that Debbie's doctors "have not ruled out the connective tissue disease disorder that was floated yesterday as a cause of the colon bleeding, but are in the dark as to how a vascular disease might be connected to the colon lesion so distant from the brain hemorrhage. Chuck overheard speculation that Ehlers-Danlos connective-tissue disease weakening arteries and veins might be the culprit."

The prospect that Debbie's entire network of veins and arteries may be corroding and collapsing due to a disease was horrible beyond words. A systemic vascular disease would expose Debbie to more hemorrhages and strokes. No treatments would be available. Dr. Dyer put this frightening scenario this way: "That this odd rupture occurred so close in time, in less than two weeks and so far, away in location, was shocking. The probabilities were extremely low. I have never seen it happen in twenty years of practice. This scares me shitless."

The climate of medical opinion was so dark that it was difficult to see grounds for optimism. One doctor was candid:

The effort to trace a cause through blood and pathology analyses was persisting, but conclusions cannot be deduced yet. We don't know how this phenomenally rare set of events may be related. We don't have answers. To be honest, we remain clueless. We have managed to reduce the number of potential causes. The data have led us to reject some propositions about a connective causal linkage. For example, we now have pretty much ruled out Ehlers-Danos. Still, tracing the presence of a specific systemic vascular disease will be extremely difficult. There are hundreds of possible vascular diseases that could be 'systemic,' and all we can do is search for clues.

This news made my heart pound and heart rate spike. Another expert was called in from Ohio State University to provide an outside opinion. His assessment was not calming. He informed me that "we have to wait for specialized pathology and biopsy reports, but I estimate that there must be some kind of linkage in the vessels, which could cause additional hemorrhages. Low-grade antibiotics should now be used to protect against infections, and the disconnected colon, of course, needs to be monitored closely."

The dark was soon partially pierced by one piece of positive news. The first rounds of laboratory screenings came back and did *not* show evidence of the presence of some form of nonarteriosclerotic and noninflammatory disease also known as segmental arterial mediolysis (SAM) which weaken blood vessel walls that are prone to form in the brain or gastrointestinal tract.

But of course there was accompanying negative news that dimmed this glimmer of light. While these tests did not reveal the presence of vasculitis, that dangerous disease nonetheless could not be ruled out. Inasmuch as the varieties of this inflammatory vessel disease are huge, the presence of each and every type could not be eliminated as possibilities. A negative—the absence of a suspected condition—cannot be proven.

The darkness was engulfing. Neurological research warns that various forms of vasculitis lead to arterial wall defects which lie dormant in blood vessels and are susceptible to bursting. Vasculitis causes intracranial aneurism formation, stenosis, and hemorrhages. In addition, it is possible that abnormal connections between veins (known as arteriovenous malformations, or AVMs) can develop anywhere, including especially in the brain, and at their sites bacteria and other impurities can accumulate in the bloodstream and pass directly through arteries into the body. If this detritus lodges in the brain, it usually leads to strokes. So there were an untold number of medical disorders beyond the varieties of vasculitis clouding diagnoses in the unsolved explanatory equation of Debbie's dysfunctions.

For example, a horrifying possibility was that Debbie's perforated aneurism was a result of an underlying hereditary hemorrhagic telangietasias (HHT) of abnormal vessels associated with Osler, Weber, or Rendu disease. This is an inherited disorder in which even the smallest vessels have thin, fragile walls that are prone to dilate and rupture. Bulges appear that often vanish but reappear seconds later and have a tendency to burst and bleed. They are most common in the brain and liver and can cause a stroke. Could this disease have been the source of Debbie's hemorrhagic aneurism, possibly inherited genetically from her mother, Fonzine, who died at the age of sixty-two from a stroke following heart problems? Diagnostics could neither prove nor disprove the presence of this disease. If Debbie was afflicted, the prospects were not good. Treatment consists primarily of closing a broken vessel with insertion of a wire coil no larger than a human hair in the abnormal vessel. The problem was that the coil can cause clots to form, blocking blood flow to precipitate additional strokes. Worse still, these kinds of vessel abnormalities either constricting or inflaming vascular channels can occur anywhere. Fears of this and other dangers undermined confidence. I could only trust that God would pierce the darkness. "I remembered the Lord, and my prayer went up to Him" (Jonah 2:7). I knew "the Lord was my only refuge" (Isa. 60:19–22).

These multiple potential defects, vulnerable to contagion, were real dangers. The road on the journey was, to say the least, bumpy at best and disastrous at worst. To grasp the gravity of Debbie's perplexing condition that fed the chronic sense of crisis, take into account that, simply put, the "known knowns" did not go very far in identifying the multiple invisible threats facing Debbie's life, rendering prognoses about her future nearly impossible.

A Problematic Terrain and Trajectory

Like every war and every life, every crisis eventually comes to an end. This last crisis was different. Its dark clouds never passed out of existence. The threat of vascular disease fomenting more strokes, potentially fatal, never disappeared. It loomed large. On top of that, the recent past posed a harbinger of probable new threats and subsequent new crises.

There existed many hurdles on Debbie's uncharted path toward recovery. Yes, thank God, she had survived this last set of life-threatening attacks. She did not die. "The Lord will be your everlasting light, and your God will be your glory" (Isa. 60:19). That indeed was what He was. It was probable that God had plans for Debbie that precluded her death.

However, we had no idea where our journey was heading. Only testing and rehabilitation treatments could reveal how far Debbie's journey would take toward regaining a portion of her former life. At this juncture (with the Lord and me by her side), nobody could tell the extent of the damage that these two latest strokes caused in either her brain's left or right hemispheres. Any or all of Debbie's brain's functions could be disabled. Needless to say, the repercussions from cell destruction in either hemisphere were dreadful. The noxious stink of high anxiety flooded the air.

Adding to the darkness was another descending storm cloud—the danger that her throat and vocal cords had been permanently damaged by the respiratory tubing into her nostrils and mouth. It was possible that Debbie might never be able to breathe or talk as she had before her long journey had begun.

This had been a hair-raising, nail-biting, fateful week. Debbie was imperiled, and her existence was precarious. Hilel reported at this crossroad the frightening circumstances:

Chuck has been at Debbie's side continuously. She continues to wink, move her left toes and hands, but doesn't have much, if any, movement on her right side. The lab is closed today, but the continuing explorations looking for the nature of her vascular problems are ongoing. Doctors have suggested that polyangitis, which could be granulomatosis with polyangitis or microscopic polyangitis, might be evident. I offer these terms to you who are less ostrich-like than I am. The bottom line is that the doctors will continue to try and determine what has caused both the problems in her brain and in colon. The swing of emotion continues. The road ahead will be very, very long and difficult.

RIDING A ROUGH ROLLERCOASTER

Debbie's fluctuating condition demonstrated that Hilel's prediction—continuing struggles with oscillating successes and setbacks—was on target. On Monday he reported,

Debbie's progress has been, and unfortunately will probably continue to be, a roller coaster ride. Whereas Sunday was a relatively good day, as night approached things went slightly downward. Her hemoglobin was low, they found an excess of spinal fluid, and the new "cocktail" to make her pulse rate a bit higher began to make her very drowsy and unresponsive to stimuli. This morning, the doctors modified the spinal fluid level in her cranium, and are addressing other issues. However, she is stable. The Doppler procedure had good results, and she began to twitch her left limbs slightly. We are all anxiously awaiting the lab results of the biopsies. Chuck, on the other hand, is a bit numb. The doctors ordered him not to rush to her side every time her eyelids rise, and to get some rest, eat properly, and take quick walks outside to get some fresh air. To say that he has been a loving, caring and attentive husband is to understate it horrifically.

Mary publicized the situation in somewhat different language:

Talked with Chuck last night and found him to be very tired, mumbling and frustrated about Debbie's prospects for long-term progress. This Monday morning his expectations for Debbie's progression sounded pessimistic. Patience is a Kegley weakness, as I well know, from living with Chuck's twin! Debbie had a round of modest physical therapy in her bed, but was unable to do most of the tasks asked of her. Chuck sensed her frustration, but she was being cheered on by all in the room. Chuck said Debbie is so weak that an anticipated move to the less-critical ICU facility would have to be deferred for at least another week, and then only if big improvements were made. She has managed to "mouth" with her lips several words, but has not actually voiced them out loud. She continues to smile when spoken to or sees a new face. She will receive more aggressive passive physical therapy. Her receptive (if not expressive) communication seems to be good.

Where was God? He was there the whole time. The sunrise was overcast with dark clouds, but the sun was shining even though it could not be seen, and I knew Jesus the Son was present despite the dark clouds shrouding my vision. God had time and time again displayed his power and grace, and I shredded some fears as I reminded myself of the Lord's promise to give "ear whenever called" (Ps. 116:1).

CHAPTER 14

DEADLINE

§

D ebbie had survived many frightening threats to her life, and these recurrent crises were catalysts to the growth of wisdom. We learn through life's most difficult moments, so these crises were not wasted. Wisdom grows in the soil of hardship, and confidence grows when we place faith in the grace of God (James 1:2–4). Aeschylus (526–456 B.C.) grasped this, writing, "Pain which cannot forget falls drop by drop upon the heart until, in our own despair, against our will, comes wisdom through the awesome grace of God."

We wanted to learn but would have preferred other means. The preceding scares had frozen my cringed and brooding face. The fright continued. The care in intensive care had been intense, and the tension after Debbie's colon-rupture surgery and her two death-defying new strokes did not abate. Doctors' whispering heightened the prevailing gravity of the situation. T. S. Eliot could have been describing our plight: Debbie "was neither living nor dead," and "I knew nothing; looking into the heart of light, the silence." I was distraught. God must have heard my desperate cries as I suffered "in the furnace of affliction" (Isa. 48:10) observing Debbie's many afflictions.

STRUCK BY MANY DEBILITIES

Annually, a third of the Americans who survive a stroke—on average eight hundred thousand—are afflicted with problems speaking, writing,

reading, and understanding language—disorders known as "aphasia."
Most also have motor and muscle disabilities. Unfortunately, following
her two new cerebral stokes, Debbie fit the profile. She suffered from
a plethora of disabilities. Unlike the promising aftermath of her first
hemorrhagic stroke and near-death sojourn, in the wake of these two
recent assaults on her brain, her chances for getting better were lower.
Most alarming was her slow responsiveness and episodic long periods of
stone-faced silence during which only her blank stare met the eye. John
and Mary lamented,

> Debbie is going through a sluggish period. She has had a few fleet-
> ing moments when there is a slight response on her left side. Several
> times when her eyes were open she did not respond at all. She still
> has the breathing apparatus inserted in her throat, which causes
> her to gag frequently. She does a lot of coughing when the pain
> medication wears off. Her blood pressure is about 156/86. The docs
> want to keep it there, and to keep the IV line to her head operating
> to boost the flow of blood through her brain vessels. All the ongo-
> ing treatments must work simultaneously. Maintaining coordina-
> tion requires maintaining a very delicate balance.

The picture of Debbie's predicaments was not very pretty. When
put together, the pieces presented a disturbing portrait of her prospects.
All one had to do was to gaze at her to see the challenges. Her motor
was running in neutral, and fuel was running low. Her neck and right
side were totally paralyzed. She was unable to swallow foods or liquids,
so to assist her survival, the NG tube from her nose to her stomach
remained continually in place to supply nutrients and fluids. The ventilator enveloping her mouth pumped the oxygen necessary for life but
prevented efforts to speak. An IV continued to feed her medications into
her arm, and another IV to her lumbar was required to regulate spinal
fluid levels in her cranium. Factor into the picture a catheter to her bladder, briefs or diapers to hold remnants of remaining bowel discharges,

a protruding colostomy bag from her abdomen to collect bowel movements, a cranial catheter to monitor changes in her ventricular system, and you can begin to picture the myriad collage of afflictions. Without real food, her weight had fallen to 106 pounds, and her ribs and bones were visible under her flaccid muscles. Debbie looked helpless and hopelessly vulnerable. However, her vitals for the most part remained within an acceptable range of variation, interrupted now and then by an occasional rise (or fall) that, when they occurred, never failed to provoke my alarm. Fortunately, I knew that a temporary rise in blood pressure, heart rate, or other indices did not a trend make.

Regular CT scans, x-rays, or MRIs filled in some of the blanks. In general, her overall condition was precarious, but thankfully she did not require full life support. The closely watched indicators suggested that the odds of another hemorrhagic aneurism were declining but remained worrisome—estimated somewhere in the 15 to 20 percent range. The frequency of further vascular spasms was also declining. In addition, the repeated pathology and biopsy reports of Debbie's vessels and veins continued to produce no evidence of the dreaded vascular disease throughout her system, and this absence of evidence modestly increased confidence. As each hour and day passed without another hemorrhage, hope expanded that maybe she was not afflicted by a diseased and deteriorating vascular system that would precipitate more uncontrollable vessel breaches. Nonetheless, the endless multiple pathology analyses could not rule out altogether the presence of untold varieties of vascular deterioration that could lie latent and suddenly breach a vessel and cause great damage.

The doctors and nurses did what they could to stimulate Debbie's responsiveness and activate her motor and mental capabilities. For example, the physical therapists deployed a machine to lift Debbie on a harness from her bed into a chair. Just attempting to sit upright was challenging. Unfortunately, Debbie's breathing was labored, her blood pressure rose during her efforts to support herself in the chair, and she had many long lapses of unresponsive inactivity, exacerbated by exhaustion and drained energy. This exercise illustrated the kinds of treatments that might be introduced to push forward what likely would be a very long recovery process.

In bed, Debbie was unresponsive most of the time. I did everything I could to push the rehabilitation needle, concentrating on passive stretching exercises to try to build Debbie's neuro connections and motor memory, and when she appeared alert, I talked to her incessantly to stimulate her thinking processes. A nurse scolded, "Chuck, you're a workaholic." "I know. I'm working on it," I retorted.

BREATHLESS AND SPEECHLESS

Debbie was downtrodden but not down and out. At this juncture of our long journey, Debbie's respiratory rate became her most pressing problem. She was unable to breathe on her own. A gas-mask-looking ventilator funneled oxygen through tubing into her lungs, while the NG tubing funneled food from her nose to her stomach. In combination, the two treatments interfered with and irritated her throat and vocal cords. Debbie could not breathe on her own, swallow, or speak, and her dependence on these dual life-sustaining devices was causing problems. What was helping her was also simultaneously causing her harm. The toll was escalating. The clock was ticking, and a deadline was approaching. These treatments could not continue without doing permanent damage.

Debbie emitted a lot of secretions into her breathing tube. The cloudy mucus in her airway passages was not good and not normal. The secretions could cause her to aspirate and choke and induce the onset of pneumonia. Moreover, her secretions were penetrating her vocal cords and, if they continued, could paralyze her vocal cords and weaken her throat muscles, compromising her capacity to swallow if and when the respirator was removed. "Chuck is still waiting impatiently for the assistive breathing ventilator supplying oxygen support to be removed," Andy explained, "because it is rubbing Debbie's throat raw, but she is still dependent on it and cannot breathe on her own."

This emergency required some kind of intervention. I soon discovered that a date with destruction, disability, or death was nearing. The deadline which made the headlines on the Internet messages would reveal Debbie's destiny. I restlessly paced the ICU corridor, nervously awaiting the surgeons' interpretation and decisions on how to contain the threat. A messenger arrived, intent on delivering a troubling message about options.

- **Meeting "the Grim Reaper"**—An anomalous visitor wearing a business suit greeted me at our ICU doorway with an icy stare. He was assigned the foreboding task of bringing dire news to the families of patients. He had a lousy job to do, which someone had to do.

   "I'm here to inform you about the options for Debra," he coldly instructed as he proceeded to define several choices that were really no choices at all. "I have looked at Debbie's charts, and you have but two choices. Your wife has been on the NG nose feeding and respiratory ventilator for fourteen days. This cannot continue. The usual maximum length is eight days. Your first choice is to authorize pulling the ventilator from her mouth and watching to see if she survives."

   "What?" I screamed. "I'm not about to risk her death. This would be a huge gamble. Her life would be put in jeopardy. The risk cannot be taken. I refuse to authorize any procedure that could be fatal."

   "Okay," the hired gun grunted. "If you insist. The second option is surgery to cut an opening in your wife's neck, from which oxygen can be pumped into her lungs. This tracheostomy, known as a 'trach,' is not simple. The odds are high that she will never be able to speak again. You may never hear her voice. She might have to be permanently connected to a breathing-supply machine and possibly confined to a bed the rest of her days. It's not much of a life—hardly worth living. The choice is yours."

   This hit hard. My rage started to boil. How could this person so callously perform his assigned role? No wonder he was a mere

131

temporary consultant hired for this painful task from an external medical-assistant employer. His voice was devoid of empathy, conjuring up images of "the Grim Reaper" summoning people about to die. He delivered his grim briefing like a heartless, obedient Nazi ordering a victim to the gas chamber. I needed a lifeline and had been thrown an anchor. I refused to budge. "Let's give my wife's doctors a better opportunity to see how she responds. Perhaps a little more time will enable her to begin to breathe some on her own and at any rate build strength if this dangerous operation proves absolutely necessary."

In the ICU hallway, I completely lost it. I cried loudly and uncontrollably. Nurse Katie heard me and rushed to my side, asking what was so disturbing and how she could help. I muttered a rehash of the down-and-out grim choices I had just been given. Katie then began to cry as well. Within a minute, five other nurses joined us. It must have been quite a sight: a group standing in a circle together, all crying.

Let me add a footnote on this miserable experience. My capacity to put aside the mean-spirited manner in which this consultant made his presentation was a challenge. I came up short on forgiveness, because I suspected that he was devoid of a moral compass after years of observing hopeless victims die or being forced to live paralyzed in mind and body. I couldn't help imagining that he was willing to rationalize the death of victims whose prolonged existence on life support were, to his mind-set, not worth the price. Maybe he believed that the world would be better without such pitiful, needy people. Perhaps he perceived disconnecting Debbie's respirator would be an act of kindness; ostensibly he deemed allowing a victim trapped in a body who doesn't have much chance of living a real life to die an act of mercy. Such a philosophy would turn the Hippocratic Oath for doctors to save lives on its head. I hope I was mistaken. If I misread his motives and was falsely blaming the messenger for the awful message, then and only then could I more readily forgive this consultant and ask for forgiveness for my anger. At this time, I was in no mood to give this "Grim Reaper" the benefit of my doubt. Moreover, I didn't want to face a harsh reality—strokes strike 20 percent of the population, 20 percent of whom survive, but only a tiny fraction of the survivors— less than 1 percent—eventually regain full cognitive or physical capabilities. Debbie's prospects undeniably were grim. Anger usually stems from fear. I *was* afraid and very angry. A deadline was approaching and might be passed with death. The future looked hopeless. I was lost. I felt suicidal. Despair and darkness smothered all light.

I prayed to God for guidance and comfort, and He must have heard my frustrated cry because I soon received some calming advice which slightly reduced my fears, sense of helplessness, and angry resentment. Adrift in a sea of torment while Debbie lay heavily sedated, I called Hilel for consolation. Hilel hit a home run. "Every hospital uses outsourced agents, assigning to outsiders the tough task of presenting worst-case scenarios to patients and their families. They are instructed to avoid any and all bases for optimism. It's partly a liability issue. If people are given false hope, and the patient fails to recover after expectations have been elevated, the caregivers will rightly complain, 'Why didn't you warn us?' Accordingly, to guard against lawsuits, hospitals' standard operating procedures dictate appointing an outsider to paint a patient's probable outcome in the darkest shades imaginable. So, Chuck, swallow the hospital's hired-gun diagnosis with a grain of salt. This 'Grim Reaper' assuredly made gruesome predictions about Debbie's likely future condition because that is what such advisors are paid to do. Relax. It is unlikely that his grim scenario will materialize."

Hilel's advice alleviated some of my dread. His update the next day showed he had clearly seen through the scene painted by the Grim Reaper:

Chuck has been riding the waves created by the terrifying report he received yesterday, but is faring better now because the doctors with whom he spoke gave a less dire analysis than yesterday's grim pronouncement. Debbie does need to get off the respirator but this does not have to be today. The important thing is for her to be strong and able to breathe on her own. I grew up in a medical family, and have children and close friends who are physicians, and know that no doctor dares to be completely sanguine in their predictions. If these don't pan out, the litigious nature of our society puts them in jeopardy.

- **Can Debbie Catch Her Breath?**—The Grim Reaper's report may have been hyperbole, but the threats he identified were steadily mounting. Debbie's fate in fact did revolve around the critical question of whether she could begin to breathe on her own volition, without any respiratory assistance, so she could begin to empower her vocal cords and possibly speak.

A neurologic-disease specialist explained why treating Debbie's breathing/respiratory problems was an urgent priority: "Normally the limit for use of a respirator and nasal feeding tube is eight days. Debbie is way beyond that boundary. This cannot help but to cause serious problems. The good part of her condition now is that when the respirator is temporarily lifted, her vocal cords appear to strengthen. This decreases the necessity to undertake a surgical tracheotomy. We aim to conduct a NIFF test tomorrow to see if she can continue breathing on her own."

Alarmingly, Debbie failed to pass that NIFF breathing test. The ENT (ears, nose, and throat) specialists said they would try to conduct another breathing-capacity test that afternoon after she has an opportunity to rest. But time for rest was not provided, because in marched the ICU physical therapists, who worked her hard. Debbie was no stranger to a tough workout and did her best. Discouragingly, Debbie again failed the second afternoon respiratory test. Her doctors' anxiety was visibly growing, and they were eager to remove Debbie's respiratory supports. They announced that still another NIFF breathing test was planned in the morning. Andy had to report,

> Chuck called and is very worried. He said the NIFF respiratory tests haven't gone well. Debbie's abdominal muscles aren't strong enough to wean her from the breathing support yet, so more time is desperately needed before the ventilator can be removed and swallow tests can be conducted. Unfortunately, after a restless night, Debbie spent most of that day sleeping, which was important for her to recoup some strength. This meant that the doctors were unable to perform the follow-on set of respiratory exercises and NIFF tests they had planned. The respiratory therapists wanted her stronger before trying the next breathing test to determine if she can temporarily breathe on her own. The number of days on respiratory support are mounting, which isn't good for the lungs or muscles. Chuck said he is on pins and needles waiting for the next test. He is hoping and praying Debbie is less restless tonight than last night, and able to meet the respiratory challenge tomorrow.

That night the attending nurse was on duty and responded promptly to my calls every two hours looking for hopeful news. I learned that Debbie's blood pressure had stabilized at 96/47, and although low, this arterial pressure was sufficient. I was not really terribly alarmed by this number, because before the strokes, Debbie's blood pressure had regularly hovered near this range; it had routinely been on the low side of the ideal 120/80 benchmark due to her extreme exercise regimen. And mercifully, the nurse told me, "Debbie is now catching some sleep, and if this rest continues, it might enable her to catch her breath during the morning respiratory tests."

- **Sprinting up a High-Altitude Mountain Marathon**—Early the next morning, I called Rev. George Crow. Brother George restored my soul. "God is on the side of those who place their trust in Him. God wants us to call on him. He will answer." Then he prayed, "We call on You, heavenly Father, to uplift Debbie, if that is Your will. Please protect her." I looked at my radiant-spirited wife, who lay looking so helpless. Yet I knew George was right: our loving God is a faithful merciful helper.

  As sure as water is wet, this prayer was answered. In my lament, God carried me through this time of Debbie's terrifying trouble. Debbie was on the threshold of an encouraging development.

  The light crushed the blackness soon thereafter. Debbie's doctors made a bold decision. Instead of conducting the postponed third NIFF test, they elected to conduct a long-shot experimental effort to determine if Debbie could breathe as her oxygen supply through the pump was very gradually reduced. The goal was to see how long Debbie could sustain breathing. Would she be able to breathe with lower levels of oxygen support?

- **Full Speed in the Fast Lane?**—Testing began. Debbie's attendants steadily diminished in increments the level of oxygen support she received. "Look, Chuck," nurse David exclaimed, "The experiment is working! Debbie is practically breathing on her own. She is receiving less than two percent of her oxygen intake from the ventilator! If she is able to maintain this performance, we may be able to take her off support!"

Andy's headline announced Debbie's breathtaking breakout:

I know many stay anxious for reports on Debbie's status and progress. Chuck just now called to say after a more rested night, Debbie's eyes have opened and the therapists are in the middle of the respiratory test. She scored a 26 which is in the upper range of the 20–30 target, so her doctors have begun testing her breathing capacity. As I write this email, she *is breathing on her own*! If she can continue this for an hour, they will remove the respiratory ventilator support and observe if and for how long she can last without more oxygen support. If successful, the roadblock will lift and Debbie can begin to stride and strive toward the distant finish line, and maybe begin the next race to see if she can eventually recover the ability to talk and eat normally. But the next hour is huge. Chuck doesn't want to give false hope, but for now, prayers are being answered. Don't stop the prayers!

Andy's follow-up e-mail soon thereafter said it all with just two words—"IT'S OUT!" He explained, "The respiratory support line was 'excavated,' that is, removed at 10:45 a.m., and Debbie is breathing on her own." I was exhilarated with joyful relief, like an alcoholic shaking off a severe hangover and swearing never to touch liquor again. Still, the doctors' warning that Debbie was "not out of the woods yet" was sobering, but optimistically they poetically added that it looked "from where she now strides in the forest, she probably can see some light." My excitement soared when I heard three attendants exclaim, "Debbie is doing even better than expected!"

- **All's Well That Ends Well?**—Debbie's throat was very sore, and the degree of recovery could not be foreseen. But I had extraordinary reason to praise God for carrying Debbie's breathing abilities so far so quickly. I concluded that this leap forward represented a huge crossing along a high bridge over very troubled waters. Debbie did her part when the breathing ventilator was extricated—her beautiful face beamed. At 12:52 p.m. she took a well-deserved nap and awoke happy at 2:05 p.m. I asked her to smile, and she did. "If you're going to be that beautiful," I joked, "I might have to get rid of you." Not wanting to waste the moment, while calling Debbie's sister, Karen, to spread the good news, I asked Debbie to smile, and she did. Her comprehension was rising in conjunction with her breathing capacity.

This bright day marked a milestone. Debbie had crossed a wide chasm. She had begun to breathe entirely on her own. This was a real breakthrough. Moreover, she had managed to breathe for a long enough period of time to justify additional experimenting by taking her off backup oxygen support for longer and longer intervals.

Mary advertised our rising spirits:

> We all knew Debbie's progress would zig and zag, have ups and downs and not be linear. Today it is all ups and hopefully the positive trend will be maintained. Today is a bold step in the right direction. The respirator is out, she is breathing on her own, and the chances that she will be able to talk are looking up when her raw vocal cords and muscles repair. Chuck is overjoyed. He believes Debbie understands her breakthrough because as he was talking with me he saw Debbie excitedly reacting by wiggling some toes on her left foot. She was smiling brightly.

The prayers of many continued to flow, and they were answered. Off had come the muzzle-like mask from Debbie's mouth. Because she had begun to breathe on her own, the tracheotomy operation was postponed. Another remarkable miracle had occurred.

ENTRY OR EXIT?

The track ahead was still littered with many obstacles. However, now that Debbie could breathe on her own, it appeared that a path to recovery was being cleared. As a precaution, when the feeding tube for liquidized food was not in use, a new plastic breathing tube in Debbie's nostrils was deployed to provide occasional bursts of oxygen support. It was hoped that this eventually could be extricated if Debbie's respiratory rate remained sufficient, but at this stage it was necessary to keep her NG tubing in place.

What commenced was an anticipated succession of peaks and valleys. If past was prologue, progress would likely be interrupted by more occasional detours and frightening crises similar to those that had episodically erupted thus far. Both advances and retreats would probably continue to line Debbie's roadway on her continuing journey. The further you fall, the higher you must climb. The path was steep and long.

The crucial factor determining whether Debbie could leave the ICU for the Acute Care stroke unit across the hallway on the same ninth floor was whether she could be weaned from *all* respiratory support to breathe entirely on her own. She succeeded in doing just that for the following forty-eight hours, with minimal and declining feeds of supplementary oxygen!

This achievement made it possible for the oxygen supply line to her nose to be removed. The stakes had been enormous. Potential recovery from throat scars and vocal-cord dysfunction were contingent upon this achievement happening. Some barriers on the path had collapsed, and it looked increasingly like it might be possible to forego the trach operation. The gateway opened to a path pointing in the right direction where Debbie could tread in order for her to regain a semblance of a meaningful life.

The next crossroad would be a transfer to the Acute Care unit if no additional roadblocks precluded that trip. Would there be an exit from the Intensive Care Unit? Nothing is assured about the future except God's everlasting love, and what you've heard many times—death and taxes. But you can probably guess what happened next.

CHAPTER 15

MOVING FORWARD OR HARDLY MOVING?

§

"Both Debbie and Chuck had a reasonably good night," Hilel reported the morning following her breakout breathing accomplishment. "Debbie's CT scan has not been fully read, but nothing seems problematic. Still no conclusions from the biopsy. They are testing her again today to see if she can still continue to handle breathing on her own, which she dramatically achieved yesterday. Forward motion is progressing. Chuck felt she was more responsive today as well."

"What goes around comes around," as the trite saying puts it. What came around next seemed to bring us back to a place we thought was behind us. Debbie was advancing when warnings suddenly appeared suggesting she might drive in reverse gear.

A SHUNT STUNT

I impatiently received from Debbie's neurosurgeons the delayed readings of her recent scan images. They were very disconcerting. They showed that the level of cerebrospinal fluid (CSF) accumulating in her brain was fluctuating outside the normal range of variation. We heard what we least wanted to hear: "The operation we have postponed is now necessary and urgent. We cannot delay any longer. A shunt must be surgically implanted in Debbie's cranium, and the surgery operation has already been scheduled on Monday. We will install a tubular vessel about an eighth of an inch in diameter. It will run under the skin from

Debbie's skull through a neck vein to her upper heart chamber where the cerebrospinal fluid will disperse into her bloodstream. The shunt tube will probably be permanent or remain implanted to function for the foreseeable future."

Dr. Scott McLanahan wanted to take no chances. I was moderately chagrined, because the external spinal-fluid bag hanging on a pole and draining tube had previously been carted away, and the replacement lumbar drain appeared to be working. I was mistaken. I should have known better. Dr. McLanahan had previously told me that eventually "a reliable means would be required to regulate the level of cerebrospinal fluids." That time had come, and a CSF shunt was that reliable means.

A mechanical cranial implant, a shunt would provide a durable safety-valve to regulate the level of cerebrospinal fluid buffering neural tissue in the brain. Known technically as a "hydrocephalus," a shunt controls excess fluids from interfering with cerebrovascular circulation and precipitating a round of new strokes. Although invasive and therefore potentially dangerous, this kind of surgery is fairly common—on average, about forty thousand are performed yearly in the United States. Because a shunt could prolong Debbie's life by deterring more brain-vessel hemorrhages, this remedial operation looked less and less like a setback and more and more like a step forward. I immediately pivoted, grateful that this precautionary intervention was now to be undertaken.

I escorted Debbie on the rolling stretcher platform to the x-ray room. After an agonizing hour-and-a-half wait, the anesthesiologist finally gave Debbie a mixture of sedatives and pain killers. After another extended nail-biting wait, the operation began. At last!

Dr. McLanahan's surgery was exceptionally fast. It only took an hour and fifteen minutes. Why? Because I had magnified in my mind the difficulties. My fears, fed by misunderstandings, were unwarranted. Dr. McLanahan relieved my stress by explaining the two treatment strategies implemented on Debbie's behalf, previously the lumbar drain and now a cerebrospinal shunt:

Their risk profiles are different. In the acute stage, we often use lumbar drains to control intracranial pressure (ICP) and promote cerebral perfusion, especially in the face of vasospasms. In the more chronic phase, we are called upon not uncommonly to implant a shunt. This is a longer-lasting (but not necessarily permanent) solution to the buildup of cerebrospinal fluid (CSF). In many ways, as I've explained to many of my patients, my placement of a CSF shunt is nothing more (or less) than very sophisticated plumbing, whereby I take cerebrospinal fluid that is accumulating in excess and deliver it to a place where it can return to the bloodstream, in Debbie's case, directly via the upper chamber of the heart. I might add that we planned from the beginning to access a vein in her neck and thread the catheter from there into the heart. The abdomen was not used due to the recent GI tract related events.

I wish I had understood this properly at the time the need for this surgery was announced, so I wouldn't have unnecessarily hit the panic button. Live and learn.

"The operation is over," Hilel's e-mail extolled, "and was a complete success. The surgeon predicts that this could contribute to Debbie's rate of recovery, if expected further advances unfold."

An imaginary bullet had been dodged, inasmuch as this shunt provided a kind of barrier to more burst aneurisms and could speed healing. Dr. McLanahan predicted that Debbie would continue using this protective mechanism "for as long as she needs it." The newly inserted shunt had a great advantage—fluid levels could be monitored externally without invasive surgery, and the pressure level could be mechanically adjusted with a magnetized device held against her head without penetration into her cranium.

When evaluating this decision, I had to question what the consequences would have been had this precautionary operation *not* been undertaken. The results were likely to have been unfavorable, maybe fatal if more strokes occurred in the absence of reliable fluid controls.

Debbie and I later met a forty-two-year-old US military officer whose surgeons, after his ruptured aneurism, chose not to implant a shunt; tragically, in a sequence he suffered four additional strokes. That tragedy could easily have also happened to Debbie. In hindsight, I am grateful that Dr. McLanahan had insisted on this invasive surgery. Thank God that He oversaw Debbie's well-being. This surgery may count as another miracle in the remarkable series of miracles that had occurred.

THE PENDULUM CONTINUES TO SWING

What lay ahead? I impatiently waited for a prognosis about what would happen next. Hopes were increasing as some new developments occurred.

- **A Skeptic Finds Faith**—A serendipitous event occurred during Debbie's relatively short shunt surgery. As I anxiously paced the waiting room, I noticed four people huddled in prayer. After their talk with God, I introduced myself and asked if I could join them. They thankfully agreed. I led another collective prayer.

  When I returned to my seat, a member of the party joined me and asked if we could talk. His name was Steve Myer. He was from New Jersey. He shared his story. A well paid high-tech expert, Steve said he was a Jew and had spent a year studying the New Testament of the Bible to prove to himself that it was false. "I failed," Steve said, "so I heard a call, accepted Jesus Christ, quit my job, and went to a Christian seminary. I am now a practicing minister." In fact, Pastor Steve was practicing his ministry as we spoke. We prayed, and Steve and I became telephone friends. He later traveled to the CMC hospital to see and spiritually support Debbie.

  Reunited with Debbie back in our cozy ICU room, I thanked God and our surgeons for this last act of deliverance. I put this operation into the elongated inventory of starts and stops on Debbie's journey. It was now a part of the past, I presumed.

- **Nursed Nerves**—One of the nurses saw the worried look on my face and said, "Chuck, I can see that you're nervous and impatient, but you should be encouraged. The chances that Debbie might be able to talk appear to be improving. She may still require modest dosages of oxygen spurts through the backup nasal tube we have made available in case the need arises. Debbie's face reflected a positive attitude that must be making a powerful contribution to her health. I admire your wife's constant smile."

  A tidal wave of reassuring calm swept over me. My nervousness declined concomitantly with rising expectations. Although paralyzed on her right side and unable to turn her thin neck more than a single half inch to her left, Debbie's doctors were excited by "the remarkable unexpected pace of her improving condition." Little signs pointed to the possibility of big progress. For example, when the stitches were removed from Debbie's shaved head where the long cranial incision had been cut, it seemed likely that other kinds of advances, both small and big, might follow. Debbie's nickname for me, "Nervous Norman," fit me a little less.

- **Poised to Perform**—Since the surgeries and some successes, the spirits of the entire medical team had steadily climbed. Debbie's receptiveness to those communicating with her and the appreciative expression shining from her face even though she could not speak in response, said it all. She was preparing to spring forward and seize every opportunity to make progress. And she was progressing, as shown by her increasing control of her left hand and arm. Highly motivated, Debbie worked so hard trying to lift her left arm that she had tremors, similar to the reflexive muscle twitches that result from vigorous isometric exercise. Her dedicated drive doing exercises paid dividends—the "physical functionality" score on her left side rose to an 8 out of a possible 10. Her ability to rub her chin with the mitten on her left hand generated additional optimism. Although prolonged passive exercises made Debbie breathe hard, a nurse interpreted Debbie's painful grimace attempting to move her right arm "as a sign that reflexes on her right side might be beginning to return."

- **Did You Hear Me?**—At the end of a promising day, I said prayers, and reminded Debbie that I would be only five hundred yards away at the Hospitality House and would be calling regularly during the night. "Okay," I thought I heard Debbie faintly whisper. Wow. Did she try to speak? Or was my imagination parenting my auditory sensation? I didn't know but held high hopes as I gazed at her beautiful face.

"Good evening," Andy's e-mail announced.

> I could tell from the first syllable out of Chuck's mouth that this day got off to a better start. Chuck thinks he might have heard Debbie try to say something, although her hushed sound was inaudible. Debbie has wiggled her left toe, and her eyes remained open the entire day. Dr. Dyer, the main neurosurgeon, dropped by late this afternoon on his way out of town (to Vail, no less, where Debbie and Chuck had skied with fraternity brothers and wives two years earlier). Dr. Dyer grasped Debbie's left hand and asked Debbie to squeeze it. He claimed he felt a slight response.

- **Friends Visit and Sing Praises**—Hilel described vividly the warming prospects in the evening that day after he, Herman Rich, and both George and Cathy Crow and their daughter, Emily, all paid another visit and got to meet each other in the waiting room. (Hilel told George his daughter was very pretty and jokingly asked George, "Is Emily spoken for?") This reunion of supportive friends made my day. After their visit, Hilel reported,

> The news today continues to be encouraging. Debbie slept well last night and is gaining some strength. Although she will continue specialized stroke care, it is beginning to look like the doctors could move her to an adjacent facility geared for

slightly more-aggressive therapies. The ICU staff has already started some modest rehabilitation work and will increase it today. Chuck is, as all of us should be, still cautious but uncharacteristically optimistic. He and Debbie are blessed with the love and prayers of his brother and sister-in-law John and Mary, his cousin Andy and great friends. Chuck constantly expresses his gratitude to you all. I think that Debbie's progress also owes much to the excellent medical care she is receiving and to Chuck's loving care and fortitude. He has been a superhero in my eyes. I can't imagine either Hollywood or a Romance writer coming up with a more heartwarming script than what I've seen and heard. They truly are a magical couple, and I hope with all my heart that they continue to be so for many, many years.

Debbie had climbed a very steep mountain and crossed many a roaring stream while on this leg of her remarkable journey. Her prospects were beginning to improve. Some severe threats were now in our rearview mirror. However, the cloud of uncertainty cast a shadow that enveloped us like a cocoon. We faced many fears that some challenges might not be overcome; the long-term possibility of a future confined to a wheelchair was one of them. And a Debbie unable to ever speak again remained an unspeakably painful possibility.

Still, Debbie's journey looked like it might resume as some barriers were lowering. Her recent steps could pave the roadway toward recovery. I knew her new accomplishments were enormous but knew all too painfully that new threats could suddenly surface. I had been on a high many times previously, only to have my hopes hit new lows. Now everyone was praying for a succession of good days in a row.

ENTERING AN EXIT RAMP?

While watching the vital indicators more closely, the staff's attention riveted on estimating how Debbie would adapt to more ambitious exercises designed to gauge the boundaries of her limitations. A previous experiment was replicated—the lift, like that used to carry heavy objects in a harness, was redeployed to move Debbie from her bed to a chair. Just sitting upright still drained much energy, but she met the goals that were set for endurance and duration. Encouraged by this achievement and others, confidence was rising that Debbie was approaching the time when she would to be able to exit the ICU and move to the next stop, Acute Care, where more ambitious physical, occupational, and speech evaluations and therapy could begin. Of course that huge step depended on no new setbacks, reversals, or accidents.

So a goal had been identified, and I eagerly spread word of this possibility. "Chuck has called with a big report," Andy announced, "including news that Debbie may be changing rooms later to another treatment center on the same floor, and that she is sitting in a chair as he talked. In addition, the docs are looking at taking some more tubes out, including the urinary track catheter. Slow movement, but forward overall."

I greeted the possibility of a transfer to the Acute Care facility with both apprehension and approval. Movement from ICU could be dangerous if it were premature; Debbie would then be deprived of the full battery of life-support devices and, more troubling, the round-the-clock dedicated attention a single nurse provided in intensive care. On the other hand, a transfer meant that new challenges might be addressed and that greater momentum toward recovery might be attained. The hanging question was whether the goal was realistic at this time.

MOVING DAY

The next morning, it began to look like the next milestone might really come into sight. At 8:10 a.m. Dr. Bernard conducted an unscheduled inspection round. He smiled, as was his custom when news was positive, which it was. He announced that the implanted shunt was working well and that probably another day or two was required before it could be ascertained whether Debbie could regain the capacity to swallow. He then revealed that Debbie might be discharged from the ICU and move to a facility with a new set of nurses and therapists. He didn't disclose any details, but his tone suggested that a transfer could be on the horizon.

Light was penetrating the darkness as a sunrise lights the dawn. Very shortly thereafter it shone brightly. The doctors abruptly burst into our ICU room and announced, "Get ready! We are about to move you two to new quarters. Gather your belongings, Chuck, you're about to move." I did a double take, like you might when you see or hear something for the first time. No time to reflect on the surprising announcement, I swung into action collecting our personal items. That task was easy; I only had to pack a few clothes, our personal computer, and the radio for Debbie I purchased to play Mozart and Beethoven because I had heard that their music cultivated brain memory even while the listener is asleep by recording the downbeat in the brain's subconscious right hemisphere.

The mechanical harness lifted Debbie's anemic emaciated body from her ICU bed to a stretcher to move her, as I watched in amazement. The next stop on our journey was really happening!

A door had opened, and the path permitted a faster pace to recovery. Uppermost in my mind then was that in her new setting with more rigorous therapeutic care, Debbie's vocal cords might begin to heal and that someday she might give clear voice to her thoughts. This was a short trip definitely worth taking. Praise God, from whom all blessings flow.

CHAPTER 16

TEN TENSE DAYS IN PURGATORY

§

Debbie's transfer from the ICU in the harness-carrier lift to Acute Care on the same floor was short—only fifty yards. Her new room was ready. My weak Debbie was to spend ten days there. The tension was thick. You may question why I call this new residence "purgatory." The reason is not hard to find—the nominal classification of Debbie's transitory circumstances in this Acute Care room fit the theological definition.

I do not know if there is really such a place as purgatory, but the noun is appropriate for labeling this part of our long journey. According to Roman Catholic doctrine, purgatory is an intermediate place or state of temporary suffering and misery where the souls of those who die in God's grace may make satisfaction for past sins and become acceptable for entry into heaven. This doctrine is based on recognition that suffering can cleanse the self of sin and selfishness.

Debbie certainly qualified for inclusion in such a place, not to cleanse sins but to mend afflictions and prepare for a renewed life. Her journey had included moments when her soul had been somewhere between life and death, and in her enervated condition, she sometimes appeared barely alive. So her travels in the Acute Care unit resembled a kind of transition, a holding place between death and sustained life. Her survival on this earth depended on her response here. What happened in Acute Care would determine her next destination, in this world or the final resting place.

Picture Debbie's new surroundings. Her new room was much smaller than the ICU room she had just left. In this cramped setting, only one nurse-attendant was available for every five patients housed in a row of adjacent rooms. The room had a small window, but the construction site that dominated the landscape made the view uninviting. To my annoyance and that of Dr. Dyer as well, the floor above Debbie's cramped room was undergoing a massive renovation, and the loud, intermittent noise of hammers, pounding, and grinding during the day was disruptive.

The monitor screens for Debbie's vital signs were no longer outside her room's doorway but instead were mounted among about eighty others on a wall behind the floor receptionist's desk, about thirty yards from her room. This was unnerving. I muttered to myself the kind of cringe-worthy things you might utter out of the corner of your mouth if you spied a fly in your coffee cup. If Debbie's pulse rose above an acceptable rate, it was not certain that the staff would notice it. So I took my concerns into my own hands and made many periodic trips from Debbie's room to the monitoring station to check her vital signs and sound the alarm if I spotted a problem. Needless to say, this habit did not make me particularly popular with the staff, although amused, they confessed they appreciated the zealous attention I paid to my beloved wife.

The Acute Care facility served two dual purposes alongside providing support for each patient's survival and strength. The first was the conduct of a series of increasingly intensive evaluations to gauge the patient's changing condition and chart potential signs of progress, guided by revision after revision of each patient's status and roadmap. The second goal was to prepare patients sufficiently so they can transfer to a full-scale in-patient rehabilitation hospital facility. Patients that fail to advance far enough to proceed with the second goal are usually discharged and routinely urged to move to an external skilled-nursing hospital closer to their residence for medical support to assist survival, sometimes for the rest of a resident's life.

Accordingly, the "purgatory" of Acute Care truly resembled a metaphorical subway stop where the traveler is required to take one or the other very different trains to two very different destinies. Unlike the theologically based definition of "purgatory," which leaves the duration indefinite, Acute Care's "purgatory" is customarily very short, with decisions about the next stop usually rendered within twenty-four to forty-eight hours. Debbie's stay was longer, a lengthy ten days, because she was struck by some unanticipated crises that mandated postponing decisions about her next destination.

SPEED ZONE AHEAD OR DEAD END?

On arrival in Acute Care, gloom pervaded her little room. I tried to hide my fears from Debbie's sight. Debbie's physical condition did not bode well for a safe and smooth visitation in this preparatory facility. The dangers could not be denied. It was traumatizing to witness the damage Debbie's strokes had precipitated. Debbie still could not speak and could barely turn her head to the left. She was paralyzed on both sides of her body. She was emaciated, having lost one-sixth of her weight, and what flesh remained hung loosely without any muscle tone. She took all medicines through an IV to her arm. A urinary tract catheter extended from her privates. Liquid nutrition was supplied through nasal tubing, which was promptly removed after use so that if needed another nasal tube could pipe oxygen to her lungs. The tubes interfered greatly with healing of Debbie's sore, red vocal cords, and the tubing inflamed her throat. Whenever my eyes gazed at her prone body, I had to look away to hide my fright.

The heart-breaking reality was that Debbie and I were "suffering grief in all kinds of trials" (1 Pet. 1:6). Seemingly random and inexplicable trials and troubles had been faced many times to get Debbie to this place, and in the Acute Care hospital wing we expected to suffer still more. Frail and fragile, Debbie was traveling on a "fearway" instead of the freeway we sought. Taking comfort in the fact that Debbie had successfully passed through many past roadblocks, we forged ahead hoping that Acute Care would serve as a highway. We trusted God would continue to shine enough light to guide Debbie on her new passageway still darkened by shadows.

STRUCK AND STUCK?

After a stroke strikes, it is usually the sad case that the brain's normally interconnected wiring or nerve circuitry is disrupted or severed. Lesions or perforations of the brain's pathways often destroy intracranial wiring, impairing or terminating motor or cognitive functions. The person struck can become "stuck," sometimes never thereafter able to see, hear, speak, or move. Consciousness can fade like the sun. In those tragic circumstances, survivors can lose some or all of their true selves—who they were capable of becoming.

Stroke survivors face three terrifying possibilities: (1) *shutdown*—all cognitive processes are forever lost, and the victim remains perpetually stuck in a vegetative condition without the ability to think or speak; (2) *slowdown*—gradually some mental capacities return, but the victims seldom recover fully their former "selves" prior to the stroke; or (3) *struggle*— some capabilities are intact, and years of rehabilitation are required to try to mend the disabilities, with no assurance that the struggle will eventually culminate in overcoming impairments. The dark future depends on the degree of damage inflicting the victim's brain and on how the survivor responds to the rehabilitative challenges they face.

Central to Debbie's capacity to travel forward were the challenges posed by the immeasurable damage that her strokes had caused. After a stroke strikes, the single most striking signpost to the future is the capacity of the brain and its neurological connections to the body to coordinate functionality. Both must connect through repeated interaction to hardwire their linkages.

This is where a stroke survivor's motivations play a crucial role. The patient must strive to rewire the connections between mind and matter. The patient's response—his or her efforts to repair the stroke's damage—is as important to recovery as is the extent of the damage. From where does this quest come? I had a definite idea of where Debbie drew her perseverance trying so hard to engineer her recovery. I was sure that she had found a reason to rehabilitate and live—God had brought her back from near death to life for a higher purpose, and to fulfill that purpose, she had to relentlessly struggle to overcome her afflictions. Grateful for her survival, she was committed to seize the opportunity provided and take an active part in her recovery.

My obsessive observation of Debbie's efforts to recover revealed small but steady steps forward in Acute Care. However, I did not anticipate that another major setback would interrupt her slow progress. Before jumping ahead to describe that obstacle, let me summarize the days that preceded it. Here's a selective travelogue of the initial starts and stops that happened the first four days in Acute Care:

- **Settling and Struggling on a Slippery Slope**—The afternoon of Debbie's arrival in the Acute Care unit put into place a new set of routines which preceded some scary new experiences. We immediately found to our satisfaction that the professional staff in this unit was attentive and consistent with its name—they provided care for those with acute infirmities.

  A physical therapist was the first to evaluate Debbie's motor skills, or more accurately her lack thereof, with the exception of Debbie's modest movement of her left arm and hand. Helpfully, the therapist showed me how to perform new passive exercises, such as lifting Debbie's arms and fingers to stimulate her atrophied muscles. This I persistently did at least three hours each day. Next, a speech therapist made a short examination of Debbie's breathing and swallowing limitations. The results were alarming. Debbie could not swallow and her respiratory tubing was cloudy, indicating that harmful secretions were causing mucus to partially block her airways. These abnormal residual secretions were aggravating the red and raw soreness that was damaging Debbie's vocal cords. Aspiration or choking could result.

- **A Throwback**—"Three strikes and you're out" is baseball's first rule. Debbie had taken many swings and had two strikes. A third would mean a strikeout. Here's what happened on the Acute Care's playing grounds the day Debbie stepped up to the plate. We made a disturbing discovery. Andy broadcasted the news: "Another set of CT scans was performed to monitor the blood vessels in Debbie's head. Chuck is nervous but glad that this is still being watched. But he was not happy with what was found—the scan had revealed another buildup of spinal fluid. This was becoming an all-too-familiar problem. As Hilel reported and Chuck just updated, 'poor Debbie just can't seem to catch a break, when something else comes along.'"

Recall that recently in ICU, Dr. McLanahan had implanted a ventricular cerebrospinal fluid shunt in Debbie's cranium. He stopped by in Acute Care to examine the atrial shunt's performance and did not like the way Debbie's cerebrospinal fluids were accumulating. "It looks like the shunt is not maintaining proper pressure," he noted. "To avoid the probability of another cerebral hemorrhage, I must adjust Debbie's shunt's settings and reduce the pressure. Don't be overly alarmed this time, Chuck. This adjustment procedure is rather routine. We will have to wait for new antibiotics to take effect before proceeding, but the wait will not be long. I will reset the settings tomorrow."

This need to reset the shunt so soon after the recent implantation ignited my fears. Why was the cranial pressure subject to so much variation? Was something larger and possibly more dangerous occurring that was causing the cerebrospinal fluid buildup? I had found something to worry about.

A host of questions came to mind. Did this adjustment mean that more adjustments were likely? Was it probable that they would grow in frequency? If so, did this decision to tinker with the shunt settings presage big problems ahead? Or might more adjustments simply spell a mechanical refining process to find the best setting, obviating the need for additional adjustments? This episode could be either good or bad. The upside was that a setting adjustment could avert a potential disaster waiting to happen; the downside was that every change of devices within the cranium entailed some risk. The good seemed to far outweigh the bad.

As night came, I said prayers, expressed loving words, and kissed Debbie good night. We would have to wait until the next day for the shunt's realignment and see if unintended consequences would result. My patience had not improved with practice. However, over-all during this first day in Acute Care, we felt we had been blessed by positive experiences.

• **Misplaced Fears**—Accustomed to the advent of occasional new achievements, we began to sense they were similar to kicking the can down the road, although it seemed at times more accurate to see the series of episodic setbacks as symbolizing cans being kicked uphill. The next day the can was kicked downhill. We experienced in rapid succession encouraging news that some potential problems were averted.

The first forward motion took place when Dr. McLanahan came by as promised and swung into action. He quickly and with surprising ease adjusted Debbie's implanted internal shunt settings using a Codman programmable valve. This hurdle was jumped easily. From about two inches from Debbie's head, Dr. McLanahan flipped on a magnetic gadget that sent painless electrical charges to the mechanized shunt. This magical reset remedied the cerebrospinal pressure problem that had been detected yesterday. For how long was anybody's guess. This was progress, nonetheless. Fears were unjustified.

While there, Dr. McLanahan kicked the can down the road further. He presented two additional pieces of encouraging news. He informed us that the wounds in Debbie's head from the initial January 8 skull surgery had healed, and the lesion where the IV catheter had been in her neck also had sealed. This was progress.

Shortly thereafter, the physical therapist used the lift machine to move Debbie from her bed to a wheelchair. She didn't last there very long. Disappointedly, Debbie's breathing became labored, and her blood pressure started rising as a result of the added energy expenditure needed for her to support herself upright in the chair. So that effort was stopped short of the goal. The can did not move.

- **Misplaced Tubing**—The next day we continued to acclimate ourselves to our new surroundings and tried to accommodate ourselves to frequent changes. Debbie had not been very responsive, perhaps in reaction to all the rushed and exhausting activities that had taken place the day before. The next discovery was bad: the nutritional feeder in Debbie's nose came loose again (at least this time not because "the Rascal" pulled it out). So it had to be replaced, which is not an easy procedure; the loose tube had to be extracted and replaced with a new tube from her nose to her stomach, with the wire enabling this insertion then withdrawn. However, the x-ray to be certain that the tube was in the right place in her stomach showed that it was bent, so the whole process had to be repeated. More x-rays showed the tubing was properly positioned in this second effort, so that problem was solved, and we could resume our slow pace ahead on the roadway.

- **"Can You Swallow This?"**—That afternoon an ENT team arrived to conduct more thorough tests. The results were very troubling. We were traveling uphill. Given ice chips, Debbie was asked to try swallowing them. She couldn't. I asked the team leader how Debbie had done, on a scale of one to ten, with ten being the best. "Oh," the doctor exaggerated giving me false hope, "about a four." Later that week, another ENT physician was painfully candid; he bluntly blurted out that Debbie had "bombed" her previous swallow test. So a remedy had to be quickly found. To my utter horror, the possibility of a tracheotomy operation to cut a hole in her throat to supply pumped oxygen was again mentioned; I had thought that that horrifying prospect had been eliminated when Debbie had begun to breathe on her own without a respirator to supply oxygen. Now the nightmare of a tracheostomy had reoccurred. The Grim Reaper's horrific prognoses of the probable consequences had come back to haunt our minds. We felt like a patient learning that a cancer presumably in remission had recurred.

- **On Track for a Trach?**—Mercifully, that tracheostomy operation was discussed but not planned, as least not yet. Instead, an alternative was identified. Since Debbie could not swallow, there was a potential other option—conducting another very different kind of surgical operation to open Debbie's abdomen and insert a "peg" tube directly into her stomach to supply food and liquids, so that Debbie's trachea would no longer be irritated by the feeding and breathing tubing from her nose.

This idea was new to me; one I had not considered. The more I thought about such an operative solution, the more aware I became of the advantages. This bypass could accelerate the healing of Debbie's vocal cords. More tests were scheduled to determine which path, trach or peg, was preferable. One of them, it appeared, would have to be eventually taken.

This long day ended on a very heartwarming note. Debbie awakened at 4:35 p.m. from another needed nap, and her voice showed growing strength despite her vocal-cord debilities. Debbie moved her stiff neck a little to the right. I was greatly encouraged by this modest accomplishment, which augured well for future progress. And when Debbie appeared anxious to tell me something, I bent down, and she whispered to me the most thrilling hushed words I could hope to hear, however faintly: "I...love...you." When Debbie's bed was lowered at 5:40 p.m. to facilitate another nap, she managed to keep her sweet eyes open for a full fifty minutes, allowing time for more prayers. Her endurance cast a ray of light through the evening dimness.

The intensifying worries about Debbie's vocal-cord dysfunctions were growing into a dark obsession. There were good reasons for my bad thoughts. Debbie was taken on another trip to the x-ray lab to take an inside look at her throat and vocal cords. The result was even worse than previously feared. Andy reported, "Chuck just learned some pretty devastating news. The throat/swallow tests indicate that Debbie's vocal cords were paralyzed, and that the paralysis could be permanent. To try to prevent this, use of the nose feeding support tube must be suspended. Instead of a trach, a peg stomach feeder will be surgically implanted." The next path had been chosen. Where would it lead?

CHAPTER 17

THE END OF THE LINE

§

D ebbie and I were growing acclimated to the persistent need to fight
fear. There were real threats to fear beyond fear itself. On the horizon now stood another steep hill. At its peak was a foreboding obstacle.
Hilel's night message pulled some punches to soften the blow:

> Chuck reported some unnerving news. Debbie's right vocal cord
> appears to be paralyzed. Initially, the doctors considered that this
> might be permanent, but several of the physicians Chuck has talked
> to are somewhat more encouraging. Her debility is called "vocal
> fold paralysis." Assuming that this goes as advertised, tomorrow
> the ENT team will again evaluate her vocal cords in preparation
> for her surgeons to insert a "peg tube" into her stomach, if the con-
> dition of her colon allows this. She may have this surgery soon. I'll
> report to you as soon as I can.

A SURGICAL SOLUTION TO A VOCAL-CORD CRISIS?
The abdominal surgery to install a peg feeder was booked for the very
next day, Thursday morning. In preparation, at midnight, Debbie was
taken off all food to allow the surgery to be performed. She got in line
with the others waiting for other kinds of surgery.

We wanted to get this operation underway immediately. But it didn't
happen. I was told it had to be postponed: "Our goal is to try to have
it performed *tomorrow* morning." So Debbie had to go without any

nourishment, waiting in a holding pattern. "As if she needed to miss food!" I thought. She was starving.

With each passing hour, liberating Debbie's throat from the nasal oxygen support and feeding tube aggravation was becoming increasingly urgent. Hilel reported, "Chuck is desperate. It is critical to squeeze Debbie into surgery for the insertion of the feeding peg in her stomach; that is complicated though by the prior colon surgery. If the peg is inserted, the nose tube can be removed, which may help with her throat recovery. Despite this uncertainty, Debbie's mood has remained upbeat. Chuck said Debbie's been beaming at the doctors and nurses today." To make this cure happen, we had to transcend a daunting series of delays.

• **A Perpetual Waiting Game**—Friday morning brought more mourning. We were informed "We will have to postpone Debbie's surgery again, until tomorrow morning." The news came down like a hammer to the head. She had been pushed to the end of the line, and, frustrated, I was nearing the end of my patience. Disappointment darkened the room like smoke from a blazing fire. My hopes vaporized. There was a vacuum in my heart.

This further delay meant that Debbie would have to go at least another thirty-six hours until she could resume receiving food. She was losing weight and strength. To try to dampen our devastating disappointment, Debbie and I tried to carry on as best we could. She mustered enough strength to withstand my passive physical therapy, and her paramedics conducted some modest exercises. Andy reported, "Although enervated and disheartened by the surgery delay, Debbie did pretty well with both physical and mental therapy today, and is sitting upright in a chair. The therapists were impressed."

Modest exercise measures were beginning to make a modest difference, especially on Debbie's relatively less-damaged left side. She could now tilt her neck leftward almost two inches. It also appeared that passive exercises were beginning to produce incrementally small reflex responses on Debbie's immobile upper right side.

In this pre-surgery interim, other activities consumed Debbie's waking moments. An ENT doctor sprayed some kind of bitter medicine into Debbie's nose to open it and numb it, but disappointedly the new swallow study revealed that the "flapper" (technically, the epiglottis that closes the airway when food is taken) was dysfunctional. It did not close automatically to prevent liquids "going down the wrong lane." If secretions seeped down her windpipe, her lungs were certain to become infected with pneumonia. The principal problem was that Debbie's throat muscles were too weak, which underscored the urgency of installing the peg feeder tube. That surgery just had to happen soon, or Debbie could never regain the capacity to swallow. Liquid nutrients continued to be cut off so the operation could proceed the next morning. We were ready. Would the operation proceed?

• **Deadlocked**—Saturday morning started with high hopes. This was to have been the day when the peg-feeder surgical insertion was scheduled so that another enormous leap away from the abyss could be taken. This also would have the advantage of permitting medications to be supplied through the peg feeder tube, eliminating the need for nasal drip-line tubing. Those were the aspirations.

The process didn't proceed as planned. As they say, "s--- happens." That morning it was what did *not* happen that struck like a rattlesnake. I escorted Debbie to the pre-operating station where the anesthetics were administered. We said prayers. They promptly took effect. The weekend doctor informed me that he would give the operation his best college try and pointed to the waiting room across the hall. That room was dim, and I was the only one in it. So I prayed and settled in for what I hoped would be a successful operation on a dark and cold weekend.

• **A Stop Sign**—Just ten minutes later, before I had had time to collect my thoughts and say prayers, the waiting-room door swung open. The surgeon bolted in. "Because of Debbie's colon and spleen operation," he announced, "a regular peg tube feeder is simply too dangerous for me to attempt. The tube will have to bypass Debbie's liver, and a pin-size puncture could be fatal. We'll have to wait until Monday, when the full A-team of surgeons will be on deck to open Debbie's stomach, make a visual inspection, and make a choice between surgically installing either a preferred G tube from her stomach to her abdomen near her colostomy bag, or a less-safe, invasive J feeding tube to her lower intestine. In the meantime, to perform the operation Monday morning, she can't have any nutritional liquids."

This dreadful extension of the end of the line extended the period without food. Could Debbie sustain life for so long without nourishment? The attending nurse reiterated the importance of avoiding further delays, stating the obvious: "Debbie really needs to be fed." The timeline was shortening.

Andy detected the terror in my voice, writing "In a matter of a few minutes Chuck has gone from another peak to the valley. He was very hopeful that the procedure to insert the stomach tube and take out the nose tube would be successful, but as the doctors began the exploratory initial part of the surgery, they concluded the location afforded too small a space and the operation was too risky, so they backed off, and will try again early next week. Pray for a successful outcome." Hilel elaborated Sunday morning:

The situation is still in a flux. Debbie has gone without any food since 1:00 a.m. Thursday. Her doctors have promised that they would make another attempt to insert the peg into her abdomen so that she could be fed that way. This next procedure is tentatively scheduled for Monday. Chuck is understandably going out of his anxious mind. I sought to reduce his desperation by pointing out that the doctors' reluctance to do anything dangerous is a sign that they think that she will improve, recover and leave the hospital. Otherwise they would be tempted to use risky procedures, such as a J-tube or tracheotomy for patients weaned from a ventilator for a long time.

• **A Dead End?**—Sunday was impatiently filled with deepening doubts as we tried to fill the waiting time with some constructive activities. There was a glimmer of joy when the attending nurse tried to apply the detangle spray I had purchased to comb out some of Debbie's remaining bird's nest hair. This helped somewhat. "I just wish," our nurse lamented, "surgeons would learn to shave a patient's entire head when they operate; that would allow all hair to regrow at the same rate, and this kind of ugly mess could be avoided." I agreed. Too many bad hair days. This gesture lifted our spirits. Yet Debbie was weakening from lack of food, and the need for her surgery operation had reached crisis proportions. The storm from the gathering clouds was darkening all hope. Hilel's e-mail account late that dark Sunday evening summarized the grim situation.

> Confusion and frustration have marked this day. Chuck was led to believe that the eating tube through Debbie's nose was fixed. It hadn't been. A wire was crimped in it and removed, but there is still no guarantee that it will work if that way of delivering food is resumed. Eventually being able to feed Debbie through a peg tube is now even more critical. An actual operation looks like it is finally going to take place. Probably tomorrow, but in light of the preceding cancellations and delays, nothing is definite. If you are confused by all of this, imagine how Chuck feels. He does think that an operation which, though it has risks, could solve the problem of getting food into Debbie, and is preferable to the "possible," "maybe," "perhaps" of other procedures, themselves marked with additional risks. I'm glad that he is trying to put a good spin on this, and perhaps he's right to do so. Imagine how much Debbie and he have been through

over the last thirty-two days. Debbie is alert and smiling and that is an enormous source of comfort to Chuck. So too are your love and prayers.

- **Nowhere to Turn**—The possible further delay that the attending nurse said following the abortive Saturday's surgery attempt should be avoided did in fact reoccur Monday. Nothing happened! A severe winter ice and snow storm smothered Charlotte, forcing a hospital lockdown requiring doctors and nurses to spend the night on sleeping cots. Only emergency operations were permitted. All other surgical operations were cancelled, including Debbie's. I furiously ruminated, "If Debbie's dire circumstance was not an emergency, what is?" This breakdown was not the breakthrough on which I had been counting. I didn't know how much more anxious pain could be suffered.

Andy sounded the distressing news: "Chuck has called in with another frustrating wait, and in fact, for the first time, he's expressing irritation at the doctors for not following through with the peg insertion like he had been promised. After hearing one surgeon tell him off-handedly this morning that the procedure was not going to happen today, one of his nurse advocates found someone who has promised Chuck to get some answers sometime today. So he's waiting."

As the darkness of night drowned Debbie's room, my terror about Debbie's weakening condition without food had hit its limit. Immediate action was critical. I doubted if Debbie could survive much longer if her surgery was postponed again. I recalled Hilel advising me to never let Debbie see my fears. I tried to heed his good advice. I exuded calm and confidence in front of Debbie, in a fake act to hide my apprehension.

But just when I was about to hit the rock bottom of despair, two doctors suddenly appeared. They were bearing what sounded like good news. "We've scheduled Debbie's surgery for 6:00 a.m. tomorrow. She will be the first in line, so her operation on Tuesday will proceed without further delay." I presumed Debbie was finally at the starting line for her race from oblivion. After all the postponements, I wasn't sure. "I plan on going up to Charlotte through this planned ordeal," Hilel reported, "to stand by and try to calm Chuck down."

- **Desperate Times and Desperate Measures**—I awoke at 3:30 a.m. on Tuesday eager to get to Debbie and oversee her surgery. I was excited. I also remained concerned, because the record snow storm that had hit Charlotte continued during the night, and the threat arose that this could once again interfere with the surgery schedule that had been planned. I submerged this ocean of fear and rearranged my face to force an optimistic expression.

  I arrived at Debbie's room at 5:00 a.m. At last, Debbie was ready for the surgery to start her life-saving trip to the operating room. Everything seemed ready. We were not left clueless about the cue, because we had been promised that Debbie would be the first in the line.

- **"The First Shall Be Last"**—That expectation did not last long. It vanished. I was informed that the surgeons had had to perform an emergency surgery on a car-accident victim in the snow storm. Debbie was no longer the first in line. However, I was told "Debbie had been rescheduled for the next available opening at 8:00 a.m."

  "Oh, well, I guess I could live with that two-hour delay," I consoled myself. At 7:00 a.m. Debbie was carried on a stretcher platform to the pre-op station with me by her side.

  My confidence rose when Dr. Beverley Paton, the head surgeon, stopped to brief us. She said, "The plan is to open Debbie's abdomen, perhaps with a horizontal incision as long as a foot, to determine if a G tube is feasible; if not, the riskier J tube to her lower intestine might be attempted. Ideally, there is about a two percent chance that the G surgery could be performed by laparoscopic procedures, which would only necessitate four or five punctures in her stomach to complete. Don't get your hopes up," she cautioned. "I hope to return as soon as possible, around eight o'clock."

- **Panic Attack**—Debbie was awake, and patient and cheerful. We prayed. And waited … and waited … and waited. Eight o'clock came and went. Still no word. I anxiously paced the hall as if walking on thumbtacks, nervously wondering if this urgent operation would actually occur. Eight o'clock became nine, and nine became ten. I lost all composure. An attending nurse informed the surgery team that "there is an extremely agitated husband in the pre-op hallway whose nerves are about to explode if his wife's operation is not undertaken."

  At 10:30 a.m. the tension in the pre-op room thickened, despite the nurses' efforts to calm me down. That was when one of the attending doctors ducked in and told me, "You may as well take your wife back to her Acute Care room, where she will be more comfortable. Too many emergencies are piling up."

  I shouted, "No way! We are staying right here. This operation will occur. It must occur. It's a matter of life or death." The doc slithered away, shrugging his shoulders.

  At 11:00 a.m. I hit the limit of my patience and endurance. What to do? I instinctively called Pastor Crow. George answered, and I explained what was happening. I heard him groan loudly enough for Debbie and half of Charlotte to overhear. "Can I offer a prayer?" George inquired.

  "Yes, of course, but please let Debbie hear it, too. She's still awake and alert. So George prayed to God, asking, "If it is Your will, let this operation proceed."

- **How Promptly Can a Pastor's Prayer Be Answered?**—No sooner than the last syllable of his last word "proceed" left George's lips, when at that very second there was a loud "whoosh." The curtain swung open. It was Dr. Paton! "Quick," she exclaimed, "we found a space. We can start preparations for Debbie's operation at once."

  Tears streaked down my face, as Debbie was rushed away in a wheelchair for pre-op by the anesthesiologists and surgery!

  George had prayed for God's help, and He responded with astonishing speed. Now I knew in my heart that God answers prayers. But this fast? The rapidity of His response was a true miracle. How promptly can God answer a pastor's prayer? Just as soon as He chooses. And God chose to answer immediately. The uniqueness of God's miracle lay in His authority over everything that happens. Debbie's deliverance had to be His doing.

- **No U-Turn**—The surgery got underway, and I paced the waiting room. At 2:45 p.m. Dr. Paton barged into the waiting room's consulting chamber to tell me what had happened. Even though exhausted, she bubbled with glee. "To our team's pleasant surprise," she proudly said, "we were able to install the less-invasive G feeding tube, without difficulty and without interference with the liver, a safe distance from her colostomy. Better still, we were able to do the surgery with laparoscopic incisions, so Debbie has only four little punctures in her stomach, which in time will heal. The peg tube is fully operational. I am so glad that this worked, and today of all days. Go back to her Acute Care room, and wait for her return in several hours. She will be heavily sedated but not in pain. Oh, by the way, better news—in the pre-operation examination, an ENT doctor and the anesthesiologist made an inspection and discovered that Debbie's vocal cords are not permanently paralyzed as originally feared. Only the right side of her cord is partially paralyzed. Because we were able to confidently remove the NG feeding tube from Debbie's nose, maybe some healing in her throat can commence."

- **Saved!**—This dizzying flood of good news was disorienting. I have no recollection how I navigated my way back to our Acute Care room. When I entered, I was stunned by the attending nurse's expression. He was mystified why all this time had passed. When I told him what had happened, he declared, "Chuck, you did exactly the right thing insisting that Debbie remain in the pre-op chamber; had you allowed the assistants to take her back here, she would have been forgotten. 'Out of sight, out of mind.' Good job. Let me know as soon as she arrives, and I'll get to work on her meds, vitals, and, at last, food and water through her new peg tube."

I was awestruck about the miracles God had chosen to perform. A sense of peace that "surpasses all understanding" (Phil. 4:7) swept over me in response to God's invisible penetration of the surgeons' minds, guiding their decision to make Debbie's life-saving surgery their first priority. Through this act God had provided a "sign"—(in Greek from the New Testament, *semeion*)—of His supernatural power to engineer miracles (Matt. 12:38–39; John 2:11; Acts 5:12; Romans 15:19). Jesus had come to earth to save, and our heavenly Father had again saved Debbie.

After witnessing God's miraculous intervention, all I desired was to come closer to the One who saved Debbie's life. God's saving grace provided a testimony to what our Lord can do. God had thrown a lifeline when Debbie was close to that fatal "one step over the line."

My faith had reached a new zenith. "I cried to you, O Lord…be my helper. And you turned my wailing into dancing. Therefore, my heart sings to you without ceasing; O Lord my God, I will give you thanks forever" (Ps. 30:8, 10-12).

Uplifted, I felt as if the dimmer-switch lighting Debbie's room had been turned to its full strength. I knew it was our Savior's light that had driven out the darkness. Everything became very bright when Debbie was carried back to me in her room. Still unconscious, nevertheless a glow seemed to radiate from her little body. This was the advent of a new beginning.

Hilel arrived in Charlotte and was waiting for me to exit the Acute Care unit to meet and greet me. He was very encouraging and comforting. His unmatchable wit sparked my rising mood. When he saw me, he apologized, explaining, "I know I'm late. I kept seeing signs on Interstate 77 saying Clean Restrooms. Do you know how long it takes to clean those things?" Hilel was never at a loss for words and cheering humor. He was exhausted. After gulping some food in the hospital cafeteria, he accepted my offer to rent him a Hospitality House room for that icy night. Encouraged, Hilel departed for Columbia the next morning since Debbie's surgery had finally, and successfully, been performed.

I was warmed and armed with the knowledge that God had provided and protected. I was not just thankful; I was sure that His purpose was to continue His healing presence and protection. My trust knew no boundaries. And I was reassured by the fact that Debbie at last was receiving food through her new G tube every three hours and breathing on her own without a nasal tube rubbing her throat raw.

A HEAD START?

The morning after the surgery began early. Debbie was sound asleep. That was fortunate, because she mercifully missed the teasing I received from the attending nurse. "Every day you come here early, Chuck, dragging that computer with you. Why? You never use it. I'll bet that you don't even know how to use it!" She had seen right through me. Thereafter, I left our PC charging in my Hospitality House room. Debbie would have enjoyed this exchange had she been awake.

A doctor arrived just after Debbie awakened that bright morning to conduct the routine evaluation. Debbie's vitals were great. She was already showing signs of gaining strength from the intake of liquid nutrition through her new peg tube to her upper stomach, protruding about three inches above her colostomy pouch.

That progress was providing evidence that Debbie was regaining her footing and starting to race ahead to a finish line. Her efforts gave her a head start, and the doctors and therapists applauded her advances. For example, several physical therapists approvingly said that my relentless passive exercises were making a measurable impact, enhanced greatly by Debbie's fierce determination. One therapist went out of her way to give Debbie helpful praise, telling her "You've got a good head on your shoulders," to which I tried to joke "That's good. I hate necks." I imagined the dialogue that would have transpired had Debbie been able to speak; her standard line would have gone something like "Now Charlie, your endeavors to be a Hilel in the joke department aren't working. Keep your day job!"

In point of fact, Debbie's therapists had a point—there were many reasons to rejoice:

- Debbie's left arm and hand muscles allowed her to initiate more movement, and she could twitch her left toe.
- She managed to move her neck to the right.
- When Debbie was transferred to a wheelchair with a neck brace, she managed to sit upright for an hour.
- Two ENT specialists inspected Debbie's throat and vocal cords. The swelling was still apparent, but Debbie voiced some sound, as if humming a tune. This achievement reduced the probabilities that a tracheotomy would be necessary.

"Chuck just called," Andy wrote, "bursting with joy over Debbie's accomplishments since her surgery. Nothing but good things to report. She's had massages and therapy, and is trying to use her voice more now that all of the tubing to her head is out. Chuck says that for once, there are no crises hanging over them, but knows it is still a long road to go." We were now again moving forward on that long road.

A BIG FORK IN THE ROAD

Hopes had crested. The next period in Acute Care saw periodic advances, and the only question was whether the pace of progress could continue or even pick up more speed. In the absence of any more detours, what would the doctors dictate? Would Debbie be evicted out of the Acute Care unit? As sure as a sunrise spells the onset of a new day, an eventual discharge was certain. But to what destination? A fork in the road was on the horizon. One path led to a skilled-nursing hospital in South Carolina. The other led nearby, to the adjacent rehabilitation hospital on the CMC campus. "Rehabilitation" had a great sound to it; "bed confinement" in a nursing hospital was as melodic sounding as teeth gnashing.

There could be no doubt about my preference. "Chuck is tirelessly advocating," Hilel e-mailed, "for Debbie to stay in Charlotte at Carolinas Rehabilitation Hospital for therapy, near the surgeons and primary care staff which has been with them these five weeks. That is the goal, over assisted treatment in Columbia. For the time being, no choices are necessary. Debbie remains in her Acute Care room, recovering from the peg tube feeding surgery."

Drs. Paton and Schiffern came by often to inspect the aftereffects of the G-tube surgery. They were very satisfied with what they observed. Dr. Paton proudly but accurately described her surgery as "a beautiful piece of work." Indeed, it was. "One day, Debbie," Dr. Schiffern cheered, "you will learn to swallow food, and the day will come when I will be able remove this annoying peg tube. I'll also bet you someday you will let me get rid of that ugly colostomy bag after I perform a colon-reversal surgery to reconnect your upper and lower intestines at the site where your aneurism burst." Of course Dr. Schiffern could not then see the future, but her optimistic prediction set in stone two major long-term goals.

Debbie was beginning to heal! In fact, her increasing capacity to control her left hand and arm presented a new kind of challenge that had to be addressed now and for months thereafter. "We need to wrap Debbie's new feeding tube in a cloth binder to prevent the tube from coming loose or, more problematically, to keep Debbie from pulling the tube out," the surgeons proclaimed. As a remedy, a large mitten was fastened around Debbie's left hand and removed only when I was exercising Debbie's hands.

The next days looked at first like an extension of the string of successes that were unwinding. More progress was made. After my indoctrination, the new attending nurses and therapists took more intense proactive involvement in Debbie's care.

Their attention was interrupted by a series of welcome visitors. The entire staff of Neurosurgery & Spine Associates came by to examine

Debbie and confer with each other. They were very encouraged—one might even say astonished. Debbie was gaining much stronger control over the entire range of her left side, from head to toe. She could turn her neck almost entirely to the left and maybe two inches to the right. Dr. Dyer requested, "Debbie, wiggle your toes," and she responded well on her left foot. He and I next looked at each other in puzzlement, wondering if we had really seen the same thing—a very slight twitch to her right toe! It then seemed as unlikely and as difficult as teaching a dog to roller skate. To this day, I'm still not sure. But Debbie's ability with her right hand to lightly touch Dr. Dyer's finger (stronger than she did for me) was another amazing sign. ("Okay, I get it," I joked, "Debbie is going to dump me and run off with you.")

Physical therapies produced surprising results as well. Debbie managed to sit upright in her chair more than five straight hours, while I administered exercises and talked to her. Better still, in another swallow test with ice chips, Debbie gagged but managed to swallow. And her voice was returning, however faintly. I put the cell phone to Debbie's mouth, and Hilel and subsequently Andy heard Debbie try to communicate with them. Hilel wrote, "Debbie in response to my usual attempts at providing good cheer actually whispered 'Hi' to me. What a joy. This makes today special." (Sadly, Debbie was too exhausted to speak loud enough to be heard by John.) Somehow, Debbie managed to speak loudly enough for George Crow to hear her feeble words, and Debbie mustered the strength to audibly say to her sister "I love you, Karen." I was thrilled. Debbie was talking, in hushed tones. After prayers, I heard her faintly say to me the words I most treasured—"I love you more than anything." I wept. Time seemed to move faster, and expectations were also rising fast.

Friday, February 14, was Valentine's Day. We did not celebrate in the usual manner, and no flowers were permitted in Debbie's room. All I could present as a present was my customary handmade card, with my personal message of love, appreciation, and devotion. It didn't matter. As it turned out, we had much to celebrate that historic day.

I bounded into Debbie's room at 6:30 a.m., energized by all the progress made the previous day. I was not there in time to hear the conversation that had taken place a few minutes earlier between the night nurse and the floor physician. But Debbie was. She had overheard enough of their conversation to understand what they were saying.

When Debbie saw me, she was bursting with excitement. She could scarcely contain herself. She had huge news to share. I jumped to her side, asking "Beautiful, what do you want to tell me?" She tried to give voice to her message, but her vocal cords were too weak for me to make out what she was saying. Something big was about to change, I inferred. But what? I bent closer, putting my ear close to her mouth. She tried again, but what she tried to say out loud was weaker still. The third effort trailed off with the faint words "at 2:00 p.m."

It took only seconds to connect the dots. Debbie had overheard the doctors' conversation and learned that she would be transferred that afternoon to the nearby rehabilitation hospital on the vast CMC complex. Putting two and two together, I deduced that all the doctors who had examined Debbie yesterday had participated in a committee-of-the-whole conference and collectively concluded that Debbie's progress had been sufficient for her to leave the Acute Care facility and transfer to the in-patient component of Carolinas Rehabilitation Hospital.

Andy spread the news: "Chuck has just called. He was so elated he could hardly speak. He thinks Debbie will be moving later today to the rehabilitation facility in an adjacent hospital building. He said that 'in the new rehabilitation facility, Debbie can receive more rigorous therapies. Trained professionals can aggressively lead her toward recovery.' He said the nurses are crying tears of joy to see her (and especially him?) leave. All in all, a terrific day."

My wish for relocation to rehabilitation treatment in Charlotte had been fulfilled. The road that opened seemed like leaving a dirt path and entering a four-lane superhighway. Barring any more setbacks, this roadway could speed Debbie's journey toward recovery. I was overjoyed. The end of the line had been extended.

We were grateful for our liberation from purgatory. A green light had magically appeared, allowing Debbie to head to a better destination. The only downside—verified by another x-ray prior to our departure— was that Debbie continued to struggle with swallowing. That problem did not dampen our spirits because we thought this challenge could be addressed by the speech-therapist professionals in rehabilitation.

We sat poised for a journey. The attendants arrived, and Debbie was carted, with me trailing, to a new habitat. The possibilities there were innumerable. The next stop was certain to prove an arduous process, but I had no doubt that my highly motivated Debbie would be diligent throughout this next phase of our long journey.

PART III: ROADWAYS TO REHABILITATION

§

"Be not afraid" is the most common single line in the Bible. . . . As we observe our mental and emotional flow over a period of disciplined time, we recognize that we largely create our own experiences. . . . We have the power to decide what each moment means and how we will respond to it.

—*FATHER RICHARD ROHR*

CHAPTER 18

A REHABILITATIVE MARATHON BEGINS

§

We exited one world, Acute Care, and entered another—Carolinas Rehabilitation Hospital. The trip literally took Debbie through a dark tunnel connecting the two buildings. There was a bright light at the end. Expectations were rising, dimmed, however, by dark memories of previous crises and remaining challenges. The past shadowed the present. The days ahead were painted in shades of black, gray, and pale white. The start of rigorous rehabilitation was welcomed, but the race was certain to be long and hard, and the route could lead anywhere.

Before hurdles could be jumped, much additional progress would be required. The damage from the bleeding inside Debbie's brain was painfully evident. Beyond dysfunctional bodily immobility, her symptoms included tiredness, imbalance, dizziness, headaches, numbness, confusion and speech impairments.

Stroke survivors spend time in the space between being a victim and being a victor. When a catastrophic stroke strikes, victims can shout in relief "I survived!" But to emerge victorious over their debilities, to become victors, survivors must struggle, strain and strive to thrive; they must get beyond the trauma they experienced and dedicate themselves to active participation in their rehabilitation.

About two-thirds of the people who survive a stroke report feeling sad and lost. They give up effort. Not Debbie. She did "not lose heart" (John 16:33). She never resigned herself to her debilities. Instead, she eagerly greeted each rehabilitative opportunity to engineer her recovery.

She heeded the warning "Fail to prepare, and prepare to fail," and prepared herself for the rigorous endeavors necessary to emerge a victor over her dysfunctions.

THE NEW SETTING

Awaiting us in room 2211 of Carolinas Rehab's C wing was an empty bed, positioned next to a second bed occupied by another patient. Only a thin curtain separated the two beds. Although excited by our arrival in our new station, I was disturbed by such crowded space. I greeted Debbie's roommate cordially but must confess that I was also upset that she had her TV blaring loudly. This is not a good idea for stroke victims, because noise and fast talking are very confusing and distracting. To make matters worse for me, the television was tuned to one of those broadcast networks blasting toxic political propaganda and hatred.

Surprise! In charged Dr. Lori Marie Grafton, who announced that the patient in the adjoining bed was scheduled to be discharged from the hospital within an hour. "Your wife, Debbie, has been through so much," Dr. Grafton lamented. "She deserves a solitary room. This room will be for Debbie's exclusive use." This decision launched a friendly and cooperative relationship with Dr. Grafton. Room 2211 suddenly seemed rather roomy. The sunlight from the room's two floor-to-ceiling windows shone brightly and afforded a cheery view. The sun was setting, but spirits were rising. We hoped this was a portent for other favorable developments to come.

Several adjustments to our new surroundings were quickly implemented. The extra bed was removed from the room, and I helped move Debbie's bed next to the doorway wall to escape the hot air vent and afford a better view of the trees outside her windows. The telephone on the new bedside table was silenced. The room had a spacious bathroom, storing a wheelchair with an adjustable brace to support Debbie's neck, as well as a recliner to facilitate short rest breaks for Debbie's back.

So we were at the starting line ready for the race to begin. What was in store for us? What did rehabilitation therapy involve? Dr. Grafton identified the most important clue: "Rehabilitation gravitates around efforts to stimulate the mind and body to work in unison—to get the brain to send signals to the body to coordinate movement. The brain is 'command central.' Enabling cerebral circuitry to relearn how to send messages to activate bodily movement is what rehabilitation is all about."

We needed to learn more. We really didn't have a very good understanding of the procedures that would guide the therapists. We were about to make important discoveries.

• **What Is Rehabilitation?**—Carolinas Rehabilitation's goals are to restore patients' capabilities for self-care, self-sufficiency, mobility, thinking, speaking, and other functions to enable survivors to live as full a lifestyle as possible. We were given an informative booklet entitled *Post-Stroke Rehabilitation* distributed by the US Department of Health and Human Services. It summarized the obstacles Debbie would try to overcome and the rehabilitative objectives our facility planned to pursue:

> The invariant goal of rehabilitation is to help survivors become as independent as possible and to attain the best possible quality of life. Even though rehabilitation does not "cure" the effects of stroke, in that it does not reverse through regeneration the dead brain tissue, rehabilitation can foster the growth of new neuronal connections and substantially help survivors achieve the best possible long-term outcome. How much can be achieved varies highly. Predictions are hard to make. The probabilities are not favorable. Pessimistically, four years after a stroke, eighty percent of patients still report impairment so severe that they have difficulty grooming, bathing, cooking and driving.
>
> Rehabilitation helps stroke survivors relearn skills that are lost when part of the brain is damaged. For example, these

skills can include coordinating leg movements in order to walk or carrying out the steps involved in any complex activity. Rehabilitation also teaches survivors new ways of performing tasks to circumvent or compensate for any residual disabilities such as learning how to bathe and dress, or how to communicate effectively when their ability to use language has been compromised. There is a strong consensus among rehabilitation experts that the most important element in any rehabilitation program is carefully directed, well-focused, repetitive practice—the same kind of practice used by all people when they learn a new skill, such as playing the piano or pitching a baseball. Rehabilitation nurses and therapists help patients who are able to perform progressively more complex and demanding tasks…to reacquire the ability to carry out basic activities of daily living which represent the first stage in a stroke survivor's return to independence.

This set of goals that define rehabilitation was precisely those that Debbie's therapists set for her. Would Debbie be one of the few victorious survivors able to reacquire the skills necessary for the resumption of living a full life? That was the daunting challenge. The distance of such a trip should not be underestimated. The booklet warns, "For some stroke survivors, rehabilitation will be an ongoing process to maintain and refine skills and could involve working with specialists for months or years after the stroke."

- **Hope Lost?**—Each year in the United States eight hundred thousand people suffer a stroke. Most strokes occur when clots stop the blood flow in some part of the brain. Less frequently, a hemorrhagic aneurism causes blood to flood the cerebrum, as happened to Debbie. Her second set of cerebral strokes caused "hemiparesis" or weakness on her left side and paralysis on her right side.

After a stroke strikes, the normally interconnected wiring or nerve circuitry is usually disrupted or severed. Blockages or ruptures of the brain's blood vessels interrupt or decimate the neural wiring controlling motor and cognitive functions. Brain cells and vessels destroyed by a stroke cannot regenerate. They die and cannot be restored. Survivors often are unable to see, hear, speak, or move. Consciousness and cognition can fade like the sun. In those tragic circumstances, survivors can lose the capabilities that make life meaningful.

A half century ago, no one thought that the growth of new neuronal connections following acute brain damage from a stroke was possible. Stroke survivors faced a dark hopeless future. Rehabilitation was not seen as a realistic goal, and recovery from a stroke was not conceived possible. Victims were routinely confined to a convalescent bed for the duration of their remaining days. That is no longer the case. Fortunately, medical science has advanced far since that time.

Or has it? True, neuro-rehabilitation science has come a long way in the past ten years. Yet many neurologists still depend almost exclusively on PET scanning of patients' brains and vascular circuitry to project the prospects of stroke survivors' recovery. Imaging provides insight but not a basis for predicting potentialities for lost functionalities to be recovered. If only the brain's circuitry is monitored, the interactive loop between brain and bodily movement will be overlooked. Neuroscience today better recognizes the importance of testing the limits to which a stroke victim's brain and body can learn to work in synergistic coordinated interaction in order to estimate the prospects for successful rehabilitation.

Stroke survivors make the most gains during the first three months. This period is crucial for recovery from disabilities and should be used to full advantage for active neuro-rehabilitation. Reversing a patient's impairments and disabilities through motor psychotherapy requires a demanding regimen. To this day, many rehabilitation clinics fail to allow a sufficient period for all the treatments necessary to reach the finish line. Frighteningly, in these antiquated rehabilitation centers, managers instruct their neurotherapists to rely on what is termed a "proportional recovery rule" to estimate the extent to which recovery can be achieved, even though this standard measure of functional impairment does not predict how far a patient's recovery can proceed. When their recovery appears to have hit a plateau in the condition of what's called the "chronic state of a stroke," the hospital's therapeutic treatment often is prematurely terminated. The discharged stroke survivor is victimized again, doomed to carry on disabled for the rest of his or her days. On top of this threat, in many irresponsible facilities over half a stroke victim's time while awake is wasted lying dormant in bed, and huge gaps of time are mistakenly consumed learning compensatory maneuvers with the strong side of survivors' bodies, sacrificing in the process the opportunity to reconstruct *all* damaged neural connections. Could Debbie bypass these obstacles in the hospital to which her travels had taken her?

- **A Safe Harbor?**—We didn't know about this sad history of poor treatment when Debbie's stay at Carolinas Rehab began. Had we known then what we now know, we would have lived in even more heightened dread that Debbie's chances for a fuller recovery could be cut short. We had no way of knowing if Carolinas Rehabilitation planned to take patients like Debbie the entire distance to reach the limits of their potential recovery.

  Hopes rose because Debbie's rehab hospital appeared to be professionally prepared to engineer her rehabilitation. Auspiciously, she was situated in a training hospital, which meant her therapists based their treatments and training on the latest research. Debbie's new home for therapy appeared to be the first-class rehabilitative facility that she needed. We were poised to learn about the procedures our rehab facility planned to implement.

A NEW ROADWAY AND A NEW ROUTINE

Day-to-day learning began immediately. The staff informed us of the new routine we would follow. Each evening at 7:00 p.m. and morning at

7:00 a.m., the nurses' twelve-hour shift rotated, and the replacing nurse was briefed on Debbie's status, and her records were updated. Each nurse attended ten patients, and the assistants collected vital statistics every four hours and gave Debbie medications and liquid nutrients through her G tube. To prevent bedsores, every two hours Debbie was to be shifted to her side, then to her back, and then her other side, with pillows supporting her new position. Pulsating pneumatic boots enveloped Debbie's legs each night to improve blood flow and help prevent clots. The bowel discharge from the colostomy bag was removed as needed, and diapers collected urine. In addition to the binder holding her tubes tightly in place, the nurses tied a padded mitten on Debbie's left hand to prevent her from pulling out her irritating ostomy pouch or her feeding funnel.

Every patient's schedule card for the next day was printed at the wing's central administrative station and circulated by 9:00 p.m. This posed a problem. I was Debbie's advocate and needed plenty of time to see that she was prepared for her first therapy appointment, which could (and sometimes did) begin as early as 7:00 a.m. I had to have the schedule before I departed the hospital wing, as required each night, and hiked to the Hospitality House. The solution: I turned what meager charm I could muster on the head receptionist, at whose desk the schedules were printed. We hit it off, and I begged her for permission to fetch Debbie's schedule as soon as all the schedules were printed. Reluctantly, she agreed. So that very first night, at about 6:00 p.m., I asked for and received at the reception desk Debbie's schedule for the next day. This practice continued throughout our stay in the rehab hospital thanks to this favored administrator, who always greeted Debbie with a smile and word of encouragement such as "Here comes that pretty Debbie in her wheelchair!" or "Look at you! Go, girl."

Each hourly session of physical therapy (PT), occupational therapy (OT), and speech therapy (ST) was scheduled Mondays through Fridays. I was chagrined to discover that no therapies were scheduled during the weekends. We would be on our own. To me, two days without professional therapy was lost time. The sessions varied widely from day to day, and I insisted on pushing Debbie in her wheelchair down the long hallways to the therapy facilities. "Oh, you can just let the therapists come to Debbie's room and transfer her," it was suggested. "No way," I insisted. "Ten precious minutes would be sacrificed from actual therapy each direction. I will handle the transportation to and from the therapy gym, so her sessions can begin right on time." They readily agreed.

Each morning and each session in speech therapy began with the same series of questions to evaluate Debbie's alertness, memory, and cognition. "What's your name? What day of the week is this? What is today's month and year? Who is the president of the United States?" When asked, "Where do you live?" Debbie showed off her growing level of comprehension, whispering, "Which one? We have one home in Virginia and another in South Carolina." When assured of Debbie's mental alertness, the various treatments would then proceed.

The first Saturday after our arrival in the rehabilitation center was an exception to the Monday through Friday schedule. This day was productively used to conduct careful evaluations of Debbie's capabilities, which would generate a benchmark against which progress might be judged. First, two hours of occupational therapy testing was performed, concentrating on the upper body. Next, Debbie's speaking and swallowing functionality were examined, which showed that her voice was very weak, her swallowing was extremely limited and caused choking, and she had a low level of double vision. Finally, a PT evaluation concentrated on sitting balance in Debbie's wheelchair. Every Wednesday, the head therapists conferred and compared their assessments and compiled a summary report, called an "FIM" (Functional Independence Measure). It covered thirty categories of functional capabilities, aggregated on a one-to-ten scale, with ten signifying 100% functional independence from assistance.

A physician made at least one evaluation each day and reported his or her findings to the surgical teams. For example, the first examining physician reported, "Debbie has a sinus tachycardia (a rapid but regular heart rate) and a damaged trachea and windpipe. Her elevated heart rate is probably induced by medications to keep the blood in her cranium flowing." Dr. Bernard also conducted his first evaluation of Debbie in her new room and said, "Chuck, I'm here to check Debbie's cerebrospinal fluid levels and remove some remaining stitches from a former IV line. I am scheduling another ultrasound and EEG to make sure there are no threatening vessel problems." This was the continuing careful medical attention we craved.

- **Hitting the Reset Button**—How difficult would be the rehabilitative struggle for the resumption of some level of a normal life? The challenges appeared daunting. Debbie would have to learn how to sit upright, stand, walk, swallow and talk all over again. But these challenges conceivably could be met. Recent neuroscience studies had illuminated an encouraging finding: when a stroke destroys tissue, the brain is programmed to begin self-repair. Like the brain's initial transformations in infancy and early childhood, after a stroke the brain triggers physiological, molecular, and structural growth. When a specific action is initiated which formerly was impaired, the behavior stimulates the formation of new brain cells and neural networks, and the compensatory rerouted neurons in time can begin to take over some of the dead cells' functions. What is destroyed can be replaced. The chances of that happening improve exponentially if aggressive rehabilitation treatments are provided for as long as they remain productive. This made Debbie's maintenance of a rigorous regimen for as long as possible imperative.
- **Cerebral and Neural Architecture**—The magnitude of the rehabilitative challenge should not be underestimated. To re-activate brain-body coordination, rehab therapists must confront the obstacles posed by human anatomy. A complex circuitry of humans' vast microscopic cellular network connects each part of the brain and body. The more neurons connect the brain's messages to other parts of the body, the more rapidly the patient will recover cognitive and motor capabilities.

Many structural barriers must be taken into account. The body depends on the brain, and the brain depends on the body. To live a meaningful life, the two must be linked. The brain and the body are inextricably interdependent, and even extreme "thick description" through the latest scanning technology cannot begin to map the dense thicket of interactive neural connections. The brain contains more than one hundred billion nerve cells, each connected to about ten thousand other cells—giving the brain approximately one thousand *trillion* neural connections. Together the brain and the spinal cord make up the central nervous system—a direct, two-way communication network that sends and receives messages to the rest of the body's peripheral nervous system. This system also is beyond the scope of measurement. The central nervous system consists of billions of neurons—cells that perform the major brain functions, the most important being the transmission of instructions to the body's muscles to make them move properly or to receive sensory impulses from the body to the brain to, for example, inform it of heat or pain. After a stroke strikes, many of these communication capabilities may be impaired, as happened to Debbie in the wake of her second set of strokes. Talk about complexity!

God has given each bodily part "the ability to do certain things well" (1 Cor. 12:4–6). Thus, each part is incomplete and dysfunctional in the absence of the others. Each person is composed of multiple parts. Rehabilitation therapy seeks to get the parts to work together. The brain—weighing less than three pounds and comprising two percent of body weight—is the most important part. It directs all of the voluntary actions of the rest of the body. Arguably the most complex piece of organized matter in the known universe, the brain is what makes people human—the only species able to use higher-level languages to communicate abstract thoughts. There can be no meaning without the brain, a God-given marvelous means to reasoning.

One of the best analogous descriptions of God's miraculous design for human anatomy underscored the mutual coordination and tight linkages between the physical and mental parts:

If there is a natural body, there is also a spiritual body....Now the body is not made up of one part but of many. If the foot should say, "Because I am not a hand, I do not belong to the body," it would not for that reason cease to be part of the body. And if the ear should say, "Because I am not an eye, I do not belong to the body," it would not for that reason cease to be part of the body. If the whole body were an eye, where would the sense of hearing be? If the whole body were an ear, where would the sense of smell be? But in fact God has arranged the parts in the body, every one of them, just as he wanted them to be. If they were all one part, where would the body be? As it is, there are many parts, but one body. Each needs the others. "The eye cannot say to the hand, I don't need you!" And the head cannot say to the feet, "I don't need you!" On the contrary, those parts of the body that seem to be weaker are indispensable, and the parts that we think are less honorable we treat with special honor. But God has combined the members of the body, so there should be no division in the body, but that its parts should have equal concern for each other (1 Cor. 15:44; 14:26; 12:15).

To regain health in mind and body, the goal set for was nothing short of recovering *all* of the capacities Debbie had lost. That would require rigorous treatments aimed at rewiring her brain, relinking her neuro-system, retooling linkages for the brain to send the right stimulus to the right muscle groups, and repetitiously to use these relearned mind-body connections so new sensory habits could take root. The course for Debbie's climb to recovery was set. It was certain to be steep. But the course was clear.

THE TRIGONOMETRY OF THERAPY

Three main types of activities defined Carolinas Rehab' primary agenda, accompanied by in-patient nursing and physician care in the hospital room.

- **Three Therapies in One**—Physical therapy (PT) aims at strengthening arms, legs, and hands through various exercises to regain a sense of balance and improve movement to reduce the risks of falling. This is the main endeavor in which I engaged at Debbie's bedside in both ICU and Acute Care—so-called passive range-of-motion exercises that I performed by moving her limbs, fingers, arms, legs, and toes to stimulate circulation, strengthen and develop tone on her atrophied flaccid muscles, and inhibit bedsores and blood clots.

  Occupational therapy (OT) provides instructions on new ways of conducting daily activities, such as showering, getting dressed, or cooking a meal. And speech therapy (ST) targets developing skills to deductively think logically, interpret inductively what is observed, speak, swallow, and read and write.

  There is no user manual or "one size fits all" treatment routine universally applicable to all stroke survivors. Because no two strokes are identical and each individual stroke survivor's neurological wiring is unique, rehabilitation therapists must work together to collectively identify the best route to recovery for each individual patient.

- **Teamwork**—From the "get-go," Debbie's therapists worked as a team, sharing their evaluations of her responses, recording her shifting functionality levels, and making recommendations to one another about subsequent treatments. Coordinated monitoring and nurturing was crucial, because what occurs within the mind and body and their respective capabilities depend to a large extent on each other. All three types of therapy involve both mental and physical treatments—activities animating cognitive thinking synergistically help control body-part motion, and both enable improvements in balance necessary to conduct everyday tasks. Progress in any one promotes progress in the others. The trick is to conduct the interactive treatments in the right sequence.

- **"Practice Makes Perfect"**—Rehabilitation is a matter of "mind over matter" because the two are interdependent. A damaged or destroyed brain will compromise or devastate mental performance, and the brain must recover capabilities to fire neural signals for sensations to be experienced and for bodily mobility to be triggered.

Carolinas Rehab's therapists acted on the axiom that Debbie's rehabilitation required restoring or reconnecting her damaged neurological network within her brain's circuitry and throughout her nervous system in order to build "mental muscle." They premised their therapies on the principle that repetitive activities would construct new compensatory neurological connections. Overcoming such impairments as paralysis depends on rewiring untethered neurological networks so that rehearsal efforts to perform voluntary acts such as waving a hand will naturally occur. Therapists call this "habituation."

Each linkage that is re-fired helps strengthen the wiring, and this connection advances exponentially the more times any particular task is repeated. Think about how an infant learns to walk, a youngster learns to ride a bicycle, or anyone learns how to use a pencil. Repetition makes each activity easier; in time, repetition permits the brain to signal the requests to the body without thinking. (Test yourself—you can readily tie your shoelaces, but if asked to show a small child how you do this task, you are likely to have to pause and think about what you're doing before you can give instructions.)

For Debbie to relearn how to undertake a task which she had lost after her strokes, such as rising to stand from a couch, she would have to succeed in an initial effort, and then repeat the maneuver to link the disconnected neural path from her brain to her body. Her neurological circuits would become "hardwired" if she managed to repeat the effort enough times so that it became an automatic mental-bodily reflex. At that point she would require less and less calculated mental concentration to control the targeted muscle group.

Taste, smell, language, thinking—you name it, any of Debbie's lost capabilities necessitated reconnecting the damaged neurological circuit network for her to restore her performance ability. Once a neural pathway is reconnected, repeated practice would lead to regained functionality. Practice makes perfect. Rebuilding neural networks when they have been damaged or destroyed by a stroke is what rehabilitation is all about.

- **Mind Over Matter**—Cognitive neuroscience seeks to uncover how sensations are transmitted to conscious mental states, and its research endeavors are central to the processes for rehabilitative procedures. However, the so-called "mind-body problem" has befuddled philosophy since antiquity, and remains poorly understood. If anyone thinks they fully understand this conundrum, they misunderstand it. Nonetheless, brain science provides a window for viewing the vital link between mind and matter underpinning approaches to rehabilitative practice.

The physical brain—the approximately one hundred billion neurons and their complex network of neural connections—gives rise to the mind: consciousness, thought, emotion, mood, and behavior which in combination shape our souls, our essential self. Without the conscious mind, life loses meaning because there can be no mind without the physical brain. The brain enables people to reason, recall memories, and communicate ideas in spoken and written words. The conscious mind is understood to originate from what happens within the brain. The mind is not a "thing," but a process emanating from how the brain processes sensations. As you read this paragraph, your mind is experiencing sensations that record the words you see on this page. This is your conscious mind processing information that no one else hears or sees, and it is occurring within the physical organ known as your brain.

If and how Debbie's nervous system and brain were able to operate after her strokes depended on the condition of an almost infinite number of factors that allowed or prevented the transmission of chemical signals to the particular regions that service specific functions. To mindfully direct her body to move on command involved unbelievably complicated processes necessitating the coordinated involvement of thousands of neurons scattered throughout her entire nervous system, with neuronal cells linked to hundreds of thousands of synaptic connections. Each neuron sends an electrical signal down its long axon. The tips of the axon then release little sacs of chemicals called neurotransmitters. Debbie's mental instructions to her body, transmitted by an intricate set of chemical signals, had to travel long distances through her neural circuitry.

This complex processual network is highly organized and mechanized, and, like a plumbing pipe or electrical circuit is vulnerable to damage or destruction when a stroke strikes. That is why a hemorrhagic stroke is often so dangerous and deadly. In the wake of Debbie's cerebral strokes, if the number of her working neurotransmitters declined or a problem interfered with the receptors, her signals could not be sent to permit her to form thoughts in her mind and express them in speech, or to activate targeted muscle groups. More troubling, her consciousness of ideas and memories stored in her brain could have been blocked from her mind, which is why her strokes could have provoked personality and belief changes that would have transformed who in essence she was. Indeed, it is highly probable that her strokes to some extent modified her soul—what Carl Jung called "the shadow self."

The intracerebral subarachnoid hemorrhages that struck Debbie opened the gates wide to a tremendous range of potential transformations in the definition of Debbie's "true self," her soul or who she was. Thanks to her heavenly Father's intercessions, whatever changed in Debbie's identity, her true self, was medicinal. She disembarked from her ride better equipped to benefit neurologically from the rehabilitative program to strengthen mind-body coordination.

- **Mood Over Mind**—To estimate Debbie's post-stroke capacity for rehabilitation, take into account the role of a survivor's attitude and drive in the rehabilitative equation.

When facing the trauma of a life-threatening stroke, overwhelmed, the victim can easily sink into the prison of hopeless despair, feeling "beside themselves," alone and alienated. This is what Martin Luther likened to the deep dread of death *(anfechtung)* which leads to paralysis of the will. Such a funk precludes rehabilitation. No stroke survivor can advance beyond their handicaps unless they liberate themselves from hopelessness and seek to push the body to function the way it was designed to perform.

If we focus only on the physical dimensions of rehabilitation, we will lose sight of the critical importance of a stroke victim's internal spirit to the recovery process. The level of determination—the will and courage to make the best of a life-threatening trauma and fight the afflictions—plays a potent but unmeasurable role. Our Swiss friend Dr. Jean Klinger underscored this principle, writing "It is interesting that a determination to survive, to overcome all obstacles, is not the privilege of us adults. As a pediatrician and neonatologist I have often observed that even very small and sick premature babies can either give in like little candles burning down or struggle, fight and win."

A key to Debbie's recovery rested in her posture toward her predicament and her motivation to engage actively in her therapies. Her mood contributed powerfully to her adaptive response. Debbie possessed a priceless drive that held the key to the door to healing. Her positive mood contributed greatly to her prospects for rehabilitation.

Our perception of our circumstances is as important as the circumstances themselves, and bad circumstances can be escaped psychologically if a stroke survivor perceives their circumstances as affording an opportunity for resuscitative rehabilitation. Debbie's mood was extraordinarily positive, for reasons that can best be accounted by the impact of her near-death sojourn on her mind.

Debbie had come as close to heaven as one can get, and assuredly retained God's uplifting presence in the deep recesses of her subconscious memory. Her cerebral neural circuitry was performing, and buried under layer after layer within her brain's storage bin, her mind could pull awareness of past sensations into consciousness. Think of how a long-forgotten tune spontaneously can suddenly pop into your head, and your brain can replay all the music and its lyrics. After her near-death sojourn outside her body, Debbie behaved like she was cognizant of that spiritual adventure, responding as if elusive subconscious recollections of her near-death experience and God's merciful grace had cycled back into her active conscious mind. Amazingly, after a stroke strikes, victims' consciousness of their previous experiential sensations often increase rather than evaporate. Debbie's did. Awareness of the Holy Spirit's escort of her soul from death's door undoubtedly contributed to the confident attitude and enthusiastic aptitude with which Debbie cheerfully pushed forward in rehabilitation. How else to explain Debbie's remarkable post-stroke motivation and fortitude?

Having looked at death in the face and surviving the scare, Debbie was armed with profound awareness that God cared for her. She was spiritually poised for her audition in the rehabilitation program, and psychologically prepared to energetically undertake the rehabilitative endeavors required to recover from her strokes' damage.

Let's retrace Debbie's journey at the rehabilitative hospital in Charlotte. Judge for yourself the extent to which the physical processes she vigorously pursued, empowered by her internal spiritual motor, would contribute to restoration of her functional capacities.

CHAPTER 19

TWO WEAK WEEKS IN REHABILITATION

§

T he start of rehabilitation featured starts and stops, successes and
setbacks, and a suspenseful mix of stresses, surprises, surgeries,
and scares. The only missing symptom of the prevailing syndrome during the slow slog was the status quo. The rehabilitative roadway led to
more changes than continuities; the route was steep, and the race is best
described as "disjointed incrementalism"—a series of small steps taken
at various stages. The only constant was awareness that we should "let
requests be known to God and be anxious for nothing" (Phil. 4:6–7),
because we could count on God for guidance.

Given the diverse events and experiences during our introduction to
rehabilitation, I will place this segment of our story into separate categories and identify the major developments in the approximate chronologi-
cal order in which they occurred. From the composite a clearer picture
comes into focus.

Debbie's travels undergoing rehabilitation included myriad experiences. Debbie benefited from three primary therapists, each assisted by a
student undergoing training who teamed together in ways that increased
their motivation. Two hands were better than one. I was allowed to contribute at two levels. First, the staff agreed with my request that I could
stand with Debbie and each therapist while the therapies were conducted and observe all that occurred, learn the techniques of each treatment, and cheer each and every small achievement. I was a participant!
Second, I fervently administered increasing amounts of passive physical

and speech exercises while at Debbie's bedside, in order to stimulate her motor and cognitive capabilities.

Debbie's symbolic voyage in rehabilitation set sail in search of a safe port. I felt the launch started very successfully. I wheeled Debbie to all her therapeutic treatments ahead of time, and she received great support. It didn't take long to get to know and respect the three primary therapists.

PHYSICAL THERAPY

Debbie's PT therapist, Erin, was a very experienced professional. The program she tailored was ambitious because there was so much distance to travel.

- Given Debbie's infirmities, as rehabilitation began, not much could be accomplished. Transferring Debbie from her wheelchair to the padded workout platform bed was a real challenge, but she made it there where her efforts focused on sitting, balance, and upper body movement. She made advances sitting up and leaning forward and backward.

  - Electrical stimulation on Debbie's immobile right arm and leg did not produce results but for the first time stimulated movement in her left leg—provoking a tirade of celebratory tears and cheers from me, the "town crier."
  - "I was instructed to try and stand upright," Debbie recounts, "rocking forward and backward counting 'one,' 'two,' and rising on 'three,' and managed with some help to sit upright, lift myself with aid, stand, and take a single step forward with my left leg. My experiment with what my PT therapist termed "pre-walking" while receiving right-leg support succeeded. I was proud."
  - Wheeled to parallel bars, Debbie was able with some assistance to stand for two minutes leaning heavily on her left leg! More tears and cheers, sobered by the effect of this effort—an

eyelid-raising heart rate of 123. At this point Debbie began to dictate her notes. She said, "My therapists concentrated on sitting and lying down while I provided support with my left arm. They electrically stimulated my right arm and saw my new responses. I also was able to rise from my wheelchair to stand holding the parallel bars, and reducing my load with my arms managed to take four steps. I was excited. I also stood upright ten minutes while placing objects into a pin-hole board. I think I am becoming more 'muscle-ready.' When a therapist told me 'stop and rest,' I refused, saying 'give me more' and 'let's not stop too soon.'"

OCCUPATIONAL THERAPY

It was our good fortune that Elizabeth, Debbie's occupational therapist, was very skilled. We appreciated her no-nonsense work ethic. Without much coaxing, Debbie responded with impressive extra effort, which Elizabeth always praised because she could see how Debbie thrived whenever she heard encouraging words.

- OT sessions concentrated on sitting upright and transferring in and out of her wheelchair. Elizabeth instructed me to back off my intensive OT and PT involvement to "give Debbie a better chance to perform at her own speed."
- A special lotion was applied to Debbie's right arm, and the stimulation generated great results—her first movement of her elbow as she bent her hand to her belly. That achievement preceded success putting puzzle pieces into a box, one at a time, for right hand control and taking a box apart and putting it back together.
- "I spent two hours in my private bathroom with the occupational therapist where I was given lessons on taking a shower. Chuck was urged to watch and learn. My therapist remained mortified at the nest of tangled hair on my head, and attempted to improve my looks

by applying massive dosages of the detangle spray and conditioner Chuck had purchased for that purpose. The results were not successful, but I must say I felt I looked slightly better."

• On the first Saturday, our frustrations mounted because no weekend therapy treatments had been scheduled. We wanted no slowdown in the progress being made. So I took an exploratory trip to the gym and asked the only person working, "Have there been any cancellations? If so, could Debbie be worked in as a substitute?" I knew I was asking a lot, and the chances were remote. "Nothing available now," I was told. "What's your wife's room number? If a cancellation does occur, we'll notify you there." Fat chance, I thought. Oh, well. I returned to Debbie's room and received a surprise! Ten minutes later, a therapist magically appeared, announcing, "My patient did not show. Debbie, I'm yours! Let's go." He was a specialist trained in both PT and OT, who worked weekends to conduct evaluations for arriving new patients. We wheeled Debbie to the gym, and she had a terrific workout that lasted an hour and a half. The therapist had a bag of new exercise tricks to try, and Debbie performed very well. For the first time, she moved her own wheelchair with her stronger left arm.

• Debbie's energy and effort amazed her therapists, who were impressed with her perseverance. Debbie recollects, "My exercises were becoming more vigorous, and I was encouraged by my therapists' encouragement. The only time a nurse suggested that I was too tired to attend a therapy session, I said 'We are going to have our first argument. I am not going to miss any sessions.' I won that altercation."

SPEECH THERAPY

Janet, a very seasoned expert, was appointed Debbie's primary speech therapist. She was very attentive but highly disturbed to find Debbie's voice so weak and her right vocal cord partially paralyzed. At the starting gate, Janet recognized the big challenge that stood in the way of Debbie's recovery.

- In the initial session, Debbie's performance was disappointing, and Janet was very discouraged. Debbie had difficulty counting to five with one breath or blowing tissue paper held in front of her mouth to make it move. Poor Debbie displayed some memory problems, undoubtedly worsened by her exhaustion after her first full-scale OT and PT sessions earlier that day. I feared that Janet may have underestimated Debbie's peak speaking and thinking capabilities when not enervated. This fear escalated in a second afternoon abortive session which had to be cut short because Debbie was too tired to focus.

- Debbie subsequently did better than initially despite her inability to count with one breath beyond 10—50 percent of the goal. Janet's expectations improved as she saw strengths emerging from Debbie that she had not previously witnessed, and treatments gradually became more fruitful. For example, Debbie answered the usual introductory questions correctly, learned to clear her throat on command, and managed to blow the tissue held in front of her mouth longer and further.

- To test and promote swallowing, Debbie was given some lemon-flavored liquid to facilitate swallowing, and in reaction Debbie vomited. She bounced back and managed to organize some pictures in proper sequence and answered questions about the location of our residences correctly but experienced a momentary memory lapse, asking me, "Is that you, Chuck?" I hid my fright.

- Debbie's vocal cords were made to gyrate with the now-familiar exercises of saying for as long and loud as possible "Eeeeeee," "Ahhhhhhhh," "Ohoooooo," and "Ah-eee, ah-eee, ah-eee." Singing "Old McDonald Had a Farm" forced these sounds to be voiced, requiring use of all the vocal muscles and engaging the full range of cord vibrations.

- Uninformed by Debbie's improving condition, a substitute speech therapist coaxed Debbie, "Try and converse with a complete sentence." That was a mistake; she underestimated Debbie's capabilities, as she soon found out. Debbie quickly blurted back, "I want you to shut up!" She had her "take that" look on her smiling face. Her humor was endearingly infectious, and this therapist could not smother her laughter. Proud of herself, Debbie enjoyed the sensations she had provoked and extended the show she had put on; she confidently commanded, "Chuck, I am ready to talk on the phone to Teresa Amick. Now!"

- John and Mary wrote, "Chuck reports more good news. During her speech therapy Debbie managed to swallow five bites of applesauce and ingest some honey-coated crumbs. She will undergo another x-ray on her vocal cords to estimate the degree to which the right side may be permanently damaged. She read and lucidly responded to all questions about content. She is not cooperating with the doctors' requests to keep her mitten on her left hand to guard against pulling out her feeding tube and colostomy pouch. Chuck says this is frustrating but a hopeful sign of Debbie's quest to sever her bonds to things which remind her of her dependence."

- Debbie's frozen right hand with which she wrote began to display growing strength. "When my regular speech therapist urged me to write a note, I wrote 'Hi, Janet.' I was making progress, slowed only by a urinary tract infection requiring antibiotics and a catheter to my bladder." (The doctors said, "Expect to catch the virus, Chuck; you are with Debbie all the time, and exposure is almost certain." Sure enough, I found myself having to "go" frequently, but this was a minor nuisance compared to real concerns.)

- In a subsequent session, Janet asked Debbie to try again writing something. Her feeble product is a treasured keepsake. In extremely tiny and faint letters, Debbie put pencil to paper and scribbled a few things or phrases that were unreadable. She tried to write "Chuck," but it came out looking something like "crucf." This was an adorably amusing start.

- Presented with some challenging deductive logic puzzles, I quietly watched over Debbie's shoulder and found she did better solving them than I could! They were difficult; even Hilel could not solve the two puzzles I described to him.
- "As my voice strength improved so did my understanding of two-way conversations. My speech therapist asked me to try to swallow some ice chips as well as some soft food with the aid of lemon swabs. These experiments were not something about which I could brag. I was embarrassed about one thing I said in ST that disturbed Chuck. To test my memory, my therapist asked 'What's your husband's name?' I must have had a memory lapse, because I answered 'Steve'—my former husband. Chuck must have been mortified. I apologized profusely. I was told that stroke survivors often suffer this kind of memory confusion, and to not worry. I did worry."

  I (Chuck) was crushed, but kept silent. After I took a few minutes to reflect about the memory problems that usually erupt for stroke survivors, I managed to bury my emotions. I calmed down further when the speech therapist saw my hurt and in private interpreted Debbie's slip of the tongue. "Don't take this personally, Chuck. Long-term or remote memory always comes back first, and more recent memories are recovered later. Debbie was just not in the here and now when she answered my question." My recovery was instant and complete. This was a principle important for other stroke survivors to learn, I thought. How odd, though—as people age, long-term memory improves, and short-term memory declines.
- Talking more frequently, Debbie was beginning to speak louder. "Chuck phoned twice," Andy reported, "and both times he proudly put the phone to Debbie's ear, I distinctly heard Debbie's voice!" Most of her thoughts made perfect sense. Other statements were mystifying. For example, when I called Hilel with an update, Debbie took the phone and said, "Hilel, I've been thinking about you and your family. How's your family?" Her train of thought was in motion, and I guess everyone is prone to a non sequitur now and then. I do it all the time.

THERAPEUTIC TREATMENTS WITH CHUCK IN CHARGE

At every opportunity when Debbie and I were alone, I tried my best to help Debbie mend. These opportunities were frequent, and I took full advantage of them administrating my own version of OT, PT, and ST treatments.

I conducted my tryout to join the varsity therapy team that first trying day. I tried my best when Debbie awoke from another nap after her elongated initial set of workouts. I jumped in with my personal treatments. Now I confess that I am prone to do everything in excess and little in moderation. And I probably overdid my work with Debbie to try to speed her recovery. John and Mary summarized: "Debbie should get an A for efforts in rehabilitation. Chuck was told to give her more rest time and not overdo his part of PT and not to talk to her if another person is in the room. Can he control himself?" Could I restrain myself? I wasn't sure. Several anecdotes illustrate my endeavors.

- My nightly passive massage exercises aided Debbie's mobility. For example, she succeeded in moving her head back and forth, fully to the left and partially to the right, as well as up and down.
- Each time I witnessed even the slightest sign of progress, I shouted in joy. This caught Debbie's attention and stimulated her to say something, which was good vocal exercise. How could she miss my loud habit? "Chuck, you react to everything so excitedly. I think the therapists and nurses have another secret nickname for you—'Ole Yeller.'" I had that one coming. At this stage, however, Debbie had great difficulties talking, and I worked her hard on the exercises, counting to twenty without taking a breath and saying "Ah-eeee" and other chants. I detected modest improvements in her communication capabilities; still mostly whispering, we managed to carry out brief conversations.
- While attending to Debbie's bedside passive exercises, I interrupted my efforts to place a call to Debbie's sister. What I overheard Debbie say confused me greatly about her state of mind. Debbie again

repeated the same thought she had expressed four days after her first January 8 hemorrhagic stroke: "K. J., I'm not supposed to be here." Did she mean on earth or the hospital? We will never know. The mystery showed how Debbie's thinking could float in strange directions.

• The best part of my assistance for Debbie came each night as the end of our time together neared. Before prying myself from her room, we kissed and said prayers. This closing ceremony was the best medicine I could provide, but parting was such sweet sorrow. I was required to leave the hospital and was always the last visitor to depart. On one occasion, I blew her another kiss from the doorway and dragged myself down the hall. I couldn't help myself—I turned around to peek inside her room to make sure she was safe and sound. She was still awake and saw me and asked, "Can you lie in bed with me?" Debbie recalls thinking, "I knew he couldn't, but desperately wanted Chuck by my side to cuddle and to keep me warm like old times. 'You better get going, before they lock the wing. I'll see you in the morning,' I told him, knowing he wanted to stay. I cried myself to sleep that night. I missed my husband and our nights in each other's arms."

PASTORAL CARE AND VISITOR SUPPORT

• Unbeknown to us, the rehab facility had a resident chaplain, Elizabeth, on the staff. She paid us the first of many regular visits to our room. We exchanged greetings and information about ourselves, our backgrounds, and our beliefs. "May I say a prayer?" Elizabeth asked. "Of course," Debbie and I both said at the same time. Her appropriate prayer was appreciated this first time and all the other times she came to see us.

• Emily Crow paid a surprise visit, and the stimulation while trying to talk energized Debbie's response. Her voice reached a new level but faded as her excited effort drained her energy. Moreover, episodically in trekked our steady stream of loyal friends spreading joy and good wishes—Hilel, Herman, and George and Cathy Crow.

- On our first Sunday in the rehab hospital, we aimed to keep the Sabbath holy. We were grateful for God's many gifts. When we discovered that Pastor Paul Doyle would be conducting a worship service, we jumped at the opportunity. Five other patients gathered with us in His name. A short sermon spoke to the healing grace of God for those afflicted with infirmities. Handouts provided the lyrics to several hymns we tried to sing to recorded background music. We said many prayers and retreated down the hall to our room, doing what scripture tells believers to do: rest and pray, keeping the Sabbath holy.

- On the following Sunday, Pastor Paul Doyle conducted another worship service. Three other patients joined singing "How Great Thou Art." Debbie sang beautifully if weakly, using her vocal cords to their greatest extent, while to spare all from my miserable singing, I mostly mouthed the words.

- Pastor Steve Meyer drove to Charlotte to see Debbie and say prayers. He was pleasantly surprised at how far Debbie had progressed in so short a time span and told her so. Debbie beamed. She was getting better displaying facial emotion and was cultivating a wonderful habit of showing off her recent accomplishments.

- The resident psychologist scheduled a special visitation for both of us. Debbie and I walked to her office, and distracted by someone, I began a conversation with that person. The psychologist saw an opportunity and seized it. "Debbie, come into my office and shut the door. I want a word or two with you in private."

Alone with Debbie, the psychologist questioned her. "I remember the conversation well. Our exchange unfolded like this: 'How is Chuck doing?' she asked. I responded, 'What do you mean?' 'Oh,' she explained, 'he seems worn down and I am concerned,' to which I replied 'Well, I think that it's understandable based on all he's been doing for me. Perhaps he's overwhelmed. My husband tends to worry, a lot. It's his nature. The initial W in his middle name should stand for Worry, not William.' The psychologist understood, saying 'I don't mean to put you on the spot but just want to make sure that he's okay. We're here for both of you.' 'I understand,' I said. 'Perhaps you should ask him how he's doing.'"

She did, giving voice to concerns about my physical and mental condition. I had heard similar concerns about my endurance, weight loss, and questionable mental and deteriorating physical condition before—from doctors and nurses as well as from the Hospitality House attendants and other guests also staying there. I guess I was paying some kind of price for our prolonged ordeal, but I was happy to pay it. All I wanted was to steer Debbie's recovery and be there for her—whatever it took. I was oblivious to my own frame of mind. My worries concentrated on Debbie, but I must admit that among my many worries was my concern about retaining my health, which was critical if I was to help Debbie meet her needs.

A Path to Recovery Paved by Doctors and Nurses
The doctors conducted a seemingly endless succession of tests and frequently modified Debbie's medications, and the nursing staff provided good advice and twenty-four-seven care.

- A preventive influenza vaccine was provided, the drug amantadine was started to booster Debbie's energy, and Keppra was prescribed to deter seizures.
- Lab technicians conducted frequent chest x-rays and CT scans. The cerebral scans focused on the sites where potential brain aneurisms were in danger of forming and hemorrhaging. As a precaution, the neurosurgery team ordered the whole gamut of available imaging screens. The results were difficult to interpret. Given their ambiguities, the neurosurgery team choose *not* to proceed at this time with the dreaded brain surgery to address the bubbled and ballooned aneurism where the first hemorrhage had occurred on January 8 and where the

danger was the greatest that the swollen vessels were most likely to rupture again. Was this delay warranted? Apparently, the doctors felt the risk was worth taking. Debbie's strength could build without a hiatus. On the other hand, postponement meant that anything could happen—the worst scenarios threatening her life.

- The clock on the discharge was ticking. Drs. Grafton and Shemtov both agreed that the brain-surgery operation should be scheduled while Debbie was still in our Charlotte rehab hospital so that the surgeons could quickly be summoned and spring into action should another vessel burst. Under no circumstances did we want to face that crisis if we were 120 miles away in Blythewood. That would be a disaster. Yet perhaps it was wise to delay; Dr. Dyer and Dr. Bernard had candidly warned that any brain surgery could result in all kinds of threats, including a loss of all the improvements that were underway or even death. Any deep penetration of the skull can damage or destroy a multitude of capabilities. Brain surgery was extraordinarily dangerous. None of us desired to confront those possibilities.

- Debbie called a night nurse to change her soiled and soaked sheets, provide a sponge bath and change her diapers, The nurse gasped in alarm when she observed poor Debbie's emaciated body. Debbie had lost so much weight she looked like a skeleton. Her condition attested to how far she needed to go to recover strength.

- In addition to the usual cleanings and colostomy bag changes, tubular feeding and dressing each morning, the nursing staff ordered Debbie to wear Tet support hose on her ankles and lower legs; they were protective, tight-fitting hose designed to deter clots. Unfortunately, because of my arthritic thumbs, I had difficulty putting the hose on and required a nurse's help most mornings.

JUDGMENT DAY

Confidence was thrown to the wind when the FIM (functional independence measure) evaluations were disclosed. The sky darkened. A composite of ten indicators on each of the three categories of therapy, the FIM index estimated Debbie's functional capabilities on a scale ranging from 0 percent (complete dependence) to 100 percent (total independence). The ultimate goal in rehabilitation was to achieve complete independence.

- Debbie's scores from the first February 15 evaluations amplified how very far she needed to travel. She was judged completely dependent (0) on others for life skills in OT, only 20 percent in PT due to her wheelchair confinement and complete dependence on her right side, and her ST functionality (comprehension, problem solving, facial expression, memory, swallowing and speech) were all ranked below 25 percent. All of Debbie's therapists reported that they were impressed with Debbie's motivation and drive.

  This evaluation was followed by a shocking announcement. "The average length of patients' stay in rehabilitation is only three weeks, and the team identified March 19 as Debbie's target discharge date. After that she will be on her own." I hit the panic button. How, possibly, could Debbie approach independence in so short a span of time, with so much to accomplish? My terror was mollified when told, "If a patient shows unusually large functional gains, then sometimes, though rare, the rehabilitation program can conceivably be extended another week or two."

  Hilel heard the anxious desperation in my voice, writing, "Chuck is devastated by these evaluations, which has forced immediate consideration of where they will stay when Debbie is discharged from the in-patient rehab hospital. He is so afraid of sudden complications that he is giving thought to selling their Blythewood home and moving to Charlotte, to be close to Debbie's neurosurgery team. The bottom line is that recovery will be long and slow, but Debbie is a fighter and perhaps can speed the pace of her rehabilitation."

  The FIM report provided powerful incentives to double up on recovery efforts, if that was possible. Debbie's discharge could be delayed if she engineered progress, and I knew she could become more independent with God's care.

- The next Wednesday's FIM calculations were more encouraging. Overall, all PT, OT, and ST scores had improved from the previous week's first accounting, but not as far as Debbie and I craved because the discharge date was approaching. Progress in speech improved to 75 percent in expression, attention, social interaction, and memory. Debbie registered her highest score, 75 percent functional independence, on the most important category, comprehension. Of all the threats posed by strokes, by far the most dreaded was disability in thinking and cognition; yet God had given Debbie protection of this vital function. Sitting, balancing, grooming, bathing, upper-body dressing, and head control had risen to 50 percent. The exception to progress was Debbie's continuing issues on her right body, especially below her hip (0 percent). She remained completely dependent transferring from her bed to her chair, and her bed mobility was gauged at only 25 percent independent. More ambitious goals were set. Debbie's doctors described her motivation as "off the charts."

SHIFTING TO SECOND GEAR

Hilel celebrated Debbie's achievements this second week but cautioned,

> Debbie continues to both struggle and improve on a daily basis. She has (with help) gotten dressed, washed herself, sat for long periods in a wheelchair, carries on conversations and seems to be in relatively good spirits. Chuck continues to ride the roller coaster through these ups and downs. Debbie is using her left hand more and more, and has movement in her right arm and hand, but not with her right leg and foot. I've been told by several physicians that while this might be permanent, it is not necessarily so. Considering that Debbie is a fighter, I'm optimistic about that as well. She'll have more x-rays to inspect her vocal cords. She is swallowing small

amounts of food, and that is very good. I gave Chuck a lecture, urging him to never let Debbie see his concerns and fears, and to fake optimism even when worries were warranted. He understood the need to raise her confidence about further recovery.

It looked like progress was trending the first two weeks in rehabilitation in the right direction. Debbie had arrived weak and was growing stronger. She had a long way to go in a short amount of time. Debbie's achievements inspired optimism. We had been carried and uplifted by God's almighty hands. We should never forget that it's the obvious that often eludes us. In this instance, God's mercy was obvious, and His presence did not elude us.

Debbie had shifted into second gear and the speedometer showed she was motoring toward rehabilitation at a faster rate. My appetite for more progress was unappeasable. It was imperative for Debbie to travel far enough on her roadway to recovery to permit a safe discharge. Progress notwithstanding, the long distance she needed to cover was frightening, and Debbie's troublesome history of improvements interrupted by threats was worrisome. Watching the evolutionary course of my Debbie's path and predicting the future based on the past was as difficult as predicting daily changes in the stock market. That principle struck like a dagger just when a new shock was least expected.

CHAPTER 20

A Dark ER Victory and Due Diligence

§

The time was nearing for our scheduled discharge from Carolinas Rehabilitation, and Debbie was not self-reliant—not even close. A great distance separated where Debbie was and where she needed to be. We proceeded as diligently as possible in our third week of rehabilitation.

A Detour to the Emergency Room

The start was a disaster. Saturday February 22 is a story unto itself. It began with promise but plummeted to a dramatic crisis that ended with a surprising climax.

Debbie was exhausted by her demanding regimen. She had earned some rest. We decided to use the weekend in the absence of scheduled therapies productively but at a slower pace. In the afternoon, I wheeled Debbie to the now-vacant therapy gym. I had hiked a half mile to a Target store and purchased some children's games similar to the sequence exercises her speech therapist had used. From her wheelchair, Debbie placed on a table some pictures in proper order, sorted colored balls into the correct holes in a box, and tried her weak right hand in a coloring book. She performed all of these tasks very well and beamed her famous smile when I praised her performance.

We returned to room 2211 at exactly 4:00 p.m. where a nurse was waiting to pour nutrition into the G tube. But first, she took Debbie's vital signs. That's when a shock struck. Given Debbie's relaxed composure,

213

her nurse could not believe that Debbie's heart rate had climbed to 175. How could this be? There were no symptoms warning that a crisis was imminent.

Dr. Rachael Shemtov was summoned at once. Assessing the situation, Dr. Shemtov concluded that Debbie's heart rate had to be lowered—immediately. She consulted other doctors, and they ordered a med to lower Debbie's rapid SVT or ventricular heart pulse. This did not sufficiently fix the problem. Debbie's fast sinus trachycardiac but regular heart pulse still hovered above 155. "I am afraid," Dr. Shemtov concluded, "that Debbie will have to go to the emergency room. It's nearby—about two hundred yards in an adjacent building—but she will have to go there in an EMS ambulance. I know, this is ridiculous, but it's the hospital's rule for medical emergencies."

I was horrified. Not Debbie. She calmly took the crisis in stride. So off we went, with me riding shotgun, forcing a reassuring facial expression as my eyes fixated on Debbie riding on the ambulance bed. The "trip" took two minutes.

• **"Try to Relax"**—When we entered the emergency room, Debbie and I were hustled into a treatment chamber. The head doctor immediately entered. "Do you know what's going on?" I asked.

"Sure I do," the physician responded. "Everyone in the hospital knows about Debbie Kegley. In fact, hospitals around the world know about her. She's famous. The extreme rarity of her hiatal hemorrhagic aneurisms in both her brain and colon has made her case worthy of study here and abroad. I have Mrs. Kegley's complete records in front of me. We will inject a liquefied pill that will cause her heart rate to drop. I must tell you, the medication will actually kill your wife for about five seconds, after which she will be okay. Be patient. First we want to give her an EKG. Then we shall proceed. Try to relax."

Debbie listened to every word. She had to understand the gravity of this scary calamity—Debbie was once again at the abyss, looking at death in the face. How could this be? My cognitive dissonance made my head spin. A number of thoughts raced through my mind: "A pill that would actually kill Debbie? Was the doctor kidding? Momentarily dead? How could this treatment be termed 'medicinal'? Okay, having identified the problem, a solution had to be found. But this?" I was beside myself.

You might have guessed it: Debbie consumed this news with as little response as she might watching grass grow. Her composure was bewildering. She was in dire danger, but you would never have known it. She was in a mental comfort zone, radiating smiles. What did she know that I didn't? Didn't she recognize the peril? Or did she have information I didn't possess, hidden within her brain cells? Did her soul exist in another realm, with spiritual knowledge that I lacked which sparked her confidence?

- **Delay in the Dark**—We were in the dark, and to my way of thinking, the sky was as black as ink. The diagnosis and treatment put my eyes on the lookout for an apocalypse, and it was impossible to bury the pall of fear. We were instructed to be patient. How? While waiting, police officers pushed two bloody chained prisoners juiced on crack cocaine into the adjoining chamber. Welcome to an Emergency Room on a Saturday night! My alarm grew by leaps and bounds. Prayers with Debbie helped. But why the delay?

"It's slightly more complicated than I thought," the doctor divulged. "Debbie's resting heart rate remains too high, about 160, but also too low. We need to get her rate back higher, to 175, in order for the magic med to work. Debbie, hold your breath and squeeze, as if you are trying to induce a bowel movement." Was he kidding? Debbie tried, without immediate success.

A half hour later, the doctor returned and said "Debbie's heart rate has finally risen, not as high as we would prefer, but high enough to try." Try? Debbie's life was at stake. What if she wasn't ready? "We need to start, now. We cannot wait any longer."

Hilel called at this critical moment and made a failing attempt to boost my confidence, claiming "these kind of problems are not unusual; the doctors can use some amazing new meds to control these kinds of threats." I was skeptical, and my panic attack persisted.

- **Deliverance**—There was no option but to accept the head doctor's risky advice. So the magic pill was administered through an IV, and before I could blink, the procedure was over. Debbie's heart rate stabilized near normal. Debbie hardly seemed to notice or to be bothered. Breathing hard in relief, I started to steady my jittering nerves. Debbie was alive and well. I was certain that once again God had delivered.

  I stood by Debbie and said a long prayer. Amazed by her composure, I said, "Debbie, you weren't the least bit worried, were you? You went through this so contentedly. I guess you left all the worrying to me." Debbie gave me a curious look and pointed her index finger toward heaven. That gesture signaled she knew God was with her all the way. She did not worry because, I surmised, during her near-death sojourn the Holy Spirit had shown her there was nothing to fear.

- **Born Again**—A dramatic transformation resulted from this experience. Like a match lighting a candle, Debbie's speaking ability took an instant turn for the better. I now could clearly understand everything she was saying. No gibberish. She had a clear head. An anticlimax accompanied this change—Debbie's wit and sense of humor hit a new high. I smiled at her, and she smiled back, teasingly. "I like that bread crumb in your teeth, Charlie." Debbie's enlivened sense of humor expelled the smell of fright from the room.

  After an unnecessarily long wait, the EMS crew finally arrived. The $1750 ambulance trip back to Debbie's rehab room was quick (of course: it doesn't take long to travel two hundred yards). About midnight Debbie was back in her bed, still animated and not ready to sleep. I was both worn out and rung out, even though the dark ordeal ended in victory. Not Debbie. She was alert and outspoken. We said prayers. I then told Debbie, "I am so blessed to have you for my wife. You are the best thing that ever happened to me." Without missing a beat, Debbie responded, "My pleasure." After all the excitement, Debbie finally drifted into a deep sleep, and I sleeplessly rejoiced throughout the night.

• **Spectral Evidence of Special Effects**—The weird thing about this emergency was that it was nothing of the sort. Debbie never went under like a drowning person gasping for breath. Instead, she emerged from submersion like a baptized believer. She was different—dare I say "reborn." I am certain her soul had been empowered and enlivened by the Holy Spirit. She changed as abruptly as the flip of a switch brings light to a dark room. She was more vocal, coherent, emotional, energetic, and confident. Debbie was aware of her "new self:" "After my pulse-rate crisis in the emergency room, I felt renewed energy and enthusiasm. Before then, I couldn't even remember what I remember. Now my memories are crystal clear."

Debbie couldn't wait to resume her therapeutic treatments. God had put fuel in her tank and ignited her cognition. It was as if she had jumped from a springboard. To mix metaphors again, the Holy Spirit had flipped her turn signal and again drove her away from harm or death. Fear of veering off course never vanished, but this turn of direction in the ER providentially heightened our expectations and trust in the Holy Spirit's continuing intercession. (A "reader alert"—because Debbie's memory and cognitive capabilities rapidly improved following her emergency room procedure, from this point forward she began to write in her own words her recollections of conversations and events for *After a Stroke Strikes*.)

The next day Hilel summarily captured the jump-start:

Debbie's strength after her detour in the Emergency Room last Saturday night is astounding. She is showing remarkable resilience and endurance. Debbie is fired up, but sometimes is worn down and too tired to engage in strenuous endeavors. She and Chuck are riding waves and their moods correspond to what is taking place. About 3:00 a.m. I was awakened by a call from

Chuck, to whom I had given permission to call anytime he felt a need to talk. He was extremely ebullient because Debbie came through this emergency better off. Debbie is driving herself at the top of her personal speed limit. However, it would be gross hyperbole to suggest that the pace is fast. It is still slow, but may gradually grow in speed.

Debbie diligently poured her newfound energy into her therapists' grinding rehabilitative regimen. Let's break the chronicle into the major categories of rehabilitative treatment, charting first the payoffs from Debbie's due diligence that unfolded this third week at Carolinas Rehab, and present a select sample of the key events that occurred.

PHYSICIAN AND NURSING TREATMENTS

- **Taking Some Tests**—The doctors detected another urinary tract infection and put Debbie on antibiotics. "It will take five to seven days," they predicted, "to affect a cure. Let's experiment with a bedpan to see if you can pee." Debbie failed that test. Debbie's vitals steadied in an acceptable range, but throat and chest x-rays showed continuing partial paralysis on her right vocal cord. Another MRI inspected Debbie's swollen brain vessels, and the shunt-pressure level was calculated.
- **Your Hands Are Tied**—One morning I arrived in Debbie's room early, eager to get the program started. Debbie was wide awake and exclaimed "Boy, Chuck, you read the riot act to the night nurse about the urgency of making sure my mittens were on all night."

  "I sure did, because it is crucial that those padded mittens remain tied to your hands to prevent you from pulling on either your G tube or your colostomy pouch. The nurses did not really believe my assertion that if you impulsively extracted the irritating tubing, the bleeding could be lethal. The tubing is adjacent to your liver. I had to defend your welfare to keep you from accidently hurting yourself."

- **The Gloves Come Off**—Unlike the others, one nurse criticized harshly my habitual administrative interruptions, berating me in no uncertain terms with an intended knockout blow: "We're professionals around here. Mind your own business. No coaching or midnight calls." I lost that battle but won the tug-of-war. Thereafter, the nurses believed me because Dr. Grafton wrote instructions informing the nurse that the mittens were an imperative precaution. My role as patient advocate could not be restrained. That's why I was always with Debbie as long as permitted and why during the wee hours I called to check to make sure all was okay.

- **Swelling Is Not Swell**—Dark dimmed some of the light that was beginning to beam. Our neurosurgeons reminded me that they must open Debbie's skull and perform another surgery to address the brain-vessel weakening and swelling, despite the risk that this surgery could set Debbie back from her recent progress—or worse. I tried to block the dark dread. But I fully understood that it was better to perform that operation soon, before she was released from the hospital, rather than having to face another emergency far from the Charlotte surgeons. If performed, it was much better to conduct this brain surgery before she was discharged from the CMC hospital.

- **The Countdown Clock Ticks Away**—Dr. Shemtov had taken the time and effort to do some research on Debbie's extremely rare consecutive aneurisms in her brain and colon. "Here's the report I found and printed for you. I read it, and it's terribly arcane and technical. It's titled 'Subarachnoid Hemorrhage in a Case of Segmented Arterial Mediolysis with Coexisting Intracranial and Intraabdominal Aneurisms.' It cites the four recorded cases prior to Debbie's. You may find it useful. But it does not provide a basis for explaining and prognosticating Debbie's condition. Her case remains a mystery, and the specialized pathology reports received so far reveal nothing definitive; some variety of systemic deteriorative vasculitis is neither verifiably present or absent. We remain in the dark. I hope we can get some answers and schedule the brain operation while Debbie is here at CMC. I'll try to lobby for that."

"Thank you," I responded. "I am very concerned that there might be another catastrophic incident."

- **No Surgical Surge**—To our disappointment, the neurosurgeons announced their decision to *not* schedule Debbie's brain surgery before her discharge: "Debbie's situation is precarious but stable, and we feel that the advantages of further delays for the operation outweigh the disadvantages." My fears could not be repressed. The clock was ticking, and the discharge date was getting closer and closer.

SPEECH AND SWALLOWING SKILLS

- **A Time of Trial**—A lot depended on Debbie's capacity to swallow food, to think abstractly, and to talk more coherently. Debbie's progress toward functional independence could not slow, because then the rehabilitation would also stop, and she would be discharged. Thankfully, periods when she sat expressionless with a blank look were diminishing in frequency and duration. She stayed in motion. Hilel wrote, "Debbie does more and more, speaks in sentences, and understands just about everything."
- **Eating like a Big Girl**—The physicians remained concerned about Debbie's persisting throat soreness and difficulty swallowing. But her capabilities were improving—Debbie managed to swallow applesauce and tiny portions of pureed oatmeal milk from a straw, ingesting 22 percent of her soft foods through her mouth and supplemented that portion with liquid nutrition through the G tube.

  Debbie was taught how to shift her head to the far left and tuck her chin when swallowing to prevent choking or aspiration. I received instructions on how to remind Debbie to tuck her chin without barking "Tuck!" My irritating habit was getting on Debbie's nerves. To avoid my alarmist shouting, the speech therapist taught Debbie to "look at your left elbow" and for me to use sign language to remind Debbie to turn and tuck her chin by lightly touching Debbie's elbow and looking at my own left elbow as a hint.

- **The Breakfast Club**—The therapy staff ordered us to participate each morning in what the rehabilitation center called "the Breakfast Club." We met with five other patients. Each member selected items to eat from a limited but appealing menu. The secondary objective was to get patients to socially interact with each other and with the attending nursing assistants. Each person was asked the usual opening questions (for example, name, date, hometown) to test comprehension and initiate conversation.

   We were encouraged. Inclusion in this "exclusive" club signaled that the therapists thought Debbie was prepared to sit in her wheelchair, eat smooth food, and swallow with chin tucks under the nurses' watchful eyes. Debbie was able to use her right hand and negotiated a fork and spoon successfully. Debbie took the lead in the group, asking the others questions.

- **Marital Bliss**—In addition to swallowing education, speech therapy sessions focused on solving crossword and sequencing puzzles. "I was shown a series of photos and put them in logical order," Debbie recalled. "I was asked 'What do you think is going on here?' I answered, 'I see in this sequence a couple putting together a bookcase,' and the therapist asked me 'do you think the couple is married?' I said 'No!' The therapist asked 'Why don't you think they are married?' I said 'because the couple appears to get along.' My stab at humor generated resounding laughter."

OCCUPATIONAL ACTIVITIES

- **Mental Gymnastics**—Debbie learned to practice the tricks of the trade she was taught. She discovered the benefits of mental methods, such as reminding herself prior to trying to stand to say "nose over toes." She recalls, "I found it helpful when facing a task I didn't think

I could perform to visualize myself doing it and saying to myself 'you can do it.' I was amazed by achievements that occurred when I put my mind to the challenge. I tried to 'think positively' and had positive results."

- **Great Is Thy Faithfulness**—A big part of rehabilitation focuses on learning to be occupied in the kinds of activity undertaken prior to a disabling stroke. Worshiping on Sunday served the dual purpose of thanking God for His blessings and for participating in the service with others. Debbie did both. Following a hearty breakfast swallowed without choking, we went to the church service held again by Pastor Paul Doyle. We were joined by eleven others. Debbie sang loudly and clearly the verses of "Great Is Thy Faithfulness," booming, "Morning by morning new mercies I see." There was no better way to occupy her time and use it to improve her occupational capabilities

- **Visitation Rewards**—Another important occupational activity is conversing with others. Debbie did just that when friends came to visit. She benefitted from a steady stream of visitors beyond the regular visits by the Crows and Hilel. She was greeted by Debbie and Dale Clark, our faithful next-farm neighbors from Wytheville, as well as Tom and Candi Hough from Hilton Head. Each couple stayed two hours. The exciting exchanges invigorated Debbie, but the stimulation wore her out. This was the first opportunity for them to see Debbie face to face since her stroke. They were alarmed by Debbie's occasional blank stares, and in private disclosed their concerns about Debbie's prospects for recovery. Their fears permeated my mind, and that night I tossed and turned until the morning.

- **How to Strike Up a Conversation**—Following these helpful but exhausting visits, our speech therapist taught us a valuable lesson about how to interact and communicate with a stroke survivor and laid down a new rule that I wish I had learned earlier. The new mandate—only one visitor in the room with Debbie at a time. Why? To ensure that visitors would not talk with and to me in Debbie's presence because such rapid conversation would be hard for Debbie to understand. Worse still, with three or more in conversation, Debbie would be isolated, a marginalized listener excluded from participating when the rapid dialogue was not directed to her alone.

Getting 'a word in edgewise' is difficult in group settings under normal circumstances—ask any politician debating other candidates for office. To strike up a conversation with Debbie, it was clear that her listening and communication skills could improve best in one-on-one exchanges. Moreover, I learned how important it was to speak slowly to Debbie and give her sufficient time to put the words together, make sense of them, and formulate a response. Just because Debbie did not reply rapidly did not mean that she did not understand; she needed time to compose her thoughts and express them. The worse-case scenario was when she was excluded because visitors conversed with each other. One-on-one conversations between Debbie and a single other visitor were best for her recovery. Hereafter, this rule would be enforced. Several prized visitors put this rule to a test and proved its worth.

- **Let's Meet on the Road to Heaven**—Two additional sets of pastors contributed to Debbie's occupational and spiritual pursuits. Pastor Steve Ridenhour and his vicar intern, Amy, visited from Wytheville. Debbie relished their inspiring prayers. Enforcing the new visitation rules requiring only a single person in conversation with Debbie to facilitate Debbie's comprehension and maximize the attention she received, I first left the ordained minister and next his vicar alone with Debbie while in the private visitor's lounge I talked with the excluded visitor.

My private exchange with Pastor Ridenhour was emotional and supportive. I told him in graphic detail about Debbie's near death in the ICU when I saw Debbie's soul rise outside her body. "I am convinced that God had returned her restored soul to me and to her earthy existence. My mind was not playing tricks on my vision." Reverend Ridenhour was not in the least skeptical. He believed me.

Then he shared his story of one of his life experiences. "Chuck," he confided, "I have never told anyone about my experience because I feared that if I told them they would think that I was losing my sanity. Years ago I had eye surgery. I was lying on the operating table, and I could hear the doctors talking. I was very nervous and afraid. That's when I saw Jesus. I don't know what Jesus looks like, of course; I still don't. But I knew it was Him. Jesus said to me, 'Do not let your heart be troubled. Trust in God; trust also in me. In my Father's house are many rooms; if it were not so, I would have told you. I am going there to prepare a place for you' (John 14:1–3). This gave me peace for the duration of the procedure, and afterward I was excited about what I had seen and heard. I know this happened. It was not a hallucination. Chuck, I believe your story." We were experiential brothers in Christ.

Debbie and I also were visited by Rev. Steve Myer, escorting his former pastor in New Jersey accompanied by his stroke-survivor wife, Victoria. While Pastor Steve and Debbie talked, the new visitor regulations allowed me to hear in another room Victoria's motivating rehabilitation story. When Victoria was discharged from her rehabilitation hospital, at home she relentlessly struggled to recover for ten years, and her perseverance was rewarded. You would never know that she had suffered a devastating stroke. "I want you to see, Chuck, what can be achieved. Do not despair," Victoria said. "Observe the rewards of hard work and faith in God. Remember the apostle Paul's epistle: 'We are hard-pressed on every side, yet not crushed; we are perplexed, but not in despair; struck down, but not destroyed.' (2 Cor. 4:7–12). Debbie should take her unspeakable troubles to the Father. "We do not know what we ought to pray for, but the Spirit Himself intercedes for us through wordless groans' (Rom. 8:26). God's power can sustain all who suffer."

- **A Balancing Act**—OT concentrated on sitting, balance, and periodic standing exercises, during which Debbie put blocks into a basket and stacked objects such as poker chips and buttons. "I was asked to tie a bow, stack buckles, and use the 'arm bike' to turn the handles against resistance," Debbie recalled. "To be immodest, I did great. In addition, while standing I placed rings on a suspended rod, with both hands."

- **A Haircut**—Bathing lessons went well. That said, Elizabeth could no longer take looking at Debbie's hairball mess. Shampoo and disentangling conditioner had not helped. She was frustrated. "Could you cut Debbie's hair nest?" I suggested as I shoved a pair of scissors into her hands. Within seconds, the glob was gone. "Hair" today, gone tomorrow. Debbie looked 200 percent better, and when she was handed a mirror and could see the great results, she was glad she had nodded her consent. This was the psychological boost that Debbie needed, as did I. To round out the achievement, Debbie was able to wash her hands in the sink and brush her teeth.

- **Kept on the Bench**—I was still prohibited from conducting bed-to-wheelchair transfers, using the peg feeding tube and changing the colostomy bag, even though the discharge date was rapidly approaching. After dismissal Debbie would have to depend on me exclusively for all tasks. I needed to learn how to manage independently, but was reduced to a mere spectator. My patience waiting for instructions was wearing thin. I couldn't wait to be allowed to perform these important procedures, which needed to be undertaken many times during the day.

- **A Bag Man**—Finally, my training in preparation for Debbie's eventual discharge began. A nurse demonstrated how to safely change Debbie's colostomy pouch collecting bowel movements. The process looked simple, but it wasn't. I had to carefully push the skin away from the barriers with one hand and slowly peel the skin barrier with the other hand; next, wipe the skin around the stoma—the open stomach hole; then cut the right size in the plastic barrier surrounding the stoma hole; and finally place a new adhesive skin barrier over the stoma and squeeze shut the replacement pouch. Cutting with scissors the proper-sized barrier was a challenge, I learned later; the trainer made it look easy. I pledged to diligently try to learn the proper procedure.

LET'S GET PHYSICAL

- **The Naked Truth**—An example of Debbie's due diligence says it all. While Debbie took a nap, I took a much-needed walk. When I returned, I was in for an amazing surprise. Debbie had managed to strip herself naked! "I have to get out of bed for my next appointment," Debbie explained. "But it's not for another hour and a half," I said. "Oh. Well, I can wait, but I'm eager to get started."
- **Rolling**—"I managed to maneuver myself in my wheelchair—maybe 30 feet." More progress seemed, literally and figuratively, just around the corner. To prove that prognosis, within days Debbie rightly bragged, "I propelled myself in my wheelchair through the gym's exit door and around the corner to the hallway. I pushed myself in my wheelchair for twenty minutes!" Debbie told her therapist "I am encouraged. Let's keep pushing. And I wheeled myself another 150 yards in my chair."
- **No Time to Waste**—Another example of Debbie's due diligence occurred during a weekend when no session was scheduled. Debbie and I ventured outside to work on wheelchair mobility, and Debbie helped me push her wheelchair up a steep sidewalk incline to the small courtyard behind the hospital, where Debbie showed off performing voice exercises, such as repeating as loud as possible, "Aaaaah eeeeee." Before returning to the room, Debbie advised, "Let's do some more OT in the gym with the new toys you purchased." Why not? We did, and she did. Pieces were stacked, cards were shuffled, words were written, and crayons brought out Debbie's latent artistic talents.
- **A Leg Up**—Debbie's right-leg immobility was her biggest handicap. If she was ever going to be able to walk, this dysfunction had to be overcome. She just had to get a leg up. The physical therapist worked especially hard on Debbie's lower right body, with me watching from the mandated twenty feet away as ordered to prevent me from interfering and distracting. Electrical stimulation was applied

to Debbie's lower right leg, without any meaningful response. The failure showed all over Debbie's disappointed face; she was extremely frustrated. She desperately wanted to regain some control over movement in her whole leg, not just above the hip. Prolonged waiting for the curse of a paralyzed leg to be lifted was like waiting for a long war to end.

- **Walking the Line**—Debbie confessed, "I didn't dare reveal my fears but knew there were growing doubts that I would ever be able to use my right leg. That meant I would never walk. I was so frustrated and depressed. I didn't want Chuck to know the depths of my despair. So I prayed silently to God, 'Please, if it is your will, grant me the power to move my right leg.' I waited for His answer."

  Thanks to God's grace, the physical therapist engineered another miracle. After electrical stimulus, she asked Debbie to try to move for the first time her lower right leg, *and she did*! "Debbie, did you see what you just did?" the therapist excitedly asked. "You moved your leg about three inches."

  Debbie replied, "I prayed all night and day that God would give me the power to move my leg, and look, I did it." I applauded while I wept a waterfall of tears. It appeared that a major challenge was being met, and prayers had been answered. Sure, this was only a start, but it was humongous. Proverbially, "a trip of a thousand miles begins with a first step." Before we can step, we have to learn to move. Was recovery of all leg control a possibility?

- **Reflex?**—Was this response a singular fluke, an isolated muscle reflex? No way. The very next day, we received telling confirmation of Debbie's breakout moment: as she lay on the platform bed, Debbie's thrilling words echoed across the gym: "I moved my right leg!" Debbie was building on her success; her modest movement the prior day had not been an induced reflex in response to electrical stimulation. She really was recovering control of her lower right leg. Andy reported, "Chuck was overjoyed and in tears when the therapists ran another electro-stimulant test that generated a response in Debbie's right leg, and she took over the reactions herself, controlling her lower leg muscles." In Debbie's own words—"I slid my entire right leg on the exercise platform, but for the first time without electrical stimulation to get the brain-to-leg neural synapses coordinated. This was a great day. I also broke my record on my arm-strength tests."

The newly joined neural links were coupling new connections and replacing the formerly severed or unwired neural networks. This gradual linkage process can be likened to that of a romantic matchmaker, bringing the two parties together through first meetings likely to promote mutual attraction. By managing to move her entire right leg, Debbie had started down the aisle to the altar, where her future would be altered because once a neural connection between brain and body is made, it is forged forever; performance depends on strengthening the linkage through repetition.

- **Wheelchair Mobility**—Lying down and rising upright, standing and propelling a wheelchair weren't easy, but Debbie refused to take her weakness lying down. She made additional gains: "I did it. I passed my 'official' wheelchair mobility test in the hallway, exceeding 370 feet, and did the heavy lifting in a wheelchair trip outside and up a sidewalk hill to the small garden behind the rehab facility."
- **Stand Tall**—"I was asked to try and straighten my right leg while standing at the parallel bars, put my mind to the challenge, and succeeded. This was a big victory. Chuck cried. I didn't stop there. With great effort, I was able to stand upright without support." This achievement presaged additional advancements in functional capabilities that soon came.
- **"I Think I'll Be Able to Walk"**—One of Hilel's many visits provided the ultimate test of adherence to the new rules. He was always irrepressibly talkative and entertaining yet supportive. So when he returned to see Debbie, tell her some jokes, and give her words of encouragement, I violated the new rule so I could overhear the conversation by standing in the background keeping my thoughts to

myself. Hilel turned up the volume. "Sweetie, I am completely certain that you will be able to walk. There's no doubt. In time you will do it."

Debbie's face lit up the room. She was thrilled to hear his bold prediction. "Thank you, Hilel. Your confidence boosts my hope." Debbie promptly and proudly informed her physical therapist, "I think I will be able to walk." Debbie's faith in her progress was a key to her recovery, and her assuring statement boded well for her promising future.

DUE PROCESS

Due diligence was being rewarded. Gains far outnumbered setbacks. Each day was getting longer and warmer, and the light was pushing away the darkness. Spring had sprung. What was coming into view cannot be described as a trend line, because the direction was not linear. If the ups and downs, advances and retreats were charted on a timeline, the connected perturbations around the trajectory would resemble a zagged line pointing toward recovery.

Time would tell if this progress would continue or if additional perforated aneurisms would again take Debbie to the abyss. What would happen? None of us can help the things that life does to us. Life has an expiration date. Awareness of our mortality helps us value life. Yet it probably is a good thing that the future could not be foreseen. We were grateful for each additional day and were learning to take one day at a time.

Some distance had to be traveled to the finish line. How far was that line? We had no way of knowing, but did know painfully well that it was not in striking distance. True, Debbie's accomplishments were wearing deep tracks in the roadway to recovery. But the alarm clock to terminate the rehabilitation process in Carolinas Rehab was set, and time was running out.

The FIM evaluations confirmed that precedents for future progress were being established. Debbie had stepped forward every time it appeared that she might be hitting a plateau. Her FIM report stated that

"Debbie is making measurable progress. She is making impressive gains in grooming, bathing, lower body dressing, toilet training, assisted transfers, sitting, head control, range of motion, cognition, standing balance, wheelchair mobility, bed-to-wheelchair transfers, bed mobility, and swallowing. All told, the progress sought (and required for continuing health insurance coverage of rehabilitation) is being realized. The indicators are excellent."

Hilel reported, "The news has been steadily positive. Debbie constantly improves on all counts. She has some feeling in her right leg, and she now writes with her right hand. Chuck is always by her side during the exercises and meals. The March 19th discharge date is still just a week away, and Chuck is nervously waiting to learn about the surgeons' projected timetable for the anticipated brain surgery." The anxiety stimulated by Hilel's concluding note cast a dark cloud over Debbie's shiny rehabilitative victories.

- **"A No-Brainer"**—On March 12, I rushed at 5:45 a.m. to get Debbie ready for her 7:00 a.m. appointment for showering practice. Breezing past the wing's central desk, I was stopped in my tracks by Dr. Shemtov. "Chuck," she said,

> lend me your ears. I have news. This morning Dr. Grafton and I met with all members of Debbie's therapy team to hold our weekly FIM consultation. You'll love our decision. We all agreed that Debbie has been making terrific progress across all categories of evaluation and that we should not interrupt her therapy treatments next week. So we agreed to extend Debbie's stay in Carolinas Rehabilitation for an additional week, until March 26. I pushed for this, but the decision was easy. It was a no-brainer. I knew you would want to know, so I'm so glad that you came by now so I could tell you the good news.

I was ecstatic. Dr. Rachel could see my excitement soaring. I thanked her but kidded, "'No brainer.' Nice choice of words."

"Yeah, you're right." She laughed. "For someone who experienced a near-fatal brain surgery, I guess I should have found another way to tell you that the team's decision did not require much thought!" No apology needed; we both enjoyed the humor.

I ran to Debbie's room. "Debbie, your doctor just leaked some great news—our stay here has been extended for an additional week." Debbie got so excited she soaked her diaper and laughed hysterically. (I never suspected that these uncontrollable laughing fits sometimes causing her to wet her pants would become one of her stroke's long-term aftereffects. Other more-subtle personality changes could be expected.) "Debbie, I am so proud of you. You have dug into your resuscitation, never complaining about grueling tasks. You have been waging a war against dysfunctions and disabilities, and your due diligence has led to steady functional improvements. Your therapists saw that you would not allow a plateau to stop your progress. That is why you have been granted an extension. You earned it."

The best way to handle past disappointments is to trump them with triumphant celebration. We celebrated the breathing space that had been provided. Debbie's extension gave her time to proceed farther down the road to recovery.

- **Breakdown or Breakthrough?**—The breaking news put the brain surgery center stage. The neurosurgery team reviewed the recent MRI and CAT scans and made a puzzling announcement: they decided to delay the follow-on brain surgery for "another two to three weeks, perhaps much longer, to give Debbie more time to heal." Say what? Why wait? Was this decision warranted? Did it mean that Debbie was too weak, so another brain surgery during our extended stay at CMC was too risky? Or alternatively, maybe the tests showed Debbie was now no longer still in a definitive danger zone necessitating the preventive brain surgery, so postponement—perhaps a lengthy one—might be beneficial.

- **In Good Hands**—Debbie's doctors couldn't identify the causes of the consecutive hemorrhagic aneurisms and remained unable to detect either the presence or absence of a deteriorative vessel disease. Another hemorrhagic aneurism in her brain could erupt if a form of vasculitis was operative. Was the surgical delay really for the best? There was no option but to trust the expert doctors' judgment, and that was not really very hard to do. We had cultivated the highest respect for these talented surgeons; they had engineered miraculous surgeries that had on at least three or four occasions saved Debbie's life. There were no better hands on which to depend.

Well, actually, there were. We had God's almighty hands on our side. Debbie and I knew that we had never been exempt from the hits that life throws at us, but God's power could sustain us. God's grace was more than sufficient. Our Lord was making us strong. Yes, there had been a series of lost melodramatic battles along the long march of Debbie's journey, but each time she had another life-threatening crisis, miraculous surgeries saved her so she could march forward. There is no doubt that Jesus had overseen the recoveries from each lost battle. We would continue to call on our Lord—the Light that knows no dark—for protection and healing.

- **Do or Die**—We managed to hold anxieties about subsequent surgeries and discharge dates in check and counted our blessings. There were many. God was turning on His light. Fortified by faith and a surge of determination, I could see vitality rising up within Debbie, mixed with defiance—the opposite of resignation. Debbie was dedicated to persevere, determined to valiantly overcome all of her disabilities. Because she would not let her morale be undermined, my morale also grew. Through the process, we were changing, becoming in our own self-images something we were not previously.
- **Identity Lost and Found**—Everyone values high self-esteem. We all make assumptions about how others perceive us. These identities usually tilt toward the positive; we naturally are inclined to imagine that others think of us favorably.

I could only guess how Debbie thought others perceived her. No one can know another person's self-image. Hers had to be positive, given the feedback she received. My own self-image was another matter. The response of friends and family to my reactions during this time of traumatized trial forced me to strike down some beliefs I had about how these dear people perceived me. Some prideful illusions were shattered.

Discovery came about when a number of friends told me that they were surprised at my dedicated forbearance attending to Debbie's perpetual nurturing. "You've been through a lot, for a long time now, Chuck," a friend asserted, painfully adding, "Many never thought you had it in you."

I was dismayed. In their eyes, who was the real me—a selfish happy-go-lucky fortunate fellow who enjoyed the good times but was not up to the task of dealing with adversity? My feelings were hurt. In my self-image, I never doubted that I could rise to the challenge of giving Debbie, without concern for my own comfort, unrelenting care in her time of greatest need.

Apparently, others' tarnished image of me improved as I responded to Debbie's plight. Friends began to see a new "me." For example, Hilel wrote, "I have now begun to appreciate Chuck's unbelievable love and fortitude. He has been a superhero in my eyes." Similarly, I was proud when Debbie overheard her nurse say, "That guy sure loves his wife. I wish my husband cared for me as much as Chuck loves Debbie."

I learned how much I loved Debbie, in ways that probably would not have been possible had we not been forced to look at death in the face. Our dark, troubled journey brought out the best in me. It is easier to be aware of headwinds—events that present heartbreaking barriers—than of tailwinds, which can give us false pride and overconfidence. Debbie's strokes produced a hurricane-level headwind, which enabled me to see myself and my life story and my identity more objectively.

Likewise, the catastrophic strokes heightened our appreciation for each other and what our treasured relationship truly was. "I always felt you loved me," Debbie told me, "but before my stroke, I did not really know that you loved me this much. Your constant loving care for me has shown me the depths of your love. Thank you for loving me." "You're welcome," I replied. "Seeing you in such desperate need has taught me, too. I have always loved you. I found out how much when I thought I might lose you. In our distress, desolation, and desperation, I found out who I am and why God brought you to me. My purpose is to love you, my loving wife, and to take care of you. I found my true self—who I was meant to be—through you, Debbie. Thank you for being my wife, and for loving me. You give me so much. What happened to you has allowed me to find myself. We are so blessed to have each other!"

We learned from our hardships. This was adversity's unforeseen gift. Hardship does not spell heartache. We compared our prior premises, reevaluated them, and deduced new meanings and self-knowledge. Our trials of troubles had not defeated us; the weary journey was not altogether dreary.

Eugene O'Neill was right when he wrote that none of us can help the things that happen to us—many things do happen in life which cannot be helped or explained. However, O'Neill was mistaken in seeing life as dark as a morgue, with the things that happen making us do other things, which inevitability lead to the loss of our true selves forever. We are not doomed to lose our souls. We can find our true selves—our souls, the person we were always meant to be—because the Holy Spirit allows us to "understand what God has freely given us" (1 Cor. 2:12). All we have to do is to lean toward the light of God's love and let the Holy Spirit within us call us "out of darkness into His wonderful light" (1 Pet. 2:9; John 14:16–17).

The horrific things that happen after a stroke strikes can empower anyone to find their true character—who they really are. Our long journey had begun with unspeakably severe pain as we faced a circumstance that belongs at the end of life. Often, at the edge of existence people sometimes wander in the dark, and fail to take advantage of their last opportunity to evaluate the meaning of life and destiny. We were not among them. In the depth of despair, our blinders came off and the darkness began to disappear. We began to extract from our seemingly intolerable crises illuminating insights. The distinct colors, like those in a rainbow, began to become visible. Night was becoming day. We untangled some of the knots in our minds. We were finding, not losing, our true selves. As we called on God for help and placed complete trust in Him, we found revelations. The words of Hebrews describe the awareness sweeping through our minds: "Now faith is the substance of things hoped for, the evidence of things not seen" (11:1). Enlightenment comes in life's darkest hour.

CHAPTER 21

THE DAWN'S EARLY LIGHT

§

Change. Starts. Stops. Surprise. Hope. Fear. Uncertainty. These were some of the salient signposts along our long night's journey into day. Our highway was liberally littered with many billboards displaying these words.

The billboard "Uncertainty Ahead" advertised the truth—we knew very little about Debbie's future fate. We knew what we didn't know, and there was almost no limit to the bottomless pit of the unknown. The hidden face of fate generates insecurities. The factors beyond control and comprehension were infinite. The only thing we knew for sure about the future was that God would remain with us and for us. That knowledge carried us forward.

The fifth week of rehabilitation in Charlotte featured some experiences that were new and some that were familiar. History was repeating itself. That augured well. Why? Because overall, despite head-scratching setbacks, Debbie's recovery was advancing. We aimed to push the achieved momentum forward at a faster pace. The new elongated discharge date was really not that long away. We were pressed to take full advantage in the remaining time of the outstanding therapy support we were receiving. But talk about the "unknown." What would happen in the wake of departure from Charlotte? Would we be prepared?

A Delayed Deadline and Enduring Dread

Every day we traveled the roadway one step at a time. Step followed step. From Andy: "A new social worker has helped with Chuck and Debbie's options after their discharge from the rehabilitation hospital, though they retain lingering hope that there could be still another extension. Chuck says they're looking less at skilled nursing facilities and more at out-patient health care options."

- **An Exit Postponed**—Progress was moving ahead rapidly. Debbie successfully worked with a calculator and handwriting despite some hand tremors, and swallowed without a full chin tuck. The occupational therapist oversaw a variety of tasks while Debbie stood at a table. Then that therapist violated protocol and leaked hints about a decision that we would hear about later. It was enough to infer that this had to be welcome news.

    We couldn't wait to hear what the staff had to say. "God, give me patience, and do it now!" Debbie teased. Then we heard the awesome news: The therapy team agreed to extend Debbie's stay at our rehab facility again—for another week, all the way to April 2! All the members of the staff supported this huge decision, which they felt would allow time for Debbie to meet some ambitious new goals. This would, we were warned, be the last extension. "We'll take it," Debbie and I both thought. We were in no hurry to exit.

    "This is great news," Hilel wrote. "Debbie's actual progress has been sensational. She is living proof that one can be inordinately sweet and nice and be tough as well. I am firmly convinced that she will be able to walk. Her cognitive powers improve daily and they are already far ahead of anything anyone could have predicted. It also gives me and many of you an opportunity to gear up and plan on helping them in real, substantive ways."

    The extension meant that it was possible to achieve more goals. However, even with the extended departure date, it was growing very unlikely that Debbie would undergo a brain-aneurism surgery before she left the hospital. Hanging over the road was the dark danger that a brain-vessel hemorrhage could again occur and that all the progress that had been achieved could be destroyed. We pledged to face the looming risks, armed with the thought that our loving God, after carrying Debbie this far, would not allow such a catastrophe to happen.

- **The Liabilities of Disabilities**—George and Cathy Crow visited and took turns talking and praying with Debbie while I conversed with this amazing couple's other half. "Chuck," George advised, "under our heavenly Father's care, Debbie has made incredible progress. However, obviously she still has a long way to go. I think you should prepare yourself for the necessity, after discharge, of placing Debbie in a skilled-nursing facility for at least two or three weeks. These have full nurse and doctor support staffs, like a regular hospital, so she will be safe. The downside is considerable, however. You could not stay with her—only visit during the day. And I must admit that the therapy is very weak—close to nonexistent. These facilities are mostly for bedridden people in their eighties and nineties."

Debbie's disabilities were transparent, but I didn't want to face the fact of Debbie's severe continuing incapacities. George's honest assessment of her functional impairments was undeniably accurate, which is why he advised that precaution should overrule risks. I hoped that George's pessimistic assessment was mistaken. His depiction of skilled-nursing facilities made them sound as appealing as a death-row prison. I was sure I needed to be with Debbie twenty-four seven, and she with me; a skilled-nursing hospital precluded that and would certainly prevent Debbie from continuing her fast pace. The only solution at the time was for Debbie and I to try, in the time that remained, to hasten her recovery so that the next step would be, instead, a home health care arrangement where I could be with her and where at least some therapy sessions could be performed.

I called Debbie Clark, seeking her expert advice. "Your friend Pastor Crow is probably correct, Chuck. Better safe than sorry. Let me do some investigative research on options in the Columbia area. All three types of facilities—skilled-nursing, home health care, and outpatient rehabilitation centers—are rated." I closed our cell phone conversation by saying, "Remember what Andy's e-mail update said about my preferences, writing, 'Chuck says they're looking less at skilled-nursing facilities and more at outpatient home health care options.'" Debbie Clark understood well our preference but did not have a say in the doctors' choices. A preference is not a plan; a posture is not a policy; a position is not a program. The therapists and doctors held our future in their hands.

I could not help brooding. We had developed a psychological dependence on our rehabilitation center and did not want to wander from our reliable setting into the vast unknown wilderness. I did not want to face this frontier. I did my best to hide from Debbie my worries about our journey's next stop. A subsequent private call to George Crow provided the comfort I needed. George sensed the desperation in my voice. "Things will work out for the best. Let's call on our Lord for recovery sufficient for Debbie to skip a detour in a skilled-nursing center. Keep the faith."

The new discharge date led to some subtle modifications in therapies, with exercises concentrating on the capabilities most required for Debbie's firmly scheduled exit, such as work on her right leg and foot, wheelchair mobility and showering. Debbie was elated, energized, and eager to get on with the needed therapies. She was all business.

PREPARING FOR A FORCED EXIT: THE WILL, THE SKILL, AND SOME THRILLS

Debbie had the will (a motivated work ethic) and the skill (resolute effort) to engineer the changes required to tenaciously move from tenuous capabilities toward greater functional autonomy. How far down the road would these traits take her? Time would tell. There wasn't much remaining time to find out.

Let the record show some significant advances that reduced some fears. You can sniff the flavor of what was brewing from some select savory highlights.

- **A Fast Break**—As Debbie sat in her wheelchair to break the fast of overnight fasting, no sooner had she swallowed small sips from a straw than we were told, "This will be the last day of your participation in the Breakfast Club. Debbie, you have met all the goals we hoped to achieve. Your supervised swallowing has succeeded, and you have been a model for social interaction for the other patients to emulate. Congratulations." Surprised, Debbie blurted, "Let me express my appreciation. I have enjoyed all of you and your company. Chuck and I are very grateful. We shall miss you and pray for you."

  Candidly, we were somewhat relieved. The Breakfast Club's rigid schedule was rather burdensome. Moreover, the benefits of participation were declining because the learning curve had flattened. To Debbie's credit, the attending staff directed more and more of the conversation to Debbie for leadership and to fill in the loud sounds of prolonged silence. That was a tribute. It was time to move on.

- **Training Trials**—The therapists were zealous in pursuit of excellence. They put me into intense training under their critical eyes. Let's just say they were demanding, and it was difficult for me to reach their high standards. I had no trouble getting most tasks done, but not at a level with which they were satisfied. This was problematic if I were to become the skilled caregiver I needed to be. In preparation for our departure, it was imperative that I could master transfers, showers, and many other procedures. I was all Debbie had, and I was not enough.

  The hill grew steeper when I was scolded, "Chuck, under no circumstances will we permit you to try to negotiate a transfer by yourself." I reluctantly submitted, even though this posed a big inconvenience when Debbie needed to transfer from her bed to her wheelchair, and I had to fetch a nurse to conduct the operation.

Debbie tried to boost my confidence, saying, "You are as capable of performing this task as well or better than some of the nurse assistants."

Our occupational therapist stepped into the breach, offering Debbie instructions to assist with her transfers. "Debbie, count 'one, two, three' each time you lean forward before rising upright to reach for your wheelchair's cross armrest, and pivot to sit in the chair." Elizabeth then observed my independent management of some trial transfers and nodded approvingly. She next oversaw Debbie try to bake brownies in the kitchen. They were delicious. Everyone wanted a taste.

- **Date Night**—The rehab center contained a separate private living area with a furnished kitchen, living room, bedroom, and restroom, which the hospital had equipped in order for patients and their spouses to simulate some degree of normalcy. The purpose went beyond the chance this would provide for intimate companionship. The "date" was designed also to test our capacity to practice regular home-living, including such tasks as administration of meals through the feeding tube and changes of Debbie's colostomy bag. Guess what? That apartment had been reserved for our use overnight on March 29. We could spend the night together! A date. We couldn't wait. Debbie wheeled herself so we could sneak a peek together. We liked what we saw. I planned ahead to purchase a candle and some matches so the setting could glow in warmth.
- **Walking the Walk**—Debbie took a big step closer to her walking goals, and was understandably proud of her accomplishment, telling John and Mary "At PT today I managed to pull myself out of my wheelchair onto the parallel bars. I was able to stand without using the bars by placing most of my weight on my left leg, and then stepped forward dragging my right leg in a simulation of actual walking." The next day Debbie took the next big step. She managed to climb unassisted out of her wheelchair, stood upright, grasped a walker, and marched forward pulling her right foot with the aid of what

Erin called a slider. Debbie shone as she declared, "Look, Chuck, look. I used the walker aided by a foot slider. This is an aid used for my 'drop foot' disability; basically it is a plastic plate strapped to my right foot which allows me to walk." "I know, darling. Didn't you see me watching and cheering? I wouldn't have missed this for anything. I am so proud of you! You will be walking in no time." The following day Debbie trudged twenty feet using her walker and slider.

- **Road Ready?**—"Chuck," Erin ordered, "tomorrow we will begin work preparing Debbie to transfer from her wheelchair to the passenger seat of your car. I want to inspect your car, give instructions, and test Debbie's ability. Have your car ready outside the rehab turnabout driveway. This process could take three days before I can check this achievement off my list."

To cut to the chase, this important experiment was undertaken the next day. Debbie jumped into the challenge with her usual enthusiasm, and we succeeded the very first try. Debbie was road ready. "No need for more of this," a relieved Erin joyfully exclaimed. "Debbie, you did great; Chuck, you did better than I expected with this transfer. We're done! Debbie will push her wheelchair back to the gym while you repark your car. Meet us. I will work on Debbie's use of her walker until you arrive." Good, bold plan, I thought as I powered our car into the parking garage.

Of course, my prized parking space near the third-floor elevator was now occupied, and I began a lengthy search in the crowded garage for another. At last I located a car exiting and approached that vacating space when, from the opposite direction, a van also made its approach. The driver pulled down his window and shouted, "It's mine. I never back up for a fool." "I always do," I responded, as I put our car in reverse gear and renewed my search. At last I found a space on the roof-top parking level. Locking our vehicle, I ran to join Debbie and Erin.

Guess what I found. Debbie was doing great walking with her walker—by herself, with Erin "spotting" her from behind in case

Debbie started to fall. She wore a bright yellow bracelet on her wrist, which read "Fall Risk" to instruct people that Debbie should be watched carefully, and to remind Debbie, in the words of St. Paul, "If you think you're standing firm, be careful you don't fall" (1 Cor. 10:12).

Debbie's accomplishment sent chills down my spine. Use of a walker could conceivably, with practice, substitute for a wheelchair. In time, I trusted, Debbie would be able to use the walker to walk farther than the twenty feet she managed this first time. More feet looked like a likely feat. No telling what might someday be achieved.

- **Hard to Swallow**—Janet was eager in ST to see how far Debbie had advanced swallowing with the chin tuck. Overall, Janet was impressed. Knowing the discharge date was only a week away, as a precaution, Janet scheduled another set of x-rays to make sure no food particles had been aspirated into her lungs. Thankfully the scans detected no substantial problems. This was a big relief. Bitter experience had taught us the risks that could suddenly appear, slowing or terminating the progress that had been made.

- **Changing a Colostomy**—The nurse coordinator came to our room full of smiles. I secretly hoped it was not because she would soon be liberated from all my bothersome inquiries. Instead, the purpose was to give me a test. With subtle sarcasm, she asked, "Chuck, can you competently change the colostomy bag?" I rose to the challenge and did it, slowly and carefully. "Okay, I think you're ready, Chuck. Practice to prepare for your exit, with a nurse watching but not coaching."

- **Heading to the Highway**—Hilel paid us another visit, and greeted Debbie with his customary "Hi, Sweetie.". They teased about having me bumped off so they could run away together. "You're doing terrifically, sweetie," Hilel applauded. His e-mail reported, "I am amazed at the incredible progress Debbie has made. She was sitting upright in her wheelchair, no longer whispering but speaking clearly, smiling and laughing. She threw one of her pillows onto a nearby chair *with* *her right arm.* She moved her right leg much more easily than she had been able to during my previous visit. She is determined to be able to walk by the time she returns to Blythewood. Chuck looks a bit thin and this is all starting to hit him."

- **Psychological Warfare and Welfare**—A session was scheduled with the resident psychologist to determine if we were mentally prepared for our approaching discharge. Disability often breeds disillusionment, depression, and a loss of self-worth; if patients lose hope that their lives will improve, they tend to retreat from interactions with others, feeling rejected and marginalized. This response can be ruinous. Psychotherapy can help victims to hang onto hope and avoid withdrawal from the world. So there were good reasons for this session.

  "It's good to see you, Chuck," our psychologist said as we entered her office, to which I joked, "That can't be true." I was curious why she addressed me first. I soon found out that my supposition was correct—that I appeared very anxious about the pending discharge. "Tell me how you feel," she pushed.

  "Oh, frankly, about like an addict trying to shake dependence on cocaine; facing our discharge, I feel a painful withdrawal about the prospect of leaving the rehab center. Debbie and I have developed a subconscious dependence on the support and medical care we receive here. It is worrisome to think about losing this. The word 'discharge' has a scary ring to it; 'an eviction notice' somehow seems more apt."

  Our shrink calmed me down and in the process reassured Debbie. "Rehabilitation," she counseled, "is never complete. It is akin to lifelong education. It should never cease. But when a crossroads is reached, the time arises to end one location for rehab and take another path to a new location. Think of your discharge as a graduation. When you graduate, usually there is a commencement. Debbie, you are about to commence the end of rehabilitation here and resume it elsewhere."

• **A Black Hole or a Rainbow?**—Dr. Grafton went out of her way to see us in our room. She had some news and wanted to inform us face to face. "The neurosurgery team," she announced, "will not perform the brain surgery during your remaining time here. They want to run some more MRI and CAT scans in radiology tomorrow morning and expect the results, when carefully reviewed, to be encouraging enough for you Chuck to bring Debbie back to CMC at 6:00 a.m. on April 8. At that time, the neurosurgeons will conduct still more images of brain vessels, compare the results with those from tomorrow, and decide whether to proceed with this surgery. So on April 8 when you return to Charlotte, be sure to pack for an extended stay in intensive care. Dr. Shemtov and I know that it would have been preferable to schedule this operation while here in CMC, instead of the next week only six days after discharge. We both recommended that. But we will just have to live with this schedule."

Our hearts sank. This decision was like a celestial black hole—a gravitational choice pulling Debbie into a dark tunnel from which light can't escape. There was no telling where the surgery would lead. It could conceivably be preemptive, repairing the blistered vessels where the first aneurism had burst January 8 to cause the stroke, to prevent new hemorrhages. Then again, the preventive operation could result in myriad new disabilities and even be lethal.

Debbie and I knew all along that this day would eventually occur. Still, given Debbie's steady progress with no serious setbacks, as each day passed, the prospects of a catastrophe seemed increasingly remote. We had dealt with the dread of potential death by denial—blocking our minds from the blinding shutter that this "black hole" surgery would exert on our sight.

Dr. Grafton was empathetic about our plight. "How does this make you feel?" she soothingly inquired. "Oh," I answered, "about like someone trying skydiving whose parachute didn't open." "But this might just possibly be the best plan," she reasoned. "Debbie has world-class surgeons in control, and they know what they're doing.

They know what they don't know, and this is a sign of wisdom. The radiology reports need to be studied and then an informed decision reached about the need for another operation. The situation is not necessarily desperate."

Dr. Grafton was right, of course. It *was* possible that Debbie was not in serious danger. Debbie and I gazed outside the window at that moment of reflection, and a ray of light—a sunbeam—broke through the clouds. A rainbow materialized. It was breathtakingly beautiful. Surely it was a sign from above, from our heavenly Father, that He was in full control. "The Lord is our light" (Ps. 27:1). This display of God's awesome power—a rainbow reminder of God's promise to protect—shattered our fears. All that was missing was the appearance of a snow white dove signifying that life could resume.

- **A Decision about the Next Destination**—Dr. Grafton placed a punctuation mark on our restored hope. She pointed to a figurative ark affording safety from drowning in a dangerous flood. She defined where our journey would take us: "You should know," she said, "that we and the therapists have seen Debbie make such great progress. For that reason, we feel confident for you to scratch from your options a skilled-nursing facility after your discharge here. As it looks now, home health care treatment appears to be the best approach when you return to your home in South Carolina. In fact, the hospital's social worker has been asked to explore facilities near your home and make some recommendations. I advise you to seek advice from friends"—a step already underway. George Crow and Debbie Clark had started to explore possibilities.

The sunbeam was so bright that the black hole blocking light imploded. We began to accept the news of the discharge date, which was starting to look less and less like an eviction notice.

Soon thereafter we heard more encouraging news—the referral to Countryside Home Health Care had been accepted. That good news eliminated any concerns about having to first travel to a skilled-nursing facility. Less reassuring was that the first member of the staff, a nurse, could not be scheduled until Friday, April 4. Maybe this wasn't so bad; it would give us a full day to recover from our homeward trip and adapt to living in our own home.

- **A Thrill**—The bottomless pit of skilled-nursing confinement was escaped. We were thrilled. Rainstorms of excited emotion washed away some doubts and dreads. "Chuck just called," Andy announced,

> to say they are 99% certain they will be returning to their home in Blythewood, and a stay in a step-down skilled nursing hospital is unnecessary. They are relieved. More positives—the therapists finally approved Chuck to assist moving/transferring Debbie from her wheelchair to bed and vice versa. Chuck understands their date night this weekend is a test to see how well they do without supervision or assistance. He said they are learning to be self-sufficient. I spoke with Debbie briefly, and she sounded remarkably great, almost as if nothing has happened. She told me "Andy, I performed squats with my stronger left leg elevated on a box while my arms were crossed. I was asked to try using the personal computer. No problem. I swung into action, and mastered each step of the experiment with ease. Chuck—a complete stranger to computer technology—was amazed."

- **Escort Service**—George and Cathy Crow came for a visit. George presented a present: "I talked with Pastor John Ropp at our church. Chuck, your sense of direction, especially under stress, is suspect. We want to drive to Charlotte the morning of Debbie's discharge, lead you back to Blythewood, and assist lifting Debbie in her wheelchair safely into your home. Okay?" Was it ever!
- **A Scary Story**—an attendant arrived next to escort Debbie, with me trailing, to the radiology station for Debbie's scheduled screenings. The escort staffer said, "So you're a professor. One of my close friends was a forty-year-old professor. He took his first overseas

vacation, assuming that he was safe flying in the plane's oxygen-pressured cabin. However, when the jet took off, he had a stroke and died." I hoped Debbie had not overheard this scary story. It reminded me that a stroke can strike anyone, anywhere at any time; there was no safe haven from such a devastating threat. We had learned the hard way that no one can prevent destruction from happening.

- **A Mitten Message**—Debbie observed the stress in my face when I asked, "Can I put on your protective mittens and tie them so they won't come off?" She knew that I knew she had learned to untie and remove her mittens at will, and that this made me anxious.

- "I'm so sorry," she said. I don't mean to give you cause for worry. The mittens do bother me. But I know I need them to prevent me from pulling my feeding tube or colostomy bag out while I sleep. I promise you I'll try not to. However, I can't really control my impulses when I'm sleeping. So please, for my protection and your peace of mind, go ahead and tie them. You can even ask our nurse to tie the mittens to the bed to increase the security." Bless her. What more could I ask of her? We made it through that night.

- **From Denial to Acceptance**—During our last weekend, Debbie and I found ourselves in a restless mood. We began to recognize the depth of disadvantages posed by the rehabilitation schedule. With nothing arranged, we were on our own. This was not a new revelation, of course; we knew weekends were largely "off days" from professional treatment. But now, from the vantage point of an approaching discharge, we asked ourselves, "What are we doing here?" We could be doing the same things at home on weekends. We mentally prepared for our exit to the next stop. It may have been our imagination, but our room began to appear much smaller—less comfortable, less attractive. And the nuisance of nurses' schedules for meals, medicines, and tubal feedings and colostomy changes began to annoy. Maybe the freedom of independent choice was to be preferred.

- **A Hot Date**—We had been eagerly looking forward to "date night." We could enjoy each other in the privacy of the hospital apartment. I was pumped. Debbie was excited. Nurse Nora packed us with medicines and supplies and bid us adieu. "Have a great night on your own," she said in her farewell. Debbie pushed her wheelchair down the hall. "If you need serious help, call us; but you shouldn't have any troubles. This is a test of your self-sufficiency when you return home."

We arrived at the apartment charged with excited anticipation. As soon as we entered, our expectations were instantly crushed. The apartment was as hot and humid as a day at the equator during monsoon season.

We were frustrated. "Hold on, Debbie," I pleaded, "I'll see what I can do to get this situation fixed. Let's unload our supplies in the bedroom, and I'll round up some help." It was then that we made another disgusting discovery: the room was not just hot. It was dirty. The bed had not even been changed, and the sink and commode were soiled. "Let me get to the bottom of this now. Can you wait for me here, or, if it's too hot, in the hallway?" I asked.

"Sure," Debbie responded. Debbie was much better than I dealing with small crises. "Don't sweat the small stuff," Debbie counseled. "It's all small stuff."

Off I bolted to the reception desk. Naturally, the staffer knew nothing about the oversight. She did not want to take any responsibility, insisting that someone else had failed to do his or her job properly. "Can you at least call the hospital electrical technician to fix the broken temperature gauge?" I pleaded. "Okay, I can do that."

What to do next? I raced back to our C wing and explained our disappointing predicament. The staff was profusely apologetic and said, "Someone let us down. The apartment was to be prepared for you. If you want, you and Debbie can return to your room for the night."

"No way—let's see if the situation can be fixed—we want to take advantage of the all-nighter that had been scheduled," I insisted.

"Okay, we'll send help to clean the room right away, and we'll call the hospital engineer to confirm that he will repair the heat/air system." This was the support we sought.

I ran back to Debbie. Turning a hallway corner, I almost knocked over Debbie's head neurosurgeon, Dr. Hunter Dyer. We were both surprised to see each other. "I was stopping over here at the rehab center to pay a visit to a friend before heading home before the Saturday-night drunks hit the road. He's not in his room, Chuck. Let me use this time while I'm here to see Debbie," Dr. Dyer said. I was thrilled. This was a silver lining to a bad circumstance.

Dr. Dyer and I hurried to the apartment, where a technician was already busy trying to repair the thermostat. Hunter greeted Debbie and was visibly amazed at Debbie's strength and healing. A huge smile graced his face. "Debbie, you're doing great! I can't wait until April 8 when our neurosurgery team will give your brain vessels a thorough examination. From what I see now, I have a measure of confidence about what we'll find that I didn't have before this meeting. Keep up the good work. You too, Chuck." Overjoyed, we thanked Dr. Dyer for his visit in his busy schedule. Hunter accepted the gratitude and said his farewell: "This event made my visit to Carolinas Rehabilitation worthwhile. I'm glad this happened. Hope your room is restored, and you can enjoy your evening date together."

To make a long story short, the technician got the air conditioner working and ordered two big fans to be delivered to our apartment to expedite the cooling (I asked both fans to be directed at our twin bed—which now had clean sheets and pillowcases.) Our "hot" date lived up to its name. We at last could hold each other in our arms. "All's well that ends well," Shakespeare wrote. The next morning, we showered and dressed in time to give more thanks to our Lord at the rehab's church service.

• **Amazing Grace**—During that final worship service, Pastor Paul Doyle gave an inspiring sermon about God's faithfulness to those in need of His healing. This message provided perfect spiritual medicine. But the sermon for the ten worshippers included a shocking revelation. "I know what you are going through," Pastor Paul disclosed, "because I am one of you. I am fighting brain cancer. I am only forty-one. But I am not afraid. I know that God will protect me, as I see Him protecting all of you. Take heart. The Lord is with you—and me."

There was not a dry eye in the room. Oddly, we felt uplifted even while we witnessed a wonderful pastor's ability through his faith to subdue his fears. If in his time of terrible trouble, Reverend Paul could so confidently place his trust in our Lord and receive relief from his suffering, so could all of us. Debbie and I had. We were pulled from the flames of fire by our faith in our God. With Him, for Him, by Him—we knew we could survive because of His grace.

This incident was another reminder that no one can count on avoiding life-threatening diseases and disasters. Who knows why bad things sometimes happen to good people? None of us really can help the things that happen to us. Adversity, however, can lead us away from earthy temptation and toward greater faith in God's ultimate glory. We should be mindful of God's grace, in good times and in bad. Paradoxically, tough times tend to make for greater appreciation of God's blessings and for preparation of our journey after life to a new eternal life. Everyone can live twice—once when they're born, and once again after death when they are reborn in communion with their Lord. After a stroke strikes, survivors can cope with impairments without being consumed or destroyed by them. Struggle makes sufferers stronger.

"HIT THE ROAD, JACK, AND DON'T COME BACK NO MORE"

"All is on track for the return to Blythewood," Andy predicted, "where the return to normalcy will take on new meaning. It sounds like Chuck is beginning to accept his new responsibilities which will be unlike the last three months. Therapy will continue, and they are anxious to begin working with the home-health staff once they are situated. Here's to their safe and quiet return home—the answer to prayers! That isn't to say there won't be many more prayers in the coming months."

- **Readied for a Road Trip**—The rehab staff allocated the remaining time preparing both of us for our approaching journey home. The therapists continued their regular drills and oversight of tasks like changing the colostomy bag. The hospital's equipment manager delivered the rental wheelchair customized to Debbie's size and weight, as well as the portable commode to deposit urine for home use. I purchased a shower bench and hauled it to our car. We were ready to return home, where home health care was scheduled to be provided.

- **Charting a Path**—Even though we had not departed, plans were already underway to finalize the next destination if and when our home care would end and rehabilitation at a new rehabilitation facility might then begin. Carolinas Rehab had jumped ahead in preparation, submitting a referral to Health South Rehabilitation in Columbia, which readily agreed to accept Debbie's eventual therapy there if and when the home health care's goals were met.

  In anticipation for that crossroad, I made a mental note to find a builder capable of constructing a ramp so we could use Debbie's wheelchair to and from our Blythewood porch to our garage without heavy-lifting by helpers to carry her up and down two sets of five steep steps. All in all, preparations were made for the path to the next station on our long journey.

- **Parting Is Such Sweet Sorrow**—We were growing confident that the need for funeral eulogies was looking increasingly premature. On April 1, the eve of our exit, a skilled musician played joyful hymns on a harp cerebrating God's glory—not music suitable for a requiem. We were given final instructions and told that the discharge "would happen after tomorrow's breakfast. Be ready and packed by 9:15 a.m."

  By sheer coincidence, the day before our discharge happened to be April Fool's Day. The last thing we expected was some kind of prank. We should have known better. Andy wrote, "Can you believe it has been 83 days since Debbie landed in Carolinas Medical

Center? Chuck told me this morning that this was his last call to me from there. Of course, not 15 minutes later, he had to call again, to pass along the trick he had fallen for: the therapists told him 'Debbie wasn't passing enough tests to go home, so they were postponing the discharge indefinitely.'"

Not to be outdone, and never missing a chance to lighten moods with his wit, Hilel jocularly added,

> the convoy back to Blythewood is about to happen. George Crow is going to go up to Charlotte and do the trailing. Having had Chuck follow me in his car here in Charlottesville, I'm glad that it will be a man of the cloth. I know that if it were me doing this, my East Bronx upbringing might lead me to utter some scatological and blasphemous words (probably no more than a hundred). Herman Rich had promised to be on a red alert during that time, and I had not only gotten the U.S. Air Force and National Guard to be prepared, but was on the verge of hiring some Native Americans ('Indians' is not politically correct anymore) to burn a path from the hospital to the Interstate. I wasn't sure about doing that for the road from the Interstate to Chuck's home, because I'm ever the optimist.

Debbie and I should have seen these stunts coming. We chuckled as we finished packing for departure. And off we went.

CHAPTER 22

HOME HEALTH CARE

❧

D ebbie and I were eager to hit the road to our home, and begin the next leg of our long journey. After our quick breakfast, many Carolinas Rehab staff members came by for a cheery but teary good-bye. Then, like clockwork, the Reverends George and John arrived early and helped load belongings, and "Hot Rod" Crow put the pedal to the metal while I tried to trail; Debbie rode shotgun, talking excitedly as she gazed upon countryside instead of a hospital campus.

AT HOME!

Debbie and I both had lumps in our throats as our house came into view. Hanging across our garage was a huge banner saying WELCOME HOME DEBBIE! Inflated balloons hung from tree limbs and shrubs. These were heartwarming. I transferred Debbie to her wheelchair, and George and John carried Debbie down and up the steps to our porch. We made it safely home!

Communications Central announced our safe return home. Andy wrote, "Chuck's message to me said he only had two near traffic accidents, and that as the discharge staff was working with them this morning, Debbie told Chuck, 'just calm down!' They are home, and here's to a very calm, quiet and healthy recovery." John and Mary added, "Chuck and Debbie finally can begin a new chapter in their lives. We are so encouraged by Debbie's progress and know that her home environment will speed her recovery and help Chuck relax a bit. We suspect that phone calls will be less frequent, as Chuck will be a busy guy in the days ahead."

Pastors George and John stayed busy helping. John installed a protective sheet and remade our king-size bed. (Later, I teased John "You had a lot of nerve—you didn't even return the next morning to make the bed; what kind of room service is that?") George meanwhile entertained Debbie and carted in huge loads from the cars. The portable commode was constructed and the shower bench put into place. Hugs were exchanged, and the four of us held hands as we prayed. "Oh," George said while exiting, "Betty Nelle Presley from Northeast Presbyterian is on the way here with a homecoming meal. Now this was one very appetizing surprise!

As predictably as a sunrise, Betty Nelle appeared, carrying wonderful covered dishes for a great dinner. She was accompanied by Renatta Loquist and Cathy Crow. We proudly displayed the beautiful quilt Cathy had made for Debbie. "Debbie," Renatta then asked, "Will you let us help you and Chuck? You know most of the women serving on the Care Team because for years you were active in the women's Focus Bible study group. When I told them about your stroke and asked the ladies who wanted to join Debbie Kegley's team, to visit and bring home-cooked meals, every hand shot up. They all love you. Are you interested?" "You bet—I am thrilled."

Renatta expected Debbie's enthusiastic approval, and put herself first in line. The next day she brought another meal and jumped into action. She presented a timetable of the Care Team's schedule for the rest of the month, and instructed "Chuck, take a break from your round-the-clock caretaking and get in a much-needed run and workout in the Cobblestone gym, unless you prefer to use your time to wash my car in the driveway." I chose the first option, and she played a disc of instrumental Christian hymns while she lovingly gave Debbie a much-needed pedicure.

Within minutes after Renatta concluded her heart-warming two-hour session with Debbie, a neighbor came to our house. He announced that many neighbors had volunteered to form a "meal train" to bring us occasional meals as a supplement to those provided by our church's Care Team. Better neighbors and friends cannot be found. "Life just got better, and living just got easier, just as I was getting started in the 'pretend chef' business," I said as I thanked him. "Now I am losing my job. Debbie will be greatly relieved."

Contributing also to our needs, Gail Doxie arrived to introduce herself and interview for a housekeeper position. Gail was accompanied by her daughter, Jasmine, carrying a darling new baby girl nicknamed "Chuckie." Gail and Jasmine did a good cleaning job, and we hired Gail to clean house every other week.

Many additional caring friends also came to our aid. They knew the real meaning of caring for those in need. For example, we heard a strange noise outside our master bedroom and wondered what it was. We soon found out: our neighborhood friends John and Cindy Voris were busy building a stone walkway to the sidewalk. It was a masterpiece, beautifully landscaped. "This is our gift for y'all," John announced. "It's my pleasure to assist you and in this way to welcome you back home."

All our caregivers shared the same vision—the purpose of life is simple, to serve others. This adhered to the injunction Jesus Christ gave to his followers—to "rule" through self-giving service (Mark 10:35–45). What a great world this earthly existence would be if everyone embraced this commitment.

HOME ALONE

After all this activity conducted by friends, the last of our visitors departed. We were then by ourselves in our home. Debbie and I stared at each other lovingly in silent amazement. It felt good to be home, yet somehow strange. We had to adjust to our old familiar surroundings and begin living despite crippling disabilities.

- **"I'm Depressed"**—Returning home had taken us to a cozy familiar setting for Debbie's energetic endeavors to rehabilitate and recover.

Or so it seemed. But that first night home after eating and bathing we settled into our own bed and snuggled. We could be together in body and spirit. As was our habit, we read a worship passage from *Our Daily Bread* prior to saying a prayer in gratitude for our deliverance. Then there was nothing but deafening silence. Perhaps we were independently assessing the paths that we had traveled to this site of deliverance. I broke the silence, asking, "Debbie, what are you thinking?" Another pregnant pause. Then Debbie revealed, "I'm depressed." Still another moment of silent reflection, when I revealed, "For some reason I am also down."

We asked each other why. The search for an answer did not take very long. "I guess," Debbie whispered, "that being in our home, at last, brings back too many fond memories of the way we were, before my stroke. We have had so many happy times here. Our days were filled with joy. Being here now reminds me of what's missing. I feel the loss." I have a very perceptive wife. "I guess you knocked the cover off the ball with that insight, Debbie. That's what I'm feeling, too. That's also why I am somewhat depressed. You put into words exactly what I'm feeling."

- **Lost and Found**—We talked more about our despondent mood to better understand it. The reality had come into focus—that we would never be quite the same as we had been before the strokes. Both of us felt part of our self was missing.

Our former lives were lost. All that remained were treasured memories. It was simply unrealistic to think that life as known previously could ever be fully recovered. The striking fact of what happens after a stroke strikes is that everything changes. We had to adjust our thinking to accommodate our new circumstances. Now the important goal was to try to live in the present, reset our compass, and to look to the future. We would strive to live as best we could.

We recognized the need to "find ourselves" by putting our heavenly Father first and letting Him guide our remaining journey. We need not be lost. Our thoughts drifted back to the central message of Thomas Wolfe's masterpiece recollections of his coming-of-age experiences as a southern country boy fleeing Ashville, North Carolina, to try to become an author in New York. Wolfe titled his original, unedited novel *Hopeless!* That described Wolfe's psychic state of mind. His thinking after many revisions was eventually published with *Look Homeward, Angel* on the dust-jacket cover, and Wolfe extended this story in the best-selling sequel *You Can't Go Home Again.* (In 2000 the complete unabridged version was published under the title *O Lost: A Story of a Buried Life.*)

Debbie and I struggled to avoid becoming lost while we had to bury parts of our previous lives. However, we saw the urgency of mentally and spiritually preparing ourselves for the kind of life that might await us after our burials—where we could find our true selves for all eternity. In our present time of troubles, we were not afraid, because we knew we had it within our God-given power to escape the prison of hopeless fear. We would only remain lost if we lost courage and faith in God's mercy. There was no chance we would let that happen. Yes, we had been "cut off from the land of the living," but our fears and despair were struck down; "Out of anguish shall be seen the light. Surely He has borne our infirmities and carried our diseases" (Isa. 53:4–12). We had seen God's grace, and the lyrics to "Amazing Grace" struck home: "How sweet the sound, that saved a wretch like me. I once was lost, and now am found; was blind, but now can see."

Why feel let down when we had been lifted up? We were somewhat ashamed of momentary sorrow and self-pity. A mortifying setback was not a dead end. We were down but not out. We had made the Lord our refuge and knew that God had proclaimed, "I will deliver those who cling to me; I will uphold them, because they know My name. They will call Me, and I will answer them" (Ps. 91:9–16).

We had many blessings. We still had each other. We were alive. God was with us. Our relationship now was stronger than ever. So was our relationship with God. We had come home, both spiritually and physically. We began to see our situation in a new light. The Chinese word "crisis" means both danger and opportunity. We had been presented with a great opportunity to rethink our lives and life's meaning. Therefore, we agreed, "Let's seize this unique opportunity that misfortune has put before us." We committed ourselves then and there to map a new route and walk forward with trust in our hearts.

• **Facing New Challenges**—Launching a new routine would take more time than anticipated. There was no time to wait. The first test occurred the next day. I managed Debbie's transfer from our bed, changed her colostomy bag, and conducted solo the first use of the feeding tube. Then it came time for me to prepare the meals that the Care Team had provided. "Give me some hints," I begged Debbie. "You are the master chef and always made all those healthy and tasty meals for us, and, as you know, I don't know my way around the kitchen very well. For starters, what's this?" I asked as I pointed my finger toward the large apparatus under the granite counter. A smirk came across Debbie's face as she said, "It's called an oven." (I am not making this up for amusement; it's that pitiful.) Debbie had to show me the basics, like the location of a can opener and how to work the settings for the microwave. The rest of my lessons went slightly better, but, truthfully, the kitchen challenge was steeper than I humbly imagined. In time I made meals that were excitingly dull. Debbie was a good sport. She was itching to "reclaim her kitchen."

We next met the major challenge head on. We pledged not to slow down the pace of our own rehabilitation program. Even though deprived of supervised therapy treatments and dependent only on my superficial understanding of how to navigate the remedial road to rehabilitation, we refused to let up or give up. "What are we waiting for?" Debbie asked. "After you give me nutrition through my feeding tube, and change my colostomy bag and diapers, let's do what we can with stretches and exercises."

It was this ambitious attitude that had served Debbie so well up to now. There was no reason to let up, so we began our own therapeutic program. Debbie was fired up and, although weak, did the best she could. We conducted self-administered efforts to replicate a version of all three of the therapies we had learned in Charlotte. Given our challenging circumstances, we judged our imitation as not altogether deficient. We may have gained a modicum of momentum. At least we were not sliding backward. We went to bed immediately thereafter. After more prayers, we fell asleep holding hands.

HOME HEALTH CARE: CARING OR CARELESS?

We pushed on the next day but encountered some bumps in the road. I called Countryside Home Health Care to confirm the schedule of visits to our house. There were *none* in place. This disconcerting news sucked the oxygen from the air and set a bad precedent that, sure enough, presaged a series of further disappointments.

• **Apprehended and Apprehensive**—Later that morning, we were charged up to begin nursing and rehabilitation with our in-house providers. We impatiently waited for one of the home-health-care therapists to arrive. No one appeared, so I again called Countryside Home Health Care, and grew anxiously apprehensive when no live person received my call. I left a voice message pleading to learn when the therapy process would commence. Finally, the phone rang, and a physical therapist informed us, "I am nearby and should be at your home soon. I live in Blythewood close to your Cobblestone Park community."

The therapist was very polite. She took a painstakingly prolonged time checking Debbie's vital signs. Then we made a shocking discovery—she had virtually no equipment with her. What? How could an unprepared home-care physical therapist provide therapy? We needed equipment as much as a tennis player needs a racket.

I rushed to purchase a walker, and the therapist then finally swung into motion. She concocted some "sliders" out of newspapers wrapping around Debbie's right foot. This improvised aid enabled Debbie to drag her lame right leg down our thirty-foot hallway and back to her wheelchair. As the therapist departed, we asked if she knew when the speech and occupational therapists would come. She didn't, cautioning, "You better call my administrators about the schedule." But I already had.

Before placing another call, the phone rang. It was a roaming home-care occupational therapy staffer. "I'm driving now to your house from Aiken," he said. Just as he arrived, a speech therapist called to report "I am on my way and will be at your home soon." Two therapists at once? Apparently, each Countryside home-health therapist intended to show up at their convenience, without appointments or warning.

Neither session was very productive because the two therapists took turns trying to accomplish something. Most of the time was again devoured checking such things as Debbie's temperature and heart rate rather than conducting therapies. I begged both therapists "Please concentrate on actual therapy," and tried to motivate them by threatening "as soon as our wheelchair ramp is built, maybe by April 14th, I plan to begin Debbie's treatment at Health South Rehabilitation." This assertion was sheer hyperbole; moving on to Health South was contingent on Debbie's improved capabilities, which could take considerable time.

We were frustrated. If this was home health care, where was the professional "care" sought for Debbie's resumed health? Our suspicions mounted. Were we imprisoned in a jail of our own making, by a poor choice of this particular home-health provider? Had Debbie's progress been arrested? Or was there an avenue out of this apprehension to a better provider? I privately made some inquiries about possible alternatives, including seeking and hiring a personal therapist. In the meantime, there was no viable option but to stay the course. Uppermost in our thinking was the upcoming critical appointment with Carolinas Neurosurgery & Spine in Charlotte. Tuesday was fast approaching, and the verdict there would determine the direction of our journey. Was there anything that could be done to speed the escape from our home-health incarceration?

- **Getting a Lift**—I was struck by the realization that there was something that could be done. In fact, it *had* to be done to expedite the beginning of professional rehabilitation at Health South. I called Jerry Sharpe, a recommended free-lance contractor, and begged him to construct a wheelchair ramp to access our garaged vehicles so I could transport Debbie to doctors and hospitals. "I'm tied up on a big job for the next forty-five days. Can you wait? If I can work on the weekend, I'll help you out." "Terrific. Thank you. It's a deal. See you as soon as possible," I responded. Late that very night Jerry appeared to design the ramp and take measurements so he could place orders for computerized, precision-cut pieces of thick plywood, posts, and guardrails.

- **A Jump Start?**—If you haven't surmised it by now, I am a rather obsessive-compulsive (add impulsive?) character. ("There's a great book about obsessive-compulsive behavior," I liked to joke; "must have read it ten times.") So when a new idea popped into my head, I sprang into action. I placed a call to the offices of Drs. Schiffern and Paton who had performed Debbie's colon and G-tube operations. "Since Debbie would be in the CMC neighborhood for her neurosurgeons' examination at 6:00 a.m. April 8, could we take advantage of this opportunity and bring her by your offices afterward in order to conduct an evaluation?" It was Saturday, so all that could be done was to leave a voice message and wait to see if my suggestion could be accommodated, however remote the odds; I thought "Why not? What's there to lose?"

- **Another Crisis?**—Monday started with a scare. I left Debbie standing at her bathroom sink to brush her teeth so that I could wash the breakfast dishes. When I returned, my heart dropped—Debbie was sitting on the floor!

"Did you fall?" I blurted. "No, not really, I just got kind of dizzy. I'm okay," Debbie said as I raised her upright, and we returned with the walker to the bed.

I had serious doubts. I am cursed with a long memory, and these were precisely the same words Debbie had uttered that fateful January 8 when she exited the interstate rest-stop restroom. Not another seizure or stroke! God would not allow a repetition. I tried to calm down. Always stoic, Debbie was very composed, telling me, "Chill out."

Soon thereafter, our physical therapist entered. Skipping greetings, I told her what had just happened. She took Debbie's vital signs, and they were normal except her heart rate was 115. "Can we ask the home-health nurse to investigate?" I urged. That went nowhere. She disclosed that a nurse was unlikely to be available until midafternoon, if then, and said that it was probably not safe to undertake PT; she was afraid of liability issues more than health risks, she admitted. What to do? We needed answers. So I called Dottie, Kim and Monique at Palmetto Internal Medicine, who swung into action and rearranged the schedule of our doctor, James Herman, in order for him to examine Debbie at 11:00 a.m.

By the time we arrived at Dr. Herman's office, all symptoms had vanished. "Debbie," Jimmy winked, "you look great. I see nothing to be worried about, but, Chuck, I know you will worry anyway. Relax. Be calm like Debbie. Go home, and take it easy. Call if any concerns more arise."

Returning home, Debbie was confident and insisted on trying modest exercises. She performed well. And at the end of the day, after a long nap, Debbie finally saw the speech therapist, who focused on Debbie's swallowing skills. So the day was not a total waste, and if the dizziness was a bomb, it failed to explode.

- **A Byway to a Bypass**—Eager to take advantage of every available moment, I anxiously placed another call to Carolinas General

Surgery to see if they had received my recorded request to examine Debbie's colostomy and G tube tomorrow. Martha answered, "Sure, this is a good idea. Can you bring Debbie to our separate two-story office building at 1:00 p.m.?"

"This is terrific," I exclaimed. "We'll be there then. Please give me details on how to get there, as I am direction impaired." She laughed and faxed the directions. Even I couldn't get lost—their office was next to one of my walking paths from the Hospitality House to the rehabilitation facility. This was the kind of break-through we needed to balance the psychological scary step backward that morning.

FACING THE SHADOW OF THE FUTURE

The CT and MRI scans to inspect Debbie's brain lesion had hung heav-ily on our minds. At 2:00 a.m. on April 8, the alarm rang. Debbie and I sprang into action. No food, as instructed, in case the brain surgery operation had to be performed. We held our breath and prayed for favorable results.

At 4:00 a.m. in the cold blackness, Herman Rich arrived to help me carry Debbie in her wheelchair down and up the steps to the garage while Debbie bravely held a flashlight to lighten our path across the dark spots. And off we went, waving good-bye. Moonlight helped guide our path.

The air in our vehicle permeated with the smell of our high anxiety. Anything could happen. We were traveling in a blind spot, from which many invisible dangers could come into view. We traveled without get-ting lost, arriving with a half hour to spare before our 6:00 a.m. appoint-ment with the radiologists.

Debbie passed all her preliminary heart-rate and blood-pressure tests, and we held hands as she approached the CMC radiology depart-ment. "Unlike Chuck, I was confident. Right on time, I transferred to the scan bed, and Chuck was expelled to the hallway." The imaging did not take very long—which was good because the 9:00 a.m. appointment with Neurosurgery & Spine necessitated a short drive. At the speed of thought, the radiology report was transmitted through the Internet to the neurosurgeons' office, so the screening results could be instantly reviewed prior to our arrival.

Larry Braccia waited to greet us at their office. "I was there," he told us, "when abdominal bleeding on January 21 put your life in peril. Debbie, you looked as if you had swallowed a basketball—nine months pregnant. All the doctors were scratching their heads trying to figure out what to do. One of them suggested an MRI, but I prevented that by saying, 'If you take time for that, she will be dead.' So that emergency surgery began at once. You were given massive blood transfusions, and Dr. Schiffern opened you up and found in your colon a hemorrhaged aneurism. She treated that rupture successfully but not in time to prevent cerebral bleeding from inducing two strokes." We reacted to this frightening retelling of what had happened the way we might if we saw a rattlesnake about to strike. We braced ourselves for the news about the morning's CT, MRI, and arteriographic x-ray scans. Was Debbie again perilously close to a precipice?

• **Two Big Breaks**—Dr. Bernard summoned us to his office. Flashing his famous broad grin, he said, "Drs. Dyer and McLanahan have joined me in reviewing the scans. I am very, very pleased to tell you that the size of the brain aneurism has diminished. Given this shrinkage, we think it is wise to postpone preemptive surgery now. We will wait and hope the healing process continues. The odds are improving. You can go home after you see Dr. McLanahan. We will schedule in mid-May another follow-up cranial screening with some new technology we will be installing. In the meantime, Debbie, you can safely start outpatient rehabilitation and cease home health care." Our sighs of relief were strong enough to start a tornado. I regretted my needless fears, which had risen fast and persisted, and now suddenly dropped like a gust of wind in a tunnel.

Down the hall, Dr. Scott McLanahan reported, "I am excited by the scans' positive vessel data. Now, here's where I come in. Debbie, you're here for me to measure your cerebrospinal fluid (CSF) levels. As you probably recall, this will take only a few seconds. Let me point the magnet machine at your head and check the settings on the ventrolateral shunt I implanted in your cranium. Uh-huh, this looks good. I just made a very modest mechanical adjustment to reduce the spinal fluid pressure. You should be good to go. No need to come back for another check until mid-May unless you experience symptoms such as the feeling that your head and face are enlarged. By the way, Debbie, you're doing great. We're really proud of your progress, especially considering the dismal near-fatal condition in which we found you last January. Keep the recovery coming."

We could never have dreamed that the news could be this good. It was better than we even dared to pray for. After trudging up many hills, the roadway finally leveled and became easier to negotiate.

I could only wonder, "What if?" What if I had gotten my preference, and the surgeons had submitted to my lobbying (and that of Drs. Shemtov and Grafton), and the brain surgery had been performed while we were still in Carolinas Rehabilitation? Perhaps an unnecessary surgery would have been undertaken—a dangerous operation that could have caused untold damage or death. God may have played a part in that surgery *not* happening. Be careful about that for which one wishes, I reckoned. I now recognized that my mistaken efforts to rush this operation while we were still in Carolinas Rehabilitation were imprudent. Hindsight has 20-20 vision.

- **Cutting the Tubes That Bind**—But wait! There was more. A third break this game-changing day followed. The breakthrough was huge. We headed to Moorhead Plaza for our checkup with the staff offices from which our general surgeons, Drs. Schiffern and Paton, worked when they were not busy performing operations.

We didn't expect much from this hastily planned visit that I had requested just three days earlier and had been officially scheduled only yesterday.

Martha was waiting, gleaming affectionately. "Debbie, you look sensational. Let's wheel you into the private office, and the physician's assistant will take a look. Chuck, come along, watch and listen, and save your funny quips until Kristen finishes her evaluation."

Kristen bounced into the examination room and inspected the sites where the PEG tube and the colostomy bag were placed. She asked the appropriate questions and took more readings of vitals. "Debbie," Kristen asked, "you are able to swallow whole food, aren't you?"

"Yes, but I have to be careful and practice a chin tuck," Debbie admitted.

"Good!" Kristen exclaimed. "Then let's get rid of that cumbersome feeder tube. Now!"

I almost fell out of my chair. Astonished, I questioned, "Wouldn't that be a major operation?" All along, I had pictured the PEG feeder as long tubing spiraling from the incision hole to the stomach, bypassing the liver and colostomy. I was wrong.

"Watch, Chuck," Kristen instructed. "Debbie, lie on your back. Here goes." And pop. It was out! Out as fast as a cork leaving a champagne bottle. My eyes widened in amazement. This feeder tube was much smaller and shorter than I had envisioned; it looked like a protruding plug with a short stem, not an elongated 1/8th-inch-wide plastic pipeline. The removal was quick—much easier to extract than I could ever have imagined. And clean. All that remained was a hole in Debbie's stomach.

Kristen was pleased and proud. "Let me give you some instructions on packing the hole and changing the dressing, Chuck. It's simple. Just be sure the hole is covered with taped plastic when you oversee Debbie's showers. And of course call if red sores or blisters appear. The wound will take about four or five weeks to heal. These wounds heal from the bottom up, so make sure this long Q-tip pushes to, but not into, the bottom. Think of pushing a plunger into a clogged drain, but not far enough to puncture Debbie's wound. Stuff the three-inch hole with the dressing tape carefully. You can do this! Here, practice while I observe your new skills."

All these events seemed too good to be true. Could this day have been any better?

We drove home, exhausted but elated and exhilarated. Along the way, I broke the law talking on our cell phone while driving, to tell "the usual suspects" the breathtaking news. Andy was the first responder. He titled his e-mail "AT HOME!"

> Chuck called sounding tired but ecstatic after their up and back trip to Charlotte to see several doctors. He said it was a pretty terrific day, they didn't get lost (!), and best of all Debbie's PEG tube was removed. She is scheduled for a new high-tech CT angiogram (I think) of her brain in about a month. The surgeons made the decision not to perform brain surgery at this time. They got back home in time for a light PT workout, with another more intensive one planned tomorrow morning. The carpenters are coming back to finish the ramp and hand rails this weekend. And the word is out that Debbie has done a little emailing too! Hopefully she will read this, and maybe hit "reply all" to everyone!

A FRESH START

The next three days, Debbie finally began receiving all three PT, OT, and ST home-health-care treatments as well as a single examination by a traveling nurse (better late than never?). Debbie and I augmented these timid treatments with our own improvised set of therapy exercises. We sought to do everything within our power to press rehabilitation forward. For this, starting therapy at Health South Rehabilitation became a pressing priority.

- **Preparing for a New Destination**—The contractor who agreed to construct the ramp from our porch to the garage so Debbie could be transported in her wheelchair came late at night to unload materials. He installed handrails and a portable showerhead and pledged to begin construction of the ramp Saturday morning. "I know you need this project ASAP to transport Debbie," he said. "I also know you're Christians, as I am. If you will give me permission to work on Sunday, I can have the ramp finished that night. Is that okay?" I quickly agreed, and because Jesus had healed the ill on the Sabbath, I assumed God would condone this work.
- **Heading to a New Beginning**—This agreement opened up a window of opportunity. I placed a call to Health South Rehabilitation and reached Terry Lundy, the coordinator of schedules for patients and staff. I learned that Debbie's referrals had been received and asked if she had been approved for treatment.

"She has," Terry confirmed. "Great," I said. "Let me ask for the impossible. Would it be possible to schedule the first evaluation as early as Monday morning?" "Let me see," Terry responded, as he stroked computer keys. "Yes, we can do that. Debbie can start on Monday, April 14, at 8:00 a.m. The first sessions focus on evaluations of her capabilities. The paperwork appears to be in order. Looking forward to seeing both of you then."

This made our day. It meant that Debbie would no longer be running in place. Frankly, with the slow-motion and erratic therapy with home health care, Debbie was actually losing ground, and her strength and mobility were regressing backward. Now, barring any disruptions or accidents, under the outpatient professional rehabilitation at Health South, she conceivably could regain the momentum she had achieved while in Carolinas Rehabilitation and build on it to speed her recovery. I called Countryside Home Health to cancel their services. You might say I "fired them with enthusiasm." I presumed their other patients probably were discovering that they also would be lucky getting Countryside to work for them.

My confidence escalated late Sunday. Our compassionate contractor met his deadline. I had gambled on that when I impetuously scheduled Debbie's initial entrance to Health South the very next morning. That wager was won. Now I could transfer Debbie in her wheelchair to our car on my own, without the need to call for help to lift her. This was the break we needed—a fresh start in professional rehabilitation.

We felt blessed. Each step in our journey moved like the seasons, connected yet separate. "There is a season, a time for every purpose under heaven" (Eccl. 3:1–8). That was certainly true for each season of our journey. Our priorities were changing as we moved from season to season, while our commitment to seek at each stage was the same but growing in intensity: "To do all to the glory of God" (1 Cor. 10:31). A time, a season, had come to put aside what had happened during this mercifully brief home-health-care excursion and funnel our energy into more productive purposes at Health South Rehabilitation.

CHAPTER 23

A New Rehabilitative Runway

§

W hat would we find at Health South Rehabilitation? It had to be a
step up from home health care. We put that disappointing experience in the rearview mirror and approached our new rehabilitation
facility with the same kind of hope and trepidation as a child on the first
day of school.

Rehabilitation at Health South

Questions were about to be answered. "Debbie," I asked from the driver's seat as I stared at her disabled condition, "do you wish we were heading back to Carolinas Rehabilitation, where you achieved so much in so
short amount of time? We could be facing another slow lane with snarls
and stops."

"I don't think so," Debbie reflected. "Who knows? Health South
might be as productive. And it has the advantage of being so near our
home, only a thirty-minute trip." We approached our new destination,
knowing we would have to accept what we would find.

- **The Rules of the Road**—Using the newly acquired "Handicapped" permit hanging from our rear-view mirror, I swung into
  the handicapped parking space outside Health South Rehabilitation
  and lifted our wheelchair out of the trunk. The wheelchair
  unfolded easily, and the transfer was rather smooth. Terry Lundy,

the office manager, warmly greeted us in the outpatient waiting room. "Pleased to meet both of you. Debbie, sign in; Chuck, here's the paperwork you probably were expecting. All authorizations have been received. Debbie, Tony will start the physical therapy evaluation first, and after that Karen will conduct the occupational therapy evaluation and Mary will assess Debbie's speaking functionality. We're ready. Chuck, you can watch and ask questions during these initial evaluations and learn about the process and procedures that will be followed."

- **Road Rage?**—Then out of Terry's mouth came unexpected instructions. "Chuck, after today you cannot be involved in Debbie's therapy treatments or even stand by to observe. We learned long ago that patients' spouses and friends interfere with treatments. With the best of intentions, your presence likely would have counterproductive effects. I hope you understand the reasons for this strict policy and will accept them. We are all business here, and our mission is to serve Debbie's best interests."

I could not hide my frown. I had expected to be allowed to do what I had done in every therapy session in Charlotte—hover, inquire, observe, worry, and tearfully applaud new achievements. I cherished my previous cheerleader role. I was shaken as if driving on a bumpy road with many potholes. I had no choice but to yield to the rules.

To be fair, I could see some merit in these regulations, however difficult they were to accept. I really did not have a legitimate reason for rage. The rationale for the policy was sound, and the part about being "all about business" was music to my ears. There was no point in objecting and ruining an auspicious beginning. I had to yield.

My mood was boosted when I was handed a printed detailed schedule of the entire month's sessions. We were pleased to discover no gaps between therapy sessions, so no time was wasted.

- **A Road Test**—"Debra Kegley," Tony said from the gym doorway. He motioned us to follow in the wheelchair. In introductions, we learned that Tony, like Debbie, hailed from Indiana, so a common ground was immediately established.

As Tony asked Debbie to try transferring from her wheelchair to the platform bed, my eyes widened. The gym was huge! Moreover, it was equipped with more machines and exercise equipment than had been available in Charlotte. This augured well. Although Debbie struggled performing platform mobility tasks, Tony praised her fierce determination.

An occupational therapist conducted the next evaluation. Karen tried to conceal her reaction to Debbie's emaciated and enervated condition, but her facial expression could not mask her dismay. As Debbie tried to sit upright in her wheelchair, Karen hid her alarm and proceeded to begin testing whatever she could conceive might be within reach of Debbie's skills. For example, Karen measured Debbie's hand strength with a squeeze-clamp measuring device and reiterated Tony's evaluation of Debbie's transfer and platform-bed mobility limitations. Notes were carefully recorded.

Finally, a friendly speech therapist escorted us into her roomy private office and put Debbie through a series of speaking and cognitive capability tests. Mary set ambitious goals; the bar was high. Mary appeared well prepared to lead Debbie on a hard drive.

- **A New Start?**—Motivated to reboot Debbie's mind and body, we didn't have a sturdy foundation on which to judge if Health South would live up to its rehabilitation potential. But the prospects looked good, and we were ready to start a run that might put Debbie's recovery on a roll.

First impressions can be misleading, but it appeared that Health South possessed many of the same positive attributes of Carolinas Rehabilitation. If there was a difference, it was with respect to size, staffing, scheduling, and equipment. Size matters, and Health South had a larger staff and a wider range of equipment. Potentially, our new facility could provide a better fit for Debbie's evolving needs. It was hard to tell. Both rehabilitation facilities specialized in particular treatments, and it was possible that Debbie could make gains because each center specialized in particular procedures which were most needed at the time for Debbie's recovery. In combination, the differences and sequence could work to Debbie's advantage, cumulatively helping her rehabilitation in ways that could not be produced had she had only one available for the duration of her long therapeutic journey.

Health South's scheduling regimen and therapeutic philosophy added value. We had hoped for as many as five treatment days, but the program permitted only three days each week (Tuesday through Thursday). However, we approved of the abbreviated allocated days because the duration of each day's sessions was long (almost always at a minimum 9:00 a.m. to 2:00 p.m.), with some day's activities extending all the way to 5:00 p.m.—like many employees' work hours. Moreover, all the sessions were ambitiously rigorous and vigorous.

It did not take us long to accommodate ourselves to this scheduling routine and appreciate its benefits. It allowed Debbie time to recover on Mondays and Fridays with a longer sleep, work in recommended personal exercises, and prepare for the stream of visitors that came to see and entertain Debbie. It appeared this part of the journey's roadway had few potholes. The road to renewal seemed to be paved and lightened from heaven above.

THE TEAM DESIGNS A STRATEGY

The first set of evaluations led the therapy team to warn that "rehabilitation would be a marathon." Debbie was certain to try to make sprints, but because her roadway featured steep hills and deep valleys, a sustained fast pace was precluded. Moreover, the clouds of another ruptured aneurism darkened the pavement. This would be a slow slog. How slow and how far to the final destination, only time would tell. The therapists' skills would have a large say in the duration.

We saw immediately that Debbie would be coached by seasoned professionals. Heading the team was Dr. Dan—a very experienced occupational therapy leader. Dan had a trained eye and had no learning curve to climb. He pushed Debbie to do things that she didn't think were possible and combined purely occupational activities such as folding clothes with very demanding, strenuous exercises. Multitasking was needed, and Dan promoted multiple approaches. Theo, the physical therapist, also was exceptionally talented. He drove Debbie to do things that she thought were beyond her capabilities. Dr. Mary, the speech therapist, was very informed, especially in sequencing increasingly difficult deductive-reasoning puzzles. She was also innovative, creatively deploying a computerized Interactive Metronome to promote neurosensory and neuro-motor coordination among bodily extremities such as hands and feet. Debbie explained, "The Metronome made a sound like a cow bell and when I heard a beat through a headphone, I was asked to tap my toes or clap hands in unison with the cadence. In another application, I was asked to perform 'cross body' movements such as waving my right hand while tapping my left toe in response to the rhythm of the musical notes. Mary knew what she was doing. I could tell from our first meeting that Mary and I would develop something special beyond a therapist-patient relationship—we would be friends."

• **Running a Road Race In Stride?**—A race had begun. The Health South therapists' professionalism shone time and time again. Here's one example: Dr. Dan and Theo at once recognized that Debbie's lower right leg and foot needed the most attention. To aid treatment, unlike the center in Charlotte, their equipment included an electrical "bioness" device to stimulate neural connections between Debbie's brain and right ankle. This sophisticated electrode mechanism pumped electric charges to energize coordinated leg and foot movement, training the brain to respond instinctively when movement was needed to negotiate walking with a walker. The bioness was promptly put into service. Debbie's advances using this assistive-training instrument immediately became apparent. "You might think about purchasing one of these for home use, Chuck," Dan and Theo suggested, "but we doubt if Blue Cross will cover the $13,000, and we don't know how long Debbie will benefit from it; she might outgrow it if our therapies produce the results we are seeking. So for now put away your credit card; let's see how well Debbie does, and then you can make the right decision." I reluctantly accepted this advice; I was prepared to do anything in my power to expedite Debbie's recovery, including purchasing a bioness. Prudence over-ruled this costly choice, because Debbie did sufficiently progress the next month for use of the bioness to end. Alternative treatments started.

- **Extracurricular Activities**—Additional types of sessions were woven into the programmatic Health South therapy fabric. One was termed the "Mobility Group." Here patients worked on control of body movement using Wii programmed games and activities. These required players to simulate with the virtual-reality activity appearing on a screen various movements such as hitting a baseball, paddling down a difficult waterway, or swinging a golf club. These games were difficult.

  Adult Daily Living (ADL) was another activity in which patients performed tasks such as vacuuming, making a bed, and cooking. In addition, Skill Builders required patients to play a variety of group games with paired partners competing with the others or baking cookies and other goodies for the hospital's monthly bake sale. Moreover, in Adjusting to Disability the resident psychologist, Rafe Ellisor, led group-therapy sessions. Participants in the group were encouraged to share their individual post-stroke experiences and receive feedback in how they were coping with their debilities.

- **Playtime on Play Day**—The Day Treatment Program was available for select patients. "I was invited to join this group the very first week, despite my weakened condition. The purpose of these supplementary sessions was to encourage the development of skills that approximated the kinds of activities that would be undertaken when I had recovered sufficiently to be discharged. Shopping, hiking, going to museums and historic places were things everyone usually does, and the program was designed to encourage disabled patients like me to undertake the usual activities they had undertaken before their strokes or spinal injuries. The programs were also designed to facilitate group social interaction."

The sessions were of two types that alternated week to week. The first were in-hospital group activities centered on deductive reasoning, memory/recall, or team competition, such as playing Scrabble or Sequence. Debbie explains:

> This was a members-only club. As a result, Chuck was excluded when at my very first event the group was required to attempt playing croquet on a grassy knoll behind the rehab build-ing—in 92-degree heat. A scary incident occurred. I lost my balance and fell to the ground. I laughed at myself, in part out of embarrassment and in part because my slip seemed funny. I was not hurt. I found my footing and my therapists helped me stand and I continued playing. It was probably a good thing that Chuck was not there to witness this accident, because I am sure his proto-paranoia would have overwhelmed him. I was right. When Chuck met me in the waiting room, I told him what happened and he went into hysterics. I calmed him down as he drove us home. Chuck approvingly complimented me, saying "That Debbie! No complaints, no regrets."

The second type of day treatment session was more adventuresome and educational, entailing an outing to some place of local interest to tourists or residents. Spouses and caregivers were encouraged to participate—an invitation "Chuck was thrilled to accept."

Debbie described these outings as "Aggressively ambitious. For example, on my very first outing, I couldn't believe the agenda.

Much labor had to be expended using my walker to hike and climb along the 'Riverwalk' adjacent to the Broad River that cuts through downtown Columbia. After transferring from my wheelchair, I used my walker to traverse about a half mile along the pathway, with Dr. Dan and Chuck keeping a watchful eye 'spotting' me in case of a fall. Chuck bragged about my accomplishment to 'Communication Central.'"

Throughout May, Health South scheduled a very diverse set of other outpatient outings that paid additional rehabilitative dividends. Conspicuous among them were a shopping trip at Walmart; a visit to a disability technological center, where many items for handicapped people could be examined and purchased; attendance in the annual Greek festival; and a tour of the South Carolina Museum of Police, where a two-hour lecture told the gruesome history of crime and punishment—the old prison cells were so barbaric that they rivaled the torture chambers Debbie and I had seen as tourists in medieval European castles.

Put this evidence together to paint a picture, and you might imagine that we felt we had been guided by divine intervention to the best place for rehabilitation for which we could ask. It was our good fortune to move forward on Health South's freeway. All things considered, it appeared that under expert supervision, we were traveling at a very productive rehabilitation facility. The journey there was to be long, very long. We felt we could beat the odds on Health South's expressway. And we were blessed that our insurance provider had not declared that Debbie's progress had flattened like a plateau and therefore that Debbie's coverage would prematurely end. This would have ended any chance for meaningful recovery. Tragically, many stroke survivors' professional therapies are stopped too soon, confining them to permanent disabilities.

To make a long story short, that "Rascal" Toby was running her race to recovery steadily over and around a number of barriers. Progress was evident, even if her ride at times included the kind of bumps someone would experience at an amusement park. It would just take time and work to near a finish line. We had both time and motivation in abundance. Debbie was in the race for the long haul. It appeared that the harder each task got, the more engaged and determined she became.

We never missed a session or arrived late. When the therapy sessions at Health South concluded or on the four days when we were traveling alone, we sought to use the time at home productively, from dawn to dusk.

Since the gun sounded to start the race on April 14, our schedules revolved around Health South's game plan. What did Debbie's long journey include when she was not in formal rehabilitation? It is helpful to fill in some blanks to better picture the kinds of activities normally attempted after a stroke strikes. This leg of these memoirs covers the period from then through May.

A Home Court Advantage

It was in the privacy of our home where almost all the "actionable" action took place when not at Health South or traveling to medical providers. We could not compete with the professional therapies at Health South, but at home we could control our schedule and attend to a range of supplementary exercises, stretches, and massages that complemented those administrated externally. A number of regularized tasks (meals, colostomy bag, showers, medications) crowded the daily agenda in our home where rehabilitative homework was performed. There were some advantages, alongside the obvious disadvantages. The major features during this prolonged interim portion of our long journey are highlighted.

- **The Care Team's Devoted Care**—The Northeast Presbyterian Church Care Team faithfully visited with Debbie on Monday and Friday afternoons between 2:00 p.m. and 4:00 p.m., and as regular as a clock, the ladies brought prepared dinners. They made important contributions to our home environment and allowed me to do some things that I otherwise could not do when attending my Debbie, such as exercising, errands, writing, and yardwork.

We could not have had better assistance, loving care, and tastier, more nourishing meals. The Care Team's participants were encouraging and entertaining. I grew very fond of all of them and affectionately nicknamed the Care Team Debbie's "Flock." We needed help, and they abundantly provided it. "I cried unto God with my voice, called unto God, and He gave ear unto me" (Ps. 77:1) described our reaction to the support that, animated by zeal to follow Christ's word, we appreciatively received from the Flock.

- **Homework and Housework**—Everyday living went on at the same time Debbie and I pursued prodigious rehabilitative efforts. Squeezing in time in the very busy health-care schedule to take care of business was hard but necessary. I had to arrange for supplies such as colostomy pouches and their accessories to be delivered; long-postponed appointments with dentists, vision care, and internal medicine and cardiologists had to be scheduled; bills had to be paid; and records had to be organized to prepare the previous year's (2013) income tax forms in time to meet the extended filing-date deadline.

Amid all the therapy activity, a number of house problems arose that somehow needed to be managed. Homes are like people. Homes need care, too. They require supplies and maintenance. Managing tasks around our house posed a big challenge because I was so unskilled with tools and technologies. Many challenges arose: staining the ramp, replacing the attic air conditioner, coordinating the annual termite inspection, installing new dryer vents and ducts, cutting entire trees and damaged limbs broken by the ice storms, restoring cable service, fixing Internet connections (so Debbie could work her magic on that bewildering technology that I had never mastered), patching porch cracks, repairing garage-door openers, ridding the attic of squirrels, and having the house pressure washed.

Andy Kegley stepped in countless times to keep our Wytheville home in order and oversaw the delivery of the special extra firm mattress Debbie would need for bed transfers, mobility, and sleep if and when we could return to our beloved Blue Ridge home. Both routine and unusual everyday jobs had to be packed into the busy schedule, including troubleshooting numerous inexplicable medical bills (for example, we were billed $25,000 for two doctors "on call" that never saw Debbie, and if you are like us, you probably are unwilling to pay for services that were neither requested nor provided. This was enough to honk off the Good Humor man. Thanks to the intervention of our insurance-coverage advocate, these charges were eventually cancelled).

- **The "Meal Train" Keeps on Track**—While I was in training trying to learn how to prepare meals, neighborhood friends provided additional dinners on many evenings when the ladies from the Care Team were not scheduled. The meals were so good and specialized to Debbie's vegetarian diet requests that I began to suspect that these caring neighbors were in some sort of secret competition with each other. This train made many stops. They saved me from certain kitchen disasters and Debbie from starvation.

- **No Breaks or Brakes**—Throughout the remaining month of May, Health South continued to conduct increasingly productive therapy sessions. The primary therapists were delighted with Debbie's aptitude and attitude. Debbie gave her best shot to every assignment. She was a real workhorse. Her commitments were rewarded with steady progress in strength, speech and mobility.

"Debbie, you are headed in the right direction," her therapy team proclaimed, "and we will stay with you for as long as possible." In all modesty, it was obvious from the therapists' reactions that Debbie was rapidly becoming their favorite patient. I am not just bragging— the therapists told me, "We wish all our patients were as cooperative and hardworking as Debbie." They told Debbie, "We can see that you are following our exercise instructions at home with Chuck, because we can see the benefits. Some of our patients complain a lot and are lazy at home, and we can see the costs. Thanks, Debbie!

Keep doing the workouts." Debbie shone every time she heard praise, encouragement, and endearment and redoubled her efforts.

- **Going Solo in the Cobblestone Gym**—Work into the diagnostic equation Debbie's fortitude and heavy lifting while with me at home. All the exercises prescribed by Health South for "homework" were performed, and others were added. They paid off.

The best example was the progression of capabilities that unfolded in Debbie's striving for walking. In April, the most distance that Debbie could travel with her walker was about 125 feet, with multiple rest breaks interspersed between each effort (30–40 feet). A milestone was reached on April 28 when we ventured outside, and Debbie carefully used her walker to reach the front of our house and managed to return to the entry porch despite the modest incline.

"Want to try the walker in the gym?" I asked a few weeks later. The heat outside was rising, and Debbie decided then and there to turn up the heat on her efforts, responding, "Why not? I am getting bored extending the walking distance within our house." We drove three blocks to the fitness center, transferred from our golf cart, and used the walker to reach the air-conditioned gym. I used a tape measure to calculate the distance around the parameters of the two basketball courts. Debbie then covered one hundred yards with her walker, with me "spotting" her. Score a big one! She had walked the length of a football field, end zone to end zone. This was something to build on—which Debbie did that summer as she cumulatively increased the distance.

To commemorate Debbie's progression to a walker, and to release both of us from the sad memories whenever we saw the now seldom-if-ever used wheelchair in our master bedroom, I folded it and stored it out of sight in the rear of our closet. It was history. Exercises with light weights and stretch bands were also introduced into the home-exercise regimen, and we practiced a series of additional yoga-type movements that the Health South therapists had recommended with printed graphic instructions.

- **In God We Trust**—Uppermost in our minds was our faith that God is "the Lord who heals you" (Exodus 15:26). From Him surely all the miraculous blessing of healing had come. If there was a single lesson extracted from this portion of our long journey, it was that trust in our Lord had carried us through every dark passage. Some people cynically maintain that faith is simply a psychological escape from fear of death. They are mistaken. Our journey cast light on a different reality. Sure, even with faith the throes of some problems persist and can make our faith grow faint, but there is no suffering that cannot be overcome when we recall God's goodness and past blessings. God's love is unfailing—"Has His promise failed? Has God forgotten to be merciful? Has He in anger withheld His compassion? (Ps. 77: 7-9)." Never! Faith conquers all fears, even of death. We are never abandoned. Therefore, no matter how severe our disappointment when hardships struck, faith sustained us; we were absolutely certain that after we died we would arrive at a secure destination—at a heavenly home in intimate relationship with our Lord.

That belief notwithstanding, I was still learning and had not escaped incarceration from pervasive fears that Debbie might undergo another devastating setback, accident, or worse. I tried to mask my chronic inner fears behind wisecracks. This was my nature; I was practiced at worrying. But practiced worship freed me from chronic anxiety.

In this leg of our long journey, the rain sometimes fell, but the stars came out and shone brighter and brighter. We were now engaged in a prolonged road trip, but still in doubt about what the future would hold. A big barrier darkened the comforting light.

A SURGICAL LOOK INTO THE DARK INSIDE
There is no sure thing, people like to say. The scheduled return to Charlotte for the CT and MRI scans on May 15 meant that the time

had come for fateful decisions about the need for another preemptive brain surgery. There was a clear and present danger ahead, and we did not look forward to going down that road. We had to; there was no available bypass.

What would these new brain tests reveal? The dark inside had to be inspected. The aneurisms were like an iceberg, 90 percent still underwater and out of sight. Debbie's cerebral vessels would continue to remain submerged and invisible unless the scanning technologies could locate them and throw light on their condition.

Concerns were well founded. The recent April 8 brain images had not eliminated the danger that another vessel might hemorrhage, destroying in its wake much, maybe all, of the progress that had been made. The past pain of old worries had returned, weighing heavily on our minds. The ghosts of January's strokes could not be exorcised. They hit as hurtfully as a finger poke in the eye. The grim memories of past dark days and crises could not be erased.

God willing, the angiogram tests could dispel some fears. We were heartened by memories of the previous emergencies that had miraculously been overcome through many surgeries. The past bore witness to bright days when there weren't many bright days.

We braced ourselves. We tried to no avail to put mental distance between the threats that now existed and the outcome we desired. The angiographic scans could either spell "Dead End" or "Proceed with Caution." The diagnostics would be a dead giveaway of some answers. Would another risky brain surgery be necessary? It seemed likely, because our surgeons had requested that we pack luggage in case surgery had to be performed. In preparation for that possibility, Debbie was prohibited from eating eight hours prior to her tests.

The CAT angiography examination went smoothly, and afterward I drove Debbie to the Carolina Neurosurgery & Spine complex for our appointment with both Dr. Hunter Dyer and Dr. Joe Bernard. Just like the April 8 examination, the radiology reports were wired ahead. By the time we arrived at our surgeons' offices, the surgeons had already reviewed the results. Debbie and I held our breath, held hands, and silently said prayers. The time for another revelation had come. Dr. Bernard spoke for both of them:

> We now know what has been hidden inside your brain, Debbie. Good news. Your vessels are not as blistered or ballooned as much as they had been five weeks ago. We did detect a little tear and a tiny bump, but this is 99.5 percent normal. We see little or no justification for operative insertions of pipelines or coils to prevent the blistered areas from bursting. No surgical intervention is recommended at this time. We will look again in July, and if those images verify the results we found today, we plan on taking another set of pictures in mid-August. Translation: the entire process would be repeated all over again. This was good. Verification through replication was the only means to confirm research results.

We classified these results as another "head start." They provoked huge sighs of relief. We could now see a clearer road on the horizon and wanted to keep traveling in that direction without using exit ramps or shifting into reverse gear. This, for now, was the best news we could receive. We darted home on the interstate. Debbie dialed the phone numbers to leave messages about this positive news for "Communications Central." Their encouraging updates went viral.

CHAPTER 24

A SUMMERTIME SOJOURN

§

Southern Carolina's climate is notoriously hot. It was fitting that Columbia had 'fessed up by adopting "Famously Hot" as the city's slogan. The heat waves during the summer of 2014 set new records. Daytime temperatures soared above a hundred degrees each day over a six-week span. This was the hottest Columbia had been since General William Tecumseh Sherman had torched the city. We felt like we were living in a sauna.

During this stretch of our long journey, Debbie was also "hot." Steaming. Sizzling. On fire. Put into focus a synopsis of the sweating and sprinting during our summertime sojourn from June through August.

- **An Impatient Patient**—The word "patient" is both a noun and an adjective. The noun applied to Debbie more than the adjective. Obviously she was *a* patient under medical care undergoing multiple treatments. However, *being* patient did not describe her disposition. She was an impatient patient—in a hurry to shed her role as *a* patient. As she put it, "I sought recovery ASAP. I was repeatedly told 'Keep your eyes on the prize.' That's what I did. I would not relent. I desperately wanted my old self back. I set my mind on working as hard as I could, just like I did at Health South's gate. I had hit major milestones and never saw any of them as an acceptable destination. I was driven to drive the full distance. I felt my confidence grow and I picked up speed after each 'pit stop' pause."

Determined, Debbie's tireless efforts to overcome her disabilities grew and grew. Time and time again, she doubled down with such zeal they made her therapists do double-takes. Her patience remaining a patient evaporated like a snowflake in the sun. She wanted to see the finish line soon. Could she get there racing ahead in the smothering South Carolina summer heat?

- **Attitudinal Adjustments**—The dog days of summer were both hot and hard. Plight produced pressures requiring adaptations to the agony of prolonged disablement. Debbie confronted the trial head on: "I knew that my attitude was a big factor in my recovery, so I tried not to let the slow grind depress my outlook. I tried to hold my frustration in check. I tried to grin and bear the burden, but couldn't conceal my grimace as I observed Chuck's perpetual worrying leading to more worries, and I began to worry about his worries."

Debbie tried to kid me to relieve my emotional anxieties. "You're living up to your nickname, 'Nervous Norman,' because you're overly nervous." The nickname fit my fits of overreaction to imagined fears like a glove fits a hand. I struggled. The worst episodes of fright occurred during Debbie's rehabilitation sessions when I couldn't be there to observe her. I filled the void most often at the university gym. The serotonin rush from exercise stimulated bursts of optimism and forced me to take my mind off worries about Debbie falling or being struck with another stroke. That hiatus ended as soon as I rushed back to Health South. My heart raced and stomach churned. Could things have gone wrong, as they had previously? Whenever I had flashbacks of Debbie's numerous close-call crises, I became as nervous as a prostitute in a confessional booth. These flashbacks were taking a toll. Imagined potential new mortal threats were like enemies: friends come and go, but enemies accumulate. I was wired to worry. If your soul mate came close to death multiple times, would you be much different? Thankfully, I did not lose my mind. Every time dread drowned my confidence, I was comforted by graphic imagery of God's protection.

Debbie's temperament was quite different from that of her paranoid husband. Other than worrying about my fright, her only major worry was about getting better. She exuded optimism, stating, "I was learning that I could go beyond what some pessimistic people had told me. As I began rehabilitation, some predicted I would forever be bound in a wheelchair and never walk with a walker or cane. I proved them wrong." Debbie put her best foot forward (wording intended) and took challenges in stride. If you are a stroke survivor, you can learn from her how a positive attitude can contribute to your rehabilitative progress.

By now it should go without saying—Debbie drew her high spirits from her spiritual beliefs. I suspect that on January 10 when Debbie had neared the other side, she subconsciously saw God by her side, and this profound truth became embedded in her brain, available to be assessed when prompted. Debbie had one of those rare cathartic experiences that produce an epiphany. She emerged from this transformative incident with fearless faith. During her near-death moment the Holy Spirit served God's primary purpose—reminding us of His presence, teaching us His word, directing our footsteps, and strengthening our resolve (Ps. 119:11, 28, 67, 133).

Debbie's stored memories had to have powerfully shaped her positive attitude. Not once did she describe herself as a victim. She accepted her plight as one of those unexpected things that can happen on life's journey, and recognized that suffering was a part of being alive. She did not look at her own frail post-stroke condition with the same sorrow and pity that many other victims felt. She faced her future with such optimism that I was beginning to suspect that the CMC therapists may have been onto something when they had questioned, "Is there something wrong with Debbie? She is constantly cheerful and confident. Does she not recognize her circumstances?" Debbie's ability to escape the crushing victimization syndrome that cripples so many survivors after a stroke strikes undoubtedly helped her adaptively face her daunting disabilities. Or did it?

- **A Momentary Maladjusted Malcontent**—Debbie craved self-sufficient independence. Who wouldn't? No one wants to be dependent on others. She complained, "I am growing very frustrated at the pace at which I am overcoming my impairments. I fear that some goals might not be achieved for a long, long time, maybe never. I am too dependent on you, Chuck, and my therapists. I never have been patient, but now I am in the summer doldrums and my confidence is starting to fade."

  Frustrated, Debbie flashed the torrid temper of a hothead. Some strange expletives ushered from her otherwise-controlled tongue. The weather was unbearably hot, but the oppressive heat was not the cause of her lost cool. She boiled with angry outbursts. Her out-of-character dark disposition was perplexing.

  I hoped these brief tantrums were compensatory and would soon pass. They did. She deflected and diverted her black moments by lacing her momentary episodic enraged outbursts with good humor. "Am I really a shrew?" she asked, laughing at herself, pivoting attitudinally to display the power of positive thinking. A five-letter word that begins with a "b" and ends with an "h" was *not* what Debbie was becoming.

  I was struck by Dr. Dyer's frightening warning that strokes can cause personality changes, sometimes so radical that others can only wonder, "Whatever happened to the person they knew?" Unfortunately, often when people suffer ruinous adversities they become ill-tempered. Fortunately, Debbie's angry phase vanished as quickly as it had appeared. It was temporary. The old sweet Debbie reappeared. Actually, my Debbie went in a different direction and came out of her brief summertime blues with an altogether new disposition: when things struck her as funny, she laughed loud and long, uncontrollably at times. Normally rather diffident and soft spoken, the "new Debbie" became a chronic comic. Once she recovered, she never lost her "happy camper" temperament. She was not becoming a clown but was finding her true self.

- **Birth of a New Day**—Newly found mirth had been given birth. On June 4 Debbie's moods shone with a new light. The timing was uncanny. It was Debbie's fifty-fifth birthday! She recollects, "We celebrated my birthday by celebrating the fact that God had given me the gift of being alive. Having stood at death's door made Chuck and I acutely aware of our mortality. Getting older was not a goal; living a meaningful life was. Our awareness that life is short helped us appreciate all the more the value of living one day at a time under God's grace. My spirits were rising."

- **An Easy Choice**—Call it a calling or whatever, but we experienced an epiphany of sorts—we felt ourselves called to serve by sharing the story of Debbie's journey from the pitch blackness of death to the light of day under God's guidance. It was then that I began transcribing my scribbled diary notes and medical records with the goal of composing for circulation a manuscript about Debbie's miraculous story. I could say I took pen to hand, and at first that was the case, but in a short time Debbie joined in converting my draft into a computer document. Debbie is the family computer whiz; I am the Komputer Klutz.

  This book's origins stemmed from that decision point. In the early stages of compiling the full story, I did most of the writing, especially when covering those early periods in ICU and Acute Care when Debbie was sedated and had no vivid recollections on which to draw. As she regained her cognitive skills and began to recover memories of passages on our long journey, Debbie contributed to our coauthorship more and more fully and stepped up to the plate editorially correcting my rough drafts and adding her voice to the narrative.

  We hosted George and Cathy Crow for dinner, and informed them of our plans to publish a memoir. The next day George e-mailed: "We absolutely loved catching up with you all. Seeing you so vibrant and alive, Debbie, is so touching to our hearts. We don't understand God's ways, but as your dear husband mentioned last night, we usually forget to be thankful for the good things. Your recovery is a 'good thing' for which we are so grateful!! I think God is going to use your story. I've heard writing a book is like being in labor, so 'push on' as they say in the birthing room. Love you guys."

- **An Anniversary**—July 6 was a special date to commemorate the value of our relationship. Twelve years earlier, Rev. George Crow had performed our wedding ceremony. Thanks to Debbie, these had been the best years of my life. Strokes and disabilities could not darken celebration of our deep mutual love on this anniversary. We fondly recalled the time our marriage had cemented our relationship in Christ. She had written,

> *My Wedding Vows to My Husband Saturday, July 6th, 2002.* I promise to God before these witnesses that from this moment, I take you, Charles, as my best friend for the rest of our lives. I pledge to honor, encourage, and support you through our walk together. When our way becomes difficult, I promise to stand by you and uplift you, so that through our union we can accomplish more than we could alone. I promise to work at our love and always make you a priority in my life. May our love only grow stronger. This is my solemn vow.

Our love did indeed grow stronger and stronger with each passing year. I thought it was at the highest peak, but suddenly Debbie's health hit bottom, and our mutual love after her stroke rose to new heights we never thought possible. Looking at death in the face had tightened our bonds. After a stroke strikes, survivors reexamine their values. I did when Debbie had stood at death's door. It was then that I discovered the depth of my love for my Debbie.

- **How "Toby" Met "Charlie"**—Curiosity once got the better of George and Cathy Crow when, soon after our wedding, we were hosting our new friends for dinner. "How did you meet Debbie?" George had asked. You might be interested, so here's a synopsis. We had met in very idiosyncratic circumstances, way beyond chance. We believe God facilitated our meeting. My friend John Clark and I went to a restaurant called The Grazin' Monkey. No other customers had yet arrived. The establishment was a tapas bar (tapas, as in Spain, not "topless"), and it was vacant. John came to cheer me up. "There's not a virtuous single woman in the entire state," I lamented. Just then in entered Debbie, alone, and she caught my eye. "Hold that thought," I exclaimed, adding, "Dibs. I saw her first." We met, exchanged a few subdued greetings, and Debbie gave John and me her telephone number with a request to share any ideas about employment opportunities—she was in the process of exploring positions since the construction firm she had served as human resource manager had closed its doors and relocated out of state.

The rest is history—a long history. Debbie wouldn't give me much attention, and we became friends before I summoned the courage to express my interests. About two year later, she accepted my proposal, and we were married the following year. We were sure that God had united us.

- **Therapeutic Innovations**—Changes in circumstances produced changes in thinking about how to cope with disability and how to overcome it. That hot summer, almost daily, the therapists introduced new exercises and different techniques. Different approaches led to new arrivals. "Different strokes for different folks"—or for different stroke survivors—was Health South's underlying therapeutic philosophy. It could be labeled pragmatism, or experimentally trying a new technique to see if it works. Many experiments did work. The path was continuously repaved. While staying the course, detours produced regular rehabilitative breakouts.

- **Mind over Matter**—To maximize rewards, the therapists stressed the importance of linking cognition to body control, explaining "Change commences when the inside and outside come together. Mind matters. Debbie, your physical goals can better be achieved if you consciously instruct your brain to perform a function that you have not previously undertaken. Think about the task that you want to perform, and then instruct your brain to react. Ask yourself, 'What can I do to set myself up for success?'"

Debbie followed this advice. For example, she told me that "Theo asked me to march by lifting my legs, which I did immediately with my left leg. 'I can't do this with my right leg,' I apologized. Theo insisted that I could. 'You tell yourself that you can't, but you can. Tell yourself that you can, and do it,' Theo insisted. 'Brain, I'm talking to you,' I said aloud. 'I want you to let me lift my right leg.' Magically, I did this the first time. I learned the power of mind over matter".

People afflicted by neuropsychiatric disturbances or brain dysfunctions are taught the importance of strengthening neural connections between mind and body, which can be empowered by mental gymnastics. A familiar mental trick is that, if stuck in a chair and unable to rise, the thing to do is to imagine getting out of the chair, and then the patient usually can rise without assistance. Athletes, especially golfers and basketball players, are well aware of the power of mental gymnastics and learn to visualize what they seek to perform. The more often a new technique is mastered, the more the repetition becomes a "natural instinct" performed by instinct because it is imprinted in the brain's neural circuitry. You have many habits of which you are not mentally aware. Ever slow down driving when you see a police car, even though you were not exceeding the speed limit? Ever lower your head driving under an overpass bridge?

- **Yes, We Can**—Health South increased regular use of the Nintendo Wii interactive simulation game where an individual performs various activities such as walking a tight-rope, moving a bubble down a canal, or playing dodge ball. Try it—it's hard. Not as hard as actually walking a tight-rope like an acrobat, but hard nonetheless. It took Debbie two months before she successfully walked the virtual reality tightrope and guided the bubble all the way to the finish line without hitting a border.

- **Value-Added Accomplishments**—We began to see how the amazing diversity and variety of therapies mutually impacted each other. Their relationships were symbiotic—their interactions contributed to one another, making the product greater than the sum of the parts. For example, multitasking exercises coupled separate activities—typically an unprecedented one and another that had already been learned. Health South creatively combined innovative new pairings, which contributed to Debbie's accumulating advances.

- **The Importance of Being Earnest**—Debbie had found her stride and was pushing hard to strive forward. The therapists exchanged approving glances and jaw-dropping looks as they witnessed Debbie master new skills. She was the sort of patient they prized. Debbie's will to win set a sterling example for other rehab patients about how to persevere. She quietly led and became a leader of a growing throng.

  Patient's earnest pursuit of recovery is of critical importance. Therapists can't do it all for stroke survivors. Patients must pitch in and participate fully. Debbie did both with her therapists and with me at home, for hour after hour daily. Everyone could see the results of her relentless efforts.

  "I recall," Debbie noted, "a conversation I had with one of my friends in my stroke-survivor group. She asked 'Debbie, how do you do it? You are doing great. I am not making progress like you.' 'Thank you,' I said. 'I work hard here but especially after our therapy sessions at home where I conduct additional intensive exercises. I do not find this difficult. Before my stroke, I had habitually worked out, so increasing the program is a kind of extension of my previous endeavors to stay in shape. Our therapists told me that my prior condition must have contributed to my survival, and is helping now. But it's all mental. I won't get better unless I try, with all my might. You can, too.'"

  "'I was afraid you would say that, Debbie,' my friend confessed. 'I don't like to exercise and work out. I have always been like that.' There our dialogue died. The elephant in the room is that some stroke survivors don't want to work hard toward recovery. At least this survivor was honest. Sadly, she had hit some kind of plateau and was content to stay there; her chances of recovery dimmed. I tried to encourage her, reciting the motto 'say no to plateau.'"

"I had another exchange with another member of my Adult Daily Living group which illustrated the importance of earnest dedication to self-rehabilitation. 'Debbie, good to see you.'

"'Likewise,' I returned. 'I am surprised to see you here, however. I thought you were discharged from Health South three weeks ago, when we said farewell. What are you doing back here?'

"She hung her head. 'Well,' she explained, 'when I got home I got kind of lazy. I became a couch potato, and sat around watching TV and reading most of the time. I went back to my lazy way of life before my stroke. I really didn't work on my therapy, and lost much of the capabilities I had developed when I was discharged. I regressed. I'm weaker and less self-sufficient now than when I left. So I had to return. Here I am, back where I started. At home I thought I was done. Now I must start all over again. If I get back to an acceptable level of independence and can go home, you can bet I'll put in more effort. I really want to recover. I will try to work harder.'"

"I told her 'That's great. You can do it if you put your mind to it. While we're here together, I'll cheer on your efforts. We can both make progress if we try. Let's get started. There's no reason we have to remain dependent on using a walker the rest of our lives.'"

- **A Home Remedy**—The escalating activities undertaken from home were making a clear difference. Debbie made substantial advancements regaining her capacity to walk. As the summer began, she was still 100 percent dependent on the use of a walker. She overcame that limitation rather rapidly. Her first venture in our gym without her walker covered a distance of three hundred feet. Within a week, she tripled that distance. By August her distance climbed to eighteen hundred feet. It wasn't long thereafter that she jettisoned her walker altogether, insisting on walking only with the assistive support of her cane. "Two steps forward and one step backward" was passé. Debbie was taking giant leaps forward, and her pace was steadily hastening.

- **Autopilot Driving**—I asked, "Debbie, do you want to try to drive to the community gym in our golf cart?" Needless to say, she was game. She did well with the use of her stronger left foot for braking and use of her weak right foot to propel the accelerator on the battery-powered cart. By August Debbie mastered driving the golf cart.

  You can guess what advancement came next. I challenged as I shoved the car keys into her hand: "Debbie, want to see if you can drive to pick up the mail?" She grabbed the chance like an alcoholic grabs the next drink. There were starts and stops accelerating and braking but few real problems. A driving-capability test at Health South was disappointing, and it was suggested that special extension pedals on both accelerator and brake could be installed. That never happened. With practice, Debbie overcame her jerking braking and fast starts and began to master the maneuvers. She drove longer and longer distances with me riding shotgun. She skipped the next formal driving exam and wouldn't have any more of "one game at a time"; she had her own game plan in mind. Several months later, strength and control of her weak right leg improved, her "lead foot" braking became steady, and she forged ahead and summoned the courage to drive on the interstate safely. "Normality" was coming. It was very becoming.

REMEMBERING THE ROAD TO RECOVERY

Looking back at the end of summer, Debbie gathered her memories of lessons learned. Hindsight provided some instructive insights. She puts her recollections at this milestone this way:

> I had to compare my stroke recovery to that of an athlete recovering from an injury. As I recall my days of long-distance running prior to my strokes, it was difficult at first to run one mile and I

had to build up to running two, three and then up to ten miles. I learned that I had to practice the same diligence if I was to recover from my strokes' damages. Every day recovery had to be my foremost priority. I put a plan in place. That plan precluded the temptation to settle for anything less than complete recovery. If I were to recover, it seemed that the following values and prerequisites were especially important:

- Putting God first and recognizing that He is in control;
- Benefitting from a dedicated caretaker and loyal advocate for my interests (my husband was off the charts in his love, dedication and loyalty);
- Making a personal commitment to get stronger and better, and acting on that motive;
- Setting realistic goals;
- Being honest about both permanent and temporary changes—the truth sets you free;
- Receiving support from family and friends;
- Rejecting the idea that post-stroke afflictions are the product of victimization; no one is to be blamed for a stroke's pains;
- Refusing to dwell on the suffering after a stroke, and keeping an eye on the possibilities of the future;
- Looking on the bright side of life and maintaining a sense of humor ('laughter is the best medicine'); and
- Placing confidence in the capacity for rehabilitation with hard work and God's will to lead to eventual recovery; believe in your ability to do whatever it takes for as long as it takes to reach recovery goals.

Admittedly, I remember how difficult it was during my journey for me to heed my own advice. I fell short many times. The key to recovery is to persevere in the effort, with as much patience as required and as much dedication as possible. Don't get down when falling down; pull yourself up and keep trying. Never give up.

I don't like to think of myself as needing help, support or encouragement from others, but I realized how important help plays in recovery. In addition, I tried to avoid viewing myself as handicapped. At first I didn't mind having a handicap permit hanging from our car's rearview mirror because I had to admit that I was really handicapped. Still, that "handicapped parking permit" was a constant reminder of my persisting limitations. As I made rehabilitative progress I insisted "Chuck, remove that symbol from our rearview mirror. Take it down! I no longer need that." It was important for me to think of myself as a recovering disabled person whose disabilities would someday disappear. Part of my cure was to picture myself as eventually capable of jogging, yoga, Pilates…you name it. Thinking I could make it was the best means to actually make it. I would never recover if I did not think that "quality of life" could be restored in my future.

CROSSING MEDICAL CROSSROADS

The heat on the roadway rose to saturate our sensations that hot and hectic summer. On two epic days, July 17 and August 12, history repeated itself. Melodramatic turning points transpired, separated in time but similar in results. They had significant long-term consequences.

- **The First Fork in the Road**—The neurosurgeons scheduled an appointment on July 17 to evaluate if the shunt was set at the right pressure level and to take another look at Debbie's brain vessels to verify that no serious enlargements of scars or tears were evident. In particular, the scans focused on the blistered sites where the aneurism had burst January 8 and brain vessels had torn after the January 21 cerebral strokes. Carolinas General Surgery had conveniently scheduled on July 17 another type of examination.

  Following the radiological scans, we hustled to the Neurosurgery & Spine offices so our surgical team could inform us of the scan results. Given the previous crises, we were almost afraid to have the brain investigated. The previous inspection had not revealed reasons to perform preemptory brain surgery. What if problems were now discovered requiring surgery?

Well, our fears were not warranted. Joe Bernard called us into his chamber. "Take a look at these images," he instructed with his characteristic hint of a grin. "Compare today's picture of the aneurism site with that in January, that taken again on April 8, and also the images inspected on May 15. Look how much smaller the bulge or bubble on the blistered aneurism vessel is now—it's much smaller! It looks like the ballooning is continuing to shrink! It is now too small to risk a surgery procedure. Better to simply wait and watch longer and see what happens again in August. Maybe the danger is passing. I hope so. This is very good news for now."

Dr. Bernard's pronouncement produced spine-tingling thrills. Oh, ye of little faith. I guessed the luggage I had packed in case a surgery was needed was for naught. Thank the Lord.

We were additionally blessed by Dr. McLanahan's encouraging news—Debbie's shunt required only a modest reduction of pressure, and the adjustment with the magnetic device took seconds. No problems were detected to give me something to worry about, so Dr. McLanahan cheerfully dismissed us, saying "Now hit the road, and drive safely. I'll see you again in mid-August for the next examination. Congratulations on the positive reports."

Before hitting the interstate, as planned we traveled back to the CMC campus for Carolinas General Surgery's follow-up examination of the remaining abdominal hole after the G tube for feeding had been removed. Was the wound healing? Had I managed the dressings properly? Were there any indications of infection? In addition, the colostomy was scheduled for inspection.

Debbie motored herself with her walker into the third floor CGS reception area. The registered nurse was amazed at how well Debbie was doing and how energetic and high spirited she appeared. Dr. Paton arrived soon thereafter. Hugs were exchanged. She had performed many operations on Debbie and knew us well. One look at Debbie, and the accolades flowed. "Debbie, I am so pleased with how wonderful you look." Debbie shone. There was nothing like applause and approval to lift her spirits. "Now let's see what's under the hood. Strip off your top, please."

Dr. Paton's trained eye looked first at the incision opening where I had stuffed the ever-shortening dressing tape, always worrying that my elongated Q-tip might have caused a puncture. "This looks good," Dr. Paton said. "It's sufficiently healed, so Chuck, you can cease the dressing and merely cover the sore with gauze tape for the next three weeks until the wound totally heals. Do not use antibiotic cream—just soap and water, like you have previously when overseeing Debbie's showers." This was great news.

Next our beloved surgeon inspected the colostomy. The ostomy hole to which the bag was attached exhibited no serious signs of redness or bleeding. That was good. However, the obtrusive bag had poised some problems beyond the messy nuisance of draining the bowel discharges in a timely manner. After showers I cleaned the ostomy surface to secure a fresh bag. Needless to say, the bag was a cosmetic disaster, protruding from Debbie's upper stomach and necessitating loose-fitting clothing to conceal the embarrassing bulge. Worse still, on three occasions during sleep, the bag had swelled with fecal discharge, breaking the plastic and, well, making a mess of poor Debbie's bedclothes and bedsheets. This was an apparatus that no one wanted attached to their body. It was a lousy substitute for discharge through the colon and anus. Yet the colostomy was indispensable for people like Debbie whose intestines were not connected, for which there was no alternative.

Or was there? Dr. Paton sprang a surprise question. "Debbie, do you want to have me operate sometime in the future to remove the colostomy? It's possible. If a surgery to reconnect the upper and lower colons succeeds, you can poop. This operation is not necessary and can be dangerous. It's purely elective. You don't have to have it done. But my guess is that, at your young age, I doubt if you want to be changing colostomy bags the rest of what may be a long life. You could live another fifty years. What do you think? Do you want to go down this road?"

Without hesitation, Debbie begged, "Please remove that ugly, messy bag. I'm ready to pack by bags—my luggage bags, not my colostomy bags—and head down this road as soon as possible."

Dr. Paton then read Debbie the riot act:

Okay, we can explore this option in time. But there's an urgent prerequisite before we can even seriously think about such a surgical operation. First you must gain weight. A lot of weight. Typically, patients lose about ten pounds from this kind of surgery and must stay in the hospital for post-surgery care about a week to ten days to recover. A lot can go wrong. So here's my demand—you *must* weigh no less than a hundred and twenty-five pounds before this operation can be scheduled. Do not even bother to come back for the next evaluation until you reach this goal. That weight must be attained, or else! Besides, you need it for your strength; you are still much too thin. My assistant will give you a handout on diet instructions, which must be followed. Chuck, don't let Debbie slip and come up short. Debbie, let me repeat my former advice—keep your eye on the prize. Oh, by the way, I love the way your hair is growing back in your cute haircut.

While driving home, Debbie said, "I am absolutely thrilled about the direction these three examinations took. To be honest, I am somewhat ambivalent about the dietary requirements." Her approach-avoidance reaction was easy to read—she desired the operation desperately but dreaded the dietary means necessary to attain the goal. Debbie really had no choice but to accommodate the doctor's weight requirements. To punctuate the demands, when we arrived home, a fax was waiting: "Please remember, Debbie, you *must* gain weight before Dr. Paton or Dr.

Schiffern will be willing to schedule another examination in preparation for your surgery. If the weight goal is met, we can think about a preparatory examination in early September to check the stoma and take rectal and colon images before scheduling the ostomy reversal."

We had a plan and a roadmap to a desired destination. The "Battle of the Bulge" began, with Debbie cooperating fully: "I looked at myself in the full-length mirror and my appearance was horrifying. I bought into the program by focusing on the treasured reward. Chuck cheered each mouthful of food I swallowed and every can of Boost I gulped to increase my calorie intake."

Pitfalls and pit stops notwithstanding, that summer the trend line was moving in the preferred direction, interrupted by modest perturbations and disruptions. Her hard work was driving rehabilitation forward. A lengthy distance had been traveled. Would that progress continue? In less than a month, Debbie's surgeons would make more examinations on which to base some informed prognoses.

- **Facing a Second Juncture**—On August 12, the second set of medical crossroads stood on the horizon, with an agenda so similar to that on July 17 that it felt like in Yogi Berra's famous statement, it was "déjà vu all over again." We took another road trip to CMC's radiology facility to estimate the feasibility of a colon reversal operation and to conduct another CT brain angiogram to determine whether more brain surgeries were necessary.

  Debbie's surgeons would once again face the necessity of making fateful decisions. Their choices were certain to steer the subsequent direction of our long journey during our summer sojourn. If more surgical interventions into Debbie's brain surgery was deemed required, what would be the probable consequences? Would more really help? Or would they prove to be historic mistakes that might end Debbie's life or leave her chained perilously close to the precipice, permanently bedridden? Which way would we head? We would soon find out.

We learned first about the "end game"—radiological news about the status of Debbie's colon. Martha's report got right to "the bottom" of the issue: "Dr. Paton was pleased with the colon images. No problems were discovered. If Debbie manages to meet her weight goal of a hundred and twenty-five pounds, a consultation about a colon reconnection surgery could be planned." She faxed a copy of the formal final written report. That report recorded, "Study performed from the rectum to the middescending colon at site of colostomy. At left midabdominal site, no bowel obstruction is evident. No persistent filling defects were seen to suggest an intraluminal mass. No constricting lesions were identified. There was no significant diverticular disease. Condition unremarkable." The path appeared clear to plan ahead for the briefing on procedures and permissions on September 4, providing all the necessary weight preconditions were fulfilled in the interim. This was great. An end was coming into sight.

The new set of CT angiogram scans used advanced new technology to better determine how the clip on Debbie's original brain aneurism was performing. At issue was the grim possibility that another major surgery requiring the opening of Debbie's skull could still be necessary. If so, the risks were infinite. Everything gained since January 8 could be lost. The operation could even be fatal. So these cerebral angiogram results held the key to Debbie's probable destiny.

We put our trust in the capable brains that would review the brain images, and accepted the delay that would be required for the entire neurosurgery team, our "brain trust," to inspect them and report the results by telephone. In the meantime, Debbie resumed her rehabilitation program back home and at Health South. We waited, hoping to take our first road trip to a destination other than a hospital in order to attend the annual St. John's Lutheran Church homecoming service in Wytheville Virginia. But on the day we planned to travel there, no word about the brain scan was forthcoming by the time the therapy sessions concluded. "Should we go anyway?" Debbie asked. "Why not? We can learn the results from our cell phone. Let's get going." And off we darted.

We drove through Charlotte and became rather unnerved when we could see the rest stop near Lake Norman where, on January 8, the life-threatening stroke had occurred. We raced past that spot as quickly as possible, recalling the crisis and the miraculous life-preserving improbability that that stroke had occurred where it did. God certainly had something to do with the location, which made possible reaching a hospital in time for Debbie's life to be saved.

With these spots in the rearview mirror, we drove on Interstate 77 toward Wytheville and were approaching the Virginia border when the cell phone rang. It was Paula from the neurosurgery office. Our hearts palpitated rapidly. "I have good news from the brain scans last Tuesday. Sorry it has taken so long for the neurosurgeon team to review the results. Are you sitting down?"

"Yes," Debbie answered, "we are now driving to Virginia."

Paula continued, "I know you'll have a wonderful time in your mountain home. Let me give you the news that will make your trip even more enjoyable. The scans showed that at the site where the clip was installed, the 'bulge' on the brain vessel, has almost disappeared. It is tiny. It appears the 'blimp' has shrunk, and the lesions have almost healed. Dr. Bernard is amazed at this incredible breakthrough. No surgery needs to be performed. The surgeons have scheduled an interview when you return again to CMC to see Dr. Paton, with whom we have been in communication, so the neurosurgeons can then also take a further peek at the vessels."

We met this news with astonished glee. The last time we were this high was on our wedding night. Whoa! We could see God's hands in this—which made this surprising, auspicious development appear less unbelievable but still a miracle. However, it did "passeth all understanding" (Phil. 4:7). For confirmation, to make sure we were not having a wishful-thinking hallucination, I asked Paula for a written report. Dated 14 August, we received in writing the best news for which we could hope. It read, "Dear Mrs. Kegley: I had the opportunity to review the CT angiogram performed on August 12, 2014. I am very pleased to let you know that there is no obvious residual or recurrent aneurism. This is fabulous. I don't see any need for a catheter placed treatment in the future, therefore, I can see you on an 'as-needed' basis. Continued follow-up with Dr. McLanahan for your shunt is encouraged. Sincerely, Joe D. Bernard MD."

TOO GOOD TO BE TRUE?

We were overwhelmed and overjoyed. All these advances forward had surprisingly taken place smoothly and safely. Did they presage more good news? I was skeptical. We had seen our hopes rise to the heights by reports in the past, only to see those hopes dashed by a major new crisis. Were these conclusions really true? It was as if we had read about them in *Ripley's Believe It or Not*.

Recall that I am a chronic worrier. Our long journey had been punctuated by a series of disappointments at various junctions that had smothered growing hopes that all was well. From them I had learned the hard way to expect the unexpected and to take nothing for granted.

I was predisposed to question the veracity of any single test. My training for my Ph. D. predisposed me to regard research findings with cautious suspicion; there was no such thing as "proof," only evidence. Moreover, I knew better than to rely on self-proclaimed expert opinion (a tongue-in-check definition of a Ph. D.—"Piled Higher and Deeper"). My practiced caution toward reported study "findings" was enhanced by the inconsistency of reported "news" in the field of health science. How many times have you read newspaper headlines proclaiming some fantastic discovery (e.g., "Study Finds That Smoking Is Good for You")? When it comes to health, everyone claims to be an expert. It sometimes seems that there are a lot of people setting health policy who can't spell "policy." It didn't reduce my lack of confidence to read a medical health care consultant warn, "Patients can't assume the health care system will work like they want it to. Patients have to manage their own health care and pay attention to detail. The sad part is, most people don't know they have to do it. If you are the patient, you need to be persistent in pestering health care providers for test results, and if you are the provider, you shouldn't assume that someone else is going to break the news to the patient."

Still haunted by fear of embracing false hopes regarding Debbie's remarkably improved medical condition, I would rather have these terrific results to question than having to face the opposite "grave" results (word choice intentional). The study's findings provided a needed springboard for high hopes. The exceptional knowledge of Debbie's doctors was as good as it gets. Moreover, just because improbable news sometimes appears to be too good to be true doesn't mean that it is false. Think of the good news of the Bible gospels; the story of Jesus had to be true, C. S. Lewis was fond of saying, because no one could make this story up.

I really had no recourse but to count on the accuracy of the findings. I began to question why I had been so pessimistic, so terrified. My chronic fears were unwarranted. It was time for me to get over my haunting terror and let Debbie speed forward in high gear. She could move downhill now; the hard drive had overnight become less hard.

Emboldened by this huge advance, we hastened the speed toward the short remaining distance to Twin Oaks, our hilltop Virginia home. Our schedule only permitted staying four nights, but we packed it with activities. We attended at Andy and Nan Kegley's historic Rose Hill family homestead a prenuptial engagement party to honor Calder Kegley and Megan Greear, who were to be married in Roanoke October 31. Sunday we attended the annual reopening of St. John's Lutheran Church for services. Our pastor announced "Debbie Kegley is here with us," and the congregation rose to applaud her return. We placed flowers on the graves of family in the 240-year-old cemetery listed on the National Historic Registry, where Debbie and I had already purchased and engraved our headstones. Following the beautiful church service, a huge picnic was held on the church grounds, where many were able to speak with Debbie for the first time since her stroke. We were so glad that we had taken this journey. This was a great homecoming.

The summertime heat was finally giving way to cooler weather, and as fall approached we looked forward to continuing our journey.

CHAPTER 25

FAST FORWARD IN THE FALL?

§

During the final four months of 2014, Debbie's condition remained in flux. It was fall. Would this be a time when Debbie would fall down? Or would she continue to rise up? Or something intermediate, with both downs and ups? Every elongated journey includes abrupt stops and resurgent starts. Our eyes were wide open, and the road on the horizon swerved in different directions. The first turn set precedents for what followed.

A SURGICAL COMING-OUT PARTY

The fall season centered on therapies and efforts to gain additional weight in preparation for the colon-reversal surgery. That operation was the departure gate for the remaining journey.

- **Weight-Watcher Blues?**—Debbie resumed her food fights in "the battle of the bulge." Gaining weight was a protracted struggle, and she fought hard, consenting to appetite-stimulation medication. We waited for weight. Hilel urged Debbie on, asking on one occasion, "Isn't it time for Debbie's feeding?"

    "'Feeding?'" I inquired. "Do you think she's a pet with a set time to be fed?" Thereafter, "Do you want to feed now?" became a frequent refrain.

The prescribed diet was religiously followed, and Debbie proudly proclaimed, "My efforts to eat larger portions are beginning to pay off. On the eve of my appointment, my weight hit 122 pounds. Was it close enough to the goal to proceed? Fortunately, the nursing staff accepted my 'white lie' that I had 'almost' crossed their high bar, and set September 4th for their consultation and evaluation."

- **"I Don't Need No Stinking Bag!"**—Debbie broke the speed limit driving toward her desired destination—removal of her bulging ostomy bag. "Chuck, I am sick and tired of that pouch collecting fecal matter, which you have to repeatedly drain and replace." So was I. The bag made no contribution to our romantic moments.

  A few pounds short of 125 pounds, we speculated what Dr. Paton would say. We powered to Charlotte to find out. Dr. Paton's look showed no sign of disapproval. "Debbie," she asked, "are you ready to proceed with the surgery?" What a relief. Then came the warnings: "There could be complications—wound infections and leakage in the colon connections. There is a five percent chance that the operation will not work, and a whole new replacement colostomy will have to be implanted. The operation is no cakewalk—it will take between three to five hours. Expect weight loss, fatigue, scar tissue, and a week or more hospital stay. You may experience bladder-control problems and diarrhea, and of course your rehabilitation therapies will have to be interrupted. Still want to go ahead?" Debbie's "Yes" echoed throughout the room. The game was on. Surgery was scheduled at the end of the month.

- **We Are Family**—Elated, and not wanting to let an opportunity pass, I placed a call to Carolinas Neurosurgery & Spine, begging like a dog asking for a walk. "Might it be possible for Dr. Dyer to see Debbie? We don't have a scheduled appointment." The receptionist said, "You can try. He is in the office seeing patients." Nothing ventured, nothing gained. We arrived within minutes and received a pleasant surprise. Our busy surgeons interrupted their schedule so they could see us. They gave Debbie hugs and praise. Thrilled by Debbie's appearance, Dr. Dyer chimed in, "Chuck, good to see you not crying for a change. Thanks for standing by Debbie every minute. You should claim the title 'Wife Reconditioning Expert.' Debbie, your rehabilitation is legendary and makes our profession worthwhile." I thanked Dr. Dyer, and he responded—"Chuck, no need for thanks. Our credo is to treat every patient as if they were a family member."

- "We feel like family," I replied. "We have seen your adherence to the Golden Rule as your team has managed seemingly intractable challenges. Your team has literally been a lifesaver."

- **Over and Out**—We returned to CMC on September 30 to attempt the colon-reversal operation. The pre-operation preparations began promptly. Debbie joked, "I get your point," as the anesthesiologists shot her painkillers. Dr. Paton dismissed me to the waiting room, urging, "Chuck, relax. We expect to start Debbie's colon-linkage surgery at 8:15 a.m. The operation will take between three and six hours, if all goes smoothly."

The time in the waiting room was similar to aging—it seemed to pass faster the longer it lasted. At 10:45 a.m. the speakers reverberated throughout the room: "Will the family of Debra Kegley come to the reception desk." What? I had waved good-bye to my precious wife a short time ago. Why so soon? Did the surgeons conclude that the operation to reconnect the upper and lower colon was too risky to perform? It couldn't be already over, could it? Or had something terrible happened?

I entered the consultation chamber feeling like a swimmer encircled by a shark. Dr. Paton was there waiting. Her post-op briefing swept my anxiety away like the air from a popped balloon. She got right to the point. "The radiology report simply stated 'no problems found,' so we began surgery immediately. The operation went extremely well, and we completed it in less than half the time than what a colon-reversal without leaks or complications normally takes. Let me abandon all humility—I am proud of how the operation went. Debbie's colon has now been sewn together and the incision site for that colostomy tube and pouch stitched closed. As long as there are no unforeseen issues, you can say good riddance to that bag. Chuck, knowing you, you probably want Debbie's last bag as a keepsake. If all heals in the next two or three days, and Debbie is able to have a bowel movement, you can take her home, make sure she regains the lost weight and allow her to gradually resume physical activity. She's come a long way, and God has been with her. Kristen and I will check on Debbie in a couple of hours in her room." Dr. Paton and I exchanged hugs. Jubilant relief pervaded the consultation chamber. God was there for us again! Our Lord never misses!

- **You Can Come Home Again, After All**—I rushed to the Hospitality House, where I had been assigned room 308—the same room where I had spent eighty consecutive days during those dark January through April 2 nights when Debbie had hung by her fingernails on the edge of eternity. Oddly, it seemed like home as memories flashed of those many sleepless nights when Debbie was so close to death's door. It was here that my relationship with God had grown stronger and stronger. Sometimes you must go into the dark in order to see the light. I had learned during those black nights in ways I could not have otherwise—that if I stood on a solid rock of trust in God (Ps. 18:2), ironically troubles would help to nourish and strengthen my bonds with my Almighty Father.

- **Coming Out**—Debbie was carried into her new hospital room, and the sun came out. As the painkillers wore off, the smiles came on. The bag was gone, and Debbie was there. I had no doubt that Debbie was ready to give recovery all she could muster. She always did. It was only a matter of how long it would take to climb back onto the roadway. This wasn't unfamiliar terrain.

The pathway forward was well lit. The doctors instructed Debbie to try to get her bowels working—to digest liquid meals and laxatives to enable defecation, without a rip or tear in the area where her colon had been stitched together. To our surprise, we learned that the best way of stimulating the digestive and colon tract into action was to attempt to walk with a walker on the two-hundred-foot loop around the square where the wing's hospital rooms were located. "This will take some courage and concentrated effort, especially at first," Dr. Paton warned that evening. "Rest today, and try tomorrow."

"I carefully climbed out of my bed, stood upright, and my nurse showed me how to cover my rear, which the hospital wrap left exposed. She tied a second wrap around my neck to form a cape." Debbie was adorable. That cape was a real pleaser. She looked like Superwoman. Slowly and painfully, step by step, Debbie circled the loop—with me tagging along prepared to catch her should she slip, saying, "I've got your back." She made it. "The Rascal" increased the distance by steadily adding more trips. Other patients were trying to conduct the same exercises, and Debbie passed them on the loop.

Finally, on Friday Debbie said, "I had my first fecal discharge. It was tiny—not something to brag about." Stronger laxatives and stool softeners did not produce the desired results. Constipation or some sort of blockage could be preventing her ability to "go," and if so, this was not good. "We may have goofed," one of the physicians confessed. "We were probably too aggressive in Debbie's diet, moving her beyond only very soft foods too soon. We'll see how she responds to a return to soft foods."

The diet was modified, and the problem "passed" late Saturday evening when a bowel movement of desired mass occurred. No tears, bleeding or fevers were evident. Fecal discharges were coming out, and this brought psychological and physical relief. If this episode wasn't the *end* all! As the flow increased, Debbie increased her walking. She was tired and still slightly bloated, yet step by step she stepped up her rehabilitative conditioning. Her outgoing personality was now matched by her bowel output.

- **Time to "Go"**—This was not exactly a "coming out" party. But it was close. The danger had begun to wane. The doctors hinted that the hospital's discharge was coming within sight. I was, as usual, paranoid—was release from hospital care premature? "We'll be careful, Chuck, and prudent," Dr. Paton promised. "We won't lie to you"—she winked—"just rearrange the facts. Just kidding. We won't discharge Debbie until we're reasonably sure she's safe to head home. Debbie, you're doing great. You have finally succeeded in realizing our goal: all tubes out. Keep you-know-what coming!"

What came was not only regularity but also an announcement that a discharge had been authorized. Dr. Paton's marching instructions included watching for a series of possible symptoms that could spell serious problems, covering the place where the stoma had been removed with gauze tape to catch any seepage, and returning for a follow-up examination. "No need to plan a funeral or write a new will—a will is a dead giveaway," she joked. "Debbie, I hope everything comes out okay. Chuck, I know you love that bag from the heart of your bottom." This humorous side to Dr. Paton's personality had been hidden while she was busy providing medical care. Now on the eve of our departure, she opened up with witty puns to brighten our bittersweet departure on a light note. They called for a rejoinder. "Beverley, you're a lot of 'pun.' What kind of a 'crack' is that?" were the best rejoinders I could roust up.

"Chuck, since around here you're so fond of Debbie's cape, I'm authorizing that you take two of the hospital bed garments with you, so you can help Debbie walk around your house wearing her 'cape.'" Elated by this affectionate gesture, we exited and excitedly hit the highway.

- **In the Passing Lane**—After successfully passing waste, Debbie didn't waste a moment recapturing her rehabilitative momentum. She reentered the passing lane and sped onward. Her perseverance and resilience were astonishing. She was overcoming each barrier on the road. All along, we both knew that God had carried and uplifted her each mile of her long journey. There was no reason to doubt that His heavy lifting would continue.

THE ROAD RACE RESUMES

There are two kinds of people—those who think there are two kinds of people and those who don't. In point of fact, there are two groups—the quick and the dead. Thanks to God's miracles, Debbie was among "the quick" and not "the dead." In the wake of her colon surgery, she spent the remaining days in the fall of 2014 expanding her exercise and spiritual agenda.

- **Walking the Walk**—The very next day after her hospital discharge, Debbie resumed her full therapy schedule at Health South. There was no stopping her. Debbie's fighting drive was best shown by increasing the distance she was walking. Walking—somewhat like someone wearing a swimmer's flipper on their right foot—but walking nonetheless. The next weekend she used her walker to cover in the Cobblestone gym fifteen hundred feet and doubled that distance—more than a half mile—a week later.

  She set sight on her next goal and reached it quickly. She discarded her walker, insisting on walking only with a support cane. With me trailing behind for safety, she covered eight hundred yards. She was not content stopping there. Debbie pledged, "I am going to try to conduct all mobility on my own so I can say good-bye to that cane." She had something to prove. You can probably guess the outcome. Success was just around the corner.

- **The Cane Mutiny**—We hosted the Crows for dinner in our home, at which time I construed a cane-retirement ceremony I titled "the cane mutiny." We convinced them to enjoy some select wine from our wine cellar to celebrate the end of Debbie's use of a cane. The four of us gave thanks to God as we recalled Debbie's breathtaking transition from a bed in ICU, to wheelchair, to walker, to a cane, and next the final step—unassisted walking. Still limping wearing her ankle brace, she was nonetheless ambulatory on autopilot.

- **Treading on the Treadmill**—Later that fall Debbie reached another milestone. "Feeling growing confidence, I asked Theo for permission to try the Health South treadmill. Hesitantly, he agreed, and was he ever impressed! Sure, my pace was slow, and I intentionally reduced it to work on controlling my gait without letting my right foot 'fling' outward. I put 'quality over quantity' by holding the treadmill's handrails and concentrating on my leg motion. My first efforts were limited to about five minutes. Gradually, my time and distance increased. Dr. Dan turned his trained eyes on my treadmill performance and suggested modifications in my walking style."

- In the process, muscle memory was being built for correct walking. To accelerate progress, Debbie began combining in a single session hikes and simulated "marching" in the gym with incremental increases in the amount of time and distance on the treadmill. Muscles were also developing in Debbie's legs, where as recently as three months ago only atrophied, flaccid pencil-thin calves and ankles could be seen; now some muscle tone and definition were evident, especially in her left leg which was noticeably larger than her right leg.

- **The Agony of "De-Feet"**—Debbie's most troubling disability was her "drop foot," which prevented her from lifting her right toes and foot. This common post-stroke affliction causes lameness and walking debilities. However, if Debbie had to suffer a prolonged disability, drop-foot was preferable to most other motor-function difficulties. To "defeat" her foot dysfunction, Health South had her use an ankle-foot orthosis, or "AFO." Debbie wrote, "The AFO was inserted into the larger gym shoes Chuck purchased for me. I immediately saw its advantages. That said, my weakness and incapacity to lift my foot and toes on command were very frustrating." We clung to the hope that total self-reliance would come in time, with hard work and hard drive.

- **The Payoff of Persistence**—"My efforts centered on physical exercises, working hardest   on my 'drop foot' dysfunctions," Debbie explained. "While exercising in the gym, I overheard a pessimistic self-appointed 'expert' proclaim 'no stroke victim with a drop-foot disability ever recovers.'"

That pessimistic person neither knew what she was talking about nor about whom she was talking. Radiating with confident determination, Debbie had things to prove. "No disabled person should ever stop trying," Debbie declared. "I would never give up! My slogan was 'Don't wait around waiting for something to happen—initiate what you want to see happen, don't look back, take advantage of every piece of good advice that comes your way, always reach beyond your grasp, and practice, practice, practice every therapy procedure.' I worked and worked on my 'drop-foot' problem, and gradually I began to realize modest results. I had learned that repeated exercise spurs the development of new neural and synapse connections, and that brains can be trained to build and strengthen particular neural pathways. Activation of my nerve wiring, what my therapists called 'habituation through repetition,' clearly was creating neuro-links from my left brain to my right toes, and I began to see some effects. Although there is not a single prescription that works for everyone, electro-stimulation and exercises were steadily working for me."

- **Take a Hike**—We purchased a less-obtrusive and less-limiting Aircast ankle-support brace to replace the foot-to-knee AFO support device. Debbie recalls, "I embraced my new brace like a puppy approaches a bowl of fresh dog food, and immediately hiked a full mile the first day. Eventually, with the aid of my new brace, I hiked the three-mile hilly 'loop' surrounding our Blue Ridge Virginia home! Following this achievement, I moved on to new reinforcing exercises. I practiced trotting, knee-bend squats, jumping in the squares on a flat plastic "agility ladder" placed on the floor, and climbing the mechanical step-master." To tweak the regime, we had heard that acupuncture sometimes works in the treatment of drop foot, and we scheduled an appointment with Dr. William Skelton to see if this approach could reduce the limp and right-toe immobility. Eight acupuncture treatments helped.

Elated with her growing speed, agility and endurance, Debbie looked at me longingly, asking, "Do you think someday we'll be able to return to our beloved chalet in Mürren Switzerland?" This is where we had celebrated many anniversaries and friends stored hiking boots and clothes for us. "You bet. I don't see why not," I optimistically predicted.

Motivated by resolve to overcome obstacles, Debbie banged on doors that could have remained locked; I believed in time she would transcend the remaining barriers. As we pictured walking paved paths in the high Swiss mountains, the Alps came alive with the sound of music.

- **Pumping the Pump**—Debbie insisted on using some of Cobblestone Park's mechanical gym equipment. She started to pump iron. As you might expect, she gradually expanded her gym routine. She began using the leg press, chest press, shoulder press, and seated leg curl and increased the number of repetitions on each machine and set of weights. Similarly, the number of new PT maneuvers introduced at Health South just grew and grew. Some of the innovations were remarkably challenging; when I learned of a new one, I wondered how Debbie was going to thread *that* needle. She never failed.

- **Helping Hands around the House**—With growing strength and mobility, Debbie escalated her contribution to home care. Making the bed, folding clothes, preparing most evening meals, running the vacuum sweeper, sorting out and taking her own medications, wiping counters, preparing the coffee maker at night for the morning's breakfast, loading and unloading the dishwasher, doing laundry, shopping for groceries, paying bills, saving me every time I had one of my frequent computer panic attacks, troubleshooting and managing the confusing remote controls for our television, showering without my hovering assistance, writing birthday and sympathy cards, helping me with these memoirs, taking her turn saying prayers at meals and reading prior to sleep the designated daily Bible lesson from *Our Daily Bread*—step by step, she began doing it all.

It was a good thing that by year's end, Debbie "reclaimed her kitchen" and took charge preparing our dinners. I was out of a job, and our need for the Care Team's meals had diminished, so their regular visits bringing meals and joy ended. To express appreciation, Debbie hosted her Flock to a luncheon, at which I improvised an emotional prayer that led to a tear or two. Observing Debbie's improving capabilities, the neighbors' "Meal Train" also rolled to a stop.

- **On the Road Again**—Debbie was on a roll, and we rolled into Charlotte for follow-up medical appointments. "I am excited to see you," Dr. Paton greeted, "and very pleased with your condition, Debbie. No more colostomy, and the stoma is healing nicely. The sad part now is that the surgical team will not have an excuse to see you unless we—or you, Chuck—invent one." I was tempted. I promised to ship our remaining supply of colostomy supplies, which Dr. Paton said could be of use to patients without the means to purchase them. We exchanged hugs and pledged to keep in contact.

We hustled from there to Carolinas Neurosurgery & Spine. Dr. Scott McLanahan checked the readings on the shunt monitor and liked what he saw. "No need for an adjustment this time, Debbie. My associates and I are very pleased to see the remarkable progress you have made. God must be looking out for you. And you are pulling your weight—but all of us wish you had more weight to pull so your strength can build faster. Let me know if you experience any of the symptoms identified in the literature you and Chuck have been provided, such as fatigue or head swelling. As for me, unless you experience problems, you won't have to see me again until a year from now, when we'll examine the shunt and, perhaps, think about surgery to remove it. I see concern on your face, Chuck. A shunt is a foreign object to the body, which it is geared to reject. Some people have shunts for years, even decades, if and when they are needed. Let's revisit this later. Good-bye for now, and keep up the fantastic recovery and rehabilitation."

- **May I Have This Dance?**—During a Health South physical therapy session, I was summoned into the treatment area for a surprise. Debbie had informed Theo that we would soon be attending a wedding in Roanoke. "Watch," Theo instructed me as he took Debbie in his arms, and they circled in a dance. "Debbie wants to be able to dance at the wedding, and look—she can."

  A big lump of pride throttled my throat. "Here, let me try," I said as I swept beautiful Debbie's slender body into my arms and swung her slowly in a small circle. She held me tightly. I dipped her, and the entire room exploded with thunderous cheering applause. Instinctively I choked up and tried to hide my moist eyes. This was shared love.

  This emotional moment preceded our trip north to the historic Roanoke hotel where the family wedding to which we had been invited was held. We were treated royally. "I was able to participate in all of the festivities," Debbie wrote, "and had a great time. We slowly danced at the reception, and I mustered the strength to use the hotel's treadmill for fifteen minutes." Motoring south toward Blythewood, Debbie urged, "Let's spend Thanksgiving at Twin Oaks. It will give us a long weekend in Virginia." We agreed on that plan.

- **Giving Thanks at Thanksgiving**—I was thankful that Debbie had insisted on preparing our Thanksgiving meal for the two of us. She made her famous green-bean casserole and was spared suffering what I would have drummed up had I been the cook. We enjoyed being alone, without company. We had each other, and that was everything we wanted. So I gave a special prayer of thanksgiving to God.

  Debbie and I worked out in the spacious Wytheville Community Center gym, where Debbie received warm welcomes from many friends who were thrilled to see her recovered enough to use some of the exercise equipment. Debbie managed twenty-five minutes on the treadmill, and I did my mirth-provoking imitation of a swimmer in the center's pool. Sunday we sat with Nancy Kegley at Holy Trinity Lutheran Church's worship service. Pastor Steve opened with announcements prior to the service. "Behold God's power—Debbie Kegley is here with us! I know almost all of you have prayed for Debbie's survival and recovery. Your prayers are being answered. Welcome home, Debbie and Chuck." Out came handkerchiefs.

- **Stayin' Alive**—Our Direct TV set had numerous commercial-free radio stations, and it was tuned to the '80s when, prior to Debbie's hike on our driveway and Rose Hill Road, the tune "Stayin' alive… stayin' alive" belted throughout the house and porches from the speakers we had installed. The refrain rang so true—I'm "dead" serious. Debbie was *staying alive* and growing stronger.

  On the return trip to South Carolina, we passed the two landmarks where our long, dark journey had begun—the interstate rest stop and Lake Norman Hospital. These were the spots on January 8 where the Lord had intervened to pull Debbie from the shadows of death. I carefully measured the distance from the rest stop to the exit for the hospital—less than two miles. We recalled our calls to our Lord and His responses. We thanked God that that near-fatal crisis had happened where it did; it was a true miracle, and not by coincidence, that when her stroke struck it was at that exact spot. Anyplace else would have meant certain death. We knew Debbie had been carried by God's almighty will.

- **Nearing a "Declaration of Independence"?**—If I could write Debbie's formal functional independence measure (FIM) evaluation, as the year's end approached, I would have put her above 90 percent in every category of assessment (except right ankle and foot) and 100 percent in many categories. The therapists at Health South did not report precisely their comparisons and individual assessments in a written summary, but there was little doubt that the evaluations were high and getting higher. The therapists said during a mid-December family conference session, "Debbie is reaching full functional independence and moving by leaps and bounds toward self-sufficiency."

Now running on high octane, Debbie's tenacity and trust in God's protection fueled her ability to put more distance between her former fragility and her desired rehabilitative destiny. She issued her "Declaration of Independence" as she strove hard toward her goal of severing dependence on help to assist daily living. The only worthy dependence was dependence on God.

A game changer on our long journey was Debbie's wonderfully cheerful attitude. She was positive during the entire first year of her trip. This helped her rehabilitation and resilience immeasurably. One conversation suffices to enable you to picture her frame of mind. I once asked her if she would, if given a choice, trade places with anyone she knew. "Absolutely not!" she exclaimed.

The rest of the year was devoted primarily to the routines that were serving Debbie so well. Health South kept up the pressure, and Debbie stepped up the rehabilitative pace, using her acquired know-how expertly. We felt blessed, as we should be. What had transpired for Debbie, now known far and wide as "the Walking Miracle," continued to remain remarkable. The advent—the coming into being— of a new beginning on this journey appeared to be happening.

- **"Exit" or "Entrance"?**—We returned to Wytheville on Christmas Eve to spend the holidays in our mountain home. The setting was perfect for prayer. We always felt somehow closer to God in the heights of the mountains. A beautiful three-inch snow covered the terrain and forests.

To our way of thinking, the Christmas holiday has a single meaningful purpose—to celebrate, in fulfillment of sacred scriptural prophecies, the birth of the incarnate Savior. We were in full spiritual gear. We placed emphasis on the new covenant God had made with humanity to save people from sin. This watershed moment was transformative. Christ's birth changed the course of history, forever. Everything changed. The eternal questions gained new, enduring answers. Christ's sacrifice on the cross created a new world. Our journey was blessed with His reassuring Word.

We were happy to be alive. It was hard, however, to simply take one day at a time. Every single day was special, of course, especially in light of how close Debbie had come to her last day on earth. A stupefying thought struck us—we were nearing a full year since January 8 when Debbie's stroke had shattered our lives. Actually, we concluded, there could be nothing better than to be present at the end of days, when Jesus returned and we could truly live twice, this time forever. We were ready!

On January 8—a year since the first brain aneurism had burst—we repressed the frightful memories. We hardly said a word. The long journey was not over. We had put many miles down the road. It appeared that there might be many more ahead. We thanked God that with His miracles the journey could continue. We couldn't wait to learn what lay ahead.

The year also concluded on a strange "role reversal." Debbie recalls, "Chuck came down with a chronic cough and virus in our Virginia home during the Christmas holidays. I had garnered sufficient strength to play the role he had so faithfully provided me for twelve months: I became his caregiver, nursing him back to health. I was thrilled to be able to give back to him some of what he had provided me. Through this role reversal, I felt in the process like my old, but better, self."

- **Lest We Forget**—Our blessings were many. God had provided protection, and we pledged we would never forget His merciful intercessions. Our Lord had pulled Debbie from death's door. These lifts from the abyss could not be seen as anything but miracles.

Not to be forgotten were the extraordinary dangers after a stroke strikes. Strokes strike thousands every week. They can happen to anyone, at anytime, anywhere. Debbie looked like she was forging an escape, but we were reminded of the probable perils by two incidents.

Debbie received the horrifying news that one of the members of her Focus women's bible study group had been struck by a stroke resulting from a ruptured aneurism in her brain stem. She died during surgery. That poor child of God was younger than Debbie and, like Debbie, had no warning symptoms. A stroke can strike at any age; strokes are one of the worst things that can happen. Debbie and I had learned to be mindful of this danger, and to use our remaining time trying to serve God's purposes.

The second incident illuminates the fact that, as Eugene O'Neill concluded, "None of us can help the things that happen to us." Nothing should be taken for granted. "One day I noticed that a member of my therapy group had missed a number of sessions," Debbie remembers, "so I asked if anybody knew why. She had made great progress recovering and was scheduled for discharge. 'Oh,' I was told, 'Joanie had a fall over the weekend in the shower. She hit her head and was rushed to an emergency room. She is still unconsciousness in the intensive care unit, on life support. She is in a coma.'" That kind of tragedy gets your attention and commands your empathy. Recovery from a stroke carries no guarantees. Life may be short. It is not prudent to make assumptions. Count your blessings, but don't count on your future health. Still, count on the Lord's love, and give thanks for His care.

We counted our blessings. We had been profoundly blessed. God had worked many miracles. Many thresholds had been crossed and many potential dangers avoided. God had hit a reset button for Debbie. There was no question in our minds that God had been our guide, uplifting and carrying Debbie great distances on our dark journey. Christ gives light "to those who sit in darkness and the shadow of death" (John 1:7; Luke 1:79). The road was shining brightly as the first year of our long journey concluded. God had provided abundant reasons for us to place complete faith in Him.

PART IV: DISPELLING DARKNESS

Your beliefs become your thoughts.
Your thoughts become your words.
Your words become your actions.
Your actions become your habits.
Your habits become your values.
Your values become your destiny.

—MAHATMA GANDHI

CHAPTER 26

"WHY ME? WHY NOT ME?"

§

"Surprise is your only teacher," Charles Sanders Pierce wrote. On January 8, 2014, Debbie's stroke struck. We didn't see this catastrophe coming. There were no symptoms. In the blink of an eye, an aneurism broke. The stroke was the nightmarish surprise of a lifetime. The shock and aftershocks drove us into an existential and spiritual schoolroom.

Debbie's stroke surprised everyone. Sadly, strokes happen frequently, but hers was as unlikely as a wildfire in a desert. Time and time again, people said, "Debbie is the last person on earth I would have guessed would have a stroke." For good reasons—Debbie was the picture of health. She was young, healthy, in superb shape, and had had no previous major illnesses.

The leading correlates of strokes are obesity, high cholesterol, smoking addiction, and high blood pressure. Debbie was devoid of them all. Genetics can play a part in a stroke as well, but lifestyle tends to play a bigger part, and Debbie was clean and lean. On the day of her devastating stroke, Debbie displayed none of the usual warnings that precede a stroke—double vision, fainting, vomiting, confusion, weakness on one side of the body, or trouble talking; she was "asymptomatic" except for slight dizziness and nausea at the interstate rest area. Why was she suddenly struck by a stroke, when none of the usual preconditions and precipitant causes were evident? How could this happen? We were forced to look at death in the face the way an imprisoned criminal on death

329

row faced an execution date, except Debbie was not a prisoner, had not committed a crime, but nonetheless had been forced to face mortality.

After a stroke strikes, all who survive sooner or later are struck with the same questions. "Why? Why did this happen? Why were dreams shattered? Why me?" No wonder. No one expects terrible things to happen. Until they do. Then comes a string of dark emotions enveloped in silent groans. In the throes of grief, surreal thoughts float to the mind's surface. "Why me?" "Will I die?" "Where does terrifying trauma fit into life's journey?" "Will the agony and adversity be relieved?" "Will my disabilities make people look away as my impairments make them fear they will face a similar fate? Or will rehabilitation ultimately triumph over perpetual disability?"

As you read our individual reactions to the "Why me?" question, keep in mind that although our long struggle to find the meaning of life's events may sound unique, it isn't. Our experience echoes conversations taking place in rehabilitation wards and homes all over the world. All who face fatality question why their final days are nearing. They instinctively dig deeply to gain awareness of who they are, what undergirds their existence, and what awaits them after death. "The unexamined life," Socrates admonished, "is not worth living." Ironically, it often takes a crushing health crisis to make us examine our lives. That kind of awakening from mental slumber strikes everyone sooner or later. When we looked at death in the face, it was our time of crisis. Never let a crisis go to waste. It was at the precipice during our life's greatest crisis that we harnessed our adversity and agony to advantage. We began to earnestly examine the meaning of existence. Suffering was our teacher.

After Debbie recovered cognition and memory, existential questions and emotions loomed large. Life's trajectory had veered off course, and contemplating "Why?" was a natural reflex, in the same way that how instrumental music is anticipated is instrumental to the cheerful or sad emotions that are experienced. Our long intellectual journey commenced. Memories make us who we are. Debbie remembered well her response to her terrifying troubles and trials and the lessons she extracted. So do I. Let her report first her reaction to the cards she had been dealt before I share mine.

"Why Me?"—Debbie's Take

Truth be told, for a long time in the aftermath of my strokes, my memory was fuzzy. My surgeons had told Chuck that stroke survivors like me never remember anything for at least two weeks after a stroke. I had three strokes, and it took me much longer. I don't have vivid recollections of anything that happened before February 21 in the Charlotte emergency room, when a drug to lower my heart rate had killed me for five seconds. Instantaneously, my pulse dropped, and my capacity to remember experiences returned. At that time, I began to think about what had happened to me. So here are my recollections of my response to my plight, which included asking myself, "Why me?" Don't get your expectations aroused. I didn't really feel that this question pertained to me. Another kind of question dominated my thinking: "Why not me?"

My strokes opened windows to new realities. From the moment I regained cognitive awareness, "Why did I have strokes leaving me incapacitated?" never captivated my mind. I never questioned why my strokes left me incapacitated. I reacted with surprise, not hopeless despair. Reconciled and resigned, I shrugged my shoulders, prayed, and thought, "Why not me?" Several months before my stroke, I heard a penetrating sermon that was titled, "Why Not Me?" Rev. John Ropp's thought-provoking sermon supplied astute wisdom and comfort. Instead of drowning myself in a sea of self-pity by asking "Why me?" I began to ask myself, "Why not me?" I decided then and there that I would turn to this way of thinking to cope with the catastrophes that had struck me.

Visitors often said, "Debbie, not you. How could this happen to you?"

I responded, "Why not me? We are all vulnerable. Anybody can suddenly be forced to face fatality and disability. Why should I be the exception? My faith shielded me from remorse when it became my turn to suffer."

An inspiring book spoke to my outlook. It is titled *A Grace Disguised: How the Soul Grows through Loss*. The author, Gerald Sittser, had compelling reasons to question the injustices that afflict the innocent. A speeding driver recklessly ran a red light, and his wife, young daughter, and mother were killed. Sittser was angry. This loss was not fair! How could God allow this terrible loss to happen? Instead of blaming and turning away from God, he questioned why he had imagined that he had an unwritten unbreakable right to fairness. "Granted," Sittser wrote, "I did not deserve to lose three members of my family. But then again, I am not sure I deserved to have them in the first place…. Perhaps I did not deserve their deaths; but I did not deserve their presence in my life either." Like Job, Sittser realized in his grief that he hadn't lost anything that God hadn't given him as His gift. Job asked the right question when he questioned his wife, "Shall we accept good from God and not trouble? The Lord gives, and the Lord takes away; blessed be the name of the Lord" (Job 2:9; 1:21).

Rev. John Ropp's sermon "Why Not Me" hit a bullseye interpreting Sittser's message about how to deal with inexplicable adversity:

Why should you and I be exempt from suffering? We are all children of Adam and Eve who fell into sin. Ever since then, people have been subject to suffering and death. People get sick and die every day. People get treated unjustly every day. Why should I expect my own life to be trouble-free? We live in a world full of pain; everything does not always go right. We live in a world of injustice; everything is not always fair. You and I may be sheltered for a while, but that doesn't mean the pain and injustice aren't there. Many of us do believe in God for as long as our lives go the way we want, and then we turn against God when things don't go our way. We have no problem believing in God as long as we're secure and its other people who are suffering pain and injustice. But if something happens to me personally, we suddenly find that we can't trust God. We may even come to hate Him. We begin to talk about undeserved suffering. What about all this undeserved happiness? Much of the grief we feel wouldn't even be possible if God hadn't been so good to us first. Why does it hurt so much to lose a loved one? Because that loved one was a precious gift from God. The size of our grief is related to the size of the gift. The greater the gift that God gives and takes away, the greater our grief will be.

Pastor Ropp's sermon put into words my perspective as I contemplated why I had suffered a devastating stroke and concluded "Why not me?" God had given me many blessings that I may not have deserved, and in my time of trouble I received an extraordinary magnitude of God's saving mercy, for reasons I don't really understand.

"No matter how bad life gets," Pastor Ropp added, "God is still good. It is better to lose everything and have God than to have everything and lose God. It is better to trust a God who gives us what we don't deserve than to insist on getting exactly what we think we do deserve." God's grace had come to me in ways I did not expect, at exactly the time I most needed His grace. I saw just how compassionately God can comfort those who sincerely seek Him (Acts 17:27; 2 Cor. 1:3-4). God's gift was for me! Those gifts shifted the ways I viewed my circumstances.

- **"I Am Not a Victim"**—The heartbreaking reality of life is that we are likely "to suffer grief in all kinds of trials" (1 Pet. 1:6). Pain and suffering comprise components of everyone's life experiences. Life is full of imponderables, and unexpected life-threatening events are some of the most puzzling. Everyone's life is unfailingly unpredictable. Mine was. The kinds of severe strokes that attacked my brain are statistically common but seldom expected; they almost always strike like lightning without clear warning. A stroke can strike anyone at any time. One in four Americans are dealt this card in their lifetimes. Many others also have looked at death in the face following an unanticipated stroke, and the majority of damaged survivors perceived themselves as victims—targets of an unjustified attack. I didn't see the onset of my inexplicable affliction that way.

My belief that I was not a victim shaped my post-stroke response to my condition. I could not and did not see myself as a victim because no one did anything to me. I had no reason to assign blame. To my way of thinking, my stroke just plain happened, for no apparent reason. I recognized that crippling events like heart attacks, malignant cancers, and hurricanes naturally transpire—events beyond comprehension for which there exist few clear-cut proximate causes. For example, my surgeons informed me that "two-thirds of the variation in cancer risk is accountable by random mutations that drive tumor growth." My stroke was probably an instance of random vessel deterioration. Who knows what dangers lie latent in our bodies, poised to ravage our health? Improbable threats are likely in the long run. Why shouldn't I accept the likelihood that harm could come my way? My stroke testified to the fact, as Eugene O'Neill argued, that "none of us can help the things that life does to us." Who's to be held responsible? No one. There was no victimization. A stroke cannot be equated with victimization.

- **What's To Bemoan or Berate?**—The hospital's handouts included the warning that following a brain injury or a stroke, "patients are likely to be angry and display anger." That also was seldom the case for me—except for a brief period when I grew extremely frustrated with the pace of my rehabilitation. I avoided the agony of anger because I didn't perceive anything or anyone warranting my anger. I was saddened by my regretful circumstances, but not overwhelmed. I reasoned that any fury I might have felt would only be self-inflicted punishment, and that would only compound my bereavement and reduce my motivation to try and make the best of my situation. So instead of falling into the pit of self-pity and sorrow, I erased from my mind my distress, accepted my condition, and looked optimistically to the future. Releasing myself from the grief of my loss, I saw myself swimming in a sea of serenity. Hereafter, when people sympathetically asked how I felt about my losses and suffering, I made a habit of responding, "I don't focus on the few things that I no longer have; instead, I focus on all of the many things that I still have."

My bliss could only have come from some sort of intuitive awareness I possessed that God was with me, and there was nothing but peace to be derived from His loving compassion. My cheerful acceptance of my circumstance manifested itself for all who looked at me to see. Time and time again, Chuck, doctors, nurses, therapists, and family and friends told me that they were mystified and unnerved at times when they observed me. Why? Because I greeted anyone and everyone who I encountered with a smile and high spirits. People expected to see despair in my face and saw instead contentment. I did not want to be seen as a victim or to be pitied. Everyone could see I knew I was in safe hands and possessed the hope necessary to cope. I just plain accepted my dire unexpected condition as a happenstance in my life. As simple as that. I got on with living as best I could, confident that eventually I could overcome my crippling disabilities.

- **Spiritual Relief**—Chuck shared his ideas about the origins of my cheerful acceptance of the dysfunctions I faced. "During your unconscious sedated state following your first hemorrhagic aneurism surgery," he told me, "I believe your soul left your body, and the Holy Spirit escorted your soul back to your body and blessed you with the gift of knowing deep down that the Holy Spirit—the same Spirit that moved in Jesus—was moving in you. God's loving presence was active, and you must have subconsciously gained firm knowledge that you had no need to worry about life after existence. You learned a profound truth during your soul's experience. I know learning theory: what people read, they forget; what they hear, they remember; what they do, they learn. Well, you heard a clear message, and learned from what you did approaching heaven's gate. You learned a priceless lesson, hermetically imprinted on your mind during your thirty-second levitation outside your body—death is a doorway to living twice, and not to be feared. The Holy Spirit carried your soul back to earthly life, and thereafter you were charged with an instinctive awareness that there was a meaningful life after life and that your resumed life could be profitably lived guided by the permanent outpouring of the Holy Spirit, through Whom anything was possible. Deep down you knew you could have a promising future. How else can your high spirits and smiling peacefulness be explained?"

Chuck was on to something. I truly felt energized by my faith in God's power. Maybe, as Chuck's vision of my near-death experience convinced him, my soul had been transported beyond my body, and this out-of-body journey had imprinted in my brain a special spiritual awareness. He probably had accurately detected the source of my inner confidence, which immeasurably enabled me to keep my chin up through my trials and tribulations as I happily strived to live a full second life.

My inner faith helped me to dedicate myself to doing what I could with my caregivers to heal and recover from my debilities. I had been given a second chance. I recognized that who I was before my stroke had vanished and would never be the same, but even when I first understood that I had been on life support, I took great courage in recognizing the opportunity that had been provided for me to become renewed and potentially even better. Oddly enough, my stroke prepared me to struggle from darkness into light. My strokes elevated my self-understanding of who I was and what I could become.

- **The Flip Side to "Why Me?**—A full year following the attack on my brain, I wrote for *After a Stroke Strikes*: "Chuck and I were able to engage in a kind of celebration of sorts. I had survived. I was recovering. My blessings were astonishing. Not only had I overcome the agony of that first burst aneurism, but also many additional life-threatening dangers requiring surgical operations. With each passing day, one at a time, the odds that I would live without going through another stroke increased."

At that juncture in my long journey, a new kind of question began to nag my mind: "Why was it me who survived, when the vast majority of stroke victims who stood at death's door perished?" I could not really understand why I deserved to be so fortunate. Indeed, I occasionally felt a tinge of guilt for being such a special exception to the general rule. Like the Jewish survivors of what looked like certain imminent death in a Nazi concentration camp during the Holocaust, I also at times wondered why I had escaped death while countless other innocent victims haven't. Was I more deserving? I doubt it.

There is only one answer why I was freed from fear. I had thrust my fears on Jesus Christ, the One who was born to die so that others could live, now and eternally. I placed my trials during my long journey before God, and Chuck and I received His great comfort amid our great suffering. Trust underpins faith, and faith provides opportunities for God to answer. "The people who walk in darkness can see a great light; those who have dwelt in a land of deep darkness, on them light can shine" (Isa. 9:2, 6–7). Vulnerability can be valuable.

The light had shined on me as prayers were answered. I was never abandoned. God's compassion was never withheld. God stood steadfast by me. To my way of thinking, God's unrestrained love and intercessions on my behalf to relieve my suffering were miraculous. God had saved me from my afflictions, and His merciful saving was all the more miraculous because I knew that God does not always respond the instant people call upon Him. God heard my groans and answered my cry, and this made His blessings all the more extraordinary because there exists no reason to expect God to obediently or automatically answer, or is obligated to answer, every petition from everyone of faith.

I believe God at times remains hidden and silent, and that in times of trial when our wishes are not fulfilled, our faith should remain firm. My faith grew, not because the God who can perform miracles (Ps. 77:14) did so for me, but because faith does not require of Him constant performance of miracles in response to every request. If God displayed His awesome power all the time, the mystery of His power would vanish. Indeed, if we could understand God fully and predict all His actions, we might even lose interest in Him. Why the righteous sometimes suffer, and why I was saved, are not questions that can be answered.

"WHY NOT ME" REDUX—CHUCK'S TAKE

Debbie's profound and adaptive response to the "Why me?" question triggered my own thinking about why Debbie had been struck by her strokes. She convinced me to not ask "Why?" and to instead ask "Why not me?"

Debbie's profound serenity spoke volumes about her inner peace and contentment despite her strokes and the miseries they caused. I was not nearly as adaptive. Unlike Debbie, I had great difficulty dealing with her pain. When the strokes struck Debbie down, I was overcome. My despair ran rampant. I thought that I might lose Debbie. That unbearable possibility overwhelmed me. I could not live without her and didn't want to continue living if she was not by my side.

I grudgingly trudged through the well-known five stages of grief identified by Swiss psychologist Elizabeth Kübler-Ross. First, at the onset of Debbie's strokes and those which followed, my first reactions were shock and incredulity—this couldn't really be happening to my Debbie. I was in *denial.* That phase of disbelief did not last long, however; the diagnoses of her doctors could not be denied or redefined as an illusion. The second stage, *anger,* also passed quickly; at whom could I blame or be angry? The third stage, *bargaining,* began soon thereafter. I had the gall to bargain with God! I pleaded for His help and loving healing and promised that I would do anything for His intervention to save Debbie's life. Thankfully, He answered my prayers without asking anything I could provide in return; His mercy had no limits. I reached the fourth stage, *depression*, next. It was deep and prolonged. I still emote despair whenever I recall all those many moments when all hope seemed lost; relief only comes when I reignite memories of the spectacular miracles that God had performed to pull Debbie from the chasm of death.

Following each of these successive four psychological stages, I eventually reached the fifth and final stage: *acceptance*. I didn't arrive at this juncture in the usual manner displayed by dying patients—surrender, consent, and detachment. My journey took me in the opposite direction. For the life of me, I could not grasp why this devastating affliction had happened to Debbie. The pain drove me to question why I had not been able to carry the cross for her. Why Debbie, instead of me?

- **It Should Have Been Me**—I looked at the question "Why not me?" from an angle divergent from Debbie's perspective. It was I who should have been in an ICU bed, not Debbie. I truly wished I could take her place and was angered that I couldn't. That was how it was supposed to be! It was supposed to be me, not her, who underwent the threat of death. I was then nearly seventy years old, whereas Debbie was in the prime of mid-life, in great health, at the mere age of fifty-four. All expectations centered prior to January 8 on the high probability that I, not Debbie, would be the first to fall from a stroke (or, as I liked to quip, "If my heart attacked me"). Debbie and I had even prepared for my pending infirmity or death. We had renewed my long-term health-care-insurance policy to assist Debbie when she became the primary caregiver; we had recently updated our last will and testament; our tombstone in Wytheville's St. John's Lutheran Church was already in place (Debbie's had engraved "Loving and Faithful Wife"); and I had drafted an obituary to lessen her burden when the time arrived for me to meet my Lord. I was prepared for my end on earth, not hers. I could sincerely ask, "Why not me?"

  Admittedly, I never realized that aging would be so fast; life is indeed short. So what? I had reached the autumn of life, and had already lived longer than I ever expected; both my Lutheran pastor grandfathers had passed at the age of fifty-seven, and my mother died after only sixty-two years. My days were surely numbered, but the figure already far surpassed my expectations, despite the fact that years of vigorous exercise had kept me in relatively good health. ("If I had known that I would live this long," my cousin, Danny Bird, liked to joke, "I would have taken better care of myself.") In short, God had granted me a longer life than expected.

Moreover, my life had already exceeded my wildest dreams—providing more than I would have dared ask for and more than I felt I deserved. My professional career had risen like a rocket from humble beginnings, modest expectations, and marginal self-confidence. My publishing endeavors culminated in more than sixty books. Scores of scholarly journal articles. Keynote speeches in fifty-seven countries. Offers of endowed chair professorships from world-class universities. Service as the youngest President of the International Studies Association. Somehow I had climbed to the very peak of my profession. None of these accomplishments really mattered after January 8. The significance of crowning career accomplishments suddenly seemed very insignificant.

If adversity was to strike Debbie or me down, it should happen to me, not her. I had tasted life and seen the best it can offer and the worst it can display. I had traveled the world and seen more of it than I had ever imagined possible. Although the bucket list Debbie and I had created included many new ambitious adventures from which we could learn and contribute to a better world, I knew that it would not be a disaster if my life on earth were to end. It had been quite a run, and if it were to end, I was acceptant.

More meaningfully, I felt that my life had been complete because it had immeasurably improved after Debbie entered it—at precisely the time I most needed a soul mate. Debbie had given me the happiest years of my life. She was the center of my thoughts and love, and I felt that my life could not have been more blessed. She was everything I dreamed of and had made my life complete. I was living the impossible dream. I could not imagine life without her and didn't want to live in her absence. So if her days were to end, I wanted mine to end too.

- **Facing the Final Curtain**—I had good reasons to wonder, "Why Debbie? Why not me?" My faith embraced the belief that the best was yet to come. When the final curtain fell, in the afterlife I knew that everything could be seen and understood. I was spiritually prepared to take the ultimate journey to life after death, when all questions would be answered. I was ready. However, as Debbie began to recover, my depression waned and thoughts of self-annihilation if Debbie died dissipated. God had lifted Debbie from the dark depths, and I mentally buried Hamlet's soliloquy "To be, or not to be?"

- **Connecting Some Dots**—Debbie's heartbreaking strokes forced me to reevaluate my priorities and rethink my values. I adopted a new perspective on life and its meaning, rearranging my mental picture of how the dots are connected, while contemplating for the first time the possibility that there might be only one dot. To conceptualize is to organize our perceptions. This is actually easier to accomplish through adversity. You can better see how the pieces fit when you see them come apart. This trial by fire enabled me to escape some of the barriers in my previous mental habits that had blinded my vision.

I knew in my heart that Debbie was correct—feeling victimized was not justified. We are not issued at birth an insurance certificate guaranteeing that we will ride on "Easy Street" without severe suffering or a premature death. Collisions, engine failures, flat tires, and many other problems are to be expected as we drive on life's roadway. We learn at an early age to resign ourselves to inevitable breakdowns, get over our agony, and push on. When adults suffer, they sometimes forget this lesson. I pledged not to become one of them. I put inevitable sufferings into a new perspective.

- **Finding New Faith**—Debbie's strokes paradoxically generated an unanticipated gift. I learned more about our heavenly Father while traveling on our mortifying journey. Terrifying troubles turned my head. I learned from adversity and suffering, gaining understandings that formerly had eluded me. God's miraculous healing enabled me to more clearly see His mercy and better appreciate God's unlimited power and sufficiency. I put into perspective the One thing that was bigger than big—God's endless love. The growth of knowledge of Him and His blessings always leave us better off spiritually (2 Pet. 3:18). The gain was worth the pain.

  My witness of Debbie's near-death sojourn strengthened the foundations of my faith. God had lifted Debbie up and protected her. I saw His miraculous intervention, and my spirits climbed to new heights. Like a football team that scores a touchdown in the final seconds to turn defeat into victory, Debbie's comeback from near death stoked my desire to live. Seeing God's loving care, I began to set my agonizing fears aside (although I continued at times to momentarily experience all the five stages of grief). God had provided many reasons to rejoice. The joy that chased away darkness was God's gift—"the serious business of heaven," as C. S. Lewis describes that joy.

- **A Purpose Driven Life**—I accepted God's providence and placed complete trust in Him, and my acceptance of His loving care brought me full comfort and confidence as I joined the fight for Debbie's rehabilitation. I discovered a primary purpose during this phase of my life. I concentrated during this toughest journey in my life on remembering how God had comforted us in our trials so that I could "comfort those in any trouble with the comfort we ourselves receive from God" (2 Cor. 1:4). Debbie was that troubled person who received most of my comforting care. I enlarged the circle in efforts to provide more care for all—especially those who have not been healed through possible but not probable divine miracles.

A TRAGEDY?

Were Debbie's strokes a "tragedy"? Not in the real sense of that word. We must confess that *After a Stroke Strikes* has been misusing this word. We have adopted it to describe what is commonly ascribed to a "tragedy"—a sad story that leads to the downfall of an individual, even death. Events are usually called "tragic" when something terrible, usually fatal, happens to someone.

This usage is really a misnomer. The Greek philosopher Aristotle specified the original meaning of a "tragedy" in the third century before Christ. Aristotle adhered to the prehistoric mythologies that celebrated, for example, the end of winter and the return of spring; these myths endorsed the belief that sacrifice and suffering lead to recognition, renewal, and, finally, redemption. Aristotle saw that trials and suffering inspire pity and fear. Anxiety arises because the causes are unknown, and he submitted that misfortunes should be traced primarily to human frailty (*hamartia*) or some "fatal flaw" such as false pride. Fear and uncertainty at the beginning of a tragedy lead directly to a mental climax, producing regret and sorrow. Ironically, this grief then leads to a purgation of those emotions (or *pathos*) through which restoration and revitalization result. How? By the perception or recognition (*antagonisa*) of truths formerly unrecognized and invisible. The loss produces a gain—learning and understanding. To Aristotle, "tragedy" meant affirmation through loss.

The "tragedy" of Debbie's strokes fit Aristotle's definition. Comforts breed the complacent illusion that they will continue. The delusion that happiness was the beneficiary's own doing invariably brings forth agonizing adversity. Aristotle called this *peripeteia*—the instant when a reversal during a tragedy changes thinking so that cognitions "veer around to its opposite." That happened after Debbie's stroke happened. Our long journey began with a catastrophic loss, but acceptance of the consequences prepared the path to new realizations about our place in God's universal schema. What, we ask, is so tragic about that? Our trauma was not a "tragedy" in the common contemporary understanding of that term. To be sure, Debbie's stroke was a calamity, a sorrowful terrifying experience. But Debbie's strokes also brought new understanding to light. Perhaps the best way of capturing this unanticipated gift of enlightenment is to label it a "catharsis." *Webster's Dictionary* defines a catharsis as a form of paradigmatic reorientation of values and outlooks—"a purification or purgation that brings about spiritual renewal or release from tension; elimination of a complex [puzzle] by bringing it to consciousness and affording it expression." In the light, we could envision the feared curse as a cure. Could this be the undetected answer to the "why?" enigma?

- **Why Not Ask the Right Questions?**—Contemporary culture misconstrues the original meaning of "tragedy" by overlooking its benefits and bemoaning its costs. Tragic experiences can produce good mental consequences.

  After a stroke strikes, victims' natural inclination is to ask, "Why?" The focus usually centers on why the terrible threat happened. Why did suffering occur? Why did this catastrophe happen? Why me?

  It gradually dawned on us that popular culture usually asks the wrong questions about the advent of adversities. The focus should not be riveted on wondering, "Why does suffering happen? Why to us?" Rather, in the aftermath of the strokes, we learned to shift focus to a series of very different questions. When the boundary between life and death grew obscure, we learned to ask ourselves these questions:

  - Why did God allow Debbie to survive?
  - Why did Debbie's near-fatal stroke happen where and when it did, permitting emergency care to prevent her death?
  - Why did God enable me to be by her side when Debbie's stroke struck, to help her travel through the valley of the shadow of death?

- Why did God lift us up from fatal danger, singling us out to carry us through this commonplace storm, when so many other stroke victims perish?
- Why were we able to see God's light in our darkness?
- Why was Debbie led to ideal places for rehabilitative therapies?
- Why did God pave the road to recovery, when so many other stroke victims never regain much or any of their former capabilities?
- Why did our suffering produce such enlightenment and understandings?

We could go on and on, identifying a multitude of additional questions our travels brought to mind. If you suffer severe afflictions and wonder why, contemplate how your suffering can create an opportunity to escape the dark. It's sometimes not bad to be sad. Consider the sorrow felt when a flower withers— is not this regret a necessary part of appreciation of its former beauty? Something similar happens when night and day are compared, and the contrast exposes the paradoxical reality. Out of the silhouette, better insight and understanding of the kind of universe God created, in all its glory, can be illuminated.

- **Count Your Blessings**—Part of humanity's rosy assumptions about how life would favorably unfold make most people forget how fragile life really is. The good life often appears certain to be our fate. It rarely is. Confidence about our promising future is usually predicated on false assumptions that we are somehow owed a fortunate journey through a long life. We are not. No one ever made that promise. We are not really deprived when we suffer a painful loss, such as always happens after a stroke strikes. It helps to turn the "Why me?" question on its head. Ask instead, "Why did we ever presume that life would be fraught with only joy, pleasure, and success?"

  The feeling of deprivation loses its suffocating force when we take the first step toward seeing that good fortune was never given to us in the first place. Rev. Ropp was right—suffering is an intrinsic part of life. There are no safeguards. Yet life can become bearable when we discover that there's really nothing we can lose. Nothing can be taken when nothing is given. And life becomes liberating when we discover through suffering and death that we can gain assurance that an eternity without pain or suffering is truly within our grasp.

Debbie's set of strokes and spine-tingling operations offered Debbie and me great instruction. There is nothing to fear. Not even death. God is always with us. The Lord always listens and cares (Jonah 2:2). The Lord loves. He *is* love.

Seek the silver lining in presumed tragedy, and you will see it. Count the blessings we receive from our Maker, and the gloomy anomie we usually feel when bad things happen will disappear. God may harness hardship for a virtuous purpose—to cultivate awareness of our Lord's loving grace. "My grace is sufficient for you," 2 Corinthians (12:9) instructs, "for My strength is made perfect in weakness." What Saint Paul wrote expressed the profound truth: only in the inner depth of the Holy Spirit within our soul can we gain knowledge of our true selves; we tend to become most conscious of that self-knowledge enabling us to see God's gifts when we face adversities.

As Debbie grew stronger and stronger, faith in God's love and power grew stronger and stronger. We both already knew that He was present—with us, in us, for us—but appreciation deepened exponentially as we witnessed what trust in Him could provide. Fears receded, and God's light drove out darkness. If we had once harbored some doubts about faith, the discoveries along our journey made them disappear. The saying "I believe. Help my unbelief" took on new meaning. God was the elixir underlying hope and undermining fear of death.

Surely, we shall never know the answers to the questions "Why me?" and "Why Debbie?" We never harbored the hubris or delusion that we were worthy or deserving of God's spectacular blessings upon us; they cannot be earned, any more than good works can purchase a first-class ticket to heaven.

What *was* now lucidly clear was that a transformed agenda had been placed at our feet. We could travel forward, not dreading death but living and loving to the fullest. We discovered a deeper sense of purpose. Having several brushes with death, who knew what might happen next? This was a time to use time wisely—not spend time on mundane inessentials. God must have had plans for us to pursue. It is our moral and spiritual duty to find and follow His goals. We prayed, "Teach us to number our days, so we can receive Your wisdom" (Heb. 12:2). We felt called to tell this story in order to offer a testimony about what God has done. Our new bucket list placed writing *After a Stroke Strikes* near the top.

To be addressed here another puzzle: why does a just God allow believers like Debbie to suffer? If He is all powerful and can do anything, why does He permit innocent believers to be struck by suffering and premature death? Why does life entail so much suffering?

CHAPTER 27

SUFFERING AND GOD

§

When problems arise, some ask, "Where was God?" This response is common after a stroke strikes or another deadly disease makes the victim suffer.

You probably have encountered people who assume that God is responsible for all that happens, including human suffering. Debbie and I are not among them. I wrote a lengthy rebuttal. "Let someone ask Chuck 'What time is it?'" Debbie kidded, "and he is likely to launch a long lecture explaining how the clock works." She was right. The issues surrounding suffering are complex. By January 2015, my unexpurgated counterarguments to God's alleged responsibility for human suffering consumed eighty pages. To spare your suffering, what follows is an abridged critique of this thesis, which applies to the larger set of questions about why terrible uncontrollable problems sometimes happen to seemingly righteous people.

THESIS

In *God's Problem: How the Bible Fails to Answer Our Most Important Question—Why We Suffer*, Dr. Bart Ehrman defines his "problem" with God thusly:

> How can God be "just" or "righteous" given the fact that there is so much suffering in the world that He allegedly created and

is sovereign over? The problem involves three assertions that all appear to be true, but if true appear to contradict one another. The assertions are these: *God is all powerful. God is all loving. There is suffering.* How can all three be true at once? If God is all powerful, then he is able to do whatever he wants (and can therefore remove suffering). If he is all loving, then he obviously wants the best for people (and therefore does not want them to suffer). And yet people suffer? How can this be explained?

God's Problem condemns God for allowing suffering, and advocates rejecting the religious doctrines on which Christianity is based.

ANTITHESIS

This theological conundrum surfaced when Debbie's stroke struck. Why did this happen to her, of all people? Where was justice? Why is there such unfairness in God's created world? Should faith be swept away because so many suffer life-shattering afflictions?

Debbie and I looked at death in the face and thought more deeply about our Savior, our relationship to Him, and the core tenets of Christian theology. Many dark issues came to light as we struggled to understand where suffering is situated in God's plan. We don't really know. But we were confident that *God's Problem* is itself problematic. Its thesis forced us to question why we had been confronted by terrifying suffering. Our journey led us to embrace an antithetical interpretation. We learned that faith in God's mercy is well placed.

- **What Is Suffering?**—There undeniably exists much human suffering in our Father's earthy world. We see pain and misery all around us and had joined the multitudes who have experienced severe suffering. But the corollary does not follow—that suffering is God's doing, His "problem."

Before complaining about suffering, keep in mind that it is a subjective sensation. It is a physio-psychological product of the mind, referring to sensations people think they experience. Such sensations are extremely variable, idiosyncratic to each individual. In much the same way as beauty lies in the eye of the beholder, one person's misery can be another person's happiness.

Suffering has at least one often-overlooked positive effect: it confers meaning on an otherwise meaningless existence. Just as darkness can be sensed only against the backdrop of light, suffering has meaning only if contrasted with pleasure. We think we suffer only when we sense that pleasure is absent, which is why people complain about illnesses because they know that good health has eluded them.

Suffering need not be pejoratively defined as an unacceptable "problem." We shouldn't assume that the world would be better if suffering didn't exist. God didn't "goof" when He created humans exposed to various levels and kinds of either physical or mental suffering. Do we really want to live in a world without suffering—a world of unmitigated perpetual pleasure? Sounds good. It wouldn't be. It would be a nightmare. Imagine every situation entirely favorable and always predictable. If we could play the game of life and never face the agony of defeat, we would have nothing to celebrate when we triumph. Motivation to overcome loss would itself be lost.

If there were no pain or suffering, we couldn't appreciate comfort and contentment. Life would be existence without sensation, as meaningless to humans as it is to a sand pebble on the beach. We could not understand pleasure without pain, any better than we can recognize what is good unless we can recognize what is bad.

The dialectical ontological principle of opposites covers much ground. No night—then what's to gain by endless day? What is summer's warmth without winter's cold? What would good health mean if there were no such thing as disease? What's to love about love if it could not be lost? Indeed, how can life be treasured if there is no such thing as death? Too much of a good thing would be a bad thing. Uniformity without diversity would not be paradise.

- **Good Grief**—From our post-stroke suffering, we learned how much we can learn from suffering. Through the fog of despair, we saw hope springing from God's merciful blessings (Matt. 7:11). We can't fully enjoy God's benevolence unless we encounter costly losses. We need suffering and loss to appreciate joy, just as a walk through a dusty desert increases appreciation of water. Debbie and I had to ask ourselves, would we have prayed so earnestly had we not withstood suffering? Without grief, there would be no basis for recognizing joy and no reason to thank God for the comforts He provides.

The apostle Paul understood adversity's advantages. He recognized how suffering builds character: "Count it all joy when you fall into various trials, for we know they can help us develop endurance; endurance develops strength of character, and character strengthens our confident hope of salvation" (Rom. 5:1–11). Elaborating, he contended, "We should even boast in our afflictions, knowing that affliction…produces hope; and hope is not put to shame, because the love of God is poured out in our hearts through the Holy Spirit that has been given to us" (Rom. 5:3–5).

St. Paul went even further when he maintained that those who suffer are best prepared to lessen others' suffering: "Blessed is God the Father…who encourages us in our every affliction to enable us to encourage others who experience every affliction with the encouragement that we ourselves have received from God. For just as the sufferings of Christ abound in us, so also the encouragement we have through Christ abounds. If we are afflicted, it is for your encouragement and salvation; if we are encouraged, it is for your encouragement, which is manifest when you endure those sufferings we ourselves experience" (2 Cor. 1:3–7). When we were weak, we were most able to see God's strength (Ps. 141). In writing this epistle, the apostle Paul was reminding people that pain provides incentives to live a more moral life and to compassionately care for the less fortunate. Love must be the underlying motive in anything we do, in everything we do (1 Cor. 13:1–4).

- **Suffering Imposed by an Angry God?**—*God's Problem* portrays our Lord as a capricious bully. At His best, God is indifferent to the plight of those He created. He is asleep at the switch, permitting the rich to exploit the poor and the powerful to dominate the weak. All suffer as they must. At His worst, God indiscriminatingly punishes both sinners and the virtuous alike. He is cruelly indifferent. God uses suffering as a means to His changing ends. So this book submits.

  This is identity theft. The mischaracterization portrays a deity unlike anything described in the New Testament. This is not the same loving God who required His only begotten Son—the most innocent man who ever lived—to suffer and die on the cross so humanity could be saved from sin and live eternally. There was no greater love than Jesus's sacrifice (John 15:13). God is animated by unlimited love—He is love. God did not create humans to make them suffer. The one true God on high puts His love high above all. He is full of mercy, and forgiving. Read holy scripture, and you will find God's real identity—a heavenly Father driven by concern, compassion, and care for all His children. Human suffering makes God suffer.

- **Injustice and Faith**—Martin Luther clearly saw the problem that "unjust" suffering posed to religious faith. In 1525, he wrote in *The Bondage of the Will*, "Inasmuch as He is the one true God, wholly incomprehensible and inaccessible to man's understanding, it is reasonable, indeed inevitable, that His justice also should be incomprehensible." Luther then confronted the transparent reality:

  > Proverbs, and experience the parent of proverbs, bear record that the more abandoned [to moral codes] men are, the more successful they are….Is it not universally held to be most unjust that bad men should prosper, and good men be afflicted? Yet

that is the way of the world. Hereupon some of the greatest minds have fallen into denying the existence of God. And a summary explanation of this whole inexplicable problem is found in a single little sentence: *There is a life after life, and all that is not punished and repaid here will be punished and repaid there.*

Sometimes the righteous suffer, and sinners prosper. Life does not always reward the virtuous and punish the wicked. Life does not seem fair. Where is justice? But here is where *God's Problem* again goes astray, boldly asserting what a just God *should* do: mechanistically make the unrighteous suffer and protect the innocent. This is not the way this world works. Why? Because God is not the exclusive determinant of everything that happens (although He is omniscient and has the omnipotent power to orchestrate everything). God did not make us puppets. God gives us free will. We can make choices. Because human nature is flawed, injustice prevails, and man's inhumanity to man never ceases. God is present and can preside, but His participation does mean that He always must exercise His power to right all wrongs. Involvement does not require His unremitting influence.

Let's not invent a problem that doesn't exist. We shouldn't expect the same God who gave everyone free will to punish all sinners and protect every righteous-driven human from suffering. The Bible is clear—God never made it His mission to assure perfection on earth. Suffering is not God's problem. To assign blame would be as fallacious as asserting that because Jesus said "the poor shall always be with us," He condoned income inequality.

- **Limits to God's Power?**—What should we expect from our Lord? Debbie and I did not see our love for our Savior as being dependent on His willingness to deploy His awesome power to provide welfare or to terminate our suffering. Some people asked us why we were so faithful to our God, who allowed us to suffer. They questioned God's power. Debbie responded, "I suffered because my health failed.

I don't know why, and neither do my doctors. But I do know all about God's extraordinary power to heal. He kept me alive. All my surgeons feared I would not make it, and some said it would take a miracle for me to survive. God performed miracles. I don't understand why you would think God is indifferent or impotent. I found that God has total power to preserve and transform life—when He chooses."

Some skeptics were not persuaded. They persisted: "There must be limits to God's power. I recently read Rabbi Harold Kushner's book *When Bad Things Happen to Good People*. Dr. Kushner argued that God's power is limited and that He would end human suffering *if only He could*. It is intimated that God is not very powerful. An all-powerful God, after all, could easily intercede to protect good people from harm." This tenet is untenable. On our journey, we began to see suffering not as a sign of God's weakness but as a consequence of the way God exercised His awesome power to create all nature.

- **Keeping Faith**—Anyone who has experienced the agony of losing a child or spouse or suffered a lifelong disability knows that suffering puts faith to a test. Nature frequently causes harm in numbers too large to count and ostensibly distributes afflictions randomly. No one is immune from the suffering that nature's natural cycle can cause. Every person stands vulnerable in harm's way; you don't have to be a hypochondriac to see why hope is an endangered emotion.

  Those who suffer should not lose faith. God should *not* be held responsible for the suffering caused by naturally occurring destructive phenomena, since He is not the sole cause of each and every natural event. If and when terrible things happen to good people, it does not mean that God has prejudicially inflicted suffering on the individual victim. God cannot be blamed for life's problems because He never assumed authority to control everybody's dangerous health threats. The fact is, God is everywhere, and that includes His presence internally within us; our sufferings are God's sufferings. As Josiah Royce describes God's vicarious participation in our experiences, "our sorrow is God's sorrow." Why would God inflict pain on Himself by authorizing our pain? That is inconceivable.

- **God's Design**—A master scientific detective such as Albert Einstein would search for and detect the elusive causes of destructive phenomena such as strokes within the ripples and waves in the stream of nature. Einstein did search the cosmos, and found answers in God's design for the universe. He concluded that the Supreme Creator unleashed the forces of nature to operate independently of His coercion. We might say that God let nature function on "remote control," releasing it from His complete control and allowing it to fluctuate on autopilot.

  In this schema, disease and death occur because they are entwined in the cyclical processes through which nature unfolds. God stands apart from His design for nature. God is omnipotent and omnipresent, and can see all that will happen, but that does not mean that God is the cause of every event that happens within His creation. The pulse of nature has much to do with what transpires. Nature took its natural course when Debbie's vascular deterioration lead to her "brain attacks" and suffering. Her strokes are attributable to natural causes. God did not cause Debbie's vascular network to balloon and burst.

- **Nature's Nurture**—By God's design, nature's natural cycles facilitate rehabilitation and health, not just destruction and death. Nature nurtures. The Creator endowed nature with remedial homeostatic or self-regulating adjustment processes which can restore a catastrophic disruption back to nature's normal range of healthy variation so that dysfunctions and the suffering they inflict can cease. For example, an infection induces a fever that kills germs, and sweat enables an overheated body to cool.

  We should give God gratitude for making healing and health possible. Hard times let us see how God created nature to permit many good, not just bad, things to happen. The suffering that nature can produce needs to be weighed against the blessings that nature bestows. Everyone can benefit from nature's healing capacities, provided by God's design. Solutions to health problems reside within nature's nurture; that product is in the process.

When Debbie neared the final abyss, God's divine intervention into nature's normal processes engineered her survival. We will never know His methodology for these miracles, which provided hope when all looked hopeless. We also will never know why God chose to answer our prayers, and not those of so many others in need. We were blessed, and knew it. God's miraculous, compassionate intervention with nature's normal rhythm carried Debbie from the edge of earthly existences. We saw God's full power activated when nature's inherent healing processes most needed a catalytic boost.

- **Adjusting to Suffering**—In hard times, 1 Peter counsels, "Do not be surprised at the fiery trial that has come upon you for your testing, as if something surprising has happened. But insofar as you partake of the sufferings of Christ, rejoice, so that you may also rejoice full of gladness at the revelation of his glory....Therefore, let those who suffer...entrust their souls to the faithful Creator by doing what is good."

Biblical scripture tells us to accept what happens to us, taking the bad with the good. Debbie grasped this: "I understood the importance of accepting what had happened. There was no advantage to complaining about my painful plight, even though my suffering was a harsh reminder that life isn't always fair. At my threshold of death, I was reminded that "The same fate comes to all, to the righteous and the wicked, to the good and the evil" (Eccl. 9:1–3). My acquiescent acceptance stemmed from a fundamental truth: "Under the sun the race is not to the swift, nor the battle to the strong nor bread to the wise, nor favor to the skillful; but time and chance happen to them all. For no one can anticipate the time of disaster. Like fish taken in a cruel net, and like birds caught in a snare, so mortals are snared at a time of calamity, when it suddenly falls upon them" (Eccl.

9:11–12). After a stroke strikes, calamity suddenly strikes; no one can escape this possibility, and no one should expect to understand *why*. Suffering can, however, undermine faith if the sufferer lets it.

We found renewed faith through tragedy and constructed a conceptual synthesis that enlightened understanding of suffering's formerly unappreciated beneficial consequences.

SYNTHESIS

There is nothing like a near-death experience to educate. Through painful suffering, we were forced to examine our prior assumptions about the mysteries enveloping the place of suffering in God's plan.

Suffering a stroke helped us grasp what we had withstood and its beneficial consequences: "Behold, I have refined you, but not as silver; I have tested you in the furnace of affliction" (Isa. 48:10). Testing helped us hear God. In *The Problem of Pain*, C. S. Lewis explains, "God whispers to us in our pleasures, speaks in our conscience, but shouts in our pains: it is His megaphone to rouse a deaf world." When coming face to face with death, we could not remain deaf.

Sometimes we have to come close to losing something in order to find something: God's light. We better visualized the value of life when it was in danger of ending. In the darkness, we relied on faith, and, magically, a mystical new light began to shine. God's miraculous healings cast a powerful beam on our Savior's work, and the light strengthened our faith. We heard His shouts.

Our remaining days will be spent reassured that our Lord's love can sustain us. We received true peace of mind from trust in our God who dwells within us. We had learned the hard way that in hard times we should focus not on what could be lost, but on what was *not* taken away. Debbie had avoided death and permanent disability. We found through our apotheosis the quintessential demonstration why God's deification was warranted: we knew God because we saw Him save. During our ordeals our gratitude expanded for the immeasurable blessings that God had provided (Prov. 3:5–6). All that was good in our lives was His doing. God's miracles intensified our faith in ways no other experience could. We "will remember the deeds of the Lord; yes, we will remember His miracles and meditate on all His mighty deeds" (Ps. 77:11-12).

We had been thrown a lifeline in our darkness—Jesus's brilliant light shined brightly like a beacon, shattering the darkness and bringing comfort. We jettisoned mourning in a new morning, just as God promised—"I will turn mourning into joy" (Jer. 31:7–14). Paradoxically, our suffering was a blessing. Our long journey may be the best thing that ever happened to us.

CHAPTER 28

A Religious Roadmap

Our efforts to grapple with the big questions about the meaning of life accelerated when Debbie stood at the threshold of losing it. The aftershocks of Debbie's strokes were seismic. They struck us with many uncustomary thoughts. We first questioned why Debbie's strokes had struck, and, as you saw in the previous chapter, we probed the causes of life's troubles and their consequences. In the strokes' aftermath, we struggled searching for answers to four "what" questions central to the meaning of life's experience and existence:

• What do we really believe in matters of faith?
• What moral code should guide our remaining days?
• What is the source of our soul—who we really are?
• What can we expect to experience in the afterlife?

We present our reflections, starting with the first question and proceeding with the others in the succeeding three chapters. We ask you to keep in mind our conviction that people should make their own choices about their beliefs. Our aim is *not* to tell any reader what to think but instead to suggest what to think *about*. We urge you to mold your own credo—your religious convictions and the philosophy that underlies them.

ON THE ROAD TO A RELATIONSHIP WITH GOD

Debbie's near death ignited our desire to see God in a proper light. Knowing that everything can be snatched away in an instant, like an insect swept away in a hurricane, was supremely motivating. Our journey propelled us into a subjective realm where spiritual and supernatural things are seldom clean and clear, where every light has its accompanying shadow. We can't accurately picture our Lord any better than we can see the equator. We had to face our intellectual limitations.

- **Creed and Confession**—Following Martin Luther, we believe that only Scripture (*solo scriptura*) provides the foundation for finding the principles of Christianity. We based our faith on the premise that the Bible held the roadmap we needed. However, the challenge is to accurately perceive what the Bible says. What exactly should we look at, look for, and accept?

    Understanding the Bible's basics is not as easy as it appears. The Bible's contents cannot simply be read to uncover its theology. Look how easy it is to read something—indeed anything—a second or third time and find that it holds new meanings that escaped your comprehension when you first read it. The exact same wording can lead to new and different ideas. The Bible isn't that different from other texts. It requires interpretation. Interpretations of all books vary—something I discovered when readers of books I had authored extracted different and unexpected lessons from those I tried to communicate when I wrote them. Likewise, each time Debbie and I tried to interpret the meaning of what happened after her strokes, insights arose that had escaped our previous understanding.

    Scripture speaks in different voices and invites discordant messages. The Bible can be unpacked and repacked, deconstructed and reconstructed, in innumerable ways. On which subset of theological opinion should believers base their faith? Personal judgment is not a good basis for reaching firm conclusions (John 9:41). "The greatest minds," Rene Descartes warned, "are open to the greatest aberrations. To be possessed of a vigorous mind is not enough. No assertion is free from any taint of falsity or uncertainty."

You might think that the creedal statements of theological belief by institutional religious authorities might clarify the Bible's meaning. Christian theologizing can aid understanding of God, but statements of doctrines and dogmas are inconsistent, downright contradictory, and far from infallible. Comparison of contending catechisms leads to a sense of futility as each new layer of ideas subverts the ones previously exposed. That can end in an intellectual quicksand, where no position remains convincing.

Your God-given ability to reason can get you to the starting line, but is insufficient to reach the finish line. "There are questions whose truth or untruth cannot be decided by men," Friedrich Nietzsche recognized. "All the supreme questions, all the supreme problems of value are beyond human reason." As St. John of Damascus warned, the mystery of "God is above all knowing and above all essence." Theology is *fides quaerens intellectum*—faith in search of understanding—but understanding cannot be obtained by intellectual inquiry and introspection. "Human salvation demands the divine disclosure of truths surpassing reason. The light of faith makes us see what we believe," St. Thomas Aquinas counseled in *Summa Theologica*. God's Spirit within us, not rational logic or church authority, must lead us to clearer understanding of articles of faith.

• **Religion Vis-ă-vis God**—But stop, you may insist. Doesn't religion provide the answers believers need? Not so fast. It is important to differentiate religion and God and distinguish the secular from the sacred and an institutionalized religion from our Lord's Word. During one cynical period in my life, unlike Debbie, I failed to see the difference; I blamed organized religion for the sins church leaders committed in the name of Christianity, and their misconduct drove me away from worship in church. I was disgusted with the inhumane effects of recurrent religious zealotry. Most Christian sects, like other religions, suffer from a checkered history of hypocrisy, sometimes sanctioning mass violence to prove that God is on their side and that their's is the one true religion of peace. The drift from biblical teaching is a too-familiar story, tarnishing religion's reputation. A well-known adage avers "Christianity is a fine religion; someone ought to try it sometime."

It is tempting to confuse the relationship of religion and God, as I had mistakenly previously done. Eric Metaxas describes why my mistake is commonplace:

> One reason that religion gets confusing is that a lot of people confuse God with religion....The major problem stems from the propensity identified by Reinhold Niebuhr: "All men like to obscure the morally ambiguous element in their political cause by investing it with religious sanctity." Abuse results in religions' ill repute. But God is separate from religion, and God's nature and character transcend religion. The best religion directs people to God, helping to clarify who God is and what he seeks from us. The worst religion calls attention to itself and glorifies human thought and tradition, obscuring our view of God. So religion can be either good or bad, while God is unconditionally good.

After strokes struck, we better understood God's unconditional goodness. That does not mean that we eradicated all doubts about the tenets within our reinvigorated faith.

- **The Benefit of the Doubt**—Faith depends on abstractions that require insight into the invisible. The very idea of God is, as George Santayana understated, "quite algebraic." With tongue in cheek, Mark Twain defined faith as "believing what you know can't be true." Doubt about what can't be seen is understandable. No wonder so many people let their doubts smother the articles of faith they recite from the Apostles' Creed or the Nicene Creed. It is not hard to see why skepticism about the Christian narrative is so ubiquitous.

You may not wish to admit that there have been times when you have questioned the doctrines of your faith. But if your faith is so unshakable that you never questioned the veracity of core Christian doctrines, you are probably an exception to the general propensity among believers.

In our post-stroke reflections, we began to understand, with Voltaire, that "doubt is not a pleasant condition, but certainty is absurd." The first key to wisdom is assiduous and frequent questioning. Pierre Abelard argued, "For by doubting we come to inquiry, and by inquiry we arrive at the truth." To believe necessitates thinking and questioning our beliefs: "To philosophize," Michel De Montaigne recognized, "is to doubt." Some measure of doubt may be necessary for faith: "I doubt, therefore I believe," was the way Frederick Marshalls put this perspective. We believe in part because we doubt, not despite it. Blind faith—that is, unquestioning faith—is not meaningful because it involves no critical thinking about that which we claim we believe.

In our moments of doubt, we drew comfort from our recollection of the counsel Martin Luther gave to a troubled woman from his Wittenberg parish. To paraphrase the account, she came to him trembling. "I sometimes have doubts about God. I fear that God knows my bursts of suspicion about His existence and will condemn me to hell," she confessed. "Please help me," she pleaded.

Luther responded,

Relax. Doubt is a natural reflex, and it is a sure sign that you are already halfway to Heaven. When you harbor doubts about God, it shows that you are thinking seriously about Him, and that is a precondition for meaningful faith. To question means that you know what is important, and your doubts disclose that you already know that the only way to seek God's grace is by calling upon Him in prayer to restore your belief. Heaven is crowded with people who have at one time or another entertained questions about God and eternity. I was once one of them. Keep praying, and let God's will be done.

Living with uncertainty is the sine qua non of faith. "Life is doubt, and faith without doubt is nothing but death," Miquel de Unamuno concluded. When we doubt, we make headway accepting the limits of what we can know. Doubt liberates the mind from the disempowering belief that we have to know everything for certain about theological conundrums before we can embrace any belief. Indeed, the Holy Spirit may encourage us to doubt so that we will enthusiastically seek God. In short, doubt produces learning, and when we suffer, we most readily learn to trust our faith. That is why there are few atheists or agnostics in an Intensive Care Unit.

After Debbie's strokes struck, we dug deeper into our superficial understanding of the principles of our faith. Struggles to comprehend religious convictions blossom like a flower during times of trouble. When we are most in need, trust of God's power climbs, in much the same way that, when we become ill, we concentrate on attaining good health.

We probed rival statements of creed, and in the process, the vague contours of some hybrid or fused combination of disparate Christian doctrines started to come into focus. The route to belief may require seeking a synthesis among alternative dogmas or biblically based statements of faith. In the last analysis, faith must rest boldly on bold assumptions. There are advantages to suspending the quest for definitive understanding and letting the mysteries remain part of scripture's mystical attraction. The unknowns stimulate curiosity, and faith grows in part because we don't have definitive answers. In our time of terrible troubles, we learned the value of doubting and questioning our religious beliefs in order to refine and strengthen them.

Onto Ontology

When we think about the religious convictions that give life meaning, we enter the realms of philosophy known as ontology and metaphysics—theories about theories regarding ultimate reality transcending the dimension of time and space, about "being" and existence in God's universe.

Debbie and I believe that there exists a one true God, who is an intelligent force that is at once immanent and transcendent—that is, prior to and independent of the universe. Accordingly, we believe that our Maker created all that exists, including space and time. Everything is a product of some first cause, and that preexistent first cause is God's divine mind, which conceived His creation, as St. Augustine put it, "like the plan of a building is conceived by the architect before it is built."

God was the architect of an atmosphere without boundaries. The connective tissue in the infinite marvel of God's created universe is nature's beautiful symmetry and rhythm. These attributes can only have been produced by His masterful intelligence, emerging by standard accounts from an inflationary Big Bang about 14,000,000,000 years ago. Ever since God unloosened in a fraction of a second celestial bodies like the earth to roam through the universe, nature has displayed some persistent regularities such as the rotation of the earth around the sun. We can predict these recurrent phenomena, which is why we "naturally" perceive them to be "natural."

What is "unnatural" are abnormal deviations from nature's rhythmic repetitions, which catch us off guard. The universe God created is subject to variation. Nature is replete with irregularities. Things happen all the time that no one could predict. Strokes are exemplary. Given a sufficiently long period of observation, sooner or later anything in nature that can happen will happen. When afflictions like a stroke strike without prior symptoms, we are prone to think of them as incredible; such events are seen as unbelievable because they lie so far beyond the "natural" or "normal" probabilities of chance that otherwise set boundaries on seeming possibilities.

God built elements of dissonance, not consonance, into nature. Nature sometimes appears "consistently inconsistent" because it provides room for every possible ingredient of the human experience, including health and disease, growth and death, and strokes and recovery. It therefore should not be shocking that surprising things sometimes happen in our life. We should rightly ask, "Why not?"

What made Debbie's aneurism rupture on that dark January day? We'll never know. Yet one simple explanation is rather compelling: nature had taken its natural course. It is not unnatural over time for brain vessels to soften and weaken or harden and narrow. This deterioration can happen to both the aged and the young, which is why unpredictable strokes like Debbie's are more frequent than most people think. Parts of everyone's body can weaken. Debbie's did. A dangerous trend in her cerebral vessels was underway, and unfortunately that dangerous trend did not reverse itself through internal healing. Disaster struck then and there. Her vascular deterioration reached its natural termination point, causing an aneurism to rupture.

Was there a connection between this terrifying experience and causes that were deeply rooted in natural phenomena? We believe that linkage was the source of Debbie's brain attack.

- **Reining in Nature?**—On our long journey, we became increasingly aware of our need to broaden and deepen our perspective on the meaning of natural events in the universe. Some aspects of nature appear "natural" because God's design made them so repetitiously regular. In this popular "design" conceptualization, by creating nature God is the ultimate "cause of causes;" singular events such as a stroke or heart attack result from the multiple interaction of secondary and tertiary causes in an enabling chain of causation originating from the divine first cause, God's creation of nature.

    Admittedly, to conceive of a cause of a cause to explain the cause of natural events takes us into an epistemological thicket outside conventional wisdom—conceptions which through millennia have befuddled philosophy. Science has barely begun to understand the place that chance and change play in nature's dynamics, which are beyond the boundaries of human logic and knowledge. Some kinds of dysfunctions and malfunctions in nature, like the decay and death that in the long run all living entities undergo, are explicable by reference to the second law of thermodynamics holding that *everything* moves toward entropy and randomness. But many unanticipated events in nature cannot be accounted for or predicted by reference to law-like patterns.

Nature provides an environment in which all phenomena, seen and unseen, can result. Nature's regularities have been termed "natural law" to reify and deify the alleged "laws of nature." "Natural law theory" is based on the premise that after God created nature He sacrificed complete control of His creation, and usually allows it to function freely. God rarely intervenes to overrule nature's routinized pulsating gyrations, so destructive disruptions or deviations outside the normal range of variation, such as strokes or earthquakes, episodically erupt. These devastating periodic disturbances causing suffering are not acts of God; they are products of nature's cyclical oscillations. It has famously been said that natural law is "neither natural nor law" to highlight nature's capricious nature and the unpredictability of particular natural events.

- **God's Free Will and Humanity's Free Will**—"Numerous people said, 'Debbie, God has a plan for you.' Of course God had plans for me, which is why he engineered my survival. God did not create me, or anyone, for the purpose of harming them. Thanks to His saving grace, I could pursue His purposes and sing His praises. I see my strokes as a product of natural processes which transpired within my vulnerable body."

The phrase "God's plan" poses a major theological puzzle—whether, and to what extent, God predetermines or preordains beforehand what happens to us in our lifetime. Is God entirely in charge? Is His unbounded will the determinant of everything we experience, so we behave as puppets in His hands? Or does He exercise His will partially? Only occasionally? Or not at all? This is the pole around which a large proportion of theological debate about teleological issues gravitates. After a stroke strikes, the victims are driven to struggle to form an opinion if they are to come to terms with their catastrophe.

Everything that humanity experiences, in all its multifarious manifestations, can be explicated by a single doctrine—God gave humans the gift of free will—the capacity to make unforced choices. Our decisions partially shape the kind of future we will inherit, with some bad choices leading to disease and premature death and other good choices to health and a long life. What happens to us is largely the combined product of our inherited genetic traits, how we live, and the extent of our exposure to nature's dangers. God does not plan or dictate how we will live, although we can rest assured that He has high expectations about the choices we will make, and can foresee them. How individuals respond to the lengthy menu of choice varies greatly across individuals. These differences are a manifestation of free will. "If He had no use for all these differences," C. S. Lewis ruminates, "I do not see why He should have created more souls than one." (In one of his books, Lewis extended this query, speculating that because each individual is unique, each saved soul may experience heaven in a unique way.)

Debbie and I could not imagine that her strokes were predestined. We attributed them to natural causes embedded in her preexisting unidentified physical vulnerabilities, themselves a product of nature's natural rhythm. God does not orchestrate each and every human event and experience. What hit our minds was that however remote our Lord may seem, He is never indifferent and always present; although invisible, He is our refuge and the answer to where the thunder hides. He can "make us ride on the heights of the earth" (Isa. 58:14), and sometimes does so by intervening to stop nature's destruction and hurt. When He does, we think of His interventions as miracles.

MIRACLES AND FAITH
C. S. Lewis predicted that none of us will probably ever observe a miracle and should not be "anxious to do so. 'Almost nothing sees miracles

but misery.' Miracles [are seen in] areas we naturally have no wish to frequent." Sure enough, we saw God's saving miracles in miserable circumstances we wished we would never have to face.

"When we see ourselves on the edge of an abyss and it seems that God has abandoned us," Marcel Proust observed, it is then that we call on Him, and "we no longer hesitate to expect a miracle." When we suffer great pain so fearful that we close our eyes to the hideous threat, we open them to God's presence "in the belief," Arthur Miller submits, "that overnight something will occur, a miracle, which will render life tolerable." We look up to divine intervention when we are down in the depths of despair.

We certainly didn't desire to become so desperate that we could see a miracle. But that was what happened every time we became desperately needy during our long journey. We looked up longingly to heaven, and we were rewarded. The many miracles that kept Debbie alive and allowed recovery enabled us to recognize that there was a supernatural force— God—operating in ways that were worthy of unlimited reverence.

Debbie and I benefited from God's miraculous intervention at many dreadfully miserable stops on our long journey. We felt the Lord's presence most keenly when we were most lost and afraid. I had ocular proof of His loving involvement and interference with the natural course of nature when I witnessed Debbie's soul rise and return from near-death. This was a true miracle. There were many other miraculous events that saved Debbie from death, but I can't provide evidence verifying that all the things that happened to prevent her death were miracles directly from God. Still, I suspect that most were divine interventions that pulled Debbie away from death's door.

These were miracles for which we wished and prayed, in adherence to holy scripture: "Humble yourselves under the mighty hand of God, that He may exalt you in due time, casting all your care upon Him, for He cares for you" (1 Pet. 5:6–7). "Ask and you will receive, that your joy may be full" (John 16:24). We called in prayer, and He answered—either through His own direct intervention or through the Holy Spirit's intercessions working through Debbie's physicians.

By definition, a miracle involves a very rare, unanticipated interruption of nature's normal processes. There can be no doubt that Debbie's miracles were exceedingly exceptional; very few individuals benefit from such divine interventions. The prolific writer Dan Wakefield, author of *Expect a Miracle*, wrote to Debbie "I always worry about people who have catastrophes who don't experience the healing and connection with God that you and your husband were blessed with. I...interviewed hundreds of people and I found only one (here and abroad) who had genuine physical healing as you did. I am truly glad that you and your husband had the blessed and wondrous experience as you did." Debbie and I know that we weren't deserving of God's improbable miraculous answers to our prayers, and this made His response that much more spectacularly meaningful.

After Debbie's strokes, we shred any latent doubts about God's capacity to perform miracles. Our journey led us to see the wisdom underlying C. S. Lewis's ontological and metaphysical thesis: "The experience of a miracle in fact requires two conditions. First we must believe in a normal stability of nature, which means we must recognize that the data offered by our senses recur in regular patterns. Secondly, we must believe in some reality beyond Nature.... Miracles in fact are a retelling in small letters of the very same story which is written across the whole world in letters too large for some of us to see." Maybe God's miracles are more frequent than suspected but elude us because we don't expect them.

Lewis calls miracles "something impossible unless the known order of nature is over-ruled or supplemented by something beyond nature. By definition, miracles must of course interrupt the usual course of nature; if they are real they must, in the very act of so doing, assert all the more the unity and self-consistency of total reality at some deeper level.... The divine art of miracle is not an art of suspending the pattern to which events conform but of feeding new events into that pattern we call 'nature.'"

By this account, miracles result from a "supernatural interruption" or "unique invasion" or "interference" in nature's normal functioning.

"God's hand" is operative in the exceptionally infrequent pauses or breaks in the way nature usually performs. This is what makes the Christian narrative the prime miracle in human history. Christianity "is precisely the story of a great miracle. A naturalistic Christianity leaves out all that is specifically Christian.... We must simply accept," Lewis contends, "that we are spirits, free and rational beings, at present inhabiting an irrational universe, and must draw the conclusion that we are *not derived from it*. We are strangers here. We come from somewhere else. Nature is not the only thing that exists. There is 'another world,' and that is where we come from. And that explains why we do not feel at home here."

This enlarged view of nature and the things that happen to us gives space to the ways spiritual interventions can momentarily intrude in and interrupt nature's repetitious regularity, without altering its fundamental dynamics. We live not just in our material world; we also concurrently exist in an entirely different realm. Cosmic physicists and the Bible concur in recognizing the reality of supernatural miraculous phenomena, whose causes cannot be ascertained. (If your faith needs further bolstering, consider a "fact" regarded by anthropologists as sacrosanct: throughout recorded history, every known culture worldwide has accepted the view that supernatural forces and paranormal phenomena exist outside sight and above human existence.)

On our long, eye-opening journey, Debbie and I felt God's invisible existence and miraculous intercessions in the overall scheme for the universe. We experienced "things which no eye has seen and no ear has heard" (1 Cor. 2:9). We needed no further proof. Our faith was not tested. It was affirmed.

Things sometimes just happen that cannot be located and dated spatially and temporally but actually do occur even though they cannot be seen. New consciousness of a new thought is one. The reality of death is another. The existence of God is a third. The concept of life created after death is a fourth—the sine qua non paragon of something that can happen beyond the limits of vision or language. Just as our brains are structured to "see" objects that are no longer present, so consciousness of "unconscious memories" rooted in our souls enable us to conceive all kinds of ideas and cognitions that lie beyond visual perception. The inability to see something does not demonstrate that it is not present—ask any blind person. After a stroke strikes, the invisible can become visible. In times of extreme stress, you might recognize the imperceptible.

Our journey illuminated many invisible and improbable life-sustaining miracles which would have remained hidden in the absence of our faith. Miracles will not be believed if minds are closed to their possibility and visual perception does not verify them. Phenomenal paranormal or supernatural events will be dismissed as delusions. My faith opened my imagination to the miracles I witnessed on Debbie's behalf, but I probably would have not defined them as "miracles" if I had relied on ocular evidence alone. C. S. Lewis writes,

> Whatever experiences we may have, we shall not regard them as miraculous if we already hold a philosophy which excludes the supernatural.... The senses are not infallible.... Experience by itself proves nothing. If a man doubts whether he is dreaming or waking, no experiment can solve his doubt, since every experiment may itself be part of the dream. Experience proves this, or that, or nothing, according to the preconceptions we bring to it.... If anything extraordinary seems to have happened, we can always say that we have been victims of an illusion.... What we learn from experience depends on the philosophy we bring to experience.

What Debbie and I learned on our journey about the meaning of existence and experience underscored the need to reconstruct and refine our moral philosophy about how we should think and act in the remaining days of our lives.

CHAPTER 29

MORALITY MATTERS

§

Those fortunate enough to exit from death's door after a stroke strikes are prone to ponder some of life's most important existential questions. "What has my life meant? What goals should I pursue beyond my parochial self-gratification? What is the primary purpose of my remaining days?"

Like all who look at death in the face, when the aftershock of Debbie's encounter with death began to lose its sting, we sought to adjust our moral compass. We set our sights on finding the best path to behaving in the ways our Savior had instructed. After we died, how we spent our post-stroke lives would be judged. Our Lord's expectations assuredly had risen after all He had done to prolong Debbie's life. Debbie's life had been spared, and we knew that "from everyone who has been given much, much will be demanded" (Luke 12:48). An opportunity had miraculously been given, and our need to give to our Savior and to others increased proportionately. We needed to align our thoughts, words, and deeds with God's will.

How? The directions stood right before us, for all to see: Christianity's moral message provides the needed moral map and is available for everyone to view. The Bible charts a pathway for acceptance into heaven. To arrive at that cherished destination, it behooves us to clearly understand Christ's ethical injunctions.

That understanding is not as hard to find as you might imagine, once the ambiguous conceptual underbrush is cleared and Christ's ethical cornerstone is allowed to shine. Holy Scripture does not mince words; it points directly to a cardinal normative rule to follow. Let's reconsider Christianity's ethical norms, as Debbie and I did after her strokes struck, rehabilitation began, and our endeavors to combine faith with action swung into high gear.

Viewing the grave is a gateway to ethical evaluation. In the aftermath of extraordinary encounters with the final abyss, we sought to reevaluate our hierarchy of values and to better distinguish right from wrong. You are invited to do so too. No need to postpone that kind of moral assessment until a stroke or some other kind of life-threatening crisis makes the search for your moral compass absolutely necessary.

But why does morality matter, you may ask. After all, isn't it through faith in Jesus Christ that all people, despite their innate wickedness, can be saved? That is what Jesus taught in the Sermon on the Mount: "He that believeth and is baptized shall be saved, but he that believeth not shall be damned" (Mark 5:3–15). Faith in our Savior comes first. Those who seek salvation must repent their sins and ask for forgiveness. Forgiven, the elect must choose to live righteously: "Faith by itself...if it is not accompanied by action, is dead" (James 2:17). "Let us not love with words or speech but with actions" (1 John 3:18). Morality matters because a believer in God is commanded to behave morally. Although salvation cannot be earned through good works, our moral obligation is to love our God with all our heart and our neighbors as ourselves. "Good works," Martin Luther summarized, "do not make a man good, but a good man does good works."

A CHRIST-CENTERED MORAL CODE

There would be no need for moral laws if all people were saints. They aren't. There has existed in all history only a single individual in human flesh without sin—Jesus Christ. At base we are all sinners. Ever since Adam's original sin, people have seemingly resisted everything except temptation. All are guilty of one or more of the seven deadly sins (greed, gluttony, envy, lust, sloth, anger, pride). St. Paul wrote, "There is none righteous, no, not one, not even me" (Rom. 3:10). He confessed, "I do not understand what I do. For what I want to do I do not do, but what I hate I do. Who will rescue me from this body of death?" (Rom. 7:15–25). Are any of us any different? Who among us has not stopped ourselves to ask, "Why did I do that, when I was born with an awareness that it was wrong?"

Humanity is incarcerated in a self-made prison. Free to choose, people repetitiously think and act sinfully. That is why in worship services Lutherans confess in the presence of God and of one another "If we say we have no sin, we deceive ourselves, and the truth is not in us. We are in bondage to sin and cannot free ourselves." You might say we are "free but shackled."

It is not difficult to see why Jesus preached about right conduct to hopelessly sinful people: Flawed people can learn to follow a righteous path (Eph. 4:29; 5:2). They can change their ways. If humans were by their nature thoroughly evil, there can be no use for Jesus's moral rules because no such corrupted person could abide by them. Conversely, if humans by their nature were thoroughly virtuous, there would be no need for His moral rules; why enunciate laws that no one breaks? Whereas Jesus above all was painfully aware that all would fail and would require forgiveness for redemption after death, Jesus asked His followers to heed what was already inherent in everyone's heart—that some actions are right, and others are wrong. We "already know the truth" (1 John 2:21). A differentiation has been recognized universally since human history began. It *is* possible for each and every sinful believer to be "justified" by our omnipotent and omniscient loving God and made eligible for salvation. What an incentive to make living a moral life a priority!

When confronting hard choices, many recommend asking, "What would Jesus do?" Often we don't know. But the beginning of wisdom starts with the preeminent primary principle Jesus proclaimed to guide decisions. We needed to look no further than Jesus Christ's most explicitly and repetitiously enunciated first principle. Jesus often cited the Old

Testament (Deut. 6:5; Prov. 6:5; Lev. 19:18) to emphasize the bedrock rule by which His followers should abide—to "do unto others as you would have them do unto you" and to "love thy neighbor as thyself." (Matt. 7:12). The preface to this injunction, of course, was the first command: "You shall love the Lord your God with all your heart and all your soul and might" (Matt. 23:37; Prov. 6:5), and then, if you do, "You should love your neighbor as yourself" (Matt. 23:39).

Jesus taught that the golden rule was the sacral moral foundational axiom on which to base all ethical ideals. The golden rule subsumes the Ten Commandments and every other subsidiary law identified in the Bible. The golden rule is golden. It blends into one statement three elements of mutuality that render it a profound moral statement: *reciprocity* (it underscores the effects of one's actions on other's subsequent reactions), a *prescription* (it instructs actors how they should act), and impartial *universality* (it is a rule for behavior applicable to all).

Jesus pronounced the golden rule many times throughout His ministry to elaborate its full meaning. "You have heard that it hath been said, 'Thou shalt love your neighbor, and hate your enemy,' Jesus told His followers; 'But I say unto you, love your enemies, bless them that curse you, do good to them that hate you, and pray for them who despitefully use you and persecute you....For if you love [only] those who love you, what reward have you?'" (Matt. 5:43–44, 46). "Therefore all things whatsoever you would that men should do to you, do ye even onto them: for this is the law of the prophets" (Luke 6:12).

Jesus identified the rewards for merciful loving: kindness would be reciprocated. "Blessed are the merciful, for they shall obtain mercy" (Matt. 5:7). Jesus's prescription implicitly makes a prediction—kindness will be returned, and meanness will provoke malice. It is in our self-interest to act with love toward others, because our loving acts will breed theirs; conversely, if we respond to others' injurious behavior with angry wrath, it will bring hurt upon us. "Give, and it shall be given unto you; good measure, pressed down, and shaken together, and running over, shall men give into your bosom" (Luke 6:38). We can help ourselves by helping other people also. If we "turn from our selfish ways…and take up the cross" (Matt. 16:24–28), love extended to others is like a contagion—the giver will receive reciprocated love. Jesus punctuated the golden rule's primacy and its medicinal effects in His last request to his disciples: "As I have loved you, you are to love one another" (John 15:12, 34).

Our Savior identified a single sure path to promote constructive relations and peace among people. The golden rule is the doctrinal cornerstone of God's moral message—the "law of laws" from which spring all other ethical norms. It reveals God's unconditional love, forgiveness, justice, and mercy. The purpose of life is to love. "To say we're on earth to serve God," Marianne Williamson clarifies, "means we're on earth to love."

Love for others can be expressed in countless ways. Pope Francis identified some of them in his 2014 speech to the US Congress: "Let us treat others with the same passion and compassion with which we want to be treated. Let us seek for others the same possibilities which we seek for ourselves. Let us help others, as we would like to be helped ourselves. In a word, if we want security, let us give security; if we want life, let us give life; if we want opportunities, let us provide opportunities. The yardstick we use for others will be the yardstick which time will use for us."

Debbie and I experienced an existential earthquake following her trip to the edge of eternity, and endeavored to broaden and deepen our moral map. How should we express love? How should the golden rule be applied? Christianity provides additional moral guidance. Let's inspect the golden rule's derivative ethical principles.

WHAT ELSE DID CHRIST TEACH?

Debbie and I heard in our hearts a calling, and, called, we endeavored to answer that call to search more deeply for clearer comprehension of Christ's moral commitments. There is much more to try to understand. After someone has a stroke, some of Christianity's ethical principles subordinate to the golden rule are likely to catch a survivor's attention. See what you think about their relevance to your life's journey.

You can better see many supplementary Christian moral precepts against the backdrop of the "love" command and reciprocity norm. "All Scripture...is profitable" (2 Tim. 3:16), but the command to love is the Bible's "principal principle"—a roadmap toward righteousness which overrules man-created institutions, traditions, and legal precepts that inhibit the formation of an inclusive community serving *all*.

Facing death makes you seriously think about the ethical obligations Jesus calls us to embrace. The obligations are binding and pose big challenges to entrenched customs. Jesus meant His words to be taken literally; they were stated with no "unless" or "except when" qualifications; they were commands, not mere suggestions. Jesus's moral message must be taken at face value. Jesus's teachings were radical when He enunciated them and remain radical today.

Jesus intentionally presented injunctions in words that could not be misunderstood, in order to make His unconventional teachings crystal clear. He was a rebel with a cause, and He "shot from the lip," arousing and alarming his audiences. To break barriers, vagueness and equivocation would not suffice. Simple declarative statements were required. Jesus knew better than all that humans' surrender to sin presented a barrier to acceptance of His moral message and that, as He said, "for from within, out of the heart of men, proceed evil thoughts" (Mark 7:21). This undoubtedly was why Jesus warned that "everyone who sins is a slave to sin" but that "if you hold to my teaching, you are really my disciples. Then you will know the truth, and the truth will set you free" (John 8:34, 31–32). In the context of His time and ours, His commands are radical: "You must love your neighbor and not hate your enemy. Love your enemies and pray for your persecutors" (Matt. 5:44–45). "Do good, and lend, hoping for nothing in return" (Luke 6:35).

These rules remain controversial because they demand so much. Are we really ready to follow the directives He asks of us? Yet we know we have no excuse but to try—it is a matter of life and death. After surviving three devastating strokes through God's loving interventions, we were primed to seek to comply with His high moral imperatives.

Jesus treated "business as usual" as a boxer treats a punching bag. Especially in auspicious times, many people turn away from the controversial ethical commitments Jesus asks of us and go about living in habitual ways that run contrary to what He commanded. That ends when near death begins. A journey then commences to strictly follow Christ's other teachings about right and wrong. Here are some highlights.

- **Judge Not**—Jesus warns, "Yea, and why even of yourselves judge ye not what is right?" (Luke 12:57). When we fail "in humility [to] value others above ourselves" (Phil. 2:3), we unwittingly inflate our own sense of superiority by judging the sinfulness of others. Jesus admonished, "Put no more judgments upon other people so that you may not have judgment passed upon you. For you will be judged by the standard you judge by, and men will pay you back with the same measure you have used with them" (Matt. 7:1–3). "Do not berate others—it only brings harm" (Ps. 37:8).

    Let God do the judging and administrate justice. On Mount Sinai, God described Himself to Moses, saying He is "compassionate and gracious, slow to anger, rich in steadfast kindness, extending kindness to the thousandth generation, forgiving iniquity, transgression, and sin; but clearing the guilty, God will not do" (Exod. 34:6–7). God will judge us by the yardstick of the golden rule. So "Do not fret because of evildoers, nor be envious of the workers of iniquity" because justice will ultimately be dealt by God: The guilty "shall soon be cut down like the grass" (Ps. 37:1).

- **A Need to Help the Needy**—Scripture tells us to "defend the cause of the weak and fatherless; maintain the rights of the poor and oppressed. Rescue the weak and needy; deliver them from the hand of the wicked" (Ps. 82:3–4). Jesus did just that. His missionary work concentrated on alleviating the agony of the poor, the sick, and the weak; it sought to help everyone, not just some. Revealingly, when a wealthy Pharisee who claimed to strictly observe all the Mosaic laws asked Jesus what he must do to enter heaven, Jesus instructed him to sell all his material goods and give the proceeds to the poor (Mark 10:17–22). "Sell what you have, and give alms" (Luke 12:34). Christ warned that whoever closes his or her eyes on the suffering of the less fortunate cannot expect the heavenly Father to forgive that person's indifference.

- **Neither Covet nor Succumb to Greed**—Jesus was sorrowed by the evidence that the rich valued their riches more than righteousness (Matt. 6:19–25; Mark 10:23–25), and condemned this proclivity. Jesus flatly asserts, "Lay not up for yourselves treasures upon earth" (Matt. 6:19); "Woe unto you that are rich!" (Luke 6:24); "Take heed, and beware of covetousness: for a man's life consists not in the abundance of things he possesses" (Luke 12:15). "For what will it profit," Jesus asked, "to gain the whole world and forfeit your life?" (Mark 8:37).

  It is impossible to worship both mammon (money and wealth) and God: "For where your treasure is, there your heart will be also" (Luke 12:34). Jesus clarifies: "No man can serve two masters; for either he will hate the one, and love the other; or else he will hold to the one, and despise the other. You cannot serve God and mammon...If therefore the light that is in thee be darkness, how great is that darkness!" (Matt. 6:12). No one ever said that that living a Christian life would be easy. At death's gate, it is easier to see the worthlessness of earthly "treasures"; they can't be taken with you, but they can be charitably distributed to the needy.

- **Live to Love and Serve**—"God is love" (1 John :16), the love instilled within our soul. "Love" is both a noun and a verb. Jesus is love. Our Savior asks us to practice selfless love, starting with the effort to see ourselves in each other. Albert Einstein understood Christ's prescription: "Only a life lived for others is a life worthwhile." Jesus was the paragon of a suffering servant and showed his love by serving others. He lovingly healed the sick, enabled the blind to see, and relieved the agony of those suffering. He made the supreme act of love, sacrificing His own life to save us from sin and death: "Greater love hath no man than this, that a man lay down his life for his friends" (John 15:13). "We have known and believed the love that God has for us; we love Him because He first loved us" (1 John 4:16, 19).

Jesus expected believers to emulate His demonstration of unconditional love, instructing His followers "All will know that you are My disciples if you have love for one another" (John 13:35), and, by implication, to do as He had done, restoring relationships between friend and foe and between neighbors and strangers, backing up words with deeds. "Let your light so shine before others, that they may see your good deeds and glorify your Father which is in heaven" (Matt. 5:16).

- **Political Power Pollutes**—Jesus condemned humans' insatiable lust for political power. Christ put his actions where his mouth was while He was in the wilderness for forty days, Satan tempted Him with the offer to gain "the kingdoms of this world" (Matt. 26). Jesus had no trouble resisting that temptation—His love of His Heavenly Father trumped any temptation to gain unbounded worldly power. He counseled passive resistance to wicked political authorities who govern, while reserving a higher jurisdiction that belongs to God. "Give to the emperor that which belongs to the emperor, and to God what belongs to God" (Matt. 22:21), He submitted (without antagonizing His Roman judges by clarifying that *everything* belongs to God and that all laws are subservient to His laws).

- **Killing Is Dead Wrong**—"Hands that shed innocent blood" are detestable to God (Prov. 6:16,17). The Ten Commandments prohibit killing, and Christ strictly forbid the taking of life and even anger—they are the devil's methods. Jesus did not mince words: "You have heard that it was said by them of old time, 'Thou shall not kill, and whosoever shall kill shall be in danger of the judgment.' But I say unto you, 'That whosoever is angry with his brother without a cause shall be in danger of the judgment.'" (Matt. 5:21–22).

- **Give Peace a Chance**—Jesus is called the "Prince of Peace" for good reasons. He preached, "Blessed are the peacemakers, for they will be called the children of God" (Matt. 4:9). It is the "meek," the humble minded, who will eventually "possess the land" (Matt. 5:5). Jesus also condemned "retributive justice": "But I tell you not to resist injury, but if anyone strikes you on the right check, turn the other to him also" (Matt. 5:39). Revenge against those who do us wrong is prohibited. Instead, Jesus embraced the spirit of holy scripture's biblical prescription for "nations to beat their swords into plowshares" (Mic. 4:3; Isa. 2:4)—timeless wisdom engraved in the entry to the United Nations headquarters.

- **Pacifism Pays**—Jesus repeatedly warned that those who engage in violence and coercive aggression will not enter God's eternal kingdom. Jesus vociferously upheld pacifism. Instructively, on the road from Gethsemane, one of His disciples took his sword and cut off the ear of the high priest's slave; this act received a harsh reprimand that reveals Jesus's immutable conviction: "Put your sword back where it belongs! For all who draw the sword will die by the sword" (Matt. 26:52).

- **Morality Applies to All Actors**—Jesus's prohibition of violence extends to relations among nations. "Whatever a man sows, that he will also reap" (Gal. 6:7). "Whoever sows generously will also reap generously" (2 Cor. 9:6). This applies to foreign policy also—in the global arena, what a country sows, so it shall reciprocally reap. Christian ethics do not differentiate one set of moral rules for individuals and another for collectivities. The golden rule applies unconditionally and absolutely to both people and entire nations; Jesus did not segregate personal from public ethical accountability. Mulford Q. Sibley writes, "Jesus accepted, as a good Jew, the interweaving of ethics, politics, and religion. When He dealt with ethical issues…He took for granted that his teaching was applicable to social organization and to politics, just as He assumed that He came not to 'destroy' the law but rather to 'fulfill' it (Matthew 5:17)." No boundaries were draw between private and public morality. Humans were instructed not to kill, and nations were not exempted from the prohibition of military force. Benjamin Franklin spoke as Christ might have when Franklin concluded, "There never was a good war or a bad peace." Erasmus rightly captured the spirit of Christ's ethical edict: "What can war beget but more war? But goodwill begets goodwill."

DISENTANGLING MORAL KNOTS

When Debbie and I began reexamining our moral vision, we were not dealing with black-and-white ethical issues. It is clearly one thing to designate "love" the foundation of your moral code; it is another to put that prescription into practice. Light can fade to gray as the cloudy panorama of scriptural morality is closely inspected. "The secret things belong to the Lord our God" (Deut. 29:29). We sought to discipline our understanding of confounding and somewhat inconsistent ethical platitudes where only hypothetical postulates come to light. The road to righteousness is shrouded with ambiguities darkening comprehension. To declare "do the right thing" and "base action on love" is the easy part. The hard part is discerning what "the right thing" is and when and where it applies in different circumstances.

Many ethical values are in potential conflict with each other. Observance of one ethical principle may require the violation of one or more others. Then a decision must be made to ascertain which moral principle should take precedence. Which value should have priority? Morality matters because, like Debbie and me, in your life you will have to make many hard choices between incompatible principles. On your life's pathway, you will cross many circumstantial crossroads. One issue illustrates the larger set of issues.

- **Cross or Country?**—Many Christians deeply love two things simultaneously, their God and their country. The potential for a value contradiction strikes home when we face the question of how far our natural inclination to love our country should extend when that loyalty requires violating the golden rule prescribing merciful love for even foreign enemies.

Especially in times of threats from abroad, many people are forced to make a choice between loyal love for their homeland and loyalty to Christ's morals. Which value would you place ahead of the other? Which is superior, and which is subordinate? This is a classic example of the kind of moral tradeoff that life presents—exemplary of a host of other hard ethical choices that inevitably arise on life's journey.

What if the interests of your nation and the ideals of Christ collide? If you value chauvinistic nationalism—"my country, right or wrong"—more highly than the glory of God and His moral commands, then you may have to repudiate the Sermon on the Mount and the golden rule. Patriotism has a problem—obedience subverts the command to love and substitutes the view that it is proper to hate every country but one's own. If you think through this troubling moral choice, take into account that all wars in the past two centuries have been fought in the name of nationalism. Unrestrained patriotism may be the last remaining religion that still demands human sacrifice. Maybe nationalism is some kind of mental disease responsible for war and death.

Jesus's injunctions make it clear how to react when a difficult choice must be made between country and Christ: "We ought to obey God rather than men" (Acts 5:29). God did not restrict His love to one nation. There exists in Christ's moral vision no contradiction between patriotism and concern for all the world's people.

- **Living Life Serenely in Gray Shadows**—Many of our cherished values clash and collide with one another. The choices we make tell us much about our moral code. The road to hell is paved with good intentions. We may have good intentions, but that does not get us off the hook when values conflict. Then a choice must be made between competing values.

Life poses an endless sequence of situations pitting one value against another, forcing difficult choices between incompatible moral principles and between incommensurate evils. Ambiguous predicaments usually necessitate choosing the lesser of two evils or the greater of two conflicting injunctions. They necessitate going beyond simple ethical platitudes such as the obligation to show compassion, minimize harm and alleviate others 'suffering. There is not only right and wrong but many shades in between. It doesn't take a stroke to make this clear, but hardships clarify. Morality requires some form of action in the face of real dilemmas, and pose difficulties for the soul to reconcile.

Jesus Christ was the only human who ever lived up to His Father's moral code, which is why someone has said that "the last Christian died on the cross." Debbie and I have fallen short time and time again, but after looking at death in the face, our efforts intensified in trying to walk in Christ's ways. His moral message was voiced to change lives. Jesus undoubtedly believed His radically subversive moral doctrines could potentially be met, perhaps because He knew that the people He loved (everyone) were capable of altering the evil behaviors toward which they were habitually inclined. "Man has free choice," St. Thomas Aquinas explains, "or otherwise counsels, exhortations, commands, prohibitions, rewards and punishments would be in vain." Jesus's injunctions were not in vain. Jesus knew that the pursuit of love in accordance with the golden rule would bring followers peace, and that peace could change the world.

Jesus's guides for action dictate that we should wrestle with the dilemmas intrinsic to moral choice. Which moral principles guide your perceptions and moral worldview? Debbie and I took comfort in our time of terrible affliction that we could trust our Lord to lead us in the right ethical direction. "The commands of the Lord are radiant, giving light to the eyes" (Ps. 19:8). We can reduce our proclivity to make poor ethical choices if we listen to God's words embedded in our spiritual mind and let the Holy Spirit guide our footsteps (Ps. 119:11, 133).

However, the problem of understanding what to think and do in cloudy circumstances where the Christian path is not clear cannot be eliminated. Reinhold Niebuhr's iconic book, *The Children of Light and the Children of Darkness*, exposed everybody's challenge of finding the correct template for moral conduct. He wrote, "It is almost impossible to be sane and Christian at the same time," and regrettably confessed that "on the whole I have been saner than Christian," placing more trust in logical reason to reduce the burdens of flawed choices than in God's ultimate justice. Every choice involves the sacrifice of one value for another. "It is an illusion," Niebuhr wrote, "to imagine that we can destroy evil merely by avowing ideals, in part because there exists a mixture of good and evil in *all* human virtue." This irony is a stubborn fact.

On our post-stroke railroad, we began to see the advantages of placing the costs of selfishness and the benefits of altruism in the spaces between the tracks. We envisioned Christian ethics in a new light. Our revelations showed us that it is man's impulse to sin that makes Christian moral constraints necessary, and it is man's capacity for upright behavior which makes Christ-centered morality possible. Our moral vision is predicated on the realism of idealism underlying Christian ethics. This view might sharpen your vision of morality matters. If in the darkness you search and find your innermost ethical values, and they conform to Jesus's morals, "shout abroad when the daybreak comes" (Matt. 16:24–28; 10:26–28). You are not doomed to remain a denizen of the dark.

Debbie and I began to accept the necessity to live with the transparent ambiguity darkening our decisions. The darkness can be escaped, but when you're facing ethical dilemmas, look for the beam of light flickering in the shadows. Goodness is stronger than evil, and light can overcome darkness.

We must attempt to adjust and adapt to life's adversities while accepting the adverse things that happen. The original wording of Reinhold Niebuhr's "Serenity Prayer" advises how to face our agonies: "God, give us the grace to accept with serenity the things that cannot be changed, the courage to change the things that should be changed, and the wisdom to know the difference." This applies to how a Christian should respond to afflictions and ambiguous ethical situations. During our long journey, we struggled to serenely confront suffering and found a measure of serenity precisely when we sincerely tried to live up to Christianity's high moral ideals.

We perceived a brighter shade of light when we strove to bury confusion by extending love toward others. In our time of terrifying need, when we were down, God lifted us up. Love is exactly what we should practice. We should reach out to people in need and extend to them the same kind of uplifting support we received from our Savior, ideally in a manner that guides the needy to His healing touch. Debbie's progressive recovery under God's care bred confidence that we, and everyone, could live more moral lives if we dedicated ourselves to that goal on a daily basis.

The point of life is to love. This was Christ's major ethical teaching. We pledged to spend our remaining days trying to act in ways that God would approve. When looking at death in the face, as Debbie and I did many times on our long journey, we concluded that we should try to live as if each day was our last, so we should take every opportunity to act with kindness, love, and charity. As someone said, "our days are numbered, so we should make each one count." "Don't wait for the last judgment," Albert Camus admonished; "it takes place every day."

We knew that Jesus is "the light of the world" (John 9:5), the Light that knows no darkness. He stated, "I have come as a light into the world, that whomever believes in Me shall not abide in darkness" (John 12:46). Jesus's Word was a lamp lighting our path to a life lived according to His ethical teachings.

Rev. George Crow offers sound advice: "How does one become more like Jesus? By developing a relationship with Him, which means growing to love Him as the God and friend that He is. We learn to worship God. We learn we can share our deepest fears with this truest of friends. We learn who He is and what He has made us to be and do." To ground our morality on Christ's Word, George recommends reading in Romans (12:1–2): "Do not be conformed to this world, but be transformed by the renewal of your mind, that by testing you may discern what is the will of God, what is good and acceptable and perfect."

The route to following Christ and scripture is shrouded in fog. We may travel on the right road but need assistance determining which direction to turn in the frequent forks that life presents. Fortunately, help is available in confronting this challenge of comprehension. Read on.

CHAPTER 30

THE HOLY SPIRIT STIRS THE SOUL

§

L ooking at death in the face, the Holy Spirit restored our souls, conveying desperately needed comfort: "Here I am with you, according to your heart" (1 Sam. 14:7). Stopping before starting to live, we thought long and hard about how the Holy Spirit stirs our souls.

The Holy Spirit's linkage to the soul is hard to comprehend. Scripture admits as much, referring to the inner peace derived from the Holy Spirit as a "peace that passes all understanding" (Phil. 4:7). A plethora of questions surround the enigmatic invisible Holy Spirit—the tertiary, oft-overlooked Third Person of the Holy Trinity (God the Father, Son, and Holy Ghost). The whole concept is mystifying, which may explain why discussion of it is often avoided. Many Christians have difficulty conceiving of God as the Son incarnate and the Holy Spirit as part of the same three-in-one unified deity.

The basic attributes of the Holy Spirit are unfathomable, mainly because the Holy Spirit is something that no mortal eye can see. Even more puzzling still are the incomprehensible processes through which the Holy Spirit penetrates the mind to generate spiritual and moral consciousness. Let us share an outline of the understandings we envisioned in the aftermath of Debbie's strokes, as informed by the Bible.

THE HOLY SPIRIT'S BIBLICAL IDENTITY

The Bible provides many insights about the Holy Spirit's capacity to telepathically influence a person's frame of mind. The Holy Spirit is within us and outside us; in the absence of God's light within us, there would be no "us." The Holy Spirit is present everywhere (Ps. 139:7–8), knows all (1 Cor. 2:6–16), possesses infinite power (Luke 1:35), gives life and protects it (Rom. 8:2), and provides understandings that cannot be discovered by reason alone (1 Cor. 2:14). The Holy Spirit enables extraordinary things to happen in our lives, teaching us (1 Cor. 2:13) and guiding us (John 16:13). If "natural insight" within the soul is unleashed through the Holy Spirit, it will guide the blessed to adhere to particular ethical principles and requirements (Rom. 2:14; Gal. 5:19–2). "The peace of God...shall guard your hearts and mind" (Phil. 4:7).

Scripture proclaims that the Holy Spirit already within us facilitates our ability "to perceive the words of understanding, to receive the instruction of wisdom, justice, judgment and equity" (Prov. 1:2–3), so that we can learn to "hate evil, love good, establish justice" (Amos 5:15) and do what is right, just and fair in our relations with all. The Holy Spirit motivates us to do God's will by leading us along a path to righteousness and to finding our purpose in life. St. Thomas Aquinas encapsulated well how the Spirit functions: "The light of faith makes us see what we believe."

After Debbie's strokes, we felt the Holy Spirit at work on our behalf. We knew we could trust God (Phil. 4:6), and this trust would let the enlightening power of the Holy Spirit supply the same lamplight that is available for anyone. Just search your heart. Release the light within you. "Walk by faith, not by sight" (2 Cor.). The Holy Spirit is available to anyone who prays for it. Jesus counsels, "Ask, and it shall be given to you; seek, and you shall find; knock, and it shall be opened unto you. For everyone that asks receives; and he that seeks finds; and to him that knocks it shall be opened" (Matt. 7:7–8); "If any man have ears to hear, let him hear" (Mark 30:16).

- **The Ghost in the Machine**—The Bible repeatedly informs us that the Holy Spirit resides *within* each and every person's soul. Scripture portrays the Holy Spirit as the source of our essence—the "self" we can become if we seek God's Word. St. Augustine maintained that everything God created was good, and what was spectacularly good was the spiritual eyesight God gave humans to look upon their purpose in life. Even fallen sinners retain a trace of the rectitude that God instilled in everyone's souls. Belief in a supreme deity and adherence to moral principles were inherited instincts, derived from inner workings where our eye cannot penetrate—"the intertwining (*perplexitas*) of veins and nerves...which satisfies the mind that uses the eyes." Thus, like "flowing water inside you" (John 4:10-14), the Holy Spirit catalytically prepares our minds to be responsive to Christ's instructions. C. S. Lewis maintained that the Holy Spirit gives us the ability to intuitively grasp a corpus of ideas and ideals that has "intrinsic reasonableness," "shines by its own light" as "a supernatural source for rational thought" as well as "a supernatural source for our ideas of good and evil."

This neo-Platonic concept of an immortal spirit from which religious ideas and moral ideals originate captures the simple version of the biblical narrative. According to this script, the spiritual soul flows *through* the mind, but spiritual consciousness is not derived *from* the mind. Logic and rational cognition do not generate our spiritual consciousness—it stems from *a priori* knowledge our Creator rooted in the soul. The soul is mediated through the physical brain but, as St. Thomas concluded, is independent of the brain. The soul is immaterial, indestructible, immortal, invisible—an underlying subjective consciousness beyond the mind that cannot be explained in physical terms. Gilbert Ryle describes the Holy Spirit as "the ghost in the machine" shaping the thoughts we conceive.

- **Spiritual Engineering**—God designed the human brain to perform like an intellectual engine, transmitting an impulse to intuitively recognize that there exists a higher power watching over us for whom we are obligated to act righteously. Spiritual awareness of our Deity and morality may be natural to us—a basic part of being human. Whenever you feel love and empathy for others, the Holy Spirit is speaking to you, inflaming your deeply entrenched emotional need to see yourself as a part of something much larger. Some situations stimulate shifts in thinking from *me* to *we*. Who hasn't gazed in awe at the stars in the vastness of space, marveled at majestic mountains, or stared at a grand vista and felt at One with the Infinite, interconnected with all? A common consequence of the "wow effect" is to feel an obligation to treat others generously and ethically, and to protect the environment God created. The Holy Spirit provides for our emancipatory inclusion in the interconnected whole, where each soul interacts with one another and yet retains a distinct identity. Similarly, in sickness we often experience transformational moments and begin to heal and regain health when we sense the Holy Spirit's capacity to uplift us from the depths of despair.

The Holy Spirit's impact is evident if we look for it. Think of young children—all seem instinctively to know that they are protected by a heavenly spirit and are connected to others. If you doubt that the Holy Spirit can neurologically wire and program the human soul to pursue a relationship with God and righteousness, consider an analog—God wired humans from birth with myriad impulses, one of which is a response to music. Mere tones and music with a beat give us the urge to move and dance. Music is intimately woven into the subconscious fabric of our lives, just like spirituality and morality.

Extend this proposition to consider also how our Creator set humans apart from other species by giving people the ability to invent words and communicate thoughts in speech. Remarkably, every human being operates from a God-given common structure for oral communication. It is evident in every known language. Every mind contains the same linguistic code, and this programmatic structure for verbal communication genetically embedded in our brains influences visual perception and shapes consistencies in humans' mode of thought. The latter impact makes it probable that certain ideas, such as the existence of a Supreme Being, originate from this communication structure unique to homo sapiens. The Holy Spirit cuts with surgical precision into this universal communication structure to drive our minds toward intuitive belief in the idea of God and the ideals of His moral code.

- **A Spiritual Motor**—Debbie and I found the apostle Paul's definition of the Holy Spirit's primary purpose persuasive: "I advise you to obey only the Holy Spirit's instructions [when you, in your heart, know what you ought to do]. He will tell you where to go and what to do, and then you won't always be doing wrong things your evil nature wants you to. For we naturally love to do evil things that are just the opposite from the things that the Holy Spirit tells us to do" (Gal. 5:16). Jesus warned, "If therefore the light that is in you is darkness, how great is that darkness" (Matt. 6:23). But light can overcome our darkness "when the Holy Spirit has his way with us....Those who belong to Christ nail their natural evil desires to his cross and crucify them there" (Gal. 5:24). Trust Christ, and then "having believed, you are sealed with the Holy Spirit" (Eph. 1:13).

  It took an encounter with nonexistence—near death—for Debbie and I to give serious thought to God's remarkable gift—our deeply interior spiritual and moral motor. You may come to other conclusions, but we doubt if a counterargument will prove convincing. Many agnostics and scientists have tried, but they have failed to produce a cogent reason for rejecting scripture's message that the Spirit living within us "intercedes with sighs too deep for words" (Rom. 8:26) to generate moral conscience and consciousness (John 14:16-17).

- **The Holy Spirit's Neurological Pathways**—What happens to the victim's soul after a stroke strikes? Nothing. It is still there, indestructible, immutable, invisible, and immaterial. A stroke may damage or destroy a region or pathway in the brain, and sensory maps for touch, vision, and thinking may be damaged or destroyed. The capacity to think abstractly can be compromised; personality can be altered. Consciousness and memory may be lost. But not the soul.

The Holy Spirit is always available to guide victims' souls, accessible both when alive or the beyond in the afterlife. Debbie's soul was independent of her mind, but her mind was always amenable to the Holy Spirit's influence. When her stroke struck, her mind retained a capacity to receive the Holy Spirit's neural messages and signals, despite her unawareness of them. Mind and Spirit are inseparable (Eph. 2:11-20).

The human brain is always accessible to the Holy Spirit. The innate Holy Spirit is believed to function somewhere near where the brain ends and the mind begins. In Debbie's case, when desperation and hope held hands after her hemorrhagic stroke, the activated Holy Spirit erased the line between consciousness and imagination.

The process through which this paranormal phenomenon happened can be traced to neurological linkages. Even in the most severe cases, stroke victims' damaged brains continue to process information, carrying this out through what neuropsychologists call "unconscious inference," without the victim being aware that underlying concepts are being formed and stored deep in their brain. A victim deemed medically unconscious and close to mortality retains the faculties of sound and sight, and sensations and experiences meld into their brains. Overheard words and impressions are combined and recombined to form and store concepts. When triggered, these imprinted conceptualizations can sometimes be retrieved to allow recollection of buried memories.

The Holy Spirit can perform this restorative service because God made the brain resilient, capable of receiving signals from new neural connections compensating for those destroyed by a stroke. Neuroscientist Eric Kandle explains: "Many sensory, motor, and cognitive functions are served by more than one neural pathway— the same information is processed simultaneously and in parallel in different regions of the brain. When one region or pathway is damaged, others may be able to compensate, at least partially, for the loss." Brain biology pictures God's ingenious design for the human brain, through which "synaptic marking" processes prime synapses connecting neurons for sufficient functionality to allow synaptic potential to stimulate reactions and sensations. The Holy Spirit can activate these processes to resuscitate a stroke survivor's mind. Thus, when a stroke destroys neural pathways, the person struck unconsciously can benefit from the Holy Spirit's intercession, even when the damage to the brain appears hopelessly irreparable.

That Debbie couldn't resurrect subconscious memories of her near-death travel to heaven's gate did not mean that her mind was not affected by her brief miraculous journey. Her spiritual soul—who she then was—had headed to heaven's door and the sojourn became intimately welded deep within her subconscious memory. It is likely that the Holy Spirit sent signals to her soul through interconnected nerve cells to her unconscious mind, probably to a specific site in the brain's right hemisphere—where impressions and cognitions are connected and stored to form what Dr. Brenda Milner terms "implicit memory." Survivors of strokes may retain subconscious memories of their experiences, submerged in their brain's deep recesses. "Preconscious unconsciousness," Dr. Lawrence Kubie submits, retains information in the temporal lobes for possible later retrieval by the conscious mind. Dr. Hermann Helmholtz agrees: "experiences are recorded and recalled not only as conscious memories, but also as unconscious memories. Unconscious memories are ordinarily inaccessible to consciousness, but they nevertheless can exert powerful effects on behavior." I was on hand to observe these effects.

- **Witness to the Holy Spirit's Intercession**—In the immediate aftermath of Debbie's devastating ruptured aneurism, not for a split-second was she in danger of becoming "soul dead." The soul is imperishable, and I saw my precious wife's soul levitate above her sedate body during her eye-popping near-death sojourn and then disappear as her soul was reunited with her body. The Holy Spirit had enveloped Debbie's soul and pulled her from the abyss. My vision provided incontestable evidence about the Holy Spirit's ability to access, intercede and resurrect the soul.

The telltale confirmatory sign of the Holy Spirit's intercession became evident the next day. Resuscitated, Debbie regained the capacity to communicate her thoughts coherently, and what she had to say revealed her astonishing contentment and peace. She exhibited no sorrow or remorse, only happiness. Why? Debbie had almost died! There is only one compelling reason—her soul had been transported to the other end of life, escorted by the Holy Spirit.

I acknowledge that this hypothesis cannot be proven and is as difficult to explain as is a subjectively inexplicable abstraction such as the origins of the unique. Nonetheless, her soul's excursion outside her body must have penetrated Debbie's subconscious mind. When Debbie's soul was suspended in the air, momentarily freed from the incarceration of the mortal world, the heavenly paradise where she would go after death was revealed. The Holy Spirit's "escort service" enabled her soul to gain kinesthetic knowledge of God, and to envision her true self in His presence. The comfort provided by this understanding cannot be surpassed. Her detour from this world and return to it is the only way of explicating the supreme serenity that infiltrated Debbie's unconscious memory of her miraculous voyage from near-death to renewed life.

The uplifting behavioral after-effects of Debbie's spiritual voyage were visible, but she was incapable of recollecting her sojourn that had provided such comfort. As her surgeons had predicted, after her brain surgery Debbie couldn't recall anything about her soul's journey outside her body. It was like a long-forgotten memory—stored so deeply in a brain that it was like one of those obscure thoughts you can't remember that you don't even remember that you once remembered it.

Everybody retains thoughts so forgotten that we forget that we forgot them, until spontaneously they suddenly spring to mind. Our recollections are like dreams—they usually fade from consciousness after we awaken, but sometimes are later vividly resurrected. Think how impressions of distant experiences, such as a bible story heard in early childhood and stored in the brain, sometimes suddenly re-emerge in our minds, word for word, and continue to speak to us (Ps. 119:130-134).

- **Cause and Consequence**—The potency by which Debbie's sub-conscious memories of the Holy Spirit lifting her soul after her brain surgery was attested by her effervescent attitude and confident comportment. This explanation conforms to Sigmund Freud's theory that subconscious memories are the basis for mental and psychological states. In absence of a more compelling explanation, the Holy Spirit's intercession most cogently explains Debbie's remarkable transformation after her stroke to a "new" or "renewed" soul or "reborn" self. Debbie was a changed person. Her contented mood was like that of St. Paul when he wrote from prison, "I have learned that whatever state I am, to be content" (Phil. 4:11). Debbie's perception of her circumstances was more important than her terrible circumstances themselves, and the Holy Spirit had colored in bright shades her perception of her dark situation. Her visible sense of serenity simply had to be the emotional consequence of the Holy Spirit's companionship during her sojourn beyond her body. She became cheerfully acceptant of her frightful circumstances, because somewhere in her subconscious mind she was intuitively able to sense her soul's inspiring near-death journey. Her fearlessness illuminates how the Holy Spirit's presence and power can be felt even though we are not fully conscious of it. When she experienced God, her soul found her true self "hidden in Christ with God" (Col. 3:3).

- **Spiritual Awakening**—"Weeping may endure for a night, but joy comes in the morning" (Ps. 30:5). Debbie had survived "in the furnace of affliction" (Isa. 48:10), and the fire had been smothered by the Holy Spirit. She came out of the night's smoldering ashes into the joy of day transformed and better prepared to resume her life journey. This miracle was followed by subsequent miracles that further demonstrated the Holy Spirit's active presence within Debbie's soul.

The Holy Spirit is a master teacher. After Debbie's strokes, our relationship with God grew exponentially. "God is our refuge and strength, a very present help in troubles" (Ps. 46:1); we knew we should "not lose heart" in times of trouble (2 Cor. 4:16). When threats strike, terrifying fears often cripple spirits, and that is when the Holy Spirit swings into action, providing assurance that God has the supreme power to make us whole again. We saw His light and were reminded of His power as Debbie's mind was renewed and restored. "He had delivered us from the power of darkness and conveyed us into the kingdom of the Son" (Col. 1:13).

We learned through our suffering how the Holy Spirit is the wellspring of our true identity, shaping who we can become through faith. "God is spirit, and those who worship Him must worship Him in spirit" (John 4:23–24). Scripture underscores this tenet repeatedly, as, for instance, when Jesus said, "The light is with you for a while longer. Walk while you have the light, lest the darkness overtake you; he who walks in the darkness does not know where he goes. While you have the light, believe in the light, that you may become sons of light" (John 12:35–36). We can call on the Holy Spirit to carry our true selves—our souls—out of darkness.

- **Signs of Spiritual Animation**—As a result of our post-stroke experiences, we perceive the Holy Spirit to be the source of the soul. Skeptics will ask, "Can the Holy Spirit really shape the human soul? Does everyone really possess a spiritual soul?" This thesis may seem far-fetched, like listening to the sounds of silence. It is not. The idea of a spiritualized soul is not a mythical fantasy. Consider some conspicuous signs that the Holy Spirit resides somewhere within the human soul:

  - All people experience spiritual sensations and make moral judgments. They don't have to, but they do. A universal impulse is evident that can only be explained by the internal composition of the human soul as our Creator designed it. The Holy Spirit has built theological ideas and ethical ideals into everyone's soul. Despite huge disparities making for differences, everyone contemplates the existence of a supreme being above themselves and cares about which ethical rules should be followed. If religious and normative ideas were irrelevant, why do so many people spend so much time debating them? People are programmed to work spirituality and moral matters into their minds—it's a matter of fact.

- Most people in most cultures in most historical epochs have believed that there truly is something called a spiritual power that solidifies our souls—our true selves. "We and God have business with each other; and in opening ourselves to His influence our deepest destiny is fulfilled," William James concluded in identifying "what I may call the instinctive belief of mankind: God is real since He produces real effects." This universality is what Carl Jung called the "collective unconscious"—an idea echoing the Platonic notion of a "world soul" connecting all created things with each other in relationship to our Maker.

- The striking diversity of human cultures notwithstanding, all people embrace some of the same values. The societies within which people live are highly variant, but the primary moral rules they endorse are very similar. If there were no such thing as a spiritual moral soul, how have similar normative moral cognitions and rules emerged in human communities that are otherwise so different?

People intuitively recognize from birth and endorse everywhere similar ideals. Why? Plausibly, the Holy Spirit programmed everyone's moral mind-set, embedding all souls with common innate ethical compulsions. All people believe that they should care for their offspring and intuitively sense that it is wrong to steal, cheat, or murder. Moreover, people everywhere value empathy for the plight of those who suffer, as well as embracing what C. S. Lewis identified as the "universal human feeling that bad men ought to suffer." Arguably, the Holy Spirit guides all humans' inner selves toward the belief that we have an inherent duty to pursue virtue and avoid vice. "The most astounding reality in all our experience," Will Durant notes, "is precisely our moral sense, our inescapable feeling, in the face of temptation, that this or that is wrong. We may yield; but the feeling is there nevertheless."

- Virtuous actions become addictively habit forming. All people experience an inner psychological reward when they undertake self-sacrificial acts of loving service toward others. A sense of peace and well-being invariably results from undertaking unnecessary acts of kindness. The giver receives psychological satisfaction in return.

  Aristotle observed, "The more virtuous a man becomes the more he enjoys virtuous actions." This is the same Aristotle who, three centuries before Christ, argued that ethical actions are guided by a distinct instinct from within, built into humans by what Aristotle called "divine providence." From a neuroscience perspective, acts of compassion develop neural connections so that the circuitry induces repetition of additional compassionate and cooperative acts. Why? This phenomenon can be explained as a consequence of God's design.

- When St. Paul spoke of "the fruits of the spirit," he identified the Holy Spirit's harvest that enables, empowers, and energizes our natural cravings to try to do what is right and practice and experience "love, joy, peace, forbearance, kindness, goodness, faithfulness, gentleness and self-control" (Gal. 5:22–23). God created us with an innate moral code. It cannot have come about through deliberative thought processes. Rationality and reason do not lead humanity to accept the same moral principles (in fact, pure reason undermines agreement). Instead, the same ethical instincts are intuited. The eternal universality of a similar moral mind-set suggests that all humanity shares a common spiritual soul.

- Throughout world history the golden rule has been deified as the worthiest guidepost for behavior. As noted, Jesus cited

Hebrew scripture to underscore the golden rule's authority and universality. But whereas Jesus voiced the golden rule's meaning more clearly than anyone, many previous thinkers from very diverse cultures since antiquity also have voiced their conviction that it is the preeminent moral norm to guide decisions. This does not diminish Jesus's importance as God's messenger. The golden rule's deep historical roots suggest that God instilled in the human soul respect for reciprocated love. We can see "the Spirit of the Lord" (Isa. 4:18) moving upon us, reigning universally in all ages, religions, and cultures, when people interact with love, forgiveness, sharing, charity, honesty, truthfulness, peace, respect, mercy, and generosity—as Jesus did when he forgave sinners, clothed the poor, and fed the hungry, in fact with compassionate love for all, irrespective of their religion, race, gender, position, wealth, culture, or nationality. The Holy Spirit's reign knows no boundaries. We can be sure that God's Spirit is God's consciousness within everyone and becomes evident in our midst whenever people behave as Jesus did and instructed. God's Spirit can be observed in all people, for some often and for those lost only occasionally; the Holy Spirit resides within everyone.

Given the golden rule's supremacy, why shouldn't God allow predecessors to proclaim its unquestionable sagacity? The Holy Spirit arguably gave the golden rule "legs" so it could travel through time and space, recognized everywhere since the beginning of human history as an inalienable valid and valuable norm for conduct.

History records numerous preceding statements of the conviction that the golden rule's premise should be preeminent. The list is rather lengthy. Here's a sample. "Is there one word which may serve as a rule of practice for all one's life?" Confucius inquired rhetorically in *The Analects*. He answered his own question: "Is not reciprocity such a word? What you do not want done to yourself, do not do to others." The legacy goes on and on. Laertius admonished, "We ought to behave to our friends…

as we wish our friends to behave toward us;" Isocrates urged, "Do not do to others what angers you if done to you by others;" Pittacus pleaded "Do not that to thy neighbor that thou wouldst not suffer for him;" Plato taught "Do to others as I would say they should do to me" as well as "Act towards me as you think I should act towards you…. Nothing in my opinion could be more valuable for us than this reciprocity;" the Pharisee philosopher Hillel pronounced that God demands, "Do not do unto others what would be hateful to you were it done to you" and that "What is hateful to thyself do not do to another. This is the whole law; every other rule is mere elaborative commentary."

This echo through the ages suggests that our Creator endowed humans with a capacity to appreciate the moral value of altruistic love underlying the golden rule long before the advent of a Christian creed. It is a timeless universal moral norm, inspired by God and implanted prior to birth in our souls. The golden rule's universality and uniformity speak to the ubiquity of the Holy Spirit's influence on the human soul.

- A universal reverence for a supreme supernatural spirit, like human's capacity to communicate through a spoken language, has often been hypothesized to originate in the brain's structure. Neuroscientist Andrew Newberg contends that humans are "wired to worship" because we were given a "spiritual brain." His account of the neural connection between cerebral function and spirituality casts light on a God-given metaphysical dimension of our essential self, from which faith originates.

Some theologians go so far as to maintain that the structure of the human mind can be understood as a parallel model of the mind of God, or a miniature version of God. St. Augustine reported that he "sought God within himself, mystery seeking mystery within mystery. You were more in me than I was in me (*interior intimo meo*)…." You remained within while I went outside (*intus eras et ego foris*)." St. Augustine conceived the inner spiritual "mind" as the source of religious belief, and concluded that precisely because the origins are inexplicable and invisible, the Holy Spirit is extant which supplies internal spiritual consciousness.

MAKE UP YOUR MIND

Most people are reluctant to call upon the Holy Spirit to awaken the consciousness within their souls. Their passion lies dormant. God will not make us live a life dedicated to giving Him the glory He deserves or make us strive to make the world a better place. We must choose to make that commitment and launch our journey. We can call on the Holy Spirit within us to prompt us to choose the path to righteousness. The Holy Spirit is alive in us, hiding in plain sight.

Oddly enough, the incentives to make that call increase when troubles increase. Sometimes we most appreciate what is good after we experience what is bad. When we suffer afflictions and loss, consciousness of our Lord's compassionate caring increases. Suffering brings out the best in us, awakens the inner ethical consciousness that often slumbers within our souls, and opens hearts and awakens minds to spiritual redirection. In the darkness, when we mourn, our tears attract God's attention: "Blessed are those who mourn, for they will be comforted" (Matt. 5:4). God is the "God of all comfort, who comforts us in all our tribulations" (2 Cor. 1:3–4).

The issue is how we then respond to pain and grief. If we are believers, our spirituality should blossom and mature. We should show our gratitude for our compassionate Savior by giving compassionate care for others. We are called to renew our commitments to Him and His goals to "bear with one another in love" (Eph. 4:2) and "Be merciful, just as your Father also is merciful" (Luke 6:36). It's ironic, but we often seem most prepared to open our spiritual souls and begin to behave ethically in our personal dealings with others when we ourselves are most in need of God's and others' loving care.

God's light shone brightly on Debbie and me, poor sinners that we knew we were, and lighted our path to righteousness. Now, recovered partially through painstakingly slow rehabilitation, it was really up to us to live up to the high standards our Lord had commanded. To be sure, our just God will judge our acts of commission and omission on Judgment Day when we die. This is a potent reason to walk a straight and narrow path while we can. Looking at death in the face makes the imperative of this choice self-evident.

Do not delay. (Don't put off until tomorrow what can be done today, like the fabled fellow who bought a book on procrastination ten years ago all the while insisting he "couldn't wait to read it.") "Now is the accepted time; behold, now is the day of salvation" (2 Cor. 6:2). Don't be like we have often been—practiced at the art of postponement. Jesus invited His followers to follow Him, but many of them, like us, voiced excuses, usually about being too busy with worldly concerns (Luke 9:59–62). Take the Lord's answer—get on with life's most important mission—preparing for death and the salvation of our souls (2 Cor. 6:2). Make up your mind. Now is the time to take a stand and invest in a ticket to paradise. The challenge could not be higher because, as Hannah Arendt suggests, fear of moral responsibility is sometimes stronger than fear of death.

You too can catch the Spirit if you don't already feel its presence or feel a need to strengthen it. Surely your aim to serve others as Jesus commanded will heighten your moral dedication, simply by asking for the Holy Spirit's help. The route to an eternal afterlife can be guided by the spiritual soul.

PART V: AFTERTHOUGHTS ON THE AFTERLIFE

My life closed twice before its close—
It yet remains to see
If immortality unveil
A third event to me.

—EMILY DICKINSON

CHAPTER 31

WHAT HAPPENS WHEN DEATH HAPPENS?

§

John Lennon wrote the lyrics for *"Imagine."* This iconic Beatle's song sparked an entire generation to *imagine* things in unfamiliar ways. He wrote:

Imagine there's no heaven
It's easy if you try
No hell below us
Above us only sky

Imagine all the people
Living for to-day…
Imagine…no religion too

Imagine all the people
Living life in peace…
Sharing all the world…

You may say I'm a dreamer
But I'm not the only one
I hope someday you'll join us
And the world will live as one.

There is a *big* problem with these lyrics. Most people throughout the world *do* accept a religion and imagine a heaven. You don't have to be a dreamer to imagine all people really sharing the world, living "as one" in heaven eternally in unity with God and with everyone. Imagine! It's not hard to do.

There is nothing quite like looking at death in the face to restore religious faith and ignite imagination about what happens after existence on earth ends. After you almost die is when you become most alert and alive. Having lived twice, escaping death, survivors are most prone to probe questions about the meaning of life and the afterlife. They confront like never previously the question "After death, is there more? If so, what will it encompass?"

After strokes took Debbie close to death, we shook paralyzing fears. In the deepest valley of fear, we looked skyward in wonder to the heavens and saw the majesty of God on high. Jesus promised, "Come to me, all you who are weary and burdened, and I will give you rest" (Matt. 11:28). We came and He provided relief. We more clearly envisioned an afterlife where God will dwell among us, wipe away our tears, and there will be "no more death or mourning or crying or pain, for the old order of things will pass away" (Rev. 21:4). After Debbie's near death, we looked forward to the time we could "pass through the door standing open to heaven" (Rev. 4:1) where our souls could escape the painful problems of earthly existence such as strokes, and come home.

The Bible calls death "the last enemy." We do not have to be afraid when we face death. Jesus's sacrifice killed death. The enemy was destroyed. A new world awaits us, altogether outside the meaning of time, space, distance and/or boundaries. All who believe in our heavenly Lord and act on His moral principles can escape the world's sorrow, suffering and fear (1 Thess. 4:13–18).

Our heightened faith in eternal existence was hardly new. *All* cultures have conceived of something higher beyond human existence. Archeological and anthropological research finds that *every* culture throughout history has imagined that there is some kind of "life after life." Those who imagine that after death there is nothing but nothingness comprises a tiny minority. Moreover, "In the long history of mankind," Hans Küng underscores, "no people or tribe has been found without any traces of religion."

On our long journey, two mysteries predominated our thoughts about heaven: (1) What will heaven be like? and (2) What will we be like if we pass through heaven's gate? You have undoubtedly wondered about these same questions. We probed the Bible for answers.

IMAGINING HEAVEN: BIBLICAL INSIGHTS

Unlike many aspects of the human experience, the nature of an afterlife requires the exercise of imagination. There is nothing about the afterworld that can be validated by spectral evidence. "No eye has seen, no ear has heard, no mind has conceived what God has prepared for those who love Him" (1 Cor. 2:9). Heaven is hidden, as impenetrable as rock and as invisible as air. All images of an afterlife are just that—images. All constructions are fabricated, many are fantastic, and none are falsifiable. The range of opinion is limited only by the imagination. Imagine!

Having said that, imagine this: The predisposition to think about the plausible attributes of the afterlife has generated a remarkably consistent consensus about some properties of an imagined heaven. Throughout recorded history people have looked to the heavens and nearly all have imagined it to be a perpetual paradise in which all is interwoven and interlaced, connected in an intimate relationship with a deity. This image conforms to Christology's view of the infinite cosmos. Imagine!

You must exercise your imagination to uncover heaven's hidden characteristics, but can draw heavily on the Holy Spirit. "He who has an ear, let him hear what the Spirit says" (Rev. 3:22). The message is loud and clear: an eternity has existed before time and will persist forever, ruled by God. After we die we can enter its flow. There is more to come! We have it on the highest authority—Jesus Christ Himself told us His death and resurrection made it possible for forgiven sinners to be saved for all eternity.

However, holy scripture and Christian doctrine do not provide a detailed authoritative definition of what immortality will be like. On the contrary, the Bible is not specific on this topic and perhaps purposively ambiguous to stimulate inquiry about God's eternal residence. The Old Testament described Heaven with suggestive allegories, and the imagery provided tantalizing simplistic similes that unsophisticated minds could comprehend. Metaphors such as "many mansions" and other symbolic allusions enabled illiterate people to envision a heaven that would await them after death, without raising doubts that would arise from abstract definitions of what had never been visible and was therefore very difficult to imagine. So the major message was serviced: belief in a promising here-after. That faith was what mattered. Mission accomplished. The details of heaven's characteristics were left to be discovered when we die.

On our long journey, our path was lighted by the Bible's multiple per-spectives on the afterlife. However, Scripture does not precisely answer the looming question: If our Lord judges us worthy to pass through the gate to heaven, what will *we* be like? The Bible provides two alterna-tive images. The first is predicated on the assumption that our rebirth in heaven will be in a *bodily* form, recognizable to other loved ones also accepted into heaven. The second image portrays a heavenly *spiritual* exis-tence after death; our bodies are barely recognizable as human bodies. Scripture supports both of these incompatible visions.

"The Christian tradition has always had *two symbols* of veritably archetypal character," Hans Küng writes, "to designate the reality of the hoped-for (or feared) hereafter," and these inconsistencies, Küng admits, are "for many people today more of a difficulty for faith than an aid to faith." C. S. Lewis similarly acknowledges that "probably every Christian now alive finds a difficulty in reconciling the two things he has been told about 'heaven'—that it is on the one hand, a life in Christ, a vision of God, a ceaseless adoration, and that it is, on the other hand, a bodily life."

In heaven, will we be as we were on earth, a whole person with both spirit and body, or will only our spiritual souls join the others saved in communion with God? Should a distinction to be drawn between a corporal and an incorporal heavenly existence? Do soul, spirit, and body combine in the next life? Do some elements persist while others are left behind? Or are the elements transfigured into something entirely new?

Scripture presents contending images. No less an authority than the apostle Paul confessed his uncertainty: "Whether in the body or apart from the body, I do not know, but God knows" (2 Cor. 12:3). No consensual Christology prevails. Juxtapose the rival biblical accounts.

- **Bodily Resurrection in a New Earth**—To help organize your perceptions of heaven, consider Dr. Randy Alcorn's biblically informed book *Heaven*. It views heavenly existence in purely material terms, and rejects the popular image of disembodied spirits floating in a celestial ethereal afterlife. He doesn't go as far as Thomas Hobbes, who maintained that everything, including our thoughts and perceptions, are nothing but matter in motion, and that even God is a physical being. But Dr. Alcorn comes close. To his way of thinking, the afterlife consists of an eternal future for fully restored human beings dwelling in a fully restored Earth.

  God's plan of the ages is 'to bring all things in heaven and on earth together under one head, even Christ'" (Eph. 1:10). Heaven will literally come to Earth, and the forgiven and blessed will live in perfect harmony in their bodies (joined with their spirits) just as they wished to live on earth during their life journeys. When you get your first glimpse of heaven, you will be amazed and delighted to find real people with real bodies enjoying close relationships with God and each other, eating, drinking, worshipping, and discovering on a New Earth. Earth as God created it. Earth as He intended it to be....Think of friends and family members who loved Jesus and are with him now. Picture them with you, walking together in this place. All of you have powerful bodies, stronger than those of an Olympic decathlete. You are laughing, playing, talking, and reminiscing.... At last, you're the person you were made for, in the place you were made to be. Everywhere there will be new people and places to enjoy, new things to discover. What's that you smell? A feast. A party's ahead. And you're invited.

We will enjoy sensations, consciousness and memories in the afterlife; our bodies remain as they were during our earthly existence. Imagine! Work imagination hard, because this interpretation will require overlooking some corollary questions. Since in this New Earth the saved will work happily with real occupations, will there also be employers and employees? Equal pay? Organized labor? All professions and all types of work? In this paradise, since all previous sins have been forgiven and forgotten, and sin is no more, will there be no rules? What? No laws? Then maybe no lawyers! Now this is heaven! (Heavenly comedians will make the saved souls howl with the lawyer jokes—"Let's ask God to manufacture some conflict, so the lawyers will have something to argue about.")

This earthly heaven will have to deal with additional employment enigmas: no disease, then no need for doctors and nurses; full knowledge, then no need for professors; no criminals, then no need for police; no war, then no need for soldiers (... hmm, now we're really getting someplace—armies of the world unite, you have nothing to lose but your jobs). Presumably, the number of occupations will plummet, and those in heaven will have to be assigned new jobs. Maybe this is where angels fit into the plan for paradise.

On a more serious level, in heaven, will there be any incentives for the pursuit of happiness, property, or status? What about pleasure from spousal sex? The imponderable questions about physical existence in a perfected New Earth really stretch the imagination.

Dr. Alcorn acknowledges other troublesome questions. "How can millions of people be with Jesus and receive personal attention?.... The issue is whether He can be in more than one place at the same time," ... walking and talking with each and every saved person. Good question. Dr. Alcorn advances a plausible answer: "It may defy our logic, but God is capable of doing far more than we can imagine. Being with Christ is the very heart of heaven, so we should be confident that we will have unhindered access to him."

Another problem is the New Earth's demographics. If the book of Revelation (7:1–7) is taken literally, heaven will not contain a "great multitude in white robes;" only 144,000 saved souls will be admitted. It is hard to imagine Dr. Alcorn's huge new cities and territorial states; not enough saved souls will pose a real problem. On the other hand, if our loving God forgives and accepts into heaven *all* who call on Him for salvation, too many people becomes a serious problem. How can room be made in the New Earth for all those bodily saints? The planet will be very crowded. How will sufficient food sustain life?

Numerous biblical passages support Dr. Alcorn's portrayal of a material bodily and physical New Earth. None is more suggestive than the resurrection of Jesus after He was crucified. He returned to earth to speak with His disciples, and, as Doubting Thomas had to be shown, the glorified Jesus came back from death in human form with a recognizable body, just as He first came to earth to share our humanity like us, "fully human in every way" (Heb. 2:17). So perhaps the Father brings those He saves to His New Earth with the same bodily appearance they had before they died. After we take our final journey, the physical self we were while still on earth could be "recycled," perhaps at the age where our health peaked, in His new kingdom on earth.

- **When the Saints Go Marching In**—Alternatively, could it be that it is primarily (maybe exclusively) our immaterial spiritual souls that will inherit the reward of an eternal relationship with God? The Bible also attests to the spiritual character of resurrected souls' heavenly existence.

After her brain surgery, I witnessed Debbie's soul rise from her body in a beam of light, and had to wonder if this signaled that in the afterlife we will be like her ascending soul appeared—not a physical body but a mobile spirit. Or was the brilliant light that blossomed into her smiling face before vanishing a sign that, had the Holy Spirit not guided her soul back to her body, her physical characteristics would have migrated to the portals of heaven?

Many biblical passages suggest that heavenly existence may not resemble our material world. Instead of portraying the otherworld far beyond this one, they picture heaven existing here right now, dwelling in us, within our soul or essential true self. There is no "hereafter." Existence on earth is commonly distortedly misperceived and misconceived; more accurately, the human soul is our true self—a "life force" existing within a material prison, a part of objective reality as imagined in mystic legends since human history began. Father Richard Rohr clarifies:

> Longing for God and longing for our True Self are the same longing. The mystics would say it is God who is even doing the longing in us and through us…. When you are living in conscious connection with [God's] Loving Inner Presence, you are in your True Self. God is forever united to this love within you…. Call the True Self the soul, the unconscious, deep consciousness, or the indwelling Holy Spirit…. Some form of suffering or death—psychological, spiritual, relational, or physical—is the only way we will loosen our ties to our small and separate false [bodily] self.

By this account, our true selves are already in God's Kingdom. Our body is little more than a shadow self. That false self will die and disintegrate—"ashes to ashes, dust to dust." Do not be distressed. The soul cannot be destroyed. At death, the physical body loses its grip on sensations, and our essential true selves, our conscious souls, leave the body and are resurrected in perpetuity. That which is divine in us returns to the imperishable divine cosmos from which everything originates. The true self that is released will experience in heaven entirely new spiritual sensations. Thus, our souls travel to where we have always belonged, spiritually joining our Father in heaven. Decay and death may kill our bodies, but the life-force comprising our energized souls survives and attains heightened consciousness, no longer subject to death.

This, of course, is a radically different way of imagining the heaven that awaits the righteous after their earthly bodily existence ends. It sees the afterlife not as a rebirth that continues our material being in paradise, but rather a reunion of our non-material spiritual soul that lives on eternally with our Maker.

The Bible abounds with many allusions to a purely spiritual, non-physical interpretation of heavenly existence. Jesus told the Pharisees, "I am not of this world" (John 8:23) and said to Pontius Pilate, "My Kingdom is not of this world" (John 18:36). Jesus prayed, "I am no longer in the world. *I do not belong to the world*.... For [humanity's] sake I sanctified myself, so that [the forgiven] also may be truly sanctified" (John 17:6–19). In this prayer to His Father prior to His supreme sacrifice, Jesus reported that His bodily incarnation was temporary, and He would return to the heavenly kingdom as spirit. Should we deduce that the saved, the sanctified, were never meant to be in the world and that their souls will enter heaven without the material entrapments of their physical bodies? If so, heaven should *not* be thought of in earthly material terms (John 18:23). God is transcendent. Those who join Him in heaven will have their souls rejoined with His *in spirit*, realizing their oneness in Jesus who is present in everything.

Other parts of scripture affirm this version of our soul's "out of body" experience at death. The Bible asserts that when we die, we will *immediately* be with our Lord (2 Cor. 5:8). What is more, St. Paul's take on this separation of the soul from the body could not be more clear: it is the soul *alone* that lives on eternally: "We are confident, yes, well pleased, to be absent from the body and to be present with the Lord." Thus, the Apostle Paul stressed the distinction between humans' physical/material natural body (*soma*), which cannot expect to inherent the kingdom of God, and the "spiritual body" which can enter God's kingdom after resurrection (1 Cor. 15:42–50). His dualistic conception highlighted the antithesis between the flesh and the spirit (Gal. 5 and Rom. 8), explicitly proclaiming "Flesh and blood will not inherit the kingdom of God" (1 Cor. 15:50).

In this conception, our Father's kingdom already resides within us—"The One who is in you is greater than the one who is in the world" (1 John 4:4). When at our death we depart from our bodies, our reunion with our Lord will not be as our corporeal beings were during our earthly existence, and heaven will not be like things were *in* or *on* this world as we know it. In the afterlife what will be restored, redeemed, renewed, and regenerated will be a unity of the saved in spiritual, not bodily or physical form. When the world ends, "we who are still alive and are left will...meet the Lord *in the air*" (1 Thess. 4:13–18). The real afterlife of the saved may be in an entirely spiritual kingdom of God.

To expand imagination about the afterlife's potential character, turn to science for additional hints and clues. Brace yourself: you might be surprised just how much science supports many biblical accounts of an afterlife, across many fields—physics, astronomy, anatomy, neurology, biology, psychology, and especially cosmology studying the origin, nature, and evolution of the universe.

IMAGINING HEAVEN: SCIENTIFIC INSIGHTS
Jesus Christ proclaimed "I am the Light of the world" (John 8:12), "the way and the truth and the life" (John 14:6). Look at His light in the light—He is everywhere. This way of thinking about God and heaven is in harmony with science. The sacred and science can be reconciled, and in many aspects are mutually supportive. Imagine! It's not hard to do. Many scientists' conclusions lend credence to John Lennon's assertion that "all the world can live as one," while undermining Lennon's denial that this peaceful harmony also exists in a heaven.

- **Viewing the Afterlife from Afar: Inferences from Astro-Science**—Henry Sidgwick recommended looking at the afterlife from "out there" far beyond in the infinite universe. He maintained that constructing a cosmic cartography from outer space allows us to recognize the seamless unity of all in the life beyond life. There is no hereafter; both the living and the dead are already immutably connected.

In 1990 the spacecraft *Voyager I* sent a picture of our planet from outer space four billion miles away, and millions took notice: God's creation looked like a tiny speck floating in airless space amid scattered rays of sunlight. Astro-scientist Carl Sagan mused in *Pale Blue Dot: A Vision of the Human Future in Space*, "Look again at that dot. That's here. That's home. That's us. Every saint and sinner in the history of our species lived here—on a mote of dust suspended in a sunbeam." To Sagan, all past and present inhabitants on earth are linked together in a timeless heavenly cosmos. This is where we are now and will be after death.

To imagine this hard-to-imagine invisible realm, consider quantum theory's postulate that just as two particles can affect each other across long distances, so too, as parapsychology maintains, total strangers sometimes appear able to communicate with each other through time and develop collective memories. The idea of connected unconscious minds joined in conversations stretches the imagination to make room for the possibility that astrophysical phenomena are real, and accordingly in the afterlife heavenly souls might relate to one another and to God through cosmological processes unbound by space, time and distance.

Sagan was not the first to look to the sky in wonder and forward these hypotheses. For example, four centuries before Christ, the Greek philosopher Plato posited that a transcendent Supreme Being existed which created the entire universe and its complete unity, and that after death everyone's soul, which he believed had a life before birth, would join this deity. Four centuries later, Epictetus maintained that at death a spiritual soul departed from earth and rose to a transcendent immaterial heaven, wherein the divine mind and the conscious human mind were forever thereafter united. In the seventeenth century Baruch Spinoza extended the idea of a unified cosmic consciousness, writing in *Viewpoint of Eternity*: "I hold that God is the immanent, and not the extraneous, cause of all things. I say, God is All; all lives and moves in God." God comprises everything that ever existed and will exist, including our souls. Hence, we are already a component of the heavenly divine. These views have come full circle, as attested by Priyamvada Natarajan's 2016 cosmic cartography *Mapping the Heavens: The Radical Scientific Ideas That Reveal the Cosmos.*

This view joins the conscious mind and soul with nature as a single entity. All things are part of God's universal order, including our consciousness. Our sense of separate individuality is illusory; we are parts of God's eternal light. We are all in this together; God—the infinite intellect—is within us, and this unified existence is eternal.

This vision of heaven as God's endless cosmic universe adheres to many biblical passages. When Jesus proclaimed that He was "the Light of the world" (John 8:12), it is likely He used this metaphor to communicate that through belief in Him we can see eternity in all its glory, with all the interdependent connections between time, space, and speed made manifest. In the light we can overcome dark ignorance and envision the entire ever-expanding heavenly universe unifying all with all in accordance with God's cosmic design. This view conceiving the cosmos as our spiritual home fits squarely into scientifically based schema.

In one variant of this conception, God is the source of all light, the light of the world, the cosmic Messenger neither reflecting nor absorbing light but the source of all visible light greater than the combined light of all the stars in the universe, and our souls are a compressed pocket of our consciousness pulled by gravitational weightless light waves traveling through empty space—tremors in the fabric of space-time—into eternal relationship with our heavenly Father. Imagine.

Stretch your imagination further, and picture our souls present in an endless multiverse containing any number of universes, each with its own laws of physics. Somewhere "out there" where these separate multiple universes intrude onto one another may be where heaven exists. Imagine! Imagine audaciously. But admit it—it's hard to do because we filter perceptions of realities through our mindsets which mask the possibility that an inclusive heaven may be the ultimate reality.

Extrapolate, and imagine after death saved souls reborn in heaven as spirits. Jesus said, "It is the spirit that gives life, the flesh is of no avail; the words that I have spoken to you are spirit and life" (John 6:71). According to the "lost" Gospel of Thomas (verse 77), Jesus said, "I am the light that is over all things. I am all; From me all has come forth, and to me all has reached. Split a piece of wood; I am there. Lift up the stone, and you will find me there." "I fill heaven and earth, says the Lord" (Jer. 23:24). God, a Supreme Being prior to His creation of the world, is Spirit—the life force that permeates everything, including everyone's higher minds making the soul the very essence of being. It is conceivable that, having seen the light, our souls will become like God's light, in constant motion everywhere for all eternity.

In this perspective, heaven is not a *place* where the soul travels after death; it is located everyplace throughout a constantly expanding universe composed of billions and billions of galaxies. It is not a site where our souls *go*; heaven is what after death we *become* as we commune with our Maker in an infinite and eternal cosmic collective consciousness. Our spirit is a moving sub-microscopic, subatomic energy flow transporting thoughts traveling throughout an endless cosmos. After life on earth ends, our souls emit energy released in what astronomy labels radiating "gravitational waves" which ripple throughout space and time faster than the speed of light in a vacuum; our spiritual souls spend eternity zooming throughout a cosmic wonderland as waves of light shining brilliantly—kinetic energized enlightenment floating in endless cosmic stream. In this kind of heaven, our soul—the part of us which departs from earth when we die—is reconnected in perpetual relationship with the Supreme Spirit of God, in a communion in which we always belonged. Michael Morwood, author of *Tomorrow's Catholic*, defines vividly this view:

> Death does not entail a journey for the soul to a place somewhere else. No, death is an entrance into a new mode of existence. It is not a physical existence. It is a new way of existing "in" God, different from the physical way we now exist "in" God. And the very fact that we Christians believe we are now living in God leads us to believe we are already participating in eternal life.

- **Insights About the Afterlife from Neuroscience**—A view of eternal possibilities from *afar* focuses on the larger picture, the whole universe. Another way of viewing these probabilities of consciousness in an afterlife is from the inside. Look inside the corporeal mind, *up close*, for additional insight into heavenly existence.

Think small. Very small—at the submicron level. This is where the body's deep-brain structure may provide clues. When scripture tells us that the kingdom of God already lies within you, that is shorthand for saying our souls derive from the Holy Spirit within us. The brain arguably is the most complex parcel of organized matter in the known universe. So what has cognitive neuroscience discovered about how the brain works, and what might happen to our consciousness—our spiritual souls—after we die?

Take the concept of human consciousness—the inner soul within everybody—below to another level. Brain scientists now "know" that the brain cannot produce thoughts by itself but suspect that the conscious mind—call it the soul—survives the death of the brain and body.

There is a living spiritual soul within our subconscious brain containing beliefs all humans already possess (Rom. 1:18). Arguably, God wired our brains to envisage an eternal afterlife—where everything is tied together with everything else in relationship with God.

From a brain-science perspective, epistemic intuitions come from within, from the ways our Creator created our brains. C. S. Lewis was an advocate of this thesis. He maintained that God created humans with an inner light of consciousness that from birth illuminates knowledge of God, heaven, goodness, and love. It is present within our brains before our development of language to put into words those things of which we are aware intuitively. "From our own childhood," Lewis contends, "we remember that before our elders thought us capable of 'understanding' anything we already had spiritual experience as pure and momentous as any we have undergone since, though not, of course, as rich in factual detail."

During our long journey, Debbie and I began to recognize that our Maker was with us and within us from the beginning, and our spiritual souls were an innate God-given gift, a part of our mental makeup which made us intuitively aware of an immortal existence. God had "set eternity in the hearts of men" (Eccl. 3:11). We cannot die but once but can live twice, here on earth and again in the heavenly afterlife, so we had no reason to "be afraid of things which kill the body because they cannot kill the soul" (Matt. 10:28).

As described in preceding chapters, this conviction was reinforced dramatically during Debbie's near-death out-of-body sojourn. The Holy Spirit is perpetually present within us and available in times of trial (John 14:16–17). The Holy Spirit had shown Debbie the glory of the afterlife—the perfect, everlasting heavenly home for our souls. Little wonder she was so confident and fearless. You would be too if your soul traveled within striking distance to blissful eternity; consoled and enlightened, your belief in the afterlife would be set in concrete. Imagine!

The critical question about life after life is whether consciousness continues after death. Cognitive neuroscience suggests it does. In *Erasing Death: The Science That Is Rewriting the Boundaries Between Life and Death*, Dr. Sam Parnia advanced "a spiritual or metaphysical perspective on the survival of our consciousness beyond death," positing that consciousness can separate from the material body. He has company. Consider one much-publicized account: Eben Alexander's *Proof of Heaven: A Neurosurgeon's Journey into the Afterlife*. Dr. Alexander was in a coma for seven days, during which the portions of his brain that enable thought and emotions completely shut down. An electroencephalogram (EEG) showed that, clinically, he was "brain dead," in a dreamless sleep incapable of thought. Miraculously, he did not die. He regained consciousness and was able to recall lucidly his spiritual journey to and within heaven in God's presence—an "experience" that could not have been produced by his brain.

Dr. Alexander overcame his previous doubts about "the soul, the spirit, or whatever you choose to call that invisible, intangible part of us that truly makes us who we are—the deep mystery at the center of existence—our consciousness." His paradigm shifted. He no longer believed that consciousness was just a by-product of material processes. "'I was blind, but now I see' took on new meaning as I understood just how blind to the full nature of the spiritual world we are on earth—especially people like I had been, who had believed that matter was the core reality, and that all else—thought, consciousness, ideas, emotions, spirit—were simply productions of it." While he was beyond his body, he received knowledge about his relationship to what he calls the larger eternal cosmic spiritual realm: "The blurring of the boundary between my awareness and the realm around me went so far at times that I *became* the entire universe." Cognitively dead, Dr. Alexander discovered that God—the divine source of the entire eternal universe—and the soul are real, and that death is only a bridge for our conscious souls to cross to a safe heavenly home. When we give up who we are, we can become what we will be—our true self.

Dr. Alexander describes heaven as a timeless dimension that moves not in sequence but all at once, so that "a moment can seem like a lifetime, and one or several lifetimes can seem like a moment." In this heavenly spiritual realm, thinking occurs instantaneously at various levels. In the afterlife, Dr. Alexander concludes, we will learn "that our eternal spiritual self is more real than anything we perceive in the physical realm, and has a direct connection to the infinite love of the Creator.… Communicating with God is the most extraordinary experience imaginable, yet at the same time it's the most natural ones of all, because God is present in us at all times. Omniscient, omnipotent, personal—and loving us without conditions. We are connected as One through our divine link with God."

Many other famous experts, including the eminent scientist Freeman Dyson and brain scientist Kevin Nelson, also are convinced of the conscious mind's survival after death. Neuroscientist Jill Taylor wrote the best-seller *My Stroke of Insight* which brought widespread attention to a spiritual interpretation of the conscious mind after life ends. She withstood a devastating stroke, and near death her brain's left hemisphere closed down and her creative right brain began to generate new ideas of which she became conscious following recovery from life-saving cerebral neurosurgery. Dr. Taylor wrote that she became aware that "I am part of a greater structure—an eternal flow of energy and molecules from which I cannot be separated. Knowing that I am a part of the cosmic flow made me feel innately safe and experience my life as heaven on earth. How can I feel vulnerable when I cannot be separated from the greater whole?… My right mind realizes that the essence of my being has eternal life."

A growing number of brain scientists accept testimonies of near-death experiences and now endorse a proposition proposed three centuries ago by Baruch Spinoza: "The human mind cannot be destroyed with the human body. There is some part of it that remains eternal." Spinoza contributed a new twist to the philosophical mind-body problem and immortality, maintaining that "the mind can neither imagine nor recollect anything save while in the body" but the mind or soul lives on in eternity after the death of a person's body.

The spiritual mind that survives death may be what becomes "us" in heaven. Evidence is accumulating that after we die our souls can travel through space and time. What's to preclude the transmigration to a heavenly new existence of subconscious electrical surges and infinitely small subatomic particles from a minute area where the brain ends and the mind begins? It is conceivable that ideas within our subconscious can be released and that our invisible spiritual souls can time travel to a new destination, speeding through and past space as do the alternating magnetic and electrical waves we call "light." Why not? Sure, no one can prove that this surreal, ostensibly supernatural, paranormal process can and does occur, but it also can't be disproven. Is that what our physical selves transport to heaven? Imagine. That's all we can do. C. S. Lewis reminds us that there are many questions "to which no answer is imaginable." The question about heavenly existence is one of those questions—one of the biggest.

IMAGINING THE FINAL DESTINATION

Scripture and science present both convergent and divergent images of heavenly existence. Some images envision body and mind resurrected together in the afterlife, whereas others portray their perpetual separation with only the spiritual soul remaining forever in relationship to and with God in a unified universe. Scripture expands the enigma further in passages (such as Matt. 18:16–19) that suggest that we can simultaneously picture heaven both ways. St. Paul usefully reminds us that scripture's varying vague pictures of the afterlife can only be seen "in a mirror dimly" (1 Cor. 13:12). We can't be sure if the ideas we can read are more accurate than what's never been written. Shakespeare adds, "There are more things in heaven and earth than are dreamt of in your philosophy."

From the beginning of our long night's journey into day, we were puzzled about heavenly existence. The only conclusion we are comfortable reaching is our unshakable belief that heaven was in us already, not a physical place so much as everyplace, because God is everywhere. We knew that a spiritual heaven is real.

That knowledge is sufficient. The long dark shadow of a meaningless afterlife in oblivion became meaningless. Stokes struck from our minds any and all thoughts of nonexistence after we die. We never would have to shudder, stagger or struggle about the afterlife again. We are convinced that everlasting life after death will be experienced in a permanent heavenly paradise by those who are saved. Beyond description—but real nonetheless. There is an eternal home for our spiritual souls. Imagine!

Nevertheless, what our ethereal and elastic *form* after death in eternity will become defies definition. God may reassemble our reborn spiritual souls and physical bodies in countless ways. The spectrum of possibilities is "out of this world," if you'll forgive the pun. Our souls may be packaged in infinite ways, ranging from a subatomic particle to a complete corporeal human body whose size, weight, height, shape, color, age, or appearance doesn't really matter. We simply have no way of knowing much about heavenly existence.

Anything is possible for our Creator. Take another heroic leap. Imagine that our Creator has created a unique heavenly home for each of us. It's possible that different souls may experience heaven in different ways, while sharing in common unity with God. Just as no two strokes are exactly alike and no two individuals are exactly the same, so too might there be different heavens for different immortal souls. All souls will be linked to each other and, more importantly, united in perennial relationship with God, but, as C. S. Lewis averred, heaven might not be the same for every soul. Lewis reasoned that God made each individual truly individual and unique and that there was a purpose behind the created differences. "Your place in heaven will seem to be made for you and you alone," Lewis argued when he spoke of "the eternal distinctness of each soul" to permit "union instead of mere sameness" with God in heaven.

> Why else were individuals created, but that God, loving all infinitively, should love each differently? And this difference floods with meaning the love of all blessed creatures for one another, the communion of all saints. If all experienced God in the same way and returned to Him in identical worship, the song of the Church triumphant would have no symphony; it would be like an orchestra in which all the instruments played the same note. Aristotle has told us that a city is a unity of unlikes, and Saint Paul that a body is a unity of different members. Heaven is a city, and a Body. The blessed may remain eternally different: a society, because each has something to tell all the others—fresh and ever fresh news of the "My God" whom each finds in Him all praise for "Our God."

C. S. Lewis's stroke of insight reminds us to keep an open mind: the Bible presents diverse ways of imagining an eternal heavenly home (Matt. 18:18). Any way you envision it, trust that the darkness will disappear, and light will shine as we are born anew, with supreme serenity and without selfishness.

Looking up over our heads to imagine heaven, Debbie and I must confess that on this inscrutable subject, we are in "over our heads." Heaven remains difficult to imagine; visualizing what cannot be seen is as hard as seeing heat. We simply don't know what God will reveal to us when we die. Only then will we learn whether the soul can exist independently of the body, or whether the conscious soul reunites with some variant of our body for all eternity. And only after death will we discover whether heaven will exist on a New Earth or if instead in heaven only our spiritual souls, absent our physical bodies, will be united in Christ. When we die, the true light will enlighten us about the afterlife's realities, which probably lay beyond our wildest dreams. We can wait. In the meantime, we feel that in the final analysis it really doesn't matter if matter matters, so long as our souls will receive the blessings of eternal peace in direct relationship with our heavenly Father. No matter what the final form of heaven and the form of our true selves in it, we can't lose if our Lord judges us acceptable for entry through heaven's gate.

Please use our ruminations about the possible contours of heavenly existence as a stimulus to frame your quest for understanding. It is up to you, dear reader, to reach your own conclusions about what happens after death. Use your imagination. You have no other option.

Of one thing you can be certain: the endgame is fraught with great promise—the start of our final never-ending journey. "There is more to life than this earthly one," theology professor Deanna Thomson reminds us; "in the life beyond there will be no more crying, no more dying, only light, only love, only joy." In heaven we are newly created: "Old things have passed away; behold, all things become new" (2 Cor. 5:17). Imagine, and rest in peace—being with Christ in heaven will be "far better" than the best circumstances we can imagine here on earth (Phil. 1:23). "There shall be no more curse" (Rev. 22:3).

"In this world," Jesus said, "you will have trouble. But take heart! I have overcome the world. In me you may have peace" (John 16:33). In the house of the Lord, in His holy, unconditional loving presence, we can finally stop thinking of a beginning and an end and start finding serenity so that in an eternal flow we can hear our souls sing; we will be free at last, at peace. We will be our true selves. We will never be alone.

EPILOGUE

I shall not die, but live, and declare the works of the Lord.

—Psalm 118:17

After a stroke strikes, dark dread strikes. Fright smothers light. All appears to be lost—even hope. Overwhelmed, survivors and loved ones cannot help but wonder what the future will bring. Our story opened with a citation of Eugene O'Neill's dire words in *A Long Day's Journey into Night*: "No one can help the things that life does to us." How true. Much of what occurs *is* beyond our control. But that does not mean, as O'Neill concluded, that what happens to us drives us irresistibly downward deeper and deeper into the dark, until we lose our true selves forever.

On our long journey from night into day, light was cast on a very different conclusion. We learned that we can shape but not determine the things that happen to us. If terrible things happen, we can choose how to respond and select a path to follow, which will powerfully affect what will happen next. Adversity creates opportunities to rethink life's purpose and to chart new paths. We will lose our "true selves" and become victims of our past only if we accept our victimization.

In the aftermath of Debbie's strokes, some of the darkness hiding our identities was lifted by the Holy Spirit's light that illuminated our roadway. We began to recognize who we were meant to be, and strived to become the persons we had always felt we should have been all along.

How? In our time of desperate need, we released ourselves into God's hands. Our Lord led us to finding our true selves as we gave unbounded love to Him and to each other. "Until you have given yourself to Him," C. S. Lewis advises, "you will not have a real self." On our long journey, we found that to "be yourself" you don't have to remain "by yourself;" you can find your true self by giving yourself to God's care and letting Him guide you toward the worthiest expressions of your identity.

Ludwig van Beethoven reportedly said, "God talks to everyone; to most, He whispers, to some, He shouts. I am deaf, but composed my music to glorify God. I heard His shouts, and tried my best to write music that would allow listeners to see His glory and sing His praise." Prior to her strokes, Debbie and I also were partially deaf to God's Word. When we hit bottom, we cried out, and God's whispers became thunderous shouts. At the edge of existence, we discovered just how responsively God's shouts ring out to those who call on Him.

Contrary to what people often think, "out of weakness we are made strong" (Heb. 11:34) and drawn by God to serve His purposes (1 Cor. 1:27–29; 2 Cor. 12:10). Debbie was dreadfully weak after her strokes struck her down. In the face of terror, we could have frozen in petrifying fear. We didn't. Knowing "the sovereign Lord is our strength" (Hab. 3:19), we were able to muster the courage to move forward. God had promised, "I am He who will sustain you. I have made you and I will carry you; I will sustain you and I will rescue you" (Isa. 46:4). After Debbie's horrific strokes took her to death's door, we were given a choice. We could either dwell on our loss or on God Himself. We chose to call on God, on whom we were completely dependent. God delivered. God shined in the darkness, broke through the shadows, and performed astounding miraculous acts which demonstrated the healing power of His divine love. The chances of survival from the kind of devastating strokes which struck Debbie were incredibly low, but she overcame the odds and slowly trod a rugged road to recovery. At each juncture along the rehabilitative highway, there can be little doubt that Debbie's close relationship with God played a huge instrumental role.

Before you can have new beliefs, you have to let some old ones lose their grip and strengthen other prior convictions. One of the most important previous beliefs we possessed was reconfirmed on our long journey—God was with us. Vivid awareness of the Lord's presence freed our minds from energy-destroying angst and anxiety. We appreciated more than ever that we could trust God's supreme power and unconditional love. This allowed us to escape addiction to that most toxic of drugs—resentful self-pity and the loneliness of self-reliance.

Debbie put her reaction to her afflictions well: "After my stroke struck, I never felt afraid. What would happen would happen, and no despair or anger was justified. I knew God could lift me and carry me through the storm. His will would be done. There was great relief in that belief. Why fear what God had in store for me? In His care, I felt I could not lose."

LIGHT IN THE DARK: A STORIED STORY

Our story began with the customary introduction "Once upon a time…" That time was January 8, 2014. That was one dark night, as black as coal. In its wake, a slow climb out of the dark commenced. This testimony covers the first twelve months following that shattering first stroke. As this book goes to press, our journey is not over—it is still unwinding. So *After a Stroke Strikes* does *not* have an ending that can now be shared.

However, we can share our motives for writing this book. We were encouraged by many to share our story of the Lord's loving response to our prayers. We felt a calling to provide a testimony to His glory, by tracing our travels down a steep mountain path to the utter dark chasm at the bottom—perhaps the best vantage point from which to clearly see atop the majestic mountain Christ's light shining brightly. The darker it got, the brighter shone God's light. God brought light to the dark arena, light that darkness could not overcome (John 1:5).

Debbie's loss of life and resumption of life were life-changing. Drawn ever nearer to God, we pledged to make productive use of our remaining time on earth serving our Savior and our neighbors – all the time perplexed why we had been granted this exceptional blessed opportunity when so many others afflicted are not thrown a lifeline.

In gratitude for God's merciful healing of our hurts, we pledged to compose a testimony of God's healing love during our time of trouble and trial. That is the main reason we made a commitment to write *After a Stroke Strikes*. We perceived a profound obligation to tell others how we moved ahead in our hike with God. "Press toward the goal," the apostle Paul urged (Phil. 3:14). This book presses that goal.

We have attempted to give the light a brighter color, so that in tough times you can learn, as did St. Paul, that "Whatever state I am in, to be content" (Phil. 4:11). At a time when she was not yet capable of participating as a coauthor, Debbie gave voice to the underlying message she wished our testimony to provide, pleading

> I ask not to be judged by my achievements, engineered with the assistance of many, to resumption of a healthy body and renewed soul. I request that I not be applauded for my successes. Please judge my story by the major times I stumbled and failed, and managed to find the strength and determination to get up and try again to regain my footing and step forward. We pray you and your loved ones can, from our story, cultivate confident faith in your capacity to carry on when catastrophes strike, and to learn to trust in God on your own journey.

If you look closely at our text, you will find a salient subtext embedded in our story: Heartbreaking struggles in the furnace of affliction made us better. We found our true selves, stronger faith, and greater love for each other. If it took a stroke to stoke the fire required to acquire new understandings, in hindsight we are oddly glad that this tinderbox ignited. Our fall into the depth had lifted us to new heights, in much the same way that ironically knowledge that we will die makes us treasure life. Our unlikely surprise gift almost made us wonder if a stroke bringing us down was a small price to pay for raising us up. We are grateful for our grief.

After a Stroke Strikes has tried to stimulate thoughtful examination of the crises that face everyone sooner or later on life's unpredictable journey. If you are among those to whom all appears dark and hopeless, this book is for you. Our goal is to provide hope to all who suffer and grieve and to provoke important questions that deserve your attention. We are fully aware of our limitations—no stroke of genius can be found from our strokes of a pen or keyboard. But if our story strikes you with new thoughts, and you derive insight and faith, then this memoir will have served its primary educational goal. It will then also serve the secondary goal of bringing comfort to those who mourn and the tertiary goal of provoking serious thought about the gift that faith in our loving God can provide.

LIVE TWICE

Debbie had lived twice, once when she was born and again when aneurisms ruptured and she (and I) looked at death in the face. When death is faced the next time, it will be for the last time (unless more of God's wondrous miracles postpone death). If the Lord then calls either of us home, we will be escorted by the Holy Spirit on a lighted path, where God will be there to greet us.

It's prudent to get ready. Scripture proclaims, "It is appointed for men to die once, but after this the judgment" (Heb. 9:27). Thanks to the Holy Spirit's miraculous intervention, judgement day had been postponed. From those great teachers, suffering and experience, we learned that our continuing journey has a clear mission: "Prepare to meet your God!" (Amos 4:12). When we die, will shall see our Lord and stand before Him to give an account about the degree to which we have lived during our earthly existence in ways that were consistent with His will (1 Cor. 3:13). If judged acceptable in His sight, tranquility, serenity, and peace will be ours for all eternity.

If we learned anything on this long journey, it was that our faith was right all along—death is only a rest stop on the road to an everlasting life after life. The gospels underscore repeatedly "the good news" that death is not the termination of our existence. "Death is a passing into God, a homecoming into God's mystery and glory," theologian Hans

Küng explicates. "Strictly speaking, only an atheist can say that death is the end of everything."

When death comes, you will not have to face its sting. The tenets of Christian faith allay all anxieties about an afterlife after death. No sensation other than sheer solace is warranted. When the world beyond and the present world are comingled in a singular cosmic unity inclusive of everyone and everything, why not look forward to it with eager anticipation? Our relationship with our Creator in everlasting peace cannot be topped.

"Do not go gentle into that good night," Dylan Thomas urged. We disagree. Why not go gently, with confident expectations? Fear of death exorcised and faith that a perfect eternity can await us, we need not dread death. Life after death has to be much better than living in darkness. After physical death our spiritual life can awaken in union with God and all creation. What can be anticipated almost makes you want to take the final journey!

The grave is a gate. Through heaven's doorway, we shall someday assuredly all pass. You can suspend many "grave" concerns that might frighten you. Such an intangible, imperceptible next world can't be seen any better than the wind blowing or ink drying, but it's there, and it's unimaginably good—unlike anything ever seen before. The road for that final journey does not lead to a dead end, to nothingness. That message alone, if you find it persuasive, may justify the time you have spent reading *After a Stroke Strikes*. We hope that, if you are a person of faith, this story has strengthened your faith; and that if you are without faith, this testimony will make you reconsider.

THE END?

The long journey reported in *After a Stroke Strikes* records what has transpired so far to provide a new beginning. But the sobering reality is that timelines are not trend lines. Is there a denouement? How will our story end? There is no telling. The future can't be foreseen.

No one can know his or her fate; everyone's days are numbered, and the number can never be known. So as our publisher was about to print these memoirs, we still faced, as always, an uncertain future. We are not "out of the woods" in spacious daylight; nobody ever is. We have to live with the malignant possibility that another setback or death could occur; strokes frequently strike previous victims after recovery. Living with uncertainty is required of everyone, the healthy and the ill, the strong and the weak, the young and the aged. Some trepidation is warranted. We still sometimes imagine dark and dangerous storm clouds gathering. We had learned from hard experience that anything can happen. Picture us trying to suspend submerged lingering fears. For example, Debbie has had a recurring nightmare about a potential fork in the road that could confront her:

After a Stroke Strikes was within weeks of printing. Chuck told me how proud he was that I had pursued our memoir's publication. We exchanged words of hope that our book would bring comfort to people who were suffering. "We will see how it will be received," he said. "Just know how wonderful it has been giving you help when you were hurting. I love you more than words can say and will be with you always. If I die first, I will be watching you from heaven, I hope, and will be waiting for you. Now Toby, I need to get in a jog. I'll be back within a half hour."

I saw him running down our long driveway, and my heart warmed. He is such a good husband. He stood by me on every step throughout my stroke recovery and was the ultimate caretaker. As I saw him disappear running around the bend, I thought how grateful I am for all the love we shared, in good times and bad. I couldn't wait for him to get back so I could give him a big hug. I waited, and waited. I wondered what was taking so long. 30 minutes became 60, and 60 became 120. Soon after the clock struck, I heard a knock on the door. To my horror and disbelief, it was a police officer. "Are you Mrs. Kegley?" the officer asked. "I have to give you some news.

Your husband was found unconscious lying on the pavement, and a Good Samaritan called 911. Your husband is in the emergency room."

My heart sank. This couldn't be happening. Why? O'Neill's haunting verse to open our book darkened my mind: "None of us can help the things that happen to us." As I gathered my purse to rush to the ER, I vowed to rise to the challenge. I knew with God's help I could. The time had come to be there for Chuck.

Fortunately, this frightening scenario did not occur. But it illustrates the kinds of threats that the future could hold. We ask you, our readers, to speculate how you think our story will end. Then examine your own life's journey, and, as a thought experiment, make a guesstimate about how your own story will end. Your answers will tell you much about your values.

ACKNOWLEDGMENTS

Our sincerest appreciation goes to you, our readers, who may be facing adversity or death and have turned to this book to find hope and faith. In our efforts to reach you without further publications delays, we acknowledge we undoubtedly have made errors of omission and commission, and ask our readers for their empathy and forgiveness.

Many people—in fact, too many to identify and thank individually—have contributed to the development of *After a Stroke Strikes*. No book can be written without the support, advice and encouragement of others, and we are indebted in countless ways to many for their generous assistance.

- To the celebrated artist who granted permission to use a digital image of *Life's Fragile Beauty* for our book's cover: our dear friend Christine Raymond—we give thanks.

- To the world-class "Lifesaver" surgeons, doctors and therapists at Carolinas Medical Center: Joe D. Bernard, Larry Braccia, Emmet Hunter Dyer, Janet Edsell, Lori Marie Grafton, Kristen Harkey, Elizabeth Houser, C. Scott McLanahan, Beverley Paton, Lynnette Schiffern, Rachel C. Shemtov, and Erin Weeks—we give thanks.

- To the extremely dedicated Health South Rehabilitation therapists and staff who skillfully paved the way to Debbie's recovery: Mary Aitchison, Horace Baker, Dan Carroll, Rafe Ellisor, Blakley Hydrick, Tomi Jackson, Tony Kochert, Cedric Luckey, Terry Lundy, Jamaine Mack, Karen McClive, Stephanie McLawhorn, Mary Newton, Theo Oates, Liza O'Cain, Jonathan Park, Allie Pedigo, Jill Polhemus, Mike Randall, David Ruthsatz, Brittney Smith, Hannah Summer, and Cheryl Varnadore—we give thanks.

- To the "Communications Central Intelligence" Internet team who kept thousands of concerned friends informed of daily, sometimes hourly, changes in Debbie's condition: Andy Kegley, John and Mary Kegley, and Hilel Salomon—we give thanks.

- To friends and associates in the publication industry who offered expert advice: Pat Coate (University of South Carolina Press), Mary B. Kegley (Kegley Books of Wytheville), Jennifer Kneer (Routledge), Barry Kight (C.C. Macgregor), Carolyn Merrill (Cengage Learning), and Janise A. Turso (W.W. Norton)—we give thanks.

- To the team at CreareSpace.com for their preparation, printing and distribution of the manuscript published by Live Twice Press—we give thanks.

- To the Pastors who lovingly provided heavy spiritual lifting inspired by their deep-seated trust in God's goodness and steadfast trust in His answers to many prayers: Revs. George Crow, Paul Doyle, Adrian Moldovan, Steve Myer, Steve Ridenhour and John Ropp—we give thanks.

- To "The Flock," the special ladies on the Northeast Presbyterian Church Care Team who, like Christ the Servant, came to serve and instruct: Cathy Crow, Rima Crow, Sharon Johnson, Ginger Kelley, Sybil Knight, Sylvia Linker, Renatta Loquist, Pam Miller, Charlotte Nickerson, Betty Nelle Presley, Sally Shealy and Laurie Walden—we give thanks.

- To our good neighbors who participated in the "Meal Train" and provided immeasurable assistive support: David and Sherri Amador, Ken and Phyllis Baldwin, Paul and Ann Childers, Ed and Jan Cox, Jerry and Kathy Davis, Ken and Phyllis Eledge, Fo and George Logan, Bob and Kathy Mangone, Mike McGinn, John and Susan Moore, Kathy Hoppe, Debra Krotish, Bethany and Ed Parlor, Allen and Carolyn Pregnall, Herman and Michelle Rich, Don and Maria Sanders, Alice and Ed Sheffington, Maggie and Mike Switzer, Tom Utroska, Cindy and John Voris, and Ginny and John White—we give thanks.

- To the multitude of people who listened to our story, urged us to publish it, and (like the Holy Spirit) in ways seen and unseen contributed to its publication: Martha Abernathy, Larry and Teresa Amick, Anita Aymer, Jim Bangle, Karen and Mark Benedict, Leslie and Mac Bennett, Mark Berkson, Danny Bird, Shannon Blanton, John and Friedie Bohraus,

Leann Brown, Ashley and Charles Butt, Hal Butt, Linda Butt, Dan and Lora Caldwell, Connie and Greg Carlson, Vaughn Cassell, Dale and Debbie Clark, John Clark, Tammy Cline, Jessica Coate, Pat and Roger Coate, Monique Council, Bobby Craig, Edwin Crow, Emily Crow, George and Cathy Crow, Peter and Suzanne Douglas, Gail and Jasmine Doxie, Joan Dunn, Pogo and Teresa Fowler, Peter French, Pierre and Jaquie Gehlen, Heinz and Lotti Gertsch, Paul Gillyard, Tom Graber, Liz Groseclose, James Herman, Chuck Hermann, Peg Hermann, Steve Hibbard, Jim Holderman, Dolph Hoehling, Candi and Tom Hough, Bob Howell, Llew and Suzy Howell, Chuck Johnson, Joan Johnson, Jack and Wanda Jones, George and Helen Keck, Danny and Sarah Kegley, George and Louise Kegley, Jackie Kegley, Marina and Stephen Kegley, Melissa and Robert Kegley, Nan Kegley, Nancy Kegley, Sissy Kegley, Cliff Kempa, Jean and Ruth Klinger, Bill Kreml, Karen and Sam Lake, Pat Larson, Alison Lockhart, Jan Love, Marink Marank, Dick and Sherri Marshall, Lisa Martin, Gregg McKenzie, Mike and Joan Meissenburg, Ashley and Brad Michie, David and Janet Miller, Adrian Moldovan, Kathy Morris, Ken and Susan Noel, Paula Parks, Mike and Rose Payton, Craig and Dawndy Mercer Plank, Shelly Powers-Pearson, Don and Jeanne Puchala, Christine and Greg Raymond, Dottie Raymond, Neil Richardson, Chuck and Dillon Robinson, Joel Rosenthal, Alpo and Leena Rusi, Joshua Salomon, Peggy and Roger Sargent, Scott Sargent, Bob Schulze, Melissa Semeniuk, Soapie Sharitz, Jerry Sharpe, Bill Skelton, Margrith Stäger, Deanna Thompson, Jim Utt, Dan Wakefield, Dottie Ward, Jackie and Winston Wright, and Kim Yandle—we give thanks.

Made in the USA
Middletown, DE
26 November 2016